IT WILL BE FUN AND TERRIFYING

Nationalism and Protest in Post-Soviet Russia

Fabrizio Fenghi

THE UNIVERSITY OF WISCONSIN PRESS

This book was published with the assistance of the Faculty Development Fund and the Humanities Research Fund, Brown University.

The University of Wisconsin Press
728 State Street, Suite 443
Madison, Wisconsin 53706
uwpress.wisc.edu

Gray's Inn House, 127 Clerkenwell Road
London EC1R 5DB, United Kingdom
eurospanbookstore.com

Printed in the United States of America

This book may be available in a digital edition.

Library of Congress Cataloging-in-Publication Data

Names: Fenghi, Fabrizio, author.
Title: It will be fun and terrifying: nationalism and protest
in post-Soviet Russia / Fabrizio Fenghi.
Description: Madison, Wisconsin: The University of Wisconsin Press, [2020]
| Includes bibliographical references and index.
Identifiers: LCCN 2019019120 | ISBN 9780299324407 (cloth)
Subjects: LCSH: Limonov, Ėduard. | Dugin, Aleksandr. | Nat͡sional-bolʹshevistskai͡a
partii͡a (Russia) | Nationalism—Russia (Federation)
| Protest movements—Russia (Federation) | Art—Political aspects—
Russia (Federation) | Politics and literature—Russia (Federation)
| Russia (Federation)—Politics and government—1991-
Classification: LCC JN6699.A8 N385 2020 | DDC 324.247/075—dc23
LC record available at https://lccn.loc.gov/2019019120

ISBN 9780299324445 (paperback)

Praise for *It Will Be Fun and Terrifying*

"Fenghi's book is successful proof that the move beyond the top-down paradigm for studying Russian political culture is long overdue."—*Ab Imperio*

"A fascinating account of the relevance of counterculture and political fringe ideas in post-Soviet Russia."—*eExtreme*

"A compelling and insightful work of scholarship. I'm particularly impressed with the fact that Fenghi manages to include sketches of individual National Bolsheviks as a seamless part of a narrative that is largely about public figures."—Eliot Borenstein, New York University

"Provides a rich and nuanced narrative filling in an important piece of the puzzle of post-Soviet Russian culture and politics. This book offers fascinating insights into the curious blend of conservative postmodernism and radical provocations that fuels the Russian far right."
—Peter Rutland, Wesleyan University

For my father

Francesco

who left for a world where it is still possible to play

Contents

Illustrations

Acknowledgments

This book was made possible by numerous encounters, social interactions, and intellectual exchanges that took place across several cultures, languages, and political beliefs. I am deeply indebted to all the people who shared with me their views and ideas, as well as their personal histories, in the course of this project. First and foremost, I am very grateful to all my anonymous informants, *natsboly* and others, for sharing their often deeply personal stories with a generosity that felt at times almost moving. This book is primarily for them. Among the book's protagonists I can name, I would like to thank in particular Aleksey Tsvetkov, for his theoretically elaborate and fully self-aware takes on his own political biography, and Aleksey Beliaev-Gintovt, for letting me participate in his "Eurasianist salon" for a little while, and for his performances. I am also grateful to Konstantin Chuvashev, Laura Ilina, and Mikhail Roshniak for giving me access to images and documents from their personal archives.

Preliminary research for the book was funded by the Ronald Muirhead Byrnes Scholarship Fund, the Nina Berberova Memorial Fund, and the University Dissertation Fellowship at Yale University. The fieldwork in Moscow was supported by the Fox International Fellowship. During the writing and publication process I received funding from the Faculty Development Fund and the Humanities Research Fund at Brown University.

The project was conceived and took its form in the Department of Slavic Languages and Literatures at Yale University. I am grateful to Katerina Clark for providing invaluable guidance throughout the process, and for being a model of dedication to scholarship and research for all of us—KC is a true academic icon. John MacKay offered deep theoretical insights during several hour-long conversations over coffee, and he made me rediscover Marxism.

Vladimir Alexandrov was a reference point since I moved to the United States ten years ago; he believed in my ideas and projects even if my approach to scholarship was very different from his own, and he taught me how to navigate American academia while periodically reminding me to take it with a grain of salt. Marijeta Bozovic convinced me that academia was the way to go after all, and that we could make it fun; she provided crucial feedback to the project and did an amazing job building networks and communities of academics working on all things postsocialist across the Northeast and beyond. Doug Rogers and Maria Sidorkina patiently answered my naïve questions about ethnography when I embarked on this project, and they offered essential advice both during my fieldwork and when it came time to actually write an ethnography. Without them I would have never found the courage to set foot in the unknown territory of cultural anthropology, which was one of the best decisions I have ever made. I would also like to express my deep appreciation to Molly Brunson, Harvey Goldblatt, and Bella Grigoryan for providing extremely useful advice not just on the writing but also on publishing strategies and fellowships and job applications. Last but not least, I'd like to thank my comrades in arms Vadim Shneyder and Roman Utkin. We have come a long way together since our very awkward early days of grad school. I am sure that this is just the beginning.

Early drafts of various sections of the book were presented at conference panels and workshops at the Institute for European, Russian, and Eurasian Studies at George Washington University; the MacMillan Center for International and Area Studies at Yale; the Davis Center for Russian and Eurasian Studies at Harvard University; the Department of Russian Studies at Davidson College; and at several ASEEES annual conventions. I am thankful to all these institutions for the opportunity to present and discuss my work. For their feedback, and for the very stimulating discussions on post-Soviet culture and society more broadly, I would like to thank all the participants at the following conferences, workshops, and events: "Locating 'Conservative Ideology' in Today's Russia," organized by Marlène Laruelle at George Washington University; the series of faculty seminars "Utopia after Utopia: Politics and Aesthetics in the Post-Socialist World," organized by Marijeta Bozovic and Marta Figlerowicz at Yale; "Russian Politics beyond the Kremlin," organized by Jessica Pisano and Doug Rogers at the MacMillan Center, also at Yale; "Cultures of Protest in Russia," organized by Ania Aizman and Maria Sidorkina at the Davis Center at Harvard; and my lecture "Post-Soviet Nationalism and Protest Culture," organized by Daria Ezerova at Davidson College.

For their feedback at various stages of this project, and for reading and commenting on various versions and sections of the manuscript, I would like to express my deep gratitude to Marta Figlerowicz, Mark Lipovetsky, Julie

Hemment, Rossen Djagalov, Serguei Oushakine, Marlène Laruelle, Maria Engström, Kevin Platt, Joan Brooks, and Eliot Borenstein. I'd also like to thank my fellow travelers and co-organizers of ASEEES panels and roundtables throughout the years, for the opportunity of building an intellectual community together, and for making this professional ritual much more enjoyable. These include, in particular, Pavel Khazanov, Maria Sidorkina, Maya Vinokour, Jason Cieply, and Maxim Hanukai. Ilya Budraitskis offered unique insights on post-Soviet politics and an outside perspective on my fieldwork during thirty-kilometer-long walks across Moscow (or sitting at a bar and drinking *kraftovoe pivo* when we got too tired) in the spring of 2015. I consider him a great ally.

The Tsentr noveishei russkoi literatury at RGGU (Russian State University for the Humanities) was my academic reference point in Moscow for many years. MGU (Moscow State University) was my host institution while I conducted my research for this project. The Tsentr sotsial'no-politicheskoi istorii and the Gosudarstvennyi tsentr sovremennogo iskusstva in Moscow gave me immediate access to the materials I needed, making my experience of Russian archives unexpectedly easy and enjoyable. From these institutions, I am particularly grateful to Elena Strukova and Olga Dementeva, respectively, for their help searching through the material, and to Ilya Budraitskis, for introducing me to both of them.

Brown University has been my academic home since 2016, and I couldn't think of a better place to pursue my research. I am thankful to my colleagues in the Department of Slavic Studies—Linda Cook, Lynne deBenedette, Svetlana Evdokimova, Masako Ueda Fidler, Vladimir Golstein, Spencer Golub, Alexander Levitsky, Michal Oklot, and Ethan Pollock—for giving me the chance to live in this true academic utopia, and for providing me with the best possible environment to complete my project. I am deeply grateful to my students for their enthusiasm and curiosity, for making teaching an absolute pleasure, and for motivating me to hone my narrative skills while keeping my facts straight.

A section of chapter 2 was first published in article form in the journal *Nationalities Papers*. I am grateful to Cambridge University Press for giving permission to reprint this material here. I would also like to express my deep appreciation to Peter Rutland for the amazing editorial work, the guidance through the publishing process, his feedback on the project, and his efforts to bring cultural studies and political science a bit closer.

At the University of Wisconsin Press, I'd like to thank my editor, Gwen Walker, who followed the publication process closely from the beginning, as well as Anna Muenchrath, who helped me bring the manuscript to the finish line. I am also grateful to Jennifer Conn, Sheila McMahon, Adam Mehring, and my copyeditor, Judith Robey, all of whom had an important role in shaping the final product, and to Laura Ilina, who gave permission to reproduce her photo on the cover of the book. A separate thanks goes to Megan Race for editing an earlier version of the manuscript.

I have an old debt of gratitude to Gian Piero Piretto, for the endless conversations about Soviet culture in Piazza Sant'Alessandro, and for introducing me to cultural studies; to Nadia Cicognini, for giving me unlimited unofficial access to all the literature I needed well before discovering the cornucopia of American libraries; and to Fausto Malcovati, for convincing me to stick to Russian during my second year of college. I'd like to thank Andrey Alikin, who made me feel like I had an old friend in Moscow for all these years, and Daria Varlamova, for the talks about Russian literature, and for getting me Limonov's phone number.

Finally, I am grateful to my mother, Patrizia, for being my main intellectual interlocutor for more than thirty-five years, and for the formal logic, and to my father, Francesco, who underneath the surface (and the tailor-made suits and English perfumes) was a true radical and would have loved to read a book about the *natsboly*. I am thankful to the cats who kept me company during the actual writing—first Jasper and then Palmiro—for teaching me the value of silence, and of chasing a feather once in a while. A special thanks goes to Alexandra, for the art and the inspiration, for keeping me sane, and for reminding me who I am.

Note on Transliteration

Transliteration of Russian words is based on the Library of Congress system, with the exception of first names, last names, and toponyms, for which I opted for the spelling most commonly used in American English. I therefore use Mayakovsky and not Maiakovskii, Navalny and not Naval'nii, Dmitry and not Dmitrii, Triumfalnaya Square and not Triumfal'naia Square. I am using Kharkov and not Kharkiv because the Ukrainian city is primarily discussed in connection with Limonov's novels. None of these exceptions apply to Russian sources cited in the notes and bibliography.

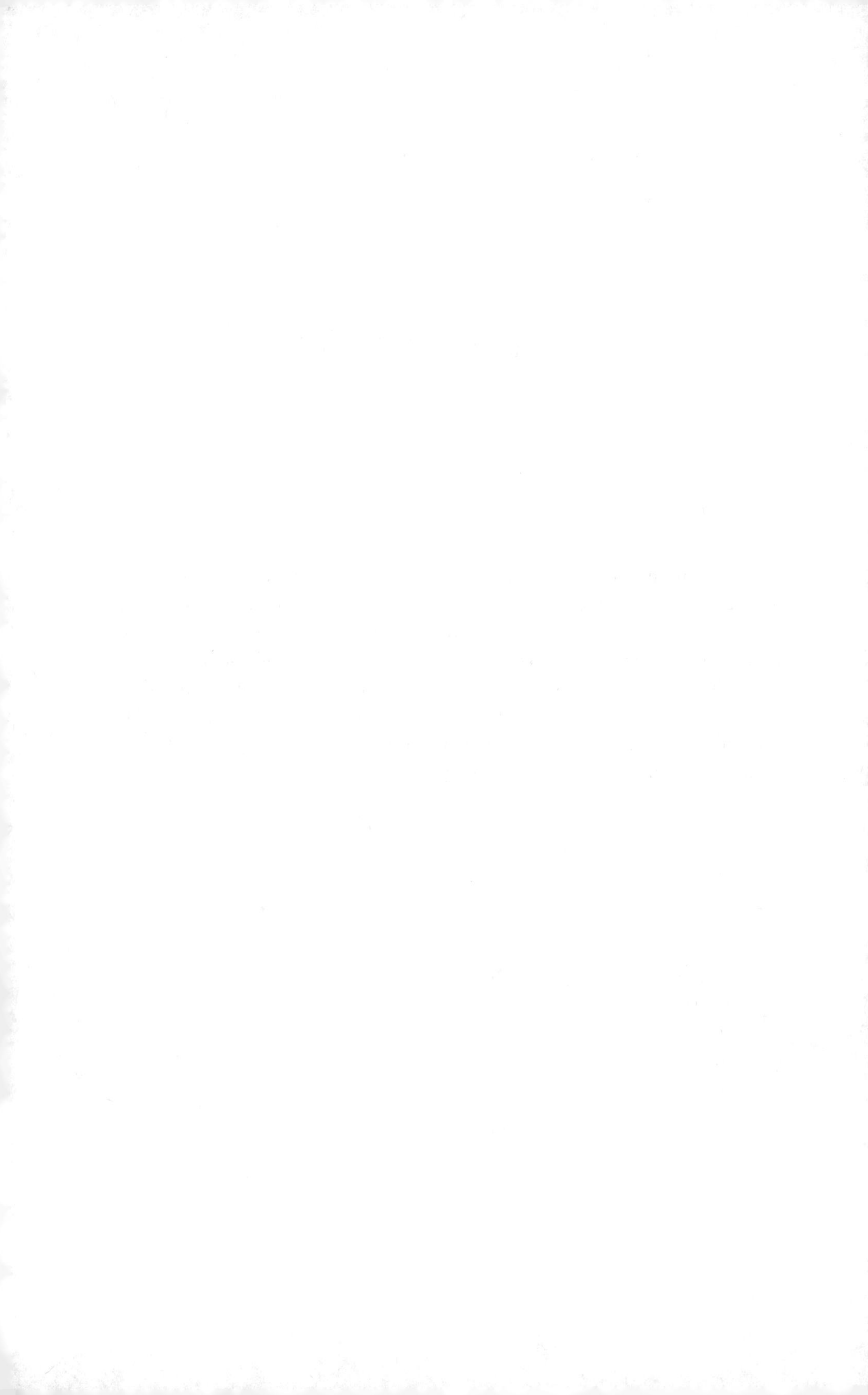

It Will Be Fun
and Terrifying

Introduction

> Gaunt napes of adolescents, / Their bony fists. / Birches. Dogs. Russia . . . / And you, like gaunt puppies . . . // You came from the slums, / From the dusk of pale cities, / From the vapors of vodka and valerian root, / From the mothers, the fathers, and the gals . . . / A row of heroic faces // I see on our hill. / Is Christ, quiet, revealed to them? / Even Christ wished he had / Such fearless apostles! // I found you all in a night humid, / Of Russia, a country of ice, / My terrible country of steel. / —I kiss your footsteps! // You, brave soldiers of the light, / Apostles, children, and sons, / Warriors of the black summer, / Like gaunt, angry puppies . . .
>
> Eduard Limonov, "Natsboly," 2009

In the winter of 2014–15, Eduard Limonov's political organization Drugaia Rossiia (The Other Russia), the current incarnation of the National Bolshevik Party (NBP), underwent a drastic change. To this moment, the *natsboly* (as the National Bolshevik activists are commonly referred to in Russia) had been among the most vocal opponents of Putin's government. In contrast to the widespread political passivity that characterized the first years of Putin's rule, they had organized numerous public protests and were subjected to harsh punishments and constant persecution by the Russian authorities. This state of affairs changed suddenly with the Russian annexation of Crimea, the beginning of the conflict in Eastern Ukraine, and Limonov's public support of Putin's foreign policy. Beginning in the spring of 2014, the organization stopped all protests against the Russian government. Instead, the *natsboly* started sending volunteer soldiers and humanitarian help to war zones in Donbass. National

Bolshevik activists began joining pro-Russian volunteer battalions in Eastern Ukraine, and photographs of heavily armed *natsboly* wearing camouflage began appearing on social media. Many *natsboly* were severely injured in the conflict. Some of them died in combat.

On December 31, 2014, I attended one of the meetings of Strategy-31, one of the *natsboly*'s initiatives, in Moscow's Triumfalnaya Square, at the center of which stands one of the city's main landmarks: a six-meter-tall monument to leading Russian avant-garde poet Vladimir Mayakovsky. Before the beginning of the conflict, when Strategy-31 had focused on advocating for freedom of speech and assembly, its unsanctioned demonstrations had been marked by regular beatings and arrests. In 2014, however, a sudden political shift occurred. The gatherings of Strategy-31 became "meetings in support of Donbass." The event I attended was sanctioned by the Moscow city government. Demonstrators stood within a fenced-in area set up by the police, who searched the participants and checked their bags at the entrance, and calmly listened to the speeches of the party leaders and representatives.

During the meeting, Beness Aijo, a black Latvian National Bolshevik, also known among the *natsboly* as "The Black Lenin," shouted from the stage that the war in Ukraine was to be seen as a class struggle between the workers and miners from the East Ukrainian region and the "Kievian oligarchs." The only way out of this conflict, he said, was to fight until the full reestablishment of the Soviet Union and its territories as they were prior to 1991. Aijo, a very committed activist, had joined the pro-Russian separatists soon after the beginning of the conflict. Like other volunteer fighters, he had been included in a list of people wanted by Interpol and would face prosecution if he were to return to Latvia.

Five months later, on May 31, 2015, I was back in the same square. This time, the public space was physically and symbolically divided into two opposing factions. On one side of the square, the *natsboly* chanted patriotic slogans, expressed their support for the pro-Russian separatists, celebrated the veterans who had returned from the war, honored those who had died, and gave speeches in support of various activists who were detained in Russian prisons for political reasons. On the other side, another type of event was taking place: the open public poetry readings called Maiakovskie chteniia (Mayakovskian readings). These readings, also started by some former members of the NBP, had been held on the last Sunday of every month since 2010.

Although the Maiakovskie chteniia had originally started as an extension of Strategy-31, the war had polarized the protesters, who took opposite positions on the conflict in Eastern Ukraine. While the *natsboly* called for the resistance against the "coup d'état of the Kievian junta," which for them embodied the unstoppable advance of global capital, the young poets gathered around Mayakovsky's monument expressed their opposition to the war. Although no real clashes between the two groups occurred, one could sense the underlying tension. At some point, an activist from Drugaia Rossiia shouted through a megaphone to the poets gathered on the other corner of the square that the *natsboly* would teach them "to be patriots." On the other side, the young poet who opened the public readings, shouting at the top of his lungs, provocatively asked to be killed by a Russian "militiaman" (*opolchenets*):

> Kill me, militiaman! / The cops will buy you the rod with state budget money. / Kill me, militiaman! / Become the punishing hand. / After all, I am not a person! Shit flows in my veins! / . . . / After all, I am not a patriot . . . or maybe you just don't like my ugly face. / Why do you need a reason? Fuck it! You don't need one! / . . . / You already tried blood! / You saw how for a brotherly people / Fighting brothers dig brotherly graves. / You turn on the TV—and you lose it, / Self-control was never your strongest side. / But then you have many other strong sides. / Kill me, volunteer! / Shoot the black sheep. / Take revenge for the crucified kid! / Save the Motherland from me! / Become a hero! / Kill me, volunteer! / Your president will be very proud of you. / Tear me to pieces! / Trample me down! / . . . // Because while you fought for Donbass, / I fucked your daughters, / And sold spice to your three-year-old son.[1]

During the reading, an excavator sent by the city administration drilled into the asphalt, producing a deafening noise. The organizers claimed that the sole purpose of the renovation was to disrupt the event, which sounded plausible, especially considering that the renovation, like the Maiakovskie chteniia, had started at 6 p.m. on a Sunday.

This moment felt revelatory. After several months spent studying intellectual and political communities built around the NBP, I witnessed how, even in a period of relative political stagnation, the culture of this radical organization had influenced Russian public life in complex and unexpected ways. These two groups of people shouting at each other and expressing diametrically opposed views on Triumfalnaya Square, a symbolic space in the history of post-Soviet protest culture, represented the two faces of the legacy of the NBP. They were living proof of the different ways in which this radical movement, in the long term, had deeply affected some of the most important political events of recent Russian history, from the wave of mass protests "for fair elections" of 2011–12 to the recent Russian intervention in Eastern Ukraine and the subsequent resurgence of nationalist and imperialist sentiments in Russian media and society.

The types of discourses that circulated and the communities that were forming on Triumfalnaya Square on those days also epitomized some of the coexisting, and deeply contradictory, elements that helped form the culture and identity of the NBP. Beness Aijo's speech and the strongly anti-Western discourses that circulated in the National Bolshevik camp reflected the way in which the NBP developed as an elaborate form of critique against capitalism and social inequality, and the fact that this form of critique was closely linked with the promotion of an aggressively nationalistic rhetoric. This specific countercultural paradigm had a deep influence both on the shaping of post-Soviet protest culture and on the development of Russian state ideology during the Putin era. The other side of the square, where young, rebellious, and at times impromptu poets turned the public space into their stage, embodied the more spontaneous and unstructured face of the NBP, which started, in fact, as a youth movement and a bohemian art project. Beyond all their ideological differences, these political communities reflected the identity and history of the NBP as a platform for political discussion that has produced new creative ways of appropriating public spaces and expressing dissent in post-Soviet Russia. The towering presence of Mayakovsky at the center of the square had an almost symbolic meaning. Both Limonov's writing and the culture of the NBP marked a return to the aesthetic posture of the Soviet avant-gardes, and to the myth of the October Revolution. The NBP could well be considered an artistic and political avant-garde, one that anticipated larger intellectual and ideological trends in Russian culture and society.

Drawing on year-long archival and ethnographic research in Moscow, *It Will Be Fun and Terrifying* examines the role of art and literary culture in the development of a post-Soviet public sphere. Specifically, it studies the making of one of the first post-Soviet "counterpublics," Limonov's National Bolshevik Party, as a network and community of radical artists, intellectuals, and political activists. I argue that, starting in the mid-1990s, the activity of this radical movement was marked by the gradual emergence of new forms of collective participation, which developed at the intersection of art, literature, performance, and political action, and which deeply affected the shaping of public culture and the formation of state ideology during the Putin era. To follow these developments, I combine textual analysis with ethnography based on participant observation, and more than forty in-depth interviews with activists and intellectuals close to the NBP and to Aleksandr Dugin's Eurasia Movement. In treating such topics as Limonov's fiction and political writings, the aesthetics of the radical newspaper *Limonka*, and Dugin's "imperial imagination," this book was conceived as a contribution to recent debates about the development of a post-Soviet public sphere and civil society, and about the applicability of such concepts to contemporary Russian society. By investigating the emergence of a "national-patriotic" opposition in the mid-1990s, *It Will Be Fun and Terrifying* also provides a new perspective on the growing role of nationalism in contemporary Russian society from the point of view of literary and cultural studies. At the same time, it offers new insights on the ways in which ideology has affected intellectual debates and the formation of opposing art and literary currents in recent Russian history.

The NBP was founded by Limonov and Dugin in the mid-1990s as an attempt to combine radical right- and left-wing ideologies. Limonov, who had just come back to Russia after several years of emigration in the United States and France, was then a scandalous writer and one of the first post-Soviet celebrities. Dugin, now frequently described by Western media as a sort of evil mastermind behind the Putin regime, was then an extravagant, mystical artist-philosopher coming from the "metaphysical" intellectual circles surrounding Soviet underground writer Yuri Mamleev. Throughout the 1990s, the NBP assumed several different identities. It was at the same time and at different stages of its existence a radical political movement, a bohemian community, and a punk squat. Before Limonov was arrested in 2001, the organization nearly turned into an illegal army, organized to start a partisan war in the mountains of Kazakhstan.

After Putin rose to power, and after Dugin left the organization, the NBP quite paradoxically fulfilled the function of a street avant-garde of the liberal opposition. The movement advocated for freedom of speech and social justice, and it protested against systematic human rights violations within Russian society. The *natsboly* became famous for staging symbolic protests against the government dubbed as *aktsii priamogo deistviia* (direct action stunts) or "tomato terrorism." In this same period, the Eurasia Movement, which was founded by Dugin and a group of former members of the NBP, had a key role in the absorption of fringe right and imperialist ideas into the Russian mainstream. Although Dugin has often been described as a sort of éminence grise of the Putin administration, his is de facto a "virtual" political movement. By sheer numbers it is absolutely marginal, comprising not so much a structured network of party activists as a small circle of right-wing intellectuals. This also applies to the Eurasian Youth Union (Evraziiskii Soiuz Molodezhi, or ESM), the "grassroots" incarnation of Dugin's neo-Eurasianism, which started as a radical, extremist, and relatively independent (from an ideological standpoint) fringe of the infamous pro-government youth movement Nashi. Like Nashi, the Eurasian Youth Union was used as an instrument of "political technology" and had significant financial and political support from the Russian government.[2] Also quite paradoxically, Dugin's small clique had even more influence on mass politics than the NBP, at least in part because of Dugin's own connections and pedagogical activities within the Russian power ministries, including the publication of his Ministry of Defense "textbook" on geopolitics.[3] Most importantly, the Eurasia Movement had an impact on Russian politics through the creation of "counterhegemonic" online networks that were explicitly aimed at infiltrating mainstream culture and legitimizing radical political ideas. This strategy was part of Dugin's "conservative postmodernism," which represented both a right-wing appropriation of Western critical theory, along with the legacy of the 1968 movement, and a conscious strategy to use postmodern irony and cynicism as an instrument to promote political violence and chaos. The idea of a conservative or reactionary form of postmodernism is also closely linked to Dugin's unique trajectory from art performance to political technology.

The impact of the NBP on contemporary Russian politics is ambiguous and problematic, in that the firmly anti-Western stance of this movement and even its specific kind of nonconformism have become part of Putin's own ideological arsenal, something that today is reflected in a widespread paradoxical vision of Russia as an "anti-imperialist Empire," a "countercultural empire," or a stronghold of both conservative and leftist (that is, in this case, anti-capitalist, anti-liberal, and anti-Western) values and beliefs.[4] On a global level, this vision in part explains the recent fascination with Russia on the part of such diverse political groups as European leftists, American white supremacists, and global hackers, which has become especially apparent since the beginning of the conflict in Eastern Ukraine, when Dugin's fringe ideas began to gain acceptance in Russia, even at the level of mainstream culture. In a way, this counterhegemonic or countercultural form of nationalism preannounced the emergence of the American alt-right, which shares with, and in part borrows from, Russian neo-Eurasianism the appropriation of postmodern provocation and alternative online networks, as well as a rejection of what is seen, broadly, as the "liberal mainstream." Both the American alt-right and Russian neo-Eurasianism have a strong connection to the European New Right, although one might argue that the American alt-right discovered the European New Right through the mediation of Russian neo-Eurasianism. Back in the 1990s, Dugin largely borrowed from the ideas of the European New Right, which emerged in France and Belgium during the 1970s, and he later reinvented and resold these fringe ideas back to the West, in the form of a new alternative to Western liberalism and civilization.

It Will Be Fun and Terrifying traces the social life of these ideas through the experience of National Bolshevik leaders and activists, as well as through cultural products that helped define the identity of the movement, including novels, newspapers, websites, paintings, political posters, and performances. This narrative follows a loosely chronological structure. The book starts with a discussion of Limonov's writing and the making of his literary and public persona in the 1970s and 1980s. Through his works, Limonov promoted a form of "dissidence within Soviet dissidence" and was a dissonant voice among Russian émigrés and the liberal intelligentsia. My analysis focuses, in particular, on Limonov's appropriation of Western countercultures and on the role played in his work by transgressive sexuality, the violation of gender boundaries, and queerness, viewed as quintessential forms of radical rejection of modernity. Limonov's writing and public activity, of course, are far from being the only forms of late Soviet dissent, but they are among the most overlooked, especially if one considers their impact on post-Soviet political activism. As a writer-provocateur, Limonov was seen as an extravagant figure who was too marginal to be taken seriously among scholars of Russian politics. A theoretical framework that could integrate his political activism with the post-Soviet reception of his works and their position within the Russian literary system was also lacking. Scholars of literature were drawn to Limonov as a radical writer playing with forms of political, sexual, and linguistic transgression and imitating Mayakovsky's provocative stance, but they became increasingly disenamored with him as soon as he started shooting machine guns and befriending war criminals in the former Yugoslavia and seeking alliance with neo-Nazis, Stalinists, and mystical far-right philosophers in Paris and Moscow. This was too much to digest, even as a provocative gesture, although one might argue that the aestheticization of violence and aggressive masculinity that Limonov embraced in this period were in fact consistent with his "sensual" quest for radicalism at all costs.

Next, I move from Limonov's lyric persona to the "early NBP" and the invention of new specifically post-Soviet modes of political protest after the fall of the Soviet Union and the parliamentary crisis of 1993. This was a time in which mass consumerism, widespread corruption, and crime, under the guise of Western liberal democracy, dominated Russian public life, a time that for many in Russia could not but be seen as a dark apocalyptic version of Francis Fukuyama's famous prophecy about the "end of history." Then, the only voices of political dissent came from the "national-patriotic" camp, which was composed of old obscurantists like the writer Aleksandr Prokhanov, hard-core Stalinists, and neo-Nazis but also by some of the same people who had enthusiastically supported Russia's transition to democracy in 1991, and who, only two years later, had become bitterly disappointed with this new state of affairs.

After Putin's rise to power, the NBP, which had started as a "political art project," turned into two very different things. In reaction to Putin's authoritarianism, the *natsboly*, who valued the revolutionary experience over ideological consistency and wanted to maintain their oppositional identity, started advocating for human rights and freedom of speech through carefully choreographed stunts, which represented some of the earliest forms of protest against the new regime, and which inspired, among other things, the emergence of radical art collectives like Voina and Pussy Riot. At the same time, Dugin and his group of National Bolshevik "schismatics" founded the fervently pro-Putin Eurasia Movement, an organization that systematically promoted and legitimized ultra-reactionary views through both mainstream and independent media.

The culture of the NBP influenced post-Soviet political processes in various and unexpected ways. By the beginning of the 2000s, the NBP had, according to various estimates, between one and five thousand deeply committed activists, although it should be noted that its real strength did not lie as much in the sheer number of supporters but in their level of commitment. As far as street politics is concerned, both the NBP and the Eurasia Movement were also recently instrumental in sending thousands of volunteers (mostly hotheads and soccer hooligans) to Crimea and Eastern Ukraine to destabilize the political situation in preparation for, and support of, Russia's covert military operations. Yet the most important way in which the NBP had a long-term impact on Russian politics was through the invention of new forms of political dissent, which later influenced, in a roundabout way, Russian public culture and mainstream politics.

In this sense, this book is about the making of a political community but also about the making of a broader public through different media. These include the above-mentioned radical newspaper *Limonka*, which had a significant influence on various youth subcultures; the *natsboly*'s public performances, which reached wide audiences through Russian and foreign media; and the neo-Eurasianists' online and offline networks. By looking closely at the culture, language, history, and everyday life of these radical communities, it is possible to better understand post-Soviet public culture in general, and the ways in which this culture eludes and differs from existing Western models of civil society.

The NBP came to fill a political void in post-Soviet public culture. In the context of the widespread political passivity that characterized Russian society between 1993 and 2011, this radical organization called for a quasi-religious commitment to a collective cause. In contrast with the general mistrust toward any form of political ideology, the *natsboly* returned to the ideals of the October Revolution and embraced a radical, "ultra-ideological" position, by reclaiming the legacy of early Soviet and Stalinist culture, the aesthetics and ideology of Italian Fascism and German Nazism, and various Western countercultures, radical political movements, and terrorist organizations. This was, first and foremost, a way of denying the possibility of a "normalized," unideological society based on a generic vision of an "imaginary Western democracy" that dominated Russian mainstream politics and media in the early post-Soviet period.[5]

The idea that post-Soviet public life is generally dominated by a fundamental political passivity and disengagement is one that is commonly accepted. Nancy Ries argues that "litanies" and "lamentations" were the main discursive genre in everyday conversations and mass media between 1989 and 1992, and she retraces the origins of this discursive mode back to Russian literary and religious traditions as well as to Soviet everyday strategies of survival.[6] Drawing on Ries, Artemy Magun claims that post-Soviet society was dominated by "depoliticization," postrevolutionary "apathy and melancholia," and "an aggressive propaganda of despair in media and in private communication."[7] For him, the catastrophic apocalyptic discourses that dominated early post-Soviet public life were fundamentally ritualistic in nature, in that they replaced "the cynical subjectivity of late socialist society, where one would pay lip service to the ideology s/he did not believe, and this sufficed for the survival of the system."[8] These post-Soviet catastrophic lamentations, "associated with prosaic consumerist enjoyment," not only served as a substitute for the participation in hollow late Soviet collective rituals but also fulfilled the function of justifying the amoral, selfish, or even openly antisocial behaviors that were becoming a common part of everyday life in Russia during the 1990s.[9]

In a similar vein, Serguei Oushakine defines the political paralysis produced by the fall of the Soviet Union and the *bespredel* (lawlessness) of the 1990s as "post-Soviet aphasia," described as the inability to find the conceptual and linguistic tools necessary to relate and elaborate on the post-Soviet condition.[10] The ideas of trauma and loss also inform Oushakine's take on the emergence of various forms of patriotism in the Russian provinces after the fall of the Soviet Union.[11] In the absence of positive political models, he argues, post-Soviet "communities of loss" based their sense of belonging on shared narratives of trauma and suffering, narratives that ultimately translated into ideas of ethnic and national distinction.[12] The trauma produced by the miserable economic conditions and the lack of social support that followed Russia's abrupt transition to capitalism has also generated a widespread distrust in politics, democracy, Western culture, and liberal values. This distrust extends to grassroots politics, foreign NGOs, and civil society organizations.[13]

Although the NBP also started in reaction to the trauma produced by the fall of the Soviet Union and the neoliberal reforms of the 1990s, the culture of this radical organization involved more positive and structured forms of political activism. At a time when political passivity dominated large segments of Russian society, the NBP functioned as a cultural and political avant-garde, not only by appropriating the aesthetic posture of the "historical avant-gardes" but also by challenging the status quo "in subversive, illegal or alternative ways."[14] Like Italian and Russian futurism and several other world avant-gardes, the NBP also indirectly contributed to the rhetoric and ideology of an authoritarian state apparatus. Like many Russian modernists, the *natsboly* often became also the victims of this authoritarian system.

Since the *natsboly* had a pioneering role within post-Soviet protest culture, everyone who later became involved in grassroots politics—the art collectives Voina and Pussy Riot, the various groups involved in the 2011–12 protest movement, and, paradoxically, Putin's government itself—had to deal with the legacy of this organization. In addition, the Eurasia Movement has attempted to "revolutionize Russia from within" state institutions, power structures, and mainstream and alternative media (even if this revolution, in Dugin's mind, would be, of course, conservative and nationalist). In both cases, the influence of these organizations on the otherwise politically passive post-Soviet public has occurred at the level of a "political unconscious." The utopian "Other Russia" of Limonov and the NBP is not just "the other Russia" of protest culture and dissent or "the other Russia" of post-Soviet nationalism but also "another," specifically post-Soviet, type of public sphere that often defies Western ideas and expectations about civil society and political activism. The goal of this book is to overcome the common tendency to see recent Russian politics as rigidly divided between "Putin's repressive government" and "spontaneous political movements," and to look at a series of gray zones of influence and contestation between state-sponsored "virtual" politics and grassroots forms of cultural resistance and civil disobedience.

Studying the social practices and cultural networks surrounding the NBP represents a way to address both how one becomes a political activist in the context of the general ideological disillusionment of the post-Soviet period and how the production, circulation, and reception of certain art and literary texts have affected contemporary Russian politics in general and grassroots politics in particular. In Russian culture, art and literature have traditionally been seen as privileged media for the discussion of social and political matters. It is a commonly accepted view that, during the nineteenth century, literature functioned as a substitute for an underdeveloped "political public sphere."[15] At the beginning of the eighteenth century, *literatura*, or *belles lettres*, came to replace *pis'mennost'*, the written language that in pre-Petrine Russia was used almost exclusively in the religious sphere and therefore had a privileged role in defining the spiritual and moral values of Russian society.[16] In the late eighteenth and the early nineteenth centuries, literary styles, genres, and currents deeply affected everyday behavior, political struggle, and the establishment of social hierarchies and rituals.[17] Of course, the question of literature's ability to transform and influence society is also of paramount importance throughout the nineteenth century, most notably in the works of Vissarion Belinsky and the Natural School and in the public and didactic activity of the "literary giants" Tolstoy and Dostoevsky. Throughout the twentieth century, art and literature not only served as media for political discussion but also affected a radical transformation of society according to "aesthetic principles," helping to establish Soviet collective rituals, traditions, and social norms.[18]

The culture of the communities under study here at the same time follows and departs from this tradition. Limonov's writing and the form of counterculture that it inspired both reinforce and deeply challenge the traditional logocentrism of Russian culture and society. On the one hand, after his return to Russia in the early 1990s, Limonov presented himself as both a literary icon and a literary hero, and the *natsboly* adopted behaviors and aesthetic postures borrowed from Limonov's prose and public self-presentation. On the other hand, in both his writing and public statements, Limonov openly challenged the classic image and value system of the Soviet and Russian *intelligent*, and the *natsboly* explicitly attacked the Russian intelligentsia for its alleged passive acceptance of the status quo, for its hypocrisy, and for its ill-concealed elitism. The cult of marginality, heroism, and political violence; the play with gender and sexuality, often in the form of aggressive masculinity; and, generally, the cult of beauty and physical strength, which the *natsboly* borrowed from Limonov's writing and public image—all of these elements represented a strong reaction against the traditional values of the Russian intelligentsia. As a "political art project," the NBP attempted to create an alternative intellectual class oriented toward political and revolutionary action, a "counter-intelligentsia."

The reception of Limonov's (and Dugin's) work not only created a readership but also gave rise to structured political communities that shared a common culture and a common set of beliefs. Both Limonov and Dugin actively tried to turn their work into a form of political action and made politics their main sphere of activity. For this reason, their work constitutes an ideal case study for understanding the way in which certain forms of art and literature turn into political action, through the creation of alternative languages, institutions, and modes of collective participation. Performativity and performance shape styles of behavior and modes of socialization within the political communities I am looking at, and play an important role in the making of the public personas of Limonov, Dugin, and the other artists, intellectuals, and political figures who populate the pages of this book. Gender and political performativity, for instance, help clarify the role of Limonov's prose within the Russian literary tradition, and the ways in which his writing imagines and projects the emergence of a community of readers founded on shared ideas and experiences of marginality and rebellion.

The making of the NBP as a countercultural movement is connected, among other things, with the emergence of a readership for Limonov's prose and for the party newspaper, *Limonka*, which gathered a diverse crowd of countercultural figures and unconventional political thinkers on both the left and the right of the political spectrum. *Limonka*, which was sold in alternative rock, punk, and heavy metal record stores, was the main instrument that the founders of the NBP used to attract new members to the party, and it soon became a cult periodical among the alternative youth of the 1990s. By combining articles about political theory, mysticism, radical right- and left-wing international movements, literature, and rock music—and by promoting emergent alternative writers, visual artists, and musicians—the newspaper helped form an alternative cultural canon for the movement. *Limonka* had a key role in the making of the NBP as a countercultural community, both through the literal collective work linked with the production of the newspaper and through the development of this shared cultural and political canon, which informed the *natsboly*'s values and lifestyles. In effect, *Limonka* translated Limonov's writing and aesthetic posture into a collective identity for the movement.

According to Benedict Anderson, in the eighteenth and nineteenth centuries, the novel and the newspaper constituted the "means for 'representing' the kind of imagined community that is the nation."[19] For Anderson, the way newspapers and novels represent simultaneous events as happening in "homogeneous, empty time" constitutes "a precise analogue of the idea of the nation, which also is conceived as a solid community moving steadily down [or up] history."[20] In addition, the simultaneous reading ritual or "mass ceremony" of the newspaper reinforced the notion of an "imagined community" of myriad unknown individual silent readers that together comprised the ideal of the nation as a secular collective.[21] Following a similar principle, the creation of the NBP as a "public" also involved the establishment of shared reading habits and rituals centering on novels and newspapers. In discussing this material, this book follows a trajectory that goes from the individual to the collective, from the elaboration of ideas and narratives by single authors to their reception and transformation within a community, including the assimilation of these ideas into mainstream and mass culture, and vice versa. In other words, the book investigates not only the ways in which the circulation of art and literary texts affected the shaping of this political community but also how the social life of this community, in turn, affected the elaboration of ideas and the production of cultural texts.

This approach applies, among other things, to the use of symbols and ideas belonging to Italian Fascism, German Nazism, and early Soviet and Stalinist culture within both the NBP and the Eurasia Movement. While these symbols and ideas featured prominently in the aesthetics and ideology of these organizations, I decided not to dwell on matters of definition or classification. Several scholars have defined Limonov's NBP and Dugin's Eurasia Movement as "fascist" or "neofascist," following different conceptions of "generic fascism." Stephen Shenfield, who wrote the first English-language book on post-Soviet far-right movements, used the following definition as a starting point: "Fascism is an authoritarian populist movement that seeks to preserve and restore premodern patriarchal values within a new order based on communities of race, nation, or faith."[22] Roger Griffin's definition of fascism, which lays claim to universality, and which has been applied, at various points, to both the NBP and the Eurasia Movement, is the following: "Fascism is a genus of political ideology whose mythic core in its various permutations is a palingenetic form of ultra-nationalism."[23] A problem with trying to apply definitions of this kind to specific movements and organizations, primarily on the basis of official statements and political programs, is that in doing so we fail to take into account the positions of these movements and organizations in relation to power structures, governmental institutions, and global and local socioeconomic trends. In the context of Russian nationalism, for example, the definition of "generic fascism" has been applied to a wide range of players: the NBP, an illegal countercultural movement vehemently opposed to Putin's regime; the Eurasia Movement, a state-funded organization that has advocated for political repressions against most opposition groups in Russia (including the NBP) and the liberal independent media; and Vladimir Zhirinovsky's LDPR (Liberal-Democratic Party of Russia)—a party that, as opposed to Dugin's and Limonov's organizations, has participated in Russian elections regularly since the mid-1990s and has maintained a significant representation in the Duma throughout the years.[24]

Using a universal definition of "generic fascism" to describe and classify political movements across the world may obscure important cultural, linguistic, and historical distinctions. Being or even calling oneself a fascist—or a democrat, liberal, or socialist—means something different in Russia today than it would in Germany, Italy, Sweden, or, say, in America in the early twentieth century, when Marcus Garvey, founder of the Universal Negro Improvement Association (UNIA), explicitly claimed ideological kinship with Italian Fascism.[25] "Fascist" is also a particularly loaded term, frequently used as a derogatory label to discredit political adversaries, and this makes its use as a scientific tool potentially problematic. This is especially true in the context of post-Soviet politics. A good example of this is the infamous mass pro-government youth movement Nashi (Ours), which was created by Putin's influential adviser Vladislav Surkov in 2005 with the surreptitious goal of preventing and repressing any form of opposition against the government. In a clear attempt to leverage the strong legacy of World War II, Nashi defined itself as "democratic" and "anti-fascist."[26] However, at the time various international commentators criticized this "anti-fascist" movement's clear resemblance to both the Komsomol (the Soviet Young Communist League) and the Hitler Youth. The organization was even dubbed "Putinjugend."[27] Nashi attacked and denigrated all extra-parliamentary opposition groups, including the NBP, which at that point was mainly focusing on issues of social justice, civil rights, and freedom of speech. Its methods were quite brutal and included hiring skinheads and soccer hooligans to savagely beat members of the opposition and raid their headquarters, and the *natsboly* became among the most frequent victims of these attacks. In order to legitimate their repressive methods, Nashi's leaders accused the members of the NBP of being fascists and even provided "scholarly evidence" to support their claims. Most significantly, Boris Yakemenko, a historian and a university professor, and the brother of the leader of Nashi, Vasily Yakemenko, published a book titled *Limonov o Limonove* (Limonov on Limonov) supporting this view; in it, he used as "historical evidence" comparisons between the symbols and aesthetics of the NBP and those of Nazi Germany.[28] The accusation of fascism extended to all members of the "liberal-fascist opposition" against Putin, which in the mind of Nashi's leaders comprised liberals, leftists, human-rights activists, independent journalists, and various international NGOs.[29] At the same time, the Russian anti-extremism law, which was formally aimed at preventing hate crimes and xenophobia, was consistently misused to imprison both nationalist and leftist members of the opposition.[30] More recently, accusations of fascism have also featured prominently in various inflamed discussions surrounding Euromaidan, the annexation of Crimea, and the conflict in Eastern Ukraine. In Russian mainstream media, the term has been used to discredit the wave of Ukrainian protests (by using as evidence the significant role played in the Maidan by ultranationalist groups). In Western media, the accusation has been leveled against Putin, on the basis of his authoritarianism and geopolitical adventures, and it has expanded to include the entirety of the Russian political system.[31]

Rather than trying to determine which organization or public figure can be defined as "objectively" fascist, this book focuses more specifically on what the use of fascist or totalitarian symbols and ideas meant for different members of these organizations in the context of the social, historical, and economic circumstances in which these movements emerged. It also considers the types of social and political practices these movements produced and how these practices helped shape post-Soviet political culture. This can be defined as a framework based on a vision of culture as a "system of meanings," as opposed to a "system of values": "To look at culture in terms of values is to approach the question from a normative and, not infrequently, ethnocentric perspective. . . . To look at it in terms of meanings, on the other hand, is to attempt to reveal the language in which people, who may disagree about values, or political ends, can do so within a shared perspective."[32]

In the case of the NBP, this has meant to trace the intellectual history of the organization, starting from its prehistory in Limonov's "poetics of marginality" to the aesthetics and the collective narratives produced in the pages of the newspaper *Limonka* and the invention of alternative lifestyles within this community. In the case of Dugin's Eurasia Movement, the book shows how this intellectual community identified with a "conservative bohemia" and an alternative intellectual and academic network, aimed at covertly influencing political processes during the Putin era. The movement "from the individual to the collective" in the case of the NBP took place through the organization of a successful grassroots political movement. Dugin's followers, in contrast, built small close intellectual circles that never became a real political force. However, the neo-Eurasianists' polarizing ideas and elaborate conspiracy theories had an influence on Russian public culture through the mediation of official mainstream media, academic institutions, and a thick network of fringe online forums and publications. The Eurasia Movement is a very useful example of the ways in which radical ideas can be assimilated into mainstream culture and used, in unexpected ways, to support power structures and repressive state apparatuses. Although they shared a common history and a common background, the NBP and the Eurasia Movement fulfilled opposite functions in the context of Russian public life. The NBP provided young disenfranchised Russians with a political platform and produced new creative forms of political dissent. Dugin's Eurasia Movement, on the other hand, supported the establishment of an authoritarian regime and the systematic repressions of its political opponents.

Dominant views about Soviet and post-Soviet politics today build, more or less explicitly, on Alexei Yurchak's concept of "living beyond [*vnye*]," defined as the main mode of collective participation in late Soviet society, or on variations of this theoretical framework. According to Yurchak, performativity deeply affected social behavior and political processes during the late Soviet period. The repetitive and formulaic language of Soviet bureaucracy, based on empty declarations of loyalty to the socialist cause, were mainly used in a ritualistic manner, as a way to confirm one's belonging to a specific social group. In particular, *stiob*, a form of parody based on "overidentification" with the object of parody (individual, institution, authority) itself, constituted a common way of subtly criticizing, and at the same time paradoxically supporting, the survival of Soviet political dogmas and institutions. *Stiob* reinforced the sense of belonging to one's community, and at the same time it allowed members of the "last Soviet generation" to provide Soviet everyday life and rituals with new and unexpected meanings. Living beyond and at the same time challenging and implicitly reinforcing the status quo characterized both the life and identity of official organizations like the Komsomol and the culture of underground art communities like the Moscow Conceptualists and the Leningrad's New Artists.[33]

Post-Soviet society appears to have inherited from "the last Soviet generation" its fundamental political passivity. Scholars in the fields of art and literary history have claimed that Moscow Conceptualism and Russian postmodernism, in their struggle against the totalitarian impulses of Stalinism and the historical avant-gardes, have remained "untainted" from any utopian impulse, producing fully "de-ideologized" art forms.[34] At the same time, political analysts have described Putin's Russia as a reign of "virtual" or "postmodern" politics, dominated by a cynical and corrupt form of authoritarianism hiding behind pure simulacra of parties, movements, and ideologies.[35]

In this context, the NBP's provocative pastiche of totalitarian symbols and ideas marked the emergence of a new form of paradoxical "militant *stiob*" or "militant living beyond" as a reaction to the early post-Soviet political impasse. At the time, the "national-patriotic" front that the NBP had emerged from represented, for better or worse, the only form of political opposition, and the NBP was the only organization in this coalition with some cultural and ideological substance. The situation changed drastically during the first decade of the 2000s, although then, also, the NBP kept playing an important role within the political opposition. On this front, some new prominent leading public figures (Garry Kasparov, Mikhail Kasyanov, Mikhail Khodorkovsky, and Anna Politkovskaya, among others) appeared, but the *natsboly* were among the few organizations that dared to take to the streets and express dissent publicly, and they certainly remained among the most vocal and most effective from the point of view of resonance and media coverage. In the pro-government camp, state-sponsored youth groups like Nashi were able to organize (mostly thanks to generous financial support from the government) huge mass demonstrations and gatherings, but they lacked any form of ideological cohesion. Surkov's neoliberal authoritarianism (or "sovereign democracy") was short-lived. Nashi and other similar organizations disappeared almost instantaneously as soon as state funding was withdrawn.[36] During his third presidential term (2012–18), Putin clearly turned to an imperialist, conservative, and overtly anti-Western rhetoric, which is definitely closer to Dugin's fringe ideas than to Surkov's vaguely patriotic promotion of markedly Western, or American, values of entrepreneurship and individual initiative.

Both the NBP and the Eurasia Movement, in different ways, have participated in a specific "culture of *stiob*." As countercultural communities born at the intersection of art and politics, these radical groups have proposed alternative lifestyles (ways of "living beyond") aimed at resisting consumerist culture and mainstream politics. The aesthetics of *Limonka*, Dugin's writing and public performances, and the art project of Aleksey Beliaev-Gintovt, the self-proclaimed stylist of the Eurasia Movement, display clear elements of *stiob* in that they provocatively appropriate, reinvent, and transform incompatible aesthetic and political stances, providing them with new unexpected meanings and calling into question traditional ideological categories. The fact that these groups applied such "flickering aesthetics" to post-Soviet grassroots and mainstream politics raises important questions about the possibility of using these discursive modes as tools of political struggle and even instruments of political repression. The National Bolsheviks' romantic utopianism and quasi-religious devotion to a collective cause, and the Eurasianists' direct involvement with power structures and repressive state apparatuses, are indications of the fact that new forms of militant or political *stiob* have emerged in the post-Soviet period. In fact, the history of these communities challenges and complicates the notion of "living beyond," by proving that "living beyond," in a space outside politics or cynically detached from moral responsibility, is in itself a political choice.[37]

Gender and sexuality; bohemianism, seen as the artistic invention of an alternative reality; and the dialectic between postmodern and avant-garde stances and sensibilities are some of the recurring categories used to define different forms of counterculture and political resistance throughout the book. The "imagined alternative communities" described in Limonov's fiction are often to be found in bohemian art milieus or among the tough kids of the Soviet industrial peripheries—or in unique, unexpected combinations of the two environments. His lyric personas borrow explicitly from the posture of the Soviet avant-gardes, freely combined with the aggressive attitude of punk subcultures. At the same time, sexuality and the systematic transgression of gender norms, in the form of either a queer sensibility or that of aggressive masculinity, play an important role both in Limonov's "poetics of marginality" and in his (not always consistent) political convictions. Limonov's rejection of modernity is largely based on a utopian vision of sexual emancipation. In reaction to a neoliberal end of history, the early NBP combined youth subcultures, the aesthetics of the historical avant gardes, and a wide range of totalitarian and extremist symbols and discourses. In the pages of *Limonka*, such avant-garde gestures are clearly described as part of a struggle against an emergent post-Soviet "society of the spectacle," and throughout their history the *natsboly* have often combined bohemian and social forms of protest against capitalism. A "search for authenticity" through bodily or physical experience, in the form of public performances or proximity to death on a battlefield, was an important element of the kind of political activism promoted by this alternative community.

Dugin's writing and public activity are dominated by a complex and paradoxical interpretation of postmodernism as a political weapon to be appropriated in a neotraditionalist struggle against modern civilization. Here, too, as in the case of the NBP, "the end of the spectacle" is realized through the "modernist" experience of (political) violence and death, which mark a return to the (premodern or analogic?) authenticity of physical experience. In their rejection of Western capitalism and modern civilization, the neo-Eurasianists see themselves as members of a "conservative bohemia"; what I describe here as their "radical political shimmering" is based in part on a specific cult of the late Soviet underground and in part on the "totalitarian queerness" of Timur Novikov's New Academy.

Sexuality, bohemianism, and the dichotomy between postmodern and avant-garde sensibilities are interconnected concepts defining the identity of these communities. In this context, the distinction between modernism, or the aesthetics of the avant-gardes, and postmodernism, which is generally associated with late capitalism and the postindustrial society, is the most potentially confusing. Neo-Eurasianism is conceived as an ideology struggling against postmodernism and postmodernity and, at the same time, as a quintessentially postmodern political theory, as the neo-Eurasianists clearly apply the strategies of postmodern art to mainstream and grassroots politics. The aesthetics and ideology of the NBP, in many respects, evokes the idea of a return to a "modernist" romantic utopianism, and, at the same time, the mix of right-wing and left-wing symbols and cultural figures produced on the pages of *Limonka* might be seen as a form of postmodern ideological pastiche.

The best way to look at this issue is through the prism of temporality and actual political practices (as opposed to programmatic statements). Following this approach, one could look at the historical avant-gardes as an embodiment of a modern faith in progress, based on a linear conception of time, and at postmodern culture as a critique of modernity and the project of the Enlightenment based on a circular conception of time. Borrowing the terminology of Mikhail Epstein, who interprets different trends in the aesthetic-ideological landscape of contemporary Russian culture in connection with their relationship with time, avant-garde political tendencies are marked by "the utopian obsession with the future" ("the happiness of coming generations"), whereas postmodern trends are characterized by the "infatuation with the present" or "the disappearance of time in a synchronic play of significations."[38] On the basis of this theoretical framework, the romantic heroism and the vision of a utopian, uninterrupted "revolutionary time" that was associated with the type of political activism promoted by the NBP defines the aesthetics and ideology of this community as closest to an avant-garde stance. In contrast, the neo-Eurasianist vision of a timeless, posthistorical, and neotraditionalist utopia, conceived as a "flourishing complexity" of cultural archetypes, clearly evokes a postmodern "synchronic play of significations." This dichotomy also impacts the kind of social practices that these communities have promoted: in the case of the NBP, the authenticity of unmediated, extreme bodily experiences; in the case of Dugin's Eurasia Movement, a visionary "intellectual game" and a form of systematic manipulation of reality through media.

This complex web of cultural categories at the same time influenced and reflected broader political trends. The ideological "queerness" or fluidity of these movements was an expression of "the extreme fluidity and plurality of the youth cultural sphere in the second half of the 1980s," which was based on continuous exchanges and overlaps between different *tusovki*, or "scenes."[39] As Hilary Pilkington points out, this fluidity reflected "a temporary suspension of the usual norms of signification" that involved both counterculture and institutional politics: "the signifier 'liberal,' for example, may be used to indicate anything from reform-communism to market-authoritarianism while that of 'democratic' is not only polysemic but omni-semic."[40] Having established itself as a pioneering political group, the NBP played an important role in the shaping of the "political grammars" and "repertoires of contention" of later political communities, such as the art groups Voina and Pussy Riot and the diverse range of groups and organizations that participated in the 2011–12 protest movement. Among other things, these later political communities displayed a similar ideological and cultural "fluidity."[41] The long-term impact of these categories is also evident in the sphere of gender and sexual politics, as is shown by the displays of aggressive masculinity and the hypersexualized representations of female bodies characterizing both the pro-government and the opposition camps under Putin.[42]

These findings confirm the importance of adopting a "bottom-up," or grounded, approach to the study of contemporary Russian politics, based on the idea of a post-Soviet transformation of culture and society rather than a normative conception of "transition" to Western models of liberal democracy.[43] Accordingly, the social and cultural networks built around the NBP, which were mapped through snowball sampling and participant observation, function as a structuring principle of this book. All of the authors, thinkers, and communities discussed in the book are or have been connected to each other and have in various ways influenced each other's work and ideas. In retracing the culture and history of these communities, the book covers a wide range of media and primary sources, including prose fiction, political writing, critical theory, journalism, visual and performance art, and ethnographic material. In moving across these different materials, it follows the ways in which ideas develop and transform when they reach different audiences and communities.

Following a common practice in cultural anthropology, I have done everything possible to protect my informants' identity by using pseudonyms and altering personal information. Even when informants gave me permission to use their real names (which was almost always the case), I erred on the side of caution. When any issue of privacy or personal danger arose, and, in fact, whenever possible, I decided to conceal the identity of my subjects. I used real names only in certain isolated cases, and exclusively when my informants' statements reflected what they had or would have shared publicly.

Both while conducting my fieldwork and while writing about these communities, I was particularly conscious of my position as a Western scholar studying both subversive and pro-government political organizations in a post-socialist country. I gave considerable thought to how interacting with, and writing about, these groups could affect them, and to the ways in which my project intervenes in local and global political processes, especially in consideration of the recent reemergence of strong geopolitical tensions between Russia and the United States.[44] Taking inspiration from Clifford Geertz's definition of culture as a "web of significance" and of cultural analysis as "an interpretive science in search of meaning," I decided to focus on what different ideological constructs meant for the members of the communities I studied and what social and political practices they produced, as opposed to identifying or defining the values that they embraced.[45]

Having conceived this as a cultural studies project, I have applied the tools of literary analysis to the interpretation of contemporary Russian political processes—like the rise of nationalism and the emergence of specifically post-socialist forms of publicity. This approach and case study make it possible to tackle questions traditionally related to literary history that would be impossible to fully grasp without resorting to extensive ethnographic fieldwork—such as the reception, consumption, and circulation of literary works, and the relationship between reading practices and political commitment. Roland Barthes famously argued that "in order to do interdisciplinary work, it is not enough to take a 'subject' (a theme) and to arrange two or three sciences around it. Interdisciplinary study consists of creating a new object, which belongs to no one."[46] The post-Soviet convergence of art, literature, radical politics, critical theory, right- and left-wing ideologies, national identity, and state propaganda described in this book is intended as just such a new object that belongs to no one.

1

"The Power of the State Should Be in the Hands of the Punks"

The Literary Origins of a Protest Movement

We have to select people for a new nation. We can call it differently, maybe not "Russians" but, say, "Eurasians" or "Scythians." It doesn't even matter that much, but the new nation should be founded on other principles, not the color of the hair or the eyes, but the courage, the loyalty, and the sense of belonging to our community. We will need children from these new people. . . . This is why we will have to allow many types of families . . . [and] polygamy, and free love. . . . We will teach boys and girls how to shoot a grenade launcher, to jump from a helicopter, to besiege villages and cities, to skin sheep and pigs, to cook tasty hot food, and to write poetry. . . . They will read the poems of Nikolay Gumilev, and the books of Lev Gumilev. Whole generations will be taught to love the East, according to the precepts of Konstantin Leontev. They will learn the beauty of the blue steppe, and the red mountains. And all the vileness of the concrete barracks, and all the vileness of Moscow slums. . . . By studying the experience of recent revolutions—the Russian Revolution of 1917, the German or National-Socialist, and the Italian Fascist revolutions, and even those that are more distant in time, like the Great French Revolution of 1789—one realizes that these were not just the revolutions, respectively, of the proletariat, of the fascists, of the bourgeoisie. These were also, in their essence, revolutions of the youth against the middle class and the old people. . . . All victorious revolutions are victories of the sons against the fathers, of youth against middle age.

Eduard Limonov, *Drugaia Rossiia*

Limonov's books are all an autobiography. He simply tells how he lives. And that's why I was interested in his books. Because he narrates his life, and he narrates in a very accessible language. He describes the smallest details, he remembers certain moments, what happened around [him], and he describes the entire situation. And Limonov's books were for me—they were like the *Tibetan Book of the Dead*. The *Tibetan Book of the Dead* is not for the dead, but for those who are alive. [It is a book about] how to live your life, a sort of instruction booklet. And all of these books that Limonov wrote were for me the same kind of instructions: "how to live." This is why I was never scared of the cops, of the police. I was never scared of ending up in prison. And in prison, I wasn't scared of my cellmates—because there's nothing to be scared of, because they are sufferers [*stradal'tsy*], just like you. And when I read his memoirs about his youth, I understand that I had the same youth—I used to steal and get into fights in backyards in the same way. And writing those books, he proved that he was exactly like you. He didn't sit there and write a book about crooks and thieves. He went and wrote *The Other Russia*: "how to educate a new generation; how to build a new country."

Aleksey, twenty-seven, artist and former member of the NBP,
Moscow, April 2015

In the opening pages of *Eto ia—Edichka* (1979), the "scandalous" novel that gave Eduard Limonov international recognition, the narrator and protagonist of the title stands, half-naked, on the balcony of the top floor of the cheap and dilapidated Hotel Winslow, between Madison Avenue and Fifty-Fifth Street in Midtown New York. It is a hot summer day, and Edichka is eating cold *shchi* (cabbage soup) directly from the pot with a traditional Russian wooden spoon decorated "with flowers of scarlet, gold, and black." As he looks defiantly at "the thousand eyes" of the employees working behind the windows of the surrounding office buildings, Edichka addresses some imagined passersby, asking them to look up:

> A nearly, sometimes entirely naked man, eating *shchi* from a pot. They don't know it's *shchi*, though. What they see is that every other day, on a hot plate there on the balcony, a man cooks a huge steaming pot of something barbaric. . . . I'm not inhibited. I am often to be found bare-assed in my shallow little room, my member pale against the background of the rest of my body, and I do not give a damn whether they see me or don't, the clerks, secretaries, and managers. I'd rather they did see me. They're probably used to me by now, and perhaps they miss me on days when I don't crawl out on my balcony. I suppose they call me "that crazy across the way." . . . I am on welfare. I live at your expense, you pay taxes and I don't do a fucking thing. . . . I consider myself to be scum, the dregs of society, I have no shame or conscience. . . . You don't like me? You don't want to pay? It's precious little—$278 a month. You don't want to pay. Then why the fuck did you invite me, entice me here from Russia, along with a horde of Jews? Present your complaints to your own propaganda, it's too effective.[1]

In Russia, Edichka used to be an underground poet, celebrated in Moscow's unofficial intellectual circles. He is now one of the many third-wave Russian émigrés with intellectual ambition who survives at the margins of American society, collecting welfare or making a living through a diverse range of low-level jobs. On the walls of Edichka's cubicle at the Hotel Winslow, a gallery of *monstres sacrés* and radical political symbols is on display, including portraits of Patricia Hearst, the surrealist artist André Breton, and Mao Tse-tung ("an object of horror to all the people who drop by to see me"); a picture of Edichka himself, "wearing a 114-patch blazer tailored by me, Limonov, monster out of the past"; a poster in support of the Workers Party and another in support of gay rights; and two shelves of poetry books.

In these opening paragraphs, the reading experience is reenacted in the form of a public performance, or an exhibitionistic act, through which Edichka, at the same time subject of a public address, protagonist, narrator, and alter ego of the author, exposes his body and thoughts to a projected audience—one that, incidentally, at this point is probably almost nonexistent considering the meager success of Limonov in the United States after he left the Soviet Union and the fact that the book was written in Russian.

These opening paragraphs produce a sort of *mise en abyme*, in that they mirror, reproduce, and at the same time establish the relationship between Edichka as a character and narrator and the imagined audience or readership of the book. They also contain, in a nutshell, some of the main elements of Limonov's poetics in general and of the novel *Eto ia—Edichka* in particular. These include the key role played by the body, violence, and sexuality in defining Limonov's aesthetics and literary persona; the attempt to turn the reading experience into a specific form of public performance through constant play on the ambiguity between fiction and autobiography; a shocking, provocative "posture," which might be interpreted as a return to the spirit of the avant-gardes; and the theme of marginality and the rejection of modern society and its values.

In the quoted passage, Edichka plays the role of the "wild" Russian émigré; he orientalizes himself. Hence, the Russian food he is eating is "something barbaric." The readers of the book, envisioned as passersby and bored office clerks who are quite literally asked to look at Edichka's naked body, are disgusted by his "uncivilized" behavior ("I consider myself to be scum, the dregs of society . . . You don't like me? . . . Then why the fuck did you invite me . . . ?") and at the same they have already paradoxically grown fond of him ("They're probably used to me by now, and perhaps they miss me on days when I don't crawl out on my balcony. I suppose they call me 'that crazy across the way'").

In this chapter, Limonov's prose and its relationship with counterculture and protest are analyzed through the prism of performativity and performance. According to Judith Butler, the performative dimension of language plays a crucial role in the imposition of social identities and the development of power dynamics. "Performativity" encompasses a wide range of phenomena: the imposition of values and social hierarchies through legal sentences, but also injurious speech, and the performance of individuals and groups in everyday life as a component of subject formation. "Gender performativity" involves the repetition of stylized behaviors and "bodily acts" that reinforce gender identity as it is imposed on the individual by social norms and conventions.[2] The "tacit performative of power" is the repetition of social rituals through which a dominant ideology or hegemonic culture establishes itself in everyday life.[3] At the same time, performativity can be used to challenge established hierarchies and values. Imposed forms of behavior can be "reappropriated," reinvented, and used to produce unexpected meanings and forms of political action. These "counter-hegemonic" or revolutionary expressions of the "political potential of the performative" include, for instance, the reappropriation and reclaiming of hate speech by its own victims as well as forms of parody of "an original or primary gender identity . . . within the cultural practices of drag, cross-dressing, and the sexual stylization of butch/femme identities."[4]

The concept of performativity can also be applied to the study of the relationship between literary culture, politics, and everyday life. In the Russian context, a form of literary performative can be retraced, for instance, in such ideas as "the poetics of everyday behavior" and "the semiotics of everyday life," concepts that Lotman uses to show how in the late eighteenth and early nineteenth century social hierarchies and codes of behavior became modeled on literary archetypes.[5] Similarly, one can recognize a performative dimension within *zhiznetvorchestvo* (life-creation), a crucial concept in the development of Russian modernism. For the Russian Symbolists, *zhiznetvorchestvo* signified, in more or less explicit terms, both a blurring of the boundary between art and everyday life and a belief in the possibility of a mystical transformation of reality through art. As an artistic principle, *zhiznetvorchestvo* also had an important role in determining the aesthetics of various Russian and Soviet avant-garde groups and movements. Later examples of *zhiznetvorchestvo* include, for instance, the Futurists' provocative street performances and their aspiration to produce a new language, new art forms, and a new way of life (by getting rid of all past traditions), as well as, in a very different form and spirit, the intrinsic theatricality of Stalinist culture.[6] The symbolist Aleksandr Blok and the futurist Mayakovsky—two poets whose life and work represented classic examples of *zhiznetvorchestvo*—were among Limonov's earliest and foremost poetic models, and Limonov's own artistic strategy can easily be seen as a form of "life-creation." As Aleksandr Skidan puts it, "Limonov's 'I' is literary through and through. Even his incarceration looks like a quotation: Avvakum, Radishchev, Dostoevsky, Chernishevsky, Sade, Genet, Cervantes, Wilde."[7]

Performativity plays a crucial role in Limonov's novels, in his politics, and in the making of his literary and public personas. Through a continuous interplay between fiction and autobiography, Limonov has carefully shaped and transformed his public image throughout the years, consistently positioning himself as an antisystemic figure at the margins of the literary system, society, and the political arena.[8] Both in his prose and poetry and in his political writings, Limonov has challenged established values and hierarchies by violating, often through the voices and bodies of his different literary personas, social taboos and literary norms. At the same time, Limonov's confessional prose is pervaded by loneliness, and by the longing for an alternative "imagined community."[9]

As Walter J. Ong points out, every writer "has to make his readers up, fictionalize them."[10] Every reading experience involves the creation of an imagined readership within the text, and the acceptance of a specific role on the part of the reader. That is, every writer creates her own audience.[11] Limonov's fiction has been deeply influenced by Western counterculture, and the punk movement in particular. Many of his major novels deal with the rejection of mainstream values and the search for an alternative community: New York's artists and outcasts; the petty criminals of the working-class periphery of Kharkov, where Limonov grew up; and Kharkov's art scene, which he joined in his early twenties after he decided to devote his life to poetry.[12]

By envisioning an ideal (transnational) audience for his writing, Limonov has developed a specific poetics of marginality, or a countercultural aesthetics, comprising a combination of recurring themes, motifs, and literary strategies from his prose and poetry, as well as from his journalistic writing and his public statements and appearances. By appropriating and adapting the aesthetics and posture of the historical avant-gardes, he has called into question the value of literary norms and cultural traditions. His works have often violated aesthetic norms and social taboos and have explored the political significance of violence, sexuality, and the body. Finally, Limonov has reclaimed and redefined the condition of marginality and "periphery"—conceived geographically, as the industrial periphery of Kharkov where Limonov grew up, and where three of his major novels take place—as well as metaphorically, as the periphery of the (Russian) literary system. Through his radical rejection of Soviet cultural institutions, the Western bourgeois way of life, and Russian émigré culture, Limonov has positioned himself and his work at the margins of society and cultural institutions, creating at the same time his own personal version of a countercultural aesthetics. Starting in the late 1980s and early 1990s, after his return to Russia and his subsequent involvement in politics, Limonov's poetics of marginality has become part of a larger political project that includes a geopolitical conception of Russia as the site for an alternative modernity. In this context, some of these recurring themes have also been absorbed into the aesthetics of the National Bolshevik Party, arguably the first post-Soviet countercultural movement.

Eros and Civilization

The strong link between Limonov's early works and the poetics of the Russian and Soviet avant-gardes is well documented.[13] Before emigrating to the United States, during his "Moscow years," Limonov was close to the neo-avant-garde group SMOG (Samoe Molodoe Obshchestvo Geniev, or Smelost', Mysl', Obraz i Glubina; The Youngest Society of Geniuses, or Courage, Idea, Image and Depth), organized by the poets Leonid Gubanov and Vladimir Aleinikov, among others. In the poem *My—natsional'nyi geroi* (We are the national hero), which circulated in samizdat, Limonov's poetic persona imagines his travels, his encounters with famous foreign artists and political leaders, the celebration of his art, and the international triumph of "the Russian popular poet and national hero Eduard Limonov and his wife-poetess and national woman Elena Shchapova."[14] Here Limonov's manner directly echoes, not without a certain dose of irony, futurist poet Vladimir Mayakovsky's juvenile heroic stance and egotistical celebration of the self: "Simple people represent life's statics. I represent its dynamics. . . . When I read—I symbolize my people's thirst for knowledge. When I make love—I symbolize the tremendous eroticism of my people. When I get drunk—I symbolize the dark sides of the Russian soul."[15] In a similar spirit, in the following passage from *Dnevnik neudachnika* (*Diary of a Loser*), a fragmented fictional diary from his "American period," Limonov returned to the rebellious celebration of youth that was typical of Russian futurism, and of Mayakovsky's poetry in particular: "Send me to the guillotine. I want to die young. Put a violent end to my life, bleed me, kill me, torture and hack me to pieces! There cannot be an old Limonov!"[16]

In the opening paragraphs of *Eto ia—Edichka*, the narrator-protagonist Edichka also re-creates, between the lines, the provocative anti-intellectualism of the historical avant-gardes: "Who was I over there? What's the difference, what would it change? I hate the past, as I always have, in the name of the present."[17] Starting with *Eto ia—Edichka*, though, Limonov's return to an avant-garde posture becomes more complex, or more subtle and "structural." By and large, in this novel Limonov did not directly emulate the style and aesthetics of the Russian avant-gardes but instead shocked his readers and critics by producing a work that was aimed at systematically breaking social and linguistic taboos and literary norms. As if following Yury Tynyanov's conception of literary evolution, *Eto ia—Edichka* produced "new forms" by including linguistic and thematic elements formerly at the margins of the literary system.[18]

Most obviously, and most famously, Limonov made extensive use of *mat*, uncensored language, in a published literary work, violating the norms of both Soviet and Russian émigré culture. He also included in his novel graphic and detailed descriptions of his alter ego's sexual encounters with both men and women. Equally shocking at the time, as Karen Ryan-Hayes points out, were Edichka's radical leftist and anti-Western views, which most dissident or émigré intellectual circles considered as morally questionable as his promiscuous sex life.[19] *Eto ia—Edichka* also forced the boundaries and norms of Western literature; from the point of view of the Western reader, "Limonov's pseudo-autobiography may be seen as a parodic commentary on contemporary Western literature. A self-proclaimed outsider, Limonov takes the conventions of Western (especially American) confessional prose to the extreme."[20]

The novel is structured as Edichka's desperate, and at times comical, first-person account of his life as a marginalized Russian émigré in New York during the 1970s. It is a confession—intimate to the point of making one cringe out of shame or disgust—of his experiences, his encounters, and his innermost thoughts and feelings. Sexuality largely determines Edichka's perception of the world, his relationships, and his convictions. Alone, destitute, and abandoned by his wife, Elena, who has left him for the luxurious and dissipated lifestyle of the fashion industry, Edichka is desperate, devoid of self-respect, and eager to share with the reader the most humiliating details of his self-abasement. At various points, Edichka implores Elena to stay and to have sex with him even if she has other partners; he alludes to the fact that, out of desperation, he thought about, and possibly tried, to rape and kill his wife; and he masturbates compulsively, often secretly wearing Elena's clothes and underwear.

Feeling too vulnerable to be with other women, he decides to have a relationship with a man. An unsuccessful attempt at a relationship with Raymond, a rich older man, eventually gives way to casual encounters with strangers—mostly strong African American men whom he randomly meets during his nighttime carousing through the streets of New York. His decision to have homosexual experiences involves a careful reconsideration of many of the male friendships that he had growing up in the working-class city of Kharkov, in Soviet Ukraine, where homosexuality was taboo, as well as a punishable crime: "Such is my history. A love for strong men. I confess, and I see it now. Sanya the Red was so strong that he used to break the bars in the fence around the outdoor dance pavilion, the bars were as thick as a big man's arm. . . . Gena was tall, well built, and looked like a young Nazi. Dark blue eyes. I never met a more handsome man."[21]

The explicit depictions of Edichka's casual homosexual encounters largely contributed to the novel's *succès de scandale*, first in Paris and Western Europe and later in post-Soviet Russia, where the book sold over half a million copies.[22] Beyond the (widely debated) question of whether these episodes should be considered autobiographical or not, the homosexual theme in the book should be seen in relation to both the protagonist's politics and the book's position vis-à-vis the Russian literary tradition. Edichka's homosexual desire is closely linked with his protest against the Western bourgeois family and way of life. After he has sex with Chris, a young black man whom he encounters by chance in an empty children's playground at night, Edichka hugs him and cries, moved by the attention and love of another human being; he then compares their condition to that of men and women who conduct a "normal" life: "Listen here, there are morals, there are decent people in the world, there are offices and banks, there are beds; sleeping in them are men and women, also very decent. It was all happening at once, and still is. And there were Chris and I, who had accidentally met there in the dirty sand, in a vacant lot in the vast Great City, a Babylon, God help me, a Babylon. There we lay, and he stroked my hair. Homeless children of the world."[23]

As Andrey Rogachevsky points out, the theme of homosexual love in the book is connected with that of Edichka's protest against capitalist society and Western bourgeois values.[24] While working as a busboy at the Hilton, Edichka explains his hatred against its customers and "the strong," or "the masters of life," as being in part motivated by what can be seen as the commodification of heterosexual relationships because, after all, Elena, Edichka's "little Russian maiden," has been bought and taken away by rich men in exchange for a pleasant and luxurious life.[25]

At the same time, violating bourgeois family values is part of Edichka's avant-garde stance, and it reflects the position of the novel within Russian literary history. After his encounter with Chris, Edichka goes to bed happy and self-complacently thinks that he is probably "the first Russian poet who managed to fuck a black man in a New York vacant lot."[26] This statement seems to ironically allude to the ambiguity between fictional and autobiographical elements in the novel, in the sense that Limonov could be either the first Russian poet to have had such an experience or the first Russian author to describe it within a literary work (or both). After the publication of the novel, and later in his career, Limonov has often played on this ambiguity, at times claiming, both in his literary works and in public interviews, that all the facts, persons, and experiences in his books are real, and at other times denying them as purely literary inventions.[27] In addition, as Olga Matich points out, the episode represented the "grossest violation of literary taboos in the novel," in that "never before in Russian literature had a homosexual encounter been portrayed so openly and in such positive terms." Hence, the inclusion of this episode is clearly part of Limonov's literary strategy.[28]

The central role played by sexuality and the body in the book is closely connected to the performative dimension of Edichka's character, which affects the way in which the protagonist experiences his own body and desire. First, homosexuality in the novel is closely linked with the desire to be or play the role of a woman. At various points throughout the narrative, Edichka violates and plays with gender roles. After being abandoned by his wife, Elena, he often wears her clothes and reenacts a sort of tragic fetishistic ritual. During his first homosexual encounter with the strong, well-built, and masculine Chris, he gladly realizes that he is finally able to behave like a woman and that he can be as seductive and beautiful as Elena, the object of his love: "At that moment I was really a woman, capricious, demanding, and probably seductive, because I remember myself playfully wiggling my *poopka* as I leaned on my hands in the sand. . . . I was behaving now exactly as my wife had when I fucked her."[29] In another passage, Edichka claims that his misogyny is caused by a sort of "vagina envy": "The biological injustice roused my indignation. Why must I love, seek, fuck, preserve . . . while she must only use. I think my hatred proceeded from envy that I had no cunt. For some reason it seemed to me that a cunt was more perfect than a prick."[30] Similarly, Edichka's performativity is mirrored by the central role played by fashion and style and his weakness for fancy and extravagant clothes: "Although I cannot afford much of anything because of my extreme poverty, still, all my shirts are lace, one of my blazers is lilac velvet, and the white suit is a beauty, my pride and joy. My shoes always have very high heels, I even own some pink ones, and I buy them where all the blacks buy theirs. . . . I want even my shoes to be a feast."[31]

These external clues and details are the most evident manifestations of deeper formal and thematic devices at work in the novel. *Eto ia—Edichka* in fact turns the reading experience simultaneously into a public session of psychoanalysis and a public performance, through which the semiautobiographical character of Edichka exposes his innermost feelings and desires, and his naked body, to his projected readers and audience. Psychoanalysis and the unconscious, in particular, have played an important role in shaping Limonov's literary persona. Discussing *Eto ia—Edichka* as an example of confessional prose, Ryan-Hayes ascribes it to the specific genre of childhood, noticing that Edichka is prone to use childlike language.[32] Cynthia Simmons draws a connection between Edichka's myth of childhood and adolescence and his narcissism.[33] Edichka's first homosexual experience takes place in a children's playground and, as mentioned, his homoerotic desire is connected with a reconsideration of the male friendships from his childhood and adolescence. In his later novel *Molodoi negodiai* (The young scoundrel), Limonov himself refers to the importance of psychoanalysis for his literary career, describing how in his youth, after discovering Freud's *Introduction to Psychoanalysis*, he decided to copy the book by hand in its entirety.[34] Freud's "discovery of the unconscious" is also discussed in Limonov's later manifesto *Drugaia Rossiia* (The other Russia), in the context of the development of a new revolutionary culture after the fall of the Soviet Union.[35] Revolutionary politics is, ultimately, the only thing that allows Edichka to overcome his obsessions and fundamental solipsism. When asked to participate in the activities of the Workers Party, Edichka is enthusiastic about the idea of protesting publicly, putting his body and mind at the service of, and risking his life for, a public cause: "A dangerous meeting was just what I needed. Admittedly, if she had said, . . . you'll receive a machine gun and cartridges, you'll participate in an action, an airplane hijacking, for example, I'd have been a lot happier. I mean it, only revolution would have fully suited my mood. But I could begin with a meeting."[36]

Edichka's radical image also contributed to the creation of Limonov's controversial public persona, which from the beginning was based on a combination of fictional and biographical elements, and on the fundamental ambiguity between the two. Long before the publication of *Eto ia—Edichka*, Limonov had already become a highly controversial figure in émigré circles because of his journalistic activity and his participation in political actions. Most famously, in his article "Razocharovanie" (Disillusionment), published in the émigré journal *Novoe russkoe slovo* (The new Russian word) on November 29, 1975, Limonov had addressed the question of the difficulties and deprivations to which Russian émigrés were subjected in the West, and had accused dissidents and the "anti-Soviet propaganda" of hiding this reality from the public view. The article had raised bitter polemics within the émigré community, especially after *Nedelia*, the Sunday supplement to *Izvestiia* (an official newspaper of the Soviet government), reprinted excerpts of the article as proof of the advantages of socialism and the failure of the capitalist system.[37] Limonov was accused of being a KGB agent, fired from *Novoe russkoe slovo*, and ostracized by the Russian émigré community. In the novel, Edichka refers directly to these and other biographical events as belonging to his past, reinforcing the confusion between the author and public figure Limonov on the one hand and his literary persona on the other. This ambiguity will be crucial to Limonov's later career as a writer, public figure, and political leader, in that elements of Limonov's extremely eventful biography will contribute to the shaping of his literary hero, and vice versa.

Marginality is another fundamental theme of Limonov's work that appeared for the first time, at least in such explicit terms, in *Eto ia—Edichka*. Edichka is naturally drawn to marginalized groups and individuals. These include the whimsical inhabitants of the Hotel Winslow, mostly impoverished and hopeless Russian intellectuals, and all his lovers, beginning with Chris, whom he suspects of being a criminal; Johnny, who is homeless; and, of course, Elena herself, whom Edichka eventually recognizes as an innocent victim of a ruthless system. He also sympathizes with ethnic minorities, and African Americans in particular. He compares, not without a certain dose of dark irony, the treatment of the Russian tenants in the Hotel Winslow to what "blacks before emancipation" had to endure. He repeatedly compares his own style to that of African Americans and, finally, he is physically attracted to African American men. His sense of belonging to, and sympathy for, marginalized groups is explicitly stated as an explanation for his decision to join the Workers Party: "For me, with my temperament, there was nothing to choose. I automatically found myself among the protesters and the dissatisfied, among the insurgents, partisans, rebels, the Reds and the gays, the Arabs and Communists, the blacks and the Puerto Ricans."[38]

Marginality is also connected to violence and its development into political action. Edichka's fascination with violence is primarily instinctive, aesthetic, and connected to human relationships and sexuality. At various points in the book he describes his plans to kill Elena and refers to the fact that he keeps a rope under his bed for this purpose. His sexual encounters with Chris and Johnny start as violent struggles, and while fighting with Chris, Edichka is clearly both scared and excited by the idea of risking his own life and, possibly, killing another man in the process.[39] He is fascinated by weapons and manifests a quasi-religious veneration for knives and pistols: "an object used to take a man's life cannot but be holy and mysterious. The very profile of a revolver, of all its parts, holds a Wagnerian horror. Cold steel, with its different profiles, is no exception."[40] In the chapter devoted to Carol and Edichka's involvement in the Workers Party, the aesthetic, quasi-sublime pleasure generated by violence and weapons turns into political action, and into a yearning for world revolution that Edichka sees as a result of his own biography and "personal tragedy": "I deduced my love for world revolution naturally from my own personal tragedy—a tragedy in which both countries were involved, both the USSR and America, and in which civilization was to blame. This civilization did not acknowledge me, it ignored my labor, it denied me my legitimate place in the sun, it had destroyed my love. . . . My craving for revolution, being built on the personal, is far more powerful and natural than any artificial revolutionary principle."[41]

At the same time, political commitment allows Edichka to fight against his solitude and to experience a sense of belonging to a community: "I needed people, lots of contacts, connections, people and more people. I dreamed about relationships with people in my sleep, I was languishing without people."[42] Ryan-Hayes argues that the novel's fragmented narrative is related to the protagonist and narrator's confused state of mind and chaotic life.[43] In addition, this fragmentariness, and the episodic structure of the book—which follows Edichka's random encounters with sexual partners, friends, and temporary colleagues—mirrors the dissolution of human bonds in the Western metropolis, as well as the character's own isolation and yearning for a missing community. The Party constitutes, among other things, a perfect remedy against solitude.

Through the Workers Party, Edichka is able to experience, at least temporarily, this sense of belonging but is also soon disappointed by the "petty bourgeois" nature of this "intellectual organization," and by its inability to communicate and reach out to the most marginalized strata of the population: "If I were making a revolution I would lean first of all on . . . people like me—the classless, the criminal, and the vicious. I would locate my headquarters in the toughest neighborhood, associate only with the have-nots." In order to do so, Edichka dreams about creating a "semi-religious Communist commune and sect" where he would want "the free and equal people living with me to love me and caress me," and where he would be able to overcome his isolation.[44]

To an extent, Edichka's relationship with the party mirrors the relationship of the book with its audience. Because of its theme and style, *Eto ia—Edichka* paradoxically (given Limonov's outspoken anti-Americanism) belongs more to the American tradition, especially that of countercultural literature of the 1950s, 1960s, and 1970s, than to the Russian tradition, even if one takes into account samizdat and Soviet underground literature. One can find evident similarities with Henry Miller, who was the first to break certain sexual taboos within a work of literature in the context of American culture, and whose novels were also based on a rough and matter-of-fact first-person narrative.[45] Limonov also recalls how he discovered and was inspired by Ernest Hemingway, Charles Bukowski, and B. Traven after moving to New York City, and Ryan-Hayes interprets Limonov's best seller as a polemical and quasi-parodic response to Norman Mailer's *An American Dream*, a major example of American countercultural literature of the period.[46]

Even more influential for him, it appears, was the discovery of Western counterculture in general, and the punk movement in particular. While in New York, Limonov was introduced by his girlfriend Julia Carpenter to Richard Hell, one of the pioneers of the punk movement, and to Marc Bell (aka Marky Ramone), the drummer of the punk band The Ramones. He was a regular at CBGB, the club on the Lower East Side where many important punk, post-punk, and new wave bands, including, among others, Television and Talking Heads, were making their debut during the 1970s. Limonov himself recognizes that his "American books" reflected and belonged to the style and spirit of the punk movement, and that the National Bolshevik Party shared with this countercultural movement its aggressive anarchist stance and radical rejection of bourgeois and mainstream values.[47]

More generally, Limonov appropriated the legacy of Western countercultural movements and combined it with the aesthetics and posture of the Russian avant-gardes. In *Eros and Civilization*, a philosophical work that has become commonly associated with the rebellious spirit of the 1968 movement, Herbert Marcuse, elaborating on Freud's theories, argues that modern society functions on the basis of a sublimation of sexual instincts, which are channeled toward industrial production and regulated through a complete organization of the time and energies devoted to leisure and work. In Marcuse's view, reproductive instincts are sublimated into the factory chain, and the priority given to the nuclear family and sex oriented toward procreation reflects the orientation of society toward production. "Polymorphous-perverse" and homoerotic expressions of sexuality and, in general, all forms of sexuality not oriented toward procreation, are a threat to the social order: "The societal perversion of the sex instinct taboos as *perversions* practically all its manifestations which do not serve or prepare for the procreative function."[48] According to Marcuse, "Freud's theory is in its very substance 'sociological,'" and it describes a political order based on the systematic repression of human happiness. Marcuse's solution to this state of affairs entails allowing the aesthetic dimension a place within the organization of society in the form of an "alliance of art and revolution." This would entail replacing the existing repressive sublimation of sexual instincts into labor with a nonrepressive sublimation of these same instincts into artistic and creative work, and it would cause "a transformation of the libido: from sexuality constrained under genital supremacy to erotization of the entire personality."[49]

Limonov's artistic and political views, and his projected vision of an imagined countercultural community, are quite consistent with Marcuse's critique. For Limonov, art and literature are instruments of sexual and political emancipation. In *Eto—ia Edichka*, his alter ego struggles to overcome his monogamous obsession and dreams about joining a polyamorous community of outcasts and rebels.[50] A few years later, this search for sexual and political emancipation translated into the quasi-sectarian vision of the NBP as an alternative community founded on military comradery and sexual promiscuity, a vision that, in a very specific way, challenged traditional gender roles and family values. Closely connected with these ideas was the idealization of childhood and youth as times of uncompromising rebelliousness and untainted promiscuity, and this also became an important component of the *natsboly*'s ethos. According to Edichka/Limonov, and to many of his followers, "all children are extremists."[51]

In the late 1970s, however, *Eto ia—Edichka* was still a countercultural book lacking its own public. The marginalized, dangerous, and extremist elements of society that Edichka refers to when he dreams of creating his own revolutionary organization made their appearance only after the fall of the Soviet Union. The emergence of this political and literary public is closely linked to further transformations of Limonov's public persona, and to the reconceptualizations of marginality taking place in the three novels that came to form his so-called *Kharkov Trilogy*.

The Periphery of the Empire

In Limonov's *Khar'kovskaia trilogiia* (The Kharkov trilogy), consisting of the novels *U nas byla velikaia epokha* (We had a great epoch, 1989), *Podrostok Savenko* (The adolescent Savenko, 1983, translated into English as *Memoir of a Russian Punk*), and *Molodoi negodiai* (The young scoundrel, 1986), the condition of marginality is associated with that of the social, cultural, and geographical periphery of the Soviet Empire.[52] While living in the United States, Limonov had positioned himself at the periphery of the literary system, producing a work that radically violated past literary norms and social taboos. In the *Kharkov Trilogy*, the condition of marginality is associated with the geographical periphery of the Soviet Union and with his hometown, the industrial city of Kharkov. The geography of Limonov's own "Childhood," "Boyhood," and "Youth" in fact determined the shaping of his literary hero as an outcast and a rebel. At the same time, by writing about his coming of age in the Soviet province, Limonov was able to provide a personal, alternative account of Soviet history that he explicitly defined in opposition to dominant narratives of everyday life during the Thaw. Finally, on a metaliterary level, the trilogy further elaborates the reflection about the impotence of the intelligentsia, the uselessness of literature, the impossibility of the novel form after modernism (broadly conceived), and the narcissism of Russian poets that Limonov started in his earlier works.

In the opening pages of *Podrostok Savenko*, the protagonist, Eddie-baby, is "standing with a disdainful expression on his face, leaning back against the wall of the building of the pharmacy—leaning and waiting."[53] It is, significantly, November 7 (1958, as we will later discover), the anniversary of the October Revolution and the beginning of a three-day holiday weekend to commemorate the historical event. A crowd of small merchants and artisans is passing in front of the bored fifteen-year-old Eddie-baby, "something on the order of a bourgeoisie" or "the goat herd," as the protagonist of the novel disdainfully calls them. They are all, fathers and sons, wearing the same boring ugly clothes, the same heavy coats and dark suits stinking of naphthalene, and shiny uncomfortable shoes—and they are about to perform their vulgar holiday rituals by swallowing shots of vodka, Olivier salad, sausages, and the "statutory herring." The young Eddie-baby distinguishes himself through his style and posture: "Eddie-baby is different from them. Which is why he's standing here in torn, wrinkled Polish velveteen pants and a yellow jacket with a hood—standing around like some Hamlet of the Saltov district and spitting with an independent air. Eddie-baby is thinking they can all go fuck themselves."[54] In a way reminiscent of what happened in the opening paragraphs of *Eto ia—Edichka*, one notices here the reappearance of one of Limonov's recurring motifs, that of the hero and the crowd—or its punk version—of the poet and his missing audiences. With his extravagant clothes, the provocative, aggressive, ill-behaved Eddie-baby embodies the original spirit of the Russian revolution. His "yellow jacket" (*zheltaia kurtka*) against the background of the gray, quiet, and conformist Khrushchev-era "middle class" is a clear allusion to the trademark "yellow blouse" (*zheltaya kofta*), the unusual outfit that Mayakovsky habitually wore to shock the Moscow bourgeoisie, and that is also commonly associated with the Russian Futurists' aspiration to turn art into a total performance of sorts.

Structured as a classic coming-of-age novel focusing on the ambitions and disillusionments of the young Eddie-baby—and on his first experiences with love, sex, and violence—*Podrostok Savenko* is also connected to the appearance of the first youth subcultures in the Soviet Union. Eddie-baby's style (the above-mentioned yellow jacket and the Polish velveteen pants) is reminiscent of that of the *stiliagi*, the young lovers of jazz and American culture who made their appearance during the 1950s and became protagonists of the "Youth Prose" of the same period, like Vasily Aksenov's 1961 iconic novel *Zvezdnyi bilet* (*A Ticket to the Stars*). Kadik (or Kadillak), one of Eddie-baby's best friends, is indeed a classic *stiliaga*. Eddie-baby's and Kadik's identical yellow jackets have been tailored by copying a model of an Austrian alpine coat that Kadik brought back from an international youth festival. Kadik is learning to play the saxophone and has been a member of the Kharkov unofficial youth organization The Blue Horse (Golubaia loshad'), which became famous in 1958 after its members were persecuted by Soviet authorities. Finally, unlike Eddie-baby, Kadik despises the hooligans of Saltovka and prefers to hang out with jazz players and better-off kids from the city center.

Eddie-baby, on the other end, clearly belongs to the working class and the underworld, even if he distinguishes himself from his peers because of his poetic talent and intellectual curiosity. Like all the other kids of Saltovka, he always carries a weapon (a straight razor), and he respects and tries to follow the honor code of the local petty criminals. He dreams of becoming a real gangster and has been discussing with his friend Kostya "Cat" the dream of reviving Russian organized crime, which has been mostly wiped out by Soviet power. In his rejection of the Soviet system, style, and behavior, Eddie-baby resembles more a *gopnik* than a classic *stiliaga*, even if the term *gopnik* is anachronistic in this context, considering that the word became commonly accepted only in the late 1980s, early 1990s.[55] A decade later, in 1994, the poet and queer performer Yaroslav Mogutin interpreted Eddie-baby as a combination of a Western punk and a skinhead. Mogutin noted that in the novel Eddie-baby likes to keep his hair almost clean shaven on the sides, which is the very same haircut Limonov prescribes in his (just written at the time) "Statute of the National Bolshevik." Obviously Mogutin himself was romanticizing the beginnings of the National Bolshevik Party, in which he was directly involved when he wrote the essay, and viewed the literary model as a source of inspiration for the political movement.[56]

The reference to the Youth Prose of the 1950s also problematizes the question of the book's historical "authenticity." On the one hand, the use of Limonov's real last name in the original title (*Podrostok Savenko*) suggests that the book should be seen as an example of documentary or memoiristic prose. Limonov's novel would be a "more authentic" account of everyday life during the Thaw (especially "far from Moscow") than the one provided by the writers of the 1950s, who in their turn had claimed that they were depicting the "real life" of Soviet people, in contrast with the "lacquered reality" of Socialist Realism.[57] On the other hand, the implicit reference to the literature of the Thaw and its attempt at creating a more "authentic" or humane form of realism could also be seen as a challenge to the possibility of authenticity itself. In fact, many details in the novel—including some of the imagery associated with the Soviet criminal underground—do suggest that here Limonov might be freely projecting ideas and situations from the early 1980s (when the book was written) to the fictional 1950s in which his characters operate.

In this novel, Limonov's *blatnaia romantika*, a "romanticism of the underworld," is combined with a cult of the poetic word and a creation of fictional mythologies surrounding the "birth of the poet."[58] Eddie-baby's father, a police officer, has named his son after the revolutionary poet Eduard Bagritsky. The choice of the name is fortuitous: the young officer is reading Bagritsky's poem "The Smugglers" ("Kontrabandisty") when they call his office from the hospital to let him know that Eddie-baby has been born: "Through the fish and the waves / Passes by the shalanda / Three Greeks to Odessa / Are carrying contraband. . . . In order for the stars to sprinkle a big profit / Cognac, stockings, and condoms."[59] Through this family legend about the choice of his own name, Limonov links his literary persona with the aesthetics and spirit of the avant-gardes and, at the same time, with imagery related to the alluring, fascinating, but not particularly morally edifying life of adventurers, outcasts, cheaters, and criminals. Describing his childhood in the novel *U nas byla velikaia epokha*, Limonov returns to this story, commenting that seventy years after the October Revolution it is finally time for the USSR to elaborate and accept all its history and cultural heritage, "both the revolutionary romantic-poets, and the counterrevolutionary romantic poets. Both Bagritsky, and Gumilev."[60] At this point in time, however, Limonov was already getting closer to the reconciliation of right- and left-wing aesthetics and ideology that a few years later became the trademark of the NBP.

The plot of *Podrostok Savenko*, one might argue, revolves entirely around the protagonist's idealization of poetry and his later disillusionment with it. It follows Eddie-baby on a path that goes from the Russian symbolists' sacred conception of literature to Limonov's own "cruel talent" or "cruel realism," and to a vision of literature as one of many forms of collective action. Eddie-baby's discovery of poetry occurs through Blok's early poems, read from a collection given to him by a local librarian who has noticed Eddie-baby's precocious intelligence. Some of Blok's lines make Eddie-baby "want to die, to die of love for Svetka, whom he had just met at the May Day celebrations." *Podrostok Savenko* depicts Eddie's poetic initiation, the discovery of his talent, and his sensitivity, which makes him fundamentally different from the other kids from Saltovka. Everyone around Eddie-baby (Asya; Captain Zilberman, the policeman chasing him for his petty crimes; and his friends Kadik and "Red" Sanya) has started to realize that he is a very talented poet. During the summer, as he reads to his friends at the beach, a "bearded man" approaches him, gives him wine, and suggests that he go to the workshop of the Kharkov poet Revol't Bunchukov. Finally, following the fashion of public readings, or the "poetry in the stadiums" that was typical of the Thaw, Eddie-baby reads his poems at the movie theater Pobeda (Victory) and manages to triumph in the local poetry contest in front of several thousand people. However, this "poetic initiation" is also marked by a series of life experiences that deeply influence and modify his perception of the world. During the three-day October holidays described in the novel, the reader witnesses Eddie-baby's transition from a romanticized vision of life and literature (that of Blok's early poems that made him want to "die of love for Svetka") to what Limonov himself once defined as a "cruel talent" (*zhestokii talant*):

> What is biographical there, and what's not—this will remain forever part of my personal history, that I am not going to share with everyone. . . . I probably have, as they used to say back in the day, a "cruel talent," that is, the ability of throwing away everything that is banal, focusing on a few extreme situations and tense moments, during which the character of an individual emerges most clearly. Autobiographical events are just a pretext, because by no means every one of them can be used for this purpose. . . . This is indeed what talent consists of: building a plot out of a multitude of sentences.[61]

After reading his poems to the crowd, and being publicly celebrated, Eddie-baby is invited to hang out with the leaders of a dangerous local gang in a park nearby. There, the gang members, on a whim, attack a group of young people—two women and a man—who are passing by; they brutally rape the two women and beat the man to death. As he witnesses this horrendous violence, Eddie-baby (from whose point of view the whole novel is told) remains indifferent and detached. At some point he even stretches his hand to touch one of the women who is being raped, as if out of curiosity. The scene is portrayed as if through the eyes of a completely cold, nonjudging, amoral viewer. The description lacks emotional involvement to the point of being purely anatomical; it conveys to the reader the experience of witnessing a horrendous crime, with no emotions attached to it. This of course makes the reading of the episode all the more disturbing and traumatic.

After this violent initiation, Eddie-baby finally reaches Svetka in her apartment and has sex with her for the first time, losing his virginity. His first sexual experience, however, is pervaded with squalor and abjection. Eddie-baby has just found out that Svetka has been lying and cheating on him and he confronts her about it. The altercation turns into a violent struggle, which turns into an ambiguously consensual encounter at best, and a tamed domestic replica of the violent scene Eddie-baby has just witnessed at worst.

The episode, like the rest of the novel, is told from the protagonist's (ingenuous) point of view, but the role of Svetka in it appears to be one of initial resistance, and subsequent passivity and resignation. The parallel with the heinous crime that Eddie-baby has just witnessed is immediate, and there is a glaring discrepancy between the character's impressions and feelings—those typically associated with an adolescent heartbreak—and the reality of what appears to be an act of normalized sexual violence. While he is having sex with Svetka, Eddie-baby fantasizes (and is aroused) by some of the sounds and vivid details of the gang rape that are still fresh in his mind, and the encounter described here clearly belongs to a world where the boundaries between pleasure, violence, and pain have become utterly indistinguishable.

Svetka, by her account, was sexually abused by a drunk friend of her late father, and later had a number of sexual experiences with several other men, but the only emotions that she displays while telling this are feigned indifference and contempt. This is seemingly a defense mechanism, and a desperate attempt at agency and power from an individual who has been forcibly deprived of both. From Eddie-baby's naïve viewpoint, however, all that happens is simply that the object of his idealized love is revealed to be a cynical, corrupted, and manipulative individual.[62] In fact, this feeling results in a complete lack of empathy on his part that precludes any form of human connection with the supposed object of his love and worship. Eddie-baby cannot love or be close to a desperate and vulnerable human being like himself; he can only be enraptured and overwhelmed by love for the distant image of a female archetype, or an idealized heroine of (neo)romantic (or early symbolist) poetry. More specifically, he cannot love or be close to a woman.

Svetka's and Eddie-baby's anaesthetized perception of violence (experienced in the role of its witness, victim, or perpetrator) mirrors the protagonist's changed attitude toward literature. The next morning, after sleeping in an abandoned shelter, he wakes up and discovers that he is being attacked by a mischief of rats. To get rid of them he starts burning pages from his notebook:

> When the blank sheets finally came to an end, Eddie, after thinking it over for a few seconds, decisively tore out the first sheet with a poem on it and lit it. The lines of "Natasha" curled and writhed in the fire: "In a white dress / on a sunny day / You've come out to take a walk . . ." "In a white dress," Eddie whispers bitterly, and hurls "Natasha" at the rats. "In a dirty dress . . . In a greasy dress . . . In a dress made of lard," he whispers angrily. "In a Ukrainian national costume, in a dress made of lard!" he said out loud, and then resolutely climbed off the door.[63]

This episode epitomizes, in fictional terms, the transition to the "cruel talent" and the "extreme situations and tense moments" that Limonov describes as the main elements of his own literary strategy.[64] The failure of the relations between genders results in self-loathing—Natasha "in a dress made of lard"—and in the impossibility of poetry after modernism (Blok's early poems, and implicitly his mystical conception of art and literature).[65] Significantly, in the novel a possibility for redemption can only be found in the sphere of political action and utopian thinking, if not in that of poetic inspiration. Eddie-baby dreams of a revolution in which "punks" will take over and keeps a red book containing the names of all the bureaucrats and state leaders that should be executed to achieve this result:

> Eddie-baby believes that the power of the state should be in the hands of the punks. There should be a dictatorship of the punks in the Soviet Union instead of a dictatorship of the proletariat. After all, the punks are much more developed, much cleverer, and much more intelligent than the proletariat. A proletarian will always back down before the knife of a punk. . . . Eddie-baby is convinced that if the leading people in the state are liquidated, there will be chaos in the country and a well-organized gang can seize power. . . . Lenin and the Bolsheviks also had a very small gang in 1917, but they still managed to seize power.[66]

Eddie-baby's discovery of poetry in the book is closely associated with an idealization of femininity. His disillusionment with literature manifests itself as misogyny. In contrast, revolutionary action is connected with a potentially homoerotic comradely love and admiration of strength. Eddie-baby can only love and show his vulnerability and despair to other marginalized comrades and boys like him, and political action appears to be truly "a men's business."[67] Ultimately, in *Podrostok Savenko* literature, or at least the kind of literature that Limonov's young alter ego idealizes, is a form of delusion, and social and spiritual redemption can only be attained through revolutionary action.

■

Molodoi negodiai explores a different "path of resistance" from the one based on youthful angst, male camaraderie, and romanticizing of the criminal underworld of Eddie-baby's "revolution of the punks": that of a bohemian lifestyle and the radical rejection of the work ethic inherent in both the Soviet and the capitalist systems. The model of this philosophy of resistance is Gena—or Genochka "the Magnificent," "Ed's"/"Limonov's"/"the poet's"/"the book peddler's" (as the protagonist is referred to at various points in the novel) best friend, who has few but ardent passions: "a beautiful landscape, cold vodka, conversation with a friend." "Genka, so it seems, is completely lacking in any form of ambition. He himself has admitted more than once that he doesn't want to be a poet, like Motrich and Ed, or an artist, like Bakhchanian.—You paint, write poetry, and I will rejoice in your successes!"[68]

Mainly devoting his life to *flânerie* (*flanirovanie*, as it is called in the book) with the poet Ed, Gena is the leader of the group of bohemians, writers, artists, and intellectuals that goes by the provocative name of SS. The group is clearly attempting to revive the "life-creation" (*zhiznetvorchestvo*) and the theatrical behavior that was common among various Russian symbolist (and later, futurist) art and literary groups in the early twentieth century. One of the members, Pol' Shemmetov, is a fanatical Francophile who speaks impeccable French and will later risk his life (and end up in prison) trying to board a ship in order to escape from the USSR; Viktorushka, or "Fritz" (a derogative word used to refer to a German person), is able to perfectly reproduce Hitler's speeches in the original German and jokingly performs them, imitating Hitler's voice and gestures, to shock the customers of a restaurant where the group is dining; Misha Basov imitates the manners of André Breton, the founder of the surrealist movement.

Here the reference to the symbolists' playful theatricality is made quite explicit: "It's just that the 'SS' and a few other kids, . . . a little bit out of boredom, . . . were playing a literary game, and decided to pretend that we lived in Kharkov at the beginning of the twentieth century, and that we were 'artist-symbolists.' . . . Len'ka Ivanov picked the name *Odeialov*. Molokhov became *Bukhankin*. And Bakhchanian proposed that they call Ed *Limonov*."[69] In one of the first interviews he gave after returning to Russia in the early 1990s, Limonov repeated this anecdote about the origins of his name almost literally, only adding a brief remark: "And the name stuck to me, it became a sort of nickname, and my second 'I' quickly replaced the first."[70]

This remark helps clarify the relationship between autobiography and fiction in Limonov's literary and political activity and the shaping of his literary and public personas over the years. Through performativity, autobiography and literary invention become closely interconnected, and the two spheres continuously influence each other; or, as Richard Borden elegantly puts it, "Eduard Savenko creates a 'real' Eduard Limonov, who, in turn, creates a literary self-fiction in which he calls himself by his created name and discusses the 'self' he invented in other fictions."[71] This plays an important role in creating a legend around Limonov's public persona and, in turn, in the making of the NBP as an artistic and political community.

The bohemian attention to clothing and style is also reflected in the account of Limonov's job as a tailor. In order to earn a living in Kharkov while trying to make a name for himself as a poet, Limonov tailored clothes for his friends and acquaintances. He then continued this activity after moving to Moscow and tailored clothes and pants for many underground writers and nonconformist artists, including, among others, Ernst Neizvestny.[72] A famous photograph from the 1970s portrays him standing in his "jacket of the national hero" and Elena Shchapova sitting at his feet "dressed as Eve" (see fig. 1). In the accounts of many members of the late Soviet artistic and literary underground, the "itinerant" Limonov of the 1970s is described as having only two possessions, "a sewing machine and a writing machine." Limonov incorporates this legend surrounding his work as a tailor here and elsewhere in his semifictional memoirs, and the biographical detail gradually becomes a metaphor for his "life-creation," in the form of a "radical change of clothing" (or masks), or a bohemian taste for disguises.[73]

In depicting the beginnings of Limonov's literary career in Kharkov, *Molodoi negodiai* deals with the question of the protagonist's creation of, and belonging to, a community of artists and intellectuals. As mentioned, Gena, Eduard, and the artist Bakhchanian consider themselves part of a collective of bohemians. In the novel, Limonov is said to have started the relationship with his first wife, Anna Rubinshtein, because of his desire to become part of her intellectual circle. Since he grew up in a working-class neighborhood and spent his youth hanging out with local criminals, and later worked in a factory and as a book-peddler, his acquaintance with a new intellectual milieu—and his relationship with Anna, the "legendary" Croatian poet Motric, and the philologist Melekhov—also marks the discovery of his first artistic models. The authors, artists, and thinkers that the young Limonov is particularly passionate about in the novel help retrace his first main literary and intellectual influences. He copies by hand two works, both given to him by Tolik Melekhov, who plays the role of the intellectual or "scholarly type" in the group. The first is Sigmund Freud's *Introduction to Psychoanalysis*, which Limonov decides to copy word for word "because I understood that I was going to need that book in the future." Next,

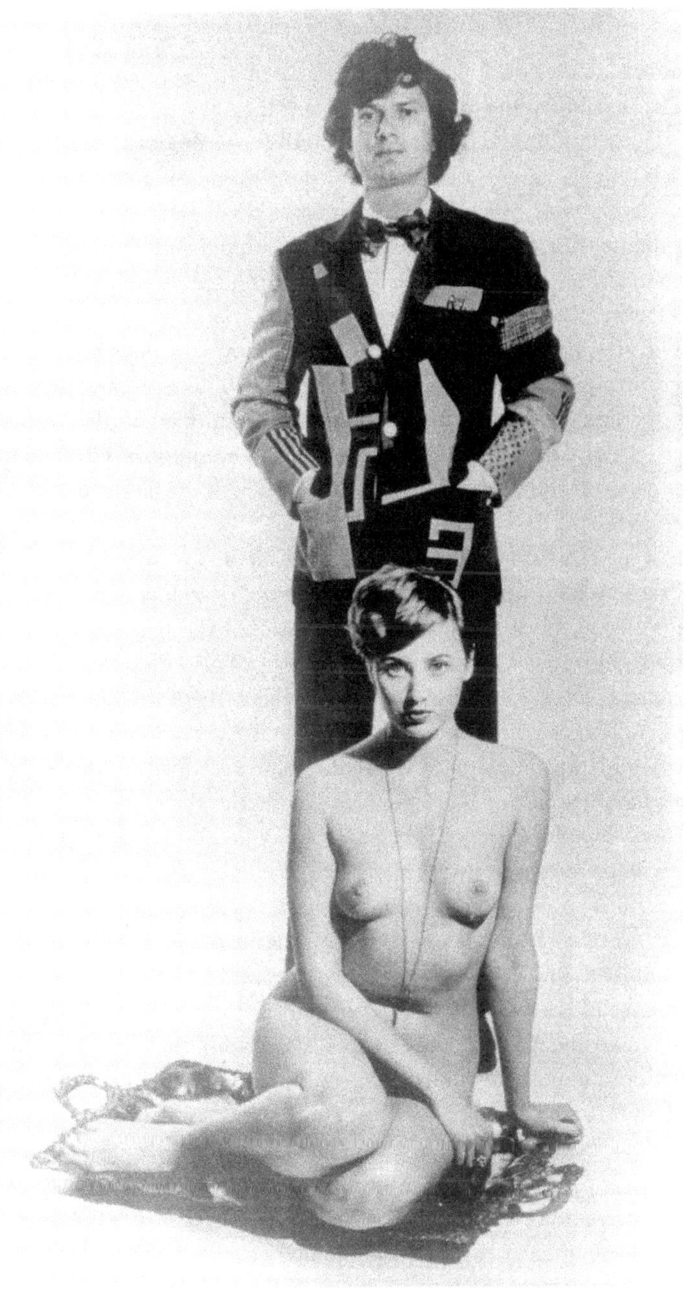

Figure 1. Eduard Limonov and Elena Shchapova in Moscow, 1974: "Me wearing the jacket of the national hero (I tailored it myself from 114 patches). Lena dressed as Eve. Moscow. 1974. Before the West." From Limonov, *Limonov v fotografiiakh* (1996).

Limonov copies out the complete works of Velimir Khlebnikov in three volumes, "excluding the footnotes."[74]

The volumes by Freud and Khlebnikov symbolically mark the beginnings of Limonov's career and its future developments. Limonov's fundamental connection with psychoanalysis emerges through the central role played by the theme of sexuality and his reflections on personal and collective memory, both in *Eto ia—Edichka* and in the *Kharkov Trilogy*, as well as in the exposure of the feelings, desires, and thoughts of a semiautobiographical lyric *I* to the public view that could be considered Limonov's own literary trademark. Even after turning to politics, when the link between his work and the exploration of the unconscious was decidedly less evident, Limonov partly attributed the cultural, social, and political backwardness of contemporary Russia to the country's general ignorance of Freud's "discoveries of the libido and the world of the unconscious."[75]

At the same time, the early love for Khlebnikov, whom Limonov considers Russia's greatest poet, marks the underlying deep link between Limonov's literary and political activity and the poetics of the Russian and Soviet avant-gardes. Through Melekhov, the young poet also discovers the works of the Russian Formalists and learns some of the rules of the literary game: "Melekhov explained to the young Savenko what is 'the automatism of perception.' . . . The young Savenko discovered that a 'blue sky' does not move the reader because after a thousand blue skies that 'blued' over the reader in a thousand books he, poor guy, does not notice the blueness of the sky anymore. The reader needs to be surprised, understood the young Savenko, who on precisely those days was turning into Limonov."[76]

In *Molodoi negodiai*, as well as in the other two books of the trilogy, the legacy of the historical avant-gardes is also inscribed into the geography and urban landscape of Kharkov. Kharkov, the narrator reminds the reader several times throughout the novel, is the birthplace of Tatlin, the "author of the project of the Monument to the Third International" who "painted all the trees in the Red Square red" to celebrate the first anniversary of the October Revolution. It is also the birthplace of Vvedensky, the "second greatest poet of the group Oberiu."[77]

Constructivist architecture dominates Kharkov's landscape and plays a major role in some of the crucial moments in the young Limonov's life. Dzerzhinsky square, "the second biggest square in the world after Tiananmen square in Bejing," is overshadowed by the "constructivist building of the State Industry, which looks like a prison—a massive and ugly construction of glass and concrete."[78] The club and movie theater Pobeda—where Eddie-baby reads his poems in front of an enthusiastic crowd in *Podrostok Savenko*—is a "product of the first period of Soviet constructivist thought, a concrete cube that towers in the center of the square where tens of thousands of people gather not only on holidays but on Saturdays as well."[79] Finally, the military headquarters described in *U nas byla velikaia epokha*, where Limonov's father was relocated with his family (as a captain of the NKVD, the Soviet secret police) soon after the war, and where Limonov spent the first years of his childhood, is a "constructivist fortress of concrete which miraculously survived [after the bombings of Kharkov]."[80] Buildings that may be construed as the ruins of constructivist architecture, physically evoking the original (betrayed) spirit of the October Revolution, overshadow the landscape of Kharkov in the trilogy and serve as a background for some of the crucial moments in the young Limonov's coming of age, like harbingers of a future radical renovation of society through the alliance of art and political struggle.

In an episode of *Molodoi negodiai*, the young poet Limonov is introduced to the avant-garde artist Vasil' Ermilov, who illustrated poetry collections by Velimir Khlebnikov and Elena Guro and was later ostracized from Soviet intellectual and artistic circles for contributing to Nazi propaganda during the German occupation of Kharkov. Walking back home from Ermilov's apartment, the protagonist discusses with Bakhchanian the relationship between avant-garde artists and Soviet institutions, on the one hand, and the realists' "seizure of power" in Soviet culture during the 1930s on the other: "I think, Vagrich, that after the civil war, after they got rid of the 'freaks' [*shizy*] who made the revolution—of people like me and you, Vagrich—different people, absolutely different people, the bureaucrats, came to power. The job of the bureaucrat is not to destroy states, but to rule them. Since bureaucrats are by nature conservative and bourgeois, they started to promote the only art that was close and accessible to them—realism."[81]

In his political manifesto, *Drugaia Rossiia*, published in 2003, Limonov still sees the October Revolution as the revolution of the marginal elements of society (the "freaks," or "*shizy*") against the bourgeois, the bureaucrats (*chinovniki*), and the silent majority (the "goat herd"). According to Limonov, Stalin was the first to betray the spirit of the revolution by starting a revival of imperial forms within Soviet culture. Later, Khrushchev and Brezhnev permanently deprived the Soviet state of all the "radical" and "heroic" elements of the October Revolution, introducing a materialistic, quasi-capitalist and bourgeois culture and ideology: "Khrushchev banalized all of us."[82] Still, while Limonov consistently interprets this era as a betrayal of the spirit of the revolution of 1917 and the final transformation of the Soviet Union into a bureaucratic state, and while his "ideal chronotope" is without any doubt that of the revolution, his relationship with Stalinism and the aesthetics of the empire is strikingly more complex and at times contradictory.[83]

Let's Go to War!

In the late 1980s and early 1990s, after his first visits to the Soviet Union, Limonov reconsidered his interpretation of Socialist Realism and his own style and position within the literary tradition. During an interview, he argued that Socialist Realism should be considered the only truly significant current in Russian art: "already now we look at these paintings not as the expression of a specific ideology, but as an exclusively aesthetic thing. And from an aesthetic point of view, Socialist Realism is both horrible, and incredibly original. And this is what enchants me."[84] Introducing himself to wider audiences in Russia, he started cultivating the image of a working class, popular, tough writer from the province, and a representative of a *zhestokii realizm* (cruel realism), in the tradition of such writers as Maksim Gorky and Sergey Esenin.[85] His last novel, he claimed, was written "in the style of late Socialist Realism. . . . I have heroes in military uniforms, with epaulets, they are all so handsome, big, and tall. . . . I am looking for an artistic, aesthetic truth, not for a historical truth."[86]

The short novel *U nas byla velikaia epokha*, Limonov's first book to be published in the Soviet Union, is a (much more concise) Soviet version of Proust's *In Search of Lost Time*, a quest for the author's memories of his childhood during the postwar years. By recreating the atmosphere of the Soviet "Great Epoch" through the viewpoint of a child, Limonov aimed to produce a personal history comprising mainly small details and flashing memories of disappeared objects, images, and *smells*: "My point of view is not that of a victim of the epoch, and is not in any way the point of view of a member of the intelligentsia, but is the point of view of somebody who lived among the common crowd. In a sense, my version of the epoch is a folkloric version."[87] Needless to say, Limonov's "populist" take on history was at this point in time quite unusual and subversive, in a way not dissimilar from Edichka's queerness and leftism in the context of Russian émigré culture of the 1970s.[88]

The image of this "lost epoch," that of the last years of Stalin's rule, is largely reconstructed on the basis of deeply personal details: the lines for bread; the beautiful uniform of his father Veniamin, senior lieutenant in the NKVD; and his father's military boots, pistol, and guitar.[89] As in Proust's *In Search of Lost Time*, memories are triggered by smells, such as that of Asidol, the product used to shine the buttons of Veniamin's uniform; the old Soviet colognes "Karmen" and "Shipr" that Veniamin applied to his face after shaving with his old-fashioned straight razor; the shoe polish of his leather boots; and the grease his father used while performing the weekly "ritual" of cleaning his duty gun. In this book, Limonov's fascination with military fashion and aesthetics, as well as his reinterpretation of Soviet history, emerges most clearly:

> In the book the reader will find a great deal of boots, *portianki*, epaulettes, breeches and weapons. Being the grandson and nephew of soldiers who died in combat, and the son of a soldier, I gave these attributes of masculinity their due, even if today's average citizen does not hold them in particularly high esteem. A burning complex of inferiority compels the contemporary individual to revise the past, including the Great Epoch—which is blamed for an abundance of blood and corpses. What are we supposed to say? Some epochs are remembered for their tragedies, others for their operettas. My personal predilections go to the army of Zhukov and the battle of Berlin, and not to the "umbrellas of Cherbourg." I actively prefer the "heroic" person to the "food-digesting" person.[90]

Through personal memory, the book establishes a system of aesthetic and moral categories and binary oppositions, including the people (*narod*) and the intelligentsia; the working class against the bourgeoisie; and the superiority of military discipline over the messiness and lack of organization of civilian life. Similarly, a moral and aesthetic reevaluation of history manifests itself in the juxtaposition of the modern capitalist world—embodied by the United States—with the Soviet Union and Germany, taken as the last representatives of a disappearing military honor code:

> "The Americans are particularly good at fighting against the civil population . . . —his father winced. The bomb is the most cowardly type of weapon. . . . [The Americans] are used to fighting with chocolate, a warm toilet, and a brothel, while listening to some Jazz. While the German is a tough opponent. . . . And now of course they have the atomic bomb. . . . The American is a shitty soldier, and this is why they like to fight by proxy . . ." Thus the first little wind of cold war passed through the room in Krasnoarmeskaa street.[91]

This nostalgic celebration of a military aesthetics and honor code, along with references to a certain heroic cult and the sharp moral and aesthetic contrast between the Soviet and German fallen empires and the cowardice and mediocrity of modern Western civilization, marks Limonov's gradual transition to politics as his main sphere of activity. In addition, it reflects his exposure to a series of cultural and political movements that have deeply affected his stance as a public intellectual in post-Soviet Russia. In Paris, Limonov had reached a certain notoriety and continued his political and journalistic activity, by collaborating with the left-wing newspaper *Libération* and, most importantly, with the radical newspaper *L'Idiot international.* Founded by the controversial writer and journalist Jean-Edern Hallier with the participation of several prominent French intellectuals, *L'Idiot international* was a highly provocative publication that proposed a renovation of the French left through a convergence of right-wing and left-wing ideas (a "red-brown ideology") and regularly published, with great scandal, contributions by both radical leftist and ultranationalist intellectuals. Through the circles close to this journal, Limonov became close to the French right-wing party National Front and was introduced to its leader, Jean-Marie Le Pen, and to the philosopher and ideologue of the French New Right Alain de Benoist.[92] At the same time, Limonov vocally criticized, in both the French and Russian presses, perestroika and the subsequent fall of the Soviet Union.[93]

The early 1990s marked a sort of macho-nationalist turn in Limonov's public image. His previous alternative, intellectual meek style was replaced by a black leather jacket, a short haircut, and military boots, which mirrored his new personal cult of strength, war, and masculinity (see figs. 2 and 3). In this period, he traveled to war zones in the former Yugoslavia, Transnistria, and Abkhazia. As he claims in his memoir, he was deeply fascinated by "war people" and by war itself, which he saw as a formative and beautiful experience.[94] In 1992 he appeared in Pawel Pawlikowski's BBC documentary *Serbian Epics*, where he was shown casually conversing with the Bosnian Serb politician Radovan Karadžić and his militia, then firing a machine gun in the direction of Sarajevo. The documentary caused outrage in the international community, further contributing to Limonov's highly controversial image.[95] Roughly at this time, the general attitude of the academic community toward him drastically changed and, by and large, literary scholars and critics started either dismissing or ignoring his work as a writer.[96]

Two of Limonov's essays from this period can help shed light on the motivations behind Limonov's transition to politics immediately after the fall of the Soviet Union: "Ischeznovenie varvarov" (The disappearance of the barbarians) and "Distsiplinarnyi sanatorii" (The disciplinary sanatorium).[97] The short piece "Ischeznovenie varvarov," which was first published in France in 1984, is a science fiction satire in which Limonov imagined the international reaction to the sudden mysterious disappearance of the Soviet Union from the face of the earth. In his polemical article, a series of institutions that mainly existed thanks to the USSR, which had been commonly perceived as a sort of geopolitical

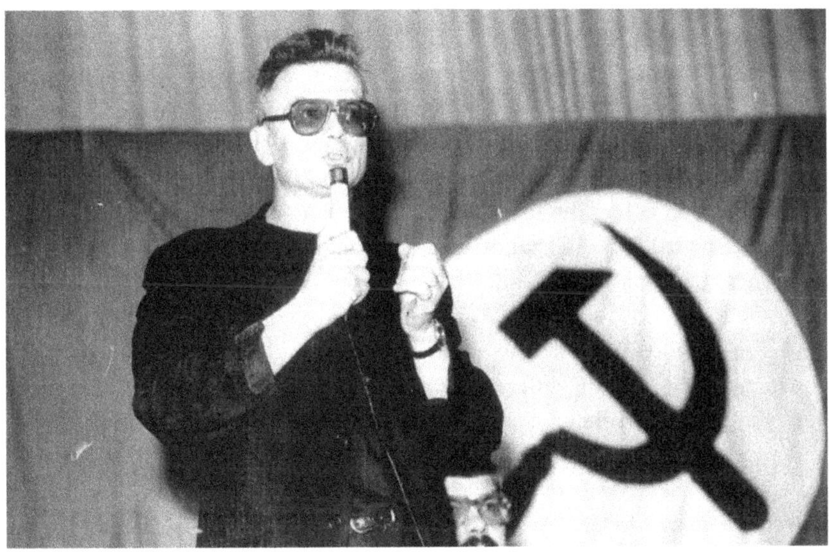

Figure 2. Eduard Limonov at the conference of the "revolutionary opposition" in Moscow on June 10, 1994, with the members of the neo-Nazi organization Russian National Unity (Russkoe Natsional'noe Edinstvo, RNE) and the communist organization Working Russia (Trudovaia Rossiia). Photo by Heidi Hollinger.

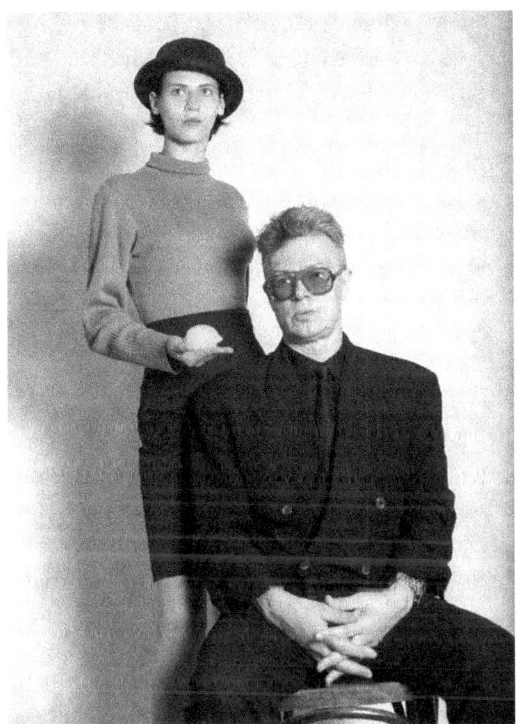

Figure 3. Eduard Limonov with his then girlfriend Elizaveta Bleze "parodying" his own older photograph "wearing the jacket of the national hero" (see fig. 1), Moscow, May 1996. Photo by Heidi Hollinger.

universal villain, are in deep crisis: the American propaganda and military industries, Radio Liberty, and the Russian dissident community. Western governments then start looking desperately for a substitute (perhaps China?) to replace the USSR as the main enemy of the Western world.

The second piece, the book-length essay "Distsiplinarnyi sanatorii," is a reflection on modern civilization and the fundamental cultural and political differences between Russia and the West. Polemicizing with George Orwell's novel *1984*, Limonov claims that, behind the surface, what distinguished the Soviet Union and the West were not their respective ideologies—totalitarianism and democracy—but the different systems of repression that their governments implemented. According to Limonov, the Soviet Union, along with other Second and Third World countries, engaged in forms of repression based on *hard* violence (police arrests and interrogations, censorship, limiting freedom of movement, etc.). Modern Western countries, on the other hand, shifted to more subtle forms of *soft* violence that turned their populations into masses of weak and sickly individuals, exclusively interested in achieving material comfort and terrified of poverty and unemployment. According to Limonov, late capitalist forms of repression are founded on the regulation of desires, mainly through mass media. More traditional and straightforward repressive measures are occasionally implemented against the "excitable people" (*vozbuzhdaiushchiesia*)—rebels, heroes, or "trouble-makers" such as Che Guevara, Yukio Mishima, and Muammar Gaddafi, who with their actions have called into question the moral and cultural foundations of modern life.

In these works, one can discern two important elements in the evolution of Limonov's aesthetics and ideology after his return to Russia in the late 1980s, early 1990s. First, both essays categorically rejected capitalism and modern civilization and celebrated heroic and highly controversial rebels as the last stronghold against the vileness and banality of modern consumerist society. Second, in these pieces Limonov envisioned the Soviet Union and Russia as a possible site for an alternative modernity and a new utopian society, distinguished from both the Soviet and the capitalist models. Later, Limonov elaborates this vision further, explicitly claiming that the outcasts (*marginaly*), and not the proletarians, should be considered the truly revolutionary class, and calling for a radical transformation of Russian society that involves, among other things, abolishing the traditional family, getting rid of traditional education, and creating new forms of collective life. Limonov also argues that no social change would be possible without truly absorbing what he evidently sees as fundamental countercultural texts: "Russia has not read the necessary books, the books that unveil and explain modernity: neither Céline, nor Miller, nor André Gide, nor Jean Genet; neither Frazer's *The Golden Bough*, nor Hitler's *Mein Kampf*, nor Julius

Evola's *Revolt Against the Modern World*. Most importantly, *She* has not read these fundamental books in time! Russia has completely ignored the truth about the powerful European nationalist movements of the twentieth century, and the revolutions that occurred during this period."[98]

These political statements combine a Nietzschean cult of the hero, radical conservative thinking, and Western critical theory. In particular, Limonov's discussion of sexuality in capitalist societies; his promotion of the *marginaly* as a revolutionary class; and his reflection on knowledge, desire, and power as closely interconnected factors in modern forms of manipulation and repression of the masses echo, respectively, the work of Herbert Marcuse and Michel Foucault. In particular, Foucault's ideas and his lectures on biopolitics at the Collège de France were being extensively published and discussed when Limonov was living in Paris during the 1980s, and *Libération*, the leftist newspaper with which he collaborated, was one of the venues for these discussions.[99]

In the late 1980s, Limonov was introduced to Russian audiences by the writer, journalist, and publisher Yulian Semyonov, famous in the Soviet Union as the author of *Seventeen Moments of Spring* (*Semnadtsat' mgnovenii vesny*), the novel and popular TV series featuring the iconic character Stierlitz, a Soviet spy working undercover as an SS officer in Nazi Germany during World War II.[100] While still based in Paris, he started visiting Russia often and getting more and more involved in its politics. In this period, he regularly published in the periodicals *Izvestiia*, *Sovetskaia Rossiia*, and *Novyi vzgliad*, harshly criticizing Russia's transition to democracy and uncritical assimilation of Western values and ideas.[101] At the same time, he started claiming that literature should be considered a dead or archaic form that is being gradually replaced by essays, "interesting thoughts," and other modes of self-expression, drawing parallels between Russian literary evolution and Western counterculture: "By the way, Russia's love for poetry during those years [the 1970s] was archaic—at that point the youth of the rest of the world already lived off another Rock 'n' Roll."[102] In the mid-1990s, with the foundation of the National Bolshevik Party, the making of one of the first post-Soviet counterpublics became Limonov's main sphere of activity. Limonov's turn to politics in the early 1990s and the emergence of this countercultural movement were anticipated and de facto made possible by the shaping of Limonov's own literary (anti-) hero, and by the projection and creation of an imagined audience of punks, outcasts, and rebels within his fiction.

Limonov's Post-Soviet Reception and Political Career

As an émigré writer, by the end of the 1980s Limonov had reached international notoriety and a certain recognition among literary scholars and critics.[103]

In post-Soviet Russia, where Limonov returned and was first published in the early 1990s, his public persona became paradoxically associated both with the anti-Yeltsin "national-patriotic opposition" (and with a certain form of nostalgia for the Soviet past) *and* with newly acquired forms of personal, cultural, and sexual freedom. The first major work by Limonov to be published in Russia, *U nas byla velikaia epokha*, depicted the rosy, everyday aspects of the Stalin era through the story of Limonov's own childhood in a provincial Soviet town. The second, *Eto ia—Edichka*, which was a literary sensation, was the first book ever officially published in Russia that explicitly dealt with the theme of homosexual desire. Mogutin, the young, openly gay journalist, performance artist, and poet who de facto introduced Limonov to the Russian public, was repeatedly prosecuted for explicitly writing about homosexuality, for trying to officially register his wedding in Moscow with his male partner, and, at the same time, for writing fiercely nationalist articles about the war in Chechnya.[104] Aleksandr Shatalov's publishing house Glagol, which published Limonov's works, specialized in transgressive, countercultural, and queer authors, including James Baldwin, William Burroughs, and Evgeny Kharitonov, who, as Laurie Essig points out, "share neither a common language nor a common culture nor historical moment. Instead, what is present in all four authors is a recognizable (at least to a Russian reader) concept of queer male sexuality. This sexuality is neither bounded nor fixed. It is not an identity, but a practice. The characters are not 'either gay or straight' but both, or neither."[105] At the same time, Limonov actively sought alliance with such nationalist politicians as Vladimir Zhirinovsky and Aleksandr Barkashov, leader of the neo-Nazi organization Russian National Unity (Russkoe natsional'noe edinstvo, RNE), and with communist nostalgics like Viktor Anpilov, leader of Trudovaia Rossiia (Working Russia).[106]

The eclectic, multifaceted nature of Limonov's public persona is reflected in the aesthetics and ideology of the NBP, which established itself, one might argue, as the quintessential post-Soviet revolutionary movement.[107] After shocking the Russian public with their violent nationalist slogans and their calls for Stalinist repressions, during the first decade of the 2000s the *natsboly* became among the most vocal opponents of Putin's government and found several allies within the liberal opposition. After spending two years in prison between 2001 and 2003 on charges of armed revolt and illegal arms trading, Limonov, along with Garry Kasparov and Mikhail Kasianov, became one of the leaders and founders of the large anti-Putin coalition Drugaia Rossiia (named after the title of Limonov's own manifesto). Drugaia Rossiia was also adopted as the official name of the party in 2010, after the NBP was outlawed in 2007.[108] After this "liberal turn," the organization started mostly focusing on issues of social inequality and freedom of speech, and the *natsboly* became famous for their *aktsii priamogo deistviia* (direct-action stunts), which included symbolic attacks against members of the establishment (involving throwing eggs at them or hitting them with roses "stripped of their thorns" in order to avoid possible violence accusations), sit-ins, and occupations of government buildings. Because of their activism, members of the NBP were frequently imprisoned and assaulted by the police and by gangs of street thugs and soccer hooligans allegedly hired by the leaders of the infamous pro-Putin youth organization Nashi.[109] The repressions against the NBP were justified by the government as part of an anti-fascist and anti-extremist policy, and pro-government media used the NBP's own nationalist rhetoric to prove Limonov's and the NBP's alleged fascism.[110] At the same time, in 2006 a group of *natsboly* who disagreed with Limonov's new liberal/leftist line left the party to found, with the support of Dugin's Eurasian Youth Union and, indirectly, that of the Putin administration, the more straightforwardly ultranationalist National Bolshevik Front.[111]

In 2009, Limonov and his followers were the initiators of "Strategy-31," a series of protests held in front of the monument to Mayakovsky on Triumfalnaya Square in Moscow on the thirty-first day of every month with thirty-one days. During these rallies, protesters claimed the right to peaceful assembly formally guaranteed by Article 31 of the Russian constitution but in fact denied by the Russian police, who regularly forcefully removed and arrested the protesters, in what soon became a ritual of Russian political life. Strategy-31 was supported and joined by several prominent figures in the Russian dissident and human rights movement, including Liudmila Alekseeva, Lev Ponomarev, and Vladimir Bukovsky, and it reclaimed the legacy of the Russian dissident movement.[112]

During the Moscow 2011–12 mass protests "for fair elections," Limonov gradually isolated himself and his followers from the opposition movement, arguably because of disagreements about its ideological orientation and political strategies. In this period, he started to publish harsh indictments of the "liberal intelligentsia" on his Facebook page and his blog on LiveJournal.[113] In 2014, because of his support of Putin's annexation of Crimea and of the separatist movement in Eastern Ukraine, he became a more acceptable figure for the Russian leadership. On May 31, 2014, for the first time in five years, Strategy-31, now renamed "Rally in Support of Donbass," was officially authorized by the Russian authorities.[114]

2

Making Post-Soviet Counterpublics

The Aesthetics of *Limonka* and the National Bolshevik Party

In Ochamchira to die is beautiful / A patch of light on the lips / In a thicket of mandarin trees / Caressing your rifle like your beloved woman / Having forgotten all the fear / That the lawless streets of Moscow / You walk as if you were naked / Good and Evil are imponderable. . . . // Let's go to war!

Natalya Medvedeva, "Poedem na voinu!" (Let's go to war!), 1995

Another one of my heroes during those years was David Bowie. This is a person who kept changing all the time. In part, I felt like I was the same way. Not that I thought that I was as talented as he was of course. . . . But I transform myself fairly easily. For instance, I remember there was a moment when I would go around wearing the fascist cap of a German *Jäger* that I had bought at some second-hand store. This doesn't mean that I was a fascist at that point, but the *style—that* I would exploit. In those years this was an element of nonconformism, because we had a dictatorship of liberal styles, not even liberal *views*, but really a "stylistic liberal dictatorship," and of course this was a form of protest. Because, on the one hand, there was a very strong Americanization in those years, and on the other, they made heroes

> out of the dissidents. That is, there was a strong cult of victims that I really didn't want to have anything to do with. And the German cap was a form of protest against both of these things.
>
> Kirill, forty-two, journalist and former member of the NBP, Moscow, February 2015

> There is no speech or performance addressed to a public that does not try to specify in advance, in countless highly condensed ways, the lifeworld of its circulation. . . . Public discourse says not only: "Let a public exist," but: "Let it have this character, speak this way, see the world in this way." It then goes out in search of confirmation that such a public exists, with greater or lesser success—success being further attempts to cite, circulate, and realize the world-understanding it articulates. Run it up the flagpole, and see who salutes. Put on a show, and see who shows up.
>
> Michael Warner, "Publics and Counterpublics"

Modern public life is characterized by the coexistence of a multiplicity of languages, styles, and modes of participation through which different social groups and individuals can express themselves and contribute to the political life of the community. Publics and counterpublics are, to use Nancy Fraser's definition, "arenas for the formation and enactment of social identities," where these different styles and languages of public participation are shaped and negotiated.[1] Publics are made of specific cultural institutions, journals, common gathering spaces, canonical books and artworks, all of which shape and mediate ideologies and generate different forms of political action. Culture and language are never socially or ideologically neutral. They enable subtle forms of exclusion. In Pierre Bourdieu's terms, "art and cultural consumption are predisposed, consciously and deliberately or not, to fulfill a social function of legitimating social differences."[2] Whereas dominant social groups and ruling classes retain the monopoly on "high culture," subaltern counterpublics are "discursive arenas where members of subordinated social groups invent and circulate counterdiscourses, which in turn permit them to formulate oppositional interpretations of their identities, interests, and needs."[3] This is why, according to Fraser, even the existence of counterpublics that promote antiliberal or antidemocratic ideas can be a good thing in the presence of social inequality, in that "assumptions that were previously exempt from contestation will now have to be publicly argued out . . . [and] the proliferation of subaltern counterpublics means a widening of discursive contestation."[4] In other words, subaltern counterpublics often give voice to disadvantaged, otherwise voiceless strata of the population and at the same time create the premises for questioning and rethinking dominant discourses and ideologies.[5]

During the 1990s, after the fall of the Soviet Union and the abrupt shift to an unbridled form of market economy, large strata of the Russian population found themselves deeply impoverished and at the same time deprived of a way of expressing political dissent (a condition that seemed paradoxical in the wake of the democratic movement of the 1980s). "Shock therapy" and what was publicly described as a form of Western liberal democracy became the banners of the Yeltsin government and the new post-Soviet ruling class. This new leadership, and the new political system that it introduced, could not be called into question inasmuch as they putatively represented (especially in the eyes of Western observers) the liberation from the yoke of Soviet totalitarianism. In this context, liberal democracy itself could be perceived by disadvantaged and marginalized social groups, and by a suddenly impoverished intelligentsia, as a system imposed from above and as an ideology aimed at justifying the privileges of the newly formed ruling class.[6] At the same time, in the ideological and symbolic void produced by the collapse of the Soviet Union, and in the absence of a collective project that went beyond passive assimilation of what were perceived to be Western cultural and political values, totalitarian symbols and aesthetics could serve as a catalyst for the creation of alternative publics and communities that resisted mainstream discourses and ideologies.

This second chapter explores the way in which the creation of a particular radical, totalitarian, and countercultural aesthetics within Eduard Limonov's National Bolshevik Party (NBP) has contributed to the shaping of new forms, styles, and languages of political dissent in post-Soviet Russia. In order to do so, it investigates the making of this radical organization, one of the first post-Soviet oppositional and subaltern publics, through the pages of its official newspaper, *Limonka*.[7] Following Michael Warner's definition of public discourse as "poetic world-making," I argue that the aesthetics of *Limonka* should be seen as an adaptation of certain themes and devices connected with Limonov's fictional and journalistic writing and with the making of his literary and public persona.[8] These themes and devices include the individual or collective condition of marginality and periphery, conceived both as geographical periphery and as the periphery of cultural systems and institutions; a provocative display of violence, sexuality, and the body, used as a form of individual and collective rebellion against artistic conventions and social norms; and a hopeless, desperate, heroic, and quasi-comical protest against cultural, institutional, and economic power, and, ultimately, against modernity in its entirety. The aggressive, "anarcho-militaristic" aesthetics of the NBP should also be seen as an adaptation of the style and posture of the historical avant-gardes to the post-Soviet political landscape, which the newspaper partly derived from Limonov's own avant-garde stance within the Russian literary system.[9] Finally, I interpret certain aspects of the aesthetics of *Limonka* as a particular kind of *stiob*, the form of parody based on overidentification with its own object that Alexei Yurchak has shown to be a fundamental feature of late Soviet public culture.[10]

According to Yurchak, the ossified, hypernormalized, and highly citational nature of late Soviet official culture caused its participants to focus, following J. L. Austin's theory of speech acts, on the performative dimension of language rather than on its constative dimension.[11] When members of the "last Soviet generation" wrote an official document, staged an unauthorized public performance, told a joke, or wrote a satirical poem, Yurchak claims, they did not mean what they said, but they performed a ritual that confirmed their belonging to a specific group or cultural milieu and defined their identity and value system. This "performative shift" affected both official forms of publicity (e.g., meetings of the Komsomol) and the cultural production and social life of underground communities that lived outside or "beyond" the boundaries of Soviet official culture.[12]

"Living *vnye*" ("living beyond"), ostensibly a widespread condition in late Soviet society, is described as the state of being at the same time "outside" and "inside" the system, formally and performatively participating in its rituals while providing them with new unexpected meanings. In addition to the Komsomol, Yurchak takes as examples of "living *vnye*" the life of various late Soviet countercultural communities, including the Necrorealists, the Leningrad underground poetic circle of the Mit'ki, and the Moscow Conceptualists. In his view, this "performative shift" had important political consequences; this form of public culture was at the same time a fundamental precondition for the existence of the Soviet system and one of the main causes of its collapse. Yet, in this narrative "living beyond" emerges as a way of existing literally outside of politics, and does not seem to include any form of active cultural or political resistance.[13] An important aspect of the condition of "living beyond" is the prominent role played in it by the discursive genre of *stiob*. *Stiob* is a parody based on overidentification with the object of the parody itself or, as the avant-garde musician and performer Sergey Kurekhin once defined it, a form of "parasitizing": "parasitizing is like looking deep into things—not negating, ridiculing, or judging them, but making visible their internal criteria."[14]

By interpreting *stiob* as a dominant discursive mode in the rhetoric of the early NBP and a subtle tactic of cultural and political resistance, this chapter shows that the appropriation and reinvention of a fascist, and in general totalitarian, aesthetics and ideology within this movement should be seen at the same time as a politically and morally disengaged act of protest (in the spirit of late Soviet underground culture) and as a return to a romanticized utopian ideal of the revolution. However, because the NBP adopted a violent and aggressive rhetoric based on a cult of war, revolution, and masculinity, and because this same rhetoric was explicitly oriented toward political action, the making of this radical community marked the emergence of a new specifically post-Soviet militant mode of collective participation, or a "post-Soviet militant *stiob*."[15] Serguei Oushakine defines the widespread inability to describe the post-Soviet condition both "on the personal level" and "on the cultural level," as "post-Soviet aphasia," and interprets nostalgic and parasitic uses of Soviet aesthetics and cultural heritage as a consequence of this symbolic and linguistic void.[16] In the case of the NBP and the newspaper *Limonka*, Soviet and totalitarian cultural symbols were in fact creatively combined in order to produce an alternative "cultural field."

The Founding Fathers

While the NBP borrowed several themes and techniques from Limonov's literary works, the shaping of the aesthetics and ideology of this organization was also the result of a collective effort. In its early stages, the emergence of this community can be explained primarily as a consequence of the appearance of a new readership for Limonov's fiction and poetry in Russia at the beginning of the 1990s. At the same time, this community reflected a convergence of various cultural formations and the collective effort of artists, intellectuals, and political thinkers seeking an alternative to what they perceived as an oppressive and all-encompassing neoliberal discourse following the parliamentary crisis of October 1993.

During Limonov's meeting with the public broadcast on Russian television in 1992, a young *neformal* (that is a member of the Soviet cultural underground or, more simply put, "an alternative kid") stood up, wearing all black clothes and thin round sunglasses, and quoted a passage from Limonov's early avant-garde poem "My—natsional'nyi geroi" (We are the national hero): "Any kind of clothes that Limonov wears become the clothes of the national hero. / T-shirts—limonovki / socks and shirts—limonki / Jackets—limon. / haircuts—ailimonov."[17] He then proposed to take inspiration from these lines and start an organization of Limonov's fans who would imitate the writer's own alternative fashion. This was not an uncommon reaction to Limonov's work and public image. In fact, many of "the old guard" of *natsboly* that I interviewed, most of whom were adolescents at the time, recalled deciding to join the party because they were attracted by Limonov's writing style, as well as by his style of clothing and self-presentation. For instance, Katya, a former member of the NBP and a doctoral student in her thirties at the time of our conversation, recalled how she started reading the Russian anarchist thinkers Kropotkin and Bakunin from a very early age. In the mid-1990s, still a teenager, she felt the need to join a political organization: "I had some sort of energy that I felt like channeling somewhere, a kind of adolescent vitality, increased by the reading of those books [by Kropotkin and Bakunin]." When she first read the party newspaper *Limonka*, Katya recalled, she was particularly attracted by the "socialist tendency" in the newspaper and by a "strange nostalgia for the Soviet past," which was conveyed through "a new and original language."

Katya had always considered herself a leftist and remarked that later in her life, "from the point of view of age and experience," she would have been much more skeptical of the NBP's flirtations with fascist symbols and ideas. However, at the time she found those same references to fascism very appealing. Limonov's "good taste," she claimed, allowed him to create an "accomplished aesthetics," which naturally attracted to the party many "creative people, writers, and artists." Katya immediately embraced the *natsboly*'s style and started wearing "a green bomber jacket, black tight short jeans, and Dr. Martens boots." She became an avid reader of Limonov's books. One of her favorites was *Diary of a Loser*, a book of fragments in which Limonov, still a destitute émigré in New York City, dreams of violence, sex, and world revolution:

> I cry for you in New York. The city of Atlantic humid winds. Where the infection flourishes boundless. Where the people-slaves serve the people-masters, who at the same time are also slaves. And at nights. I, in my dirty hotel. Lonely, Russian, stupid. I dream of you, dream of you, dream. Who innocently died young—beautiful, smiling, still alive. With scarlet lips, white-necked tender being. Scratched hands on the rifle strap—Russian-speaking—Revolution—my love![18]

Another early member of the NBP, forty-two-year-old journalist Kirill, also remembered how as an adolescent he had identified with Limonov's isolation, tragic heroism, and disillusionment with life and women. Kirill recalled seeing Limonov for the first time at a public event in Moscow in the late 1980s. First and foremost, he said, he was struck by Limonov's attitude, by the new and simple way in which the writer talked and interacted with the public, and by the way he dressed ("all in black and with a bright red shirt"), which was so different from that of the Soviet journalists, congressmen, and members of the *nomenklatura* he saw there. Limonov's short stories and books, which Kirill had later read, made a strong impression on him because they were written in a "different language," "not very literary at times, but also precise and vivid" and far from the Soviet literary style he had been used to.

The discovery of Limonov's fiction coincided with Kirill's coming of age. As an adolescent, he was looking for a "masculine principle in himself," and Limonov offered a "version of a masculine approach to life." Like Ernest Hemingway for the Soviet generation of the 1960s, Kirill told me, Limonov showed him and many other Russian men of his generation a particular "attitude toward women, toward danger, toward risk, toward misfortune and disillusionment." Kirill's fascination with Limonov was also linked with a taste for adventure, which drew him to journalism, and which he had previously found in the heroes of classic adventure fiction who had populated his childhood imagination. Although later he read all "the classics of world literature," the authors that he read as a child—Alexandre Dumas, Arthur Conan Doyle, Robert Louis Stevenson, and Henry Rider Haggard—determined his "basic moral values" as well as his male adventurous role models: Eduard Limonov, the Russian bard Vladimir Vysotsky, and the Japanese writer and adventurer Yukio Mishima. Like Mishima, during his adolescence Kirill started practicing bodybuilding, something that he felt was part of a process of spiritual and physical improvement and transformation.

In a way not dissimilar from Limonov's literary persona, during his years as a young NBP activist Kirill frequently saw himself "from the outside," "like the hero of a film." He changed frequently, as if playing different roles. Although, as he told me, Kirill was never a fascist or a "Hitler-admirer" (*Gitleropoklonnik*), he could appreciate the "fascist style" and "use some of the elements" of this style as a form of protest against what he called a "stylistic liberal dictatorship," that is, a massive "Westernization, or, better, Americanization" of post-Soviet culture and society.

Finally, forty-one-year-old Anton, another member of the NBP old guard with strong academic interests who later pursued a career in journalism, told me something that echoed what many other National Bolshevik activists of different ages and backgrounds said about Limonov's work. Upon reading *Eto ia—Edichka* as a sixteen-year-old, Anton immediately recognized himself and other young Muscovites—impoverished, isolated, and marginalized in their own city—in the desperate protagonist of the book. Like Edichka, Anton and his peers saw themselves as victims of social injustice and social inequality. Like Edichka, they could only imagine escaping their condition by transgressing social norms and rejecting mainstream values.

In Anton's description, the capitalist, Babylon-like, post-Soviet Moscow of his adolescence becomes strangely similar to the alienating New York City of the 1970s, where Edichka, as a miserable third-wave Russian émigré, is unable to find a place for himself. As an image symbolically reflecting the feeling of complete hopelessness that he and his peers experienced during the 1990s, Anton recalled how he once stood at the entrance of a Moscow metro station with his friends—tired, penniless, and drinking the "cheapest possible beer"—and looked at the shiny Mercedes that would pass by, understanding that, "no matter what," he and his peers would never be able to cross the line that separated them from the oligarchs, the privileged, and the powerful:

> It felt like this had been written *for me.* I found these vibrations absolutely relevant to my own. Especially of course that feeling—that feeling, when he describes himself in New York . . . In *Edichka,* yes? . . . That feeling when he describes himself in New York as a normal guy, in this city absolutely foreign and incomprehensible to him—in principle, this is exactly how we felt in Moscow, in a strange way. Although we were born here, and we had lived here 13–16 years . . . All of a sudden we started feeling in our own home like Limonov in New York, you know? And because of this, this subject resonated with us. It was about a sort of ontological awareness and position that you can do whatever you like, you can go "to the end of the night," like in Céline, and still you'll never be able to get out of this "Hotel Winslow," you'll never move to the Upper West Side. And this *abyss*—it is absolutely *insurmountable.* And here at your place, "at the hotel Winslow," how can I say, in this sort of "nocturne," go ahead and find some adventures for yourself [*ty ishchi sam sebe prikliucheniia*], yes? That's all. . . . And of course Moscow in the 1990s, and our journeys through it, they were absolutely the same kind of story [*iz takoi zhe opery*].

The emergence of the NBP as a more structured political entity took place in the aftermath of the constitutional crisis of October 1993. This was, according to many, the event that marked the premature failure of Russia's liberal reforms—effectively the original sin of Russian democracy. The crisis took place only two years after the (mostly) bloodless revolution of 1991 that put an end to the Soviet Union, when Yeltsin famously stood alongside a peaceful crowd of Muscovites in front of the parliament building, also known as the "White House," to defend the democratic reforms against the coup organized by a group of hardliners that included the heads of the military, the intelligence, and the police forces.[19]

Between the spring and fall of 1993, as a result of the disastrous consequences of the market reforms—which had caused dramatic inflation, widespread poverty and criminality, a severe health crisis, and the sudden collapse of the military-industrial complex and educational system—Yeltsin tried on several occasions to abolish the first Russian parliament (the Supreme Soviet), which was threatening a vote of no confidence against him. After Yeltsin issued a decree that would have immediately dissolved the parliament, the congress declared his power illegitimate and his actions unconstitutional. On September 21, under the leadership of Vice President Aleksandr Rutskoy and Chairman of the Supreme Soviet Ruslan Khasbulatov, the members of the parliament barricaded themselves in the White House, the same building that only two years earlier had come to embody the victory of democratic reforms. Ultranationalists, like the members of Barkashov's Russian National Unity and of the National Salvation Front (Front natsional'nogo spaseniia), along with communist nostalgics, like the members of Anpilov's Working Russia, gathered in front of the building to protest the actions of the president and started building barricades to defend the Supreme Soviet from a possible incursion of the army. It was reported that some of the neofascists from Barkashov's organization and groups of soldiers who had been fighting in interethnic conflicts in the former Soviet regions of Abkhazia and Transnistria and in the Baltic states were carrying automatic rifles.

The standoff culminated in the events of October 3–5, 1993. On October 3, some of the White House "defenders" (who according to some sources had been lured outside as part of a strategic maneuver of the military and police units loyal to Yeltsin) headed toward Ostankino, the TV tower from which all the major Russian TV and radio channels broadcast, with the intention of taking over the Russian media. Some of the protesters marched in crowds toward the building; others drove there on trucks that the police had left unattended in front of the parliament building before withdrawing. When the protesters (a crowd of several thousand people, and some of them—the minority—armed) tried to break into the building, police special forces started shooting into the crowd from inside the building and from armored vehicles surrounding it. The next day, Yeltsin declared a state of emergency and gave the order to storm the parliament. The White House was bombarded from tanks and other armored vehicles for several hours before catching on fire and being seized by troops loyal to the president. According to official estimates, 159 people (131 civilians and 28 police officers and members of the military) lost their lives and 423 (321 civilians and 102 police officers and members of the military) were wounded during the events of September 21–October 5, 1993, in Moscow.[20] Following the bombing of the White House there were numerous unconfirmed reports from eyewitnesses about a much higher number of casualties, summary executions, beatings of deputies and other White House defenders, and secret coordinated police operations aimed at disposing unidentified bodies through mass cremations.[21]

After the end of the conflict, Yeltsin temporarily banned all the nationalist and communist newspapers and organizations that had sided with the defenders of the White House. The 1993 constitution implemented after the confrontation guaranteed extraordinarily strong powers to the president, who could override all other branches of the government and the legislative body. In addition to the fact that the standoff with the parliament had been resolved through violent means, the virtually unlimited powers that the new constitution guaranteed to the president hindered the full development of democratic institutions and paved the way for the emergence of an autocratic system in Russia.[22] More generally, the events of October 1993, combined with the disastrous consequences of the liberal reforms and the widespread corruption of Yeltsin's government, also fundamentally discredited the idea of democracy in the eyes of most Russians.[23]

The National Bolshevik Party started its activities in November 1994, only one year after the siege of the Russian parliament. Beyond Limonov, the founders of the party included the radical right-wing philosopher Aleksandr Dugin—today widely known as the leader of the Eurasia Movement and commonly described by Western commentators and journalists as an ideological mastermind behind Putin's regime—Taras Rabko, then a law student and a fan of Limonov; and Egor Letov, the lead singer of the legendary Soviet underground punk band Grazhdanskaia oborona (Civil Defense). Limonov and Dugin, who acted respectively as the political leader and the ideologue of the party, conceived the NBP as a combination of radical right- and left-wing ideologies, supporting a nationalist and imperialist foreign policy, together with strong social welfare and equal distribution of wealth. In Limonov's and Dugin's eyes, the party was supposed to carry on the legacy of the Red-Brown coalition that had emerged during the violent confrontation of 1993 and to realize its revolutionary potential.

The emblem of the party was taken from the back cover of *Ischeznovenie varvarov* (The disappearance of the barbarians), a tongue-in-cheek science fiction essay, written in the mid-1980s, in which Limonov imagined the nefarious consequences of the sudden disappearance of the Soviet Union from the geopolitical landscape. The symbol of the NBP, an encircled black hammer and sickle on a red background, evoked Nazi and Soviet aesthetics in a very immediate and somewhat uncanny way (see fig. 4). The poet, visual artist, performer, and queer activist Yaroslav Mogutin proposed the name for the party newspaper, borrowing it from Limonov's poem "My—natsional'nyi geroi," in which Limonov childishly dreamt of becoming a rock star of sorts.[24] The graphic designer Konstantin Chuvashev, at the time one of Aleksandr Dugin's closest "disciples," drew the masthead for the newspaper, including the iconic hand grenade that became the other main symbol of the movement (see fig. 5).

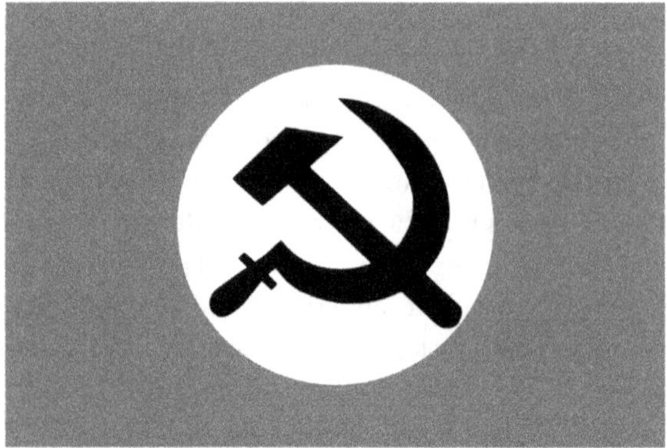

Figure 4. Symbol of the NBP/Drugaia Rossiia (hammer and sickle).

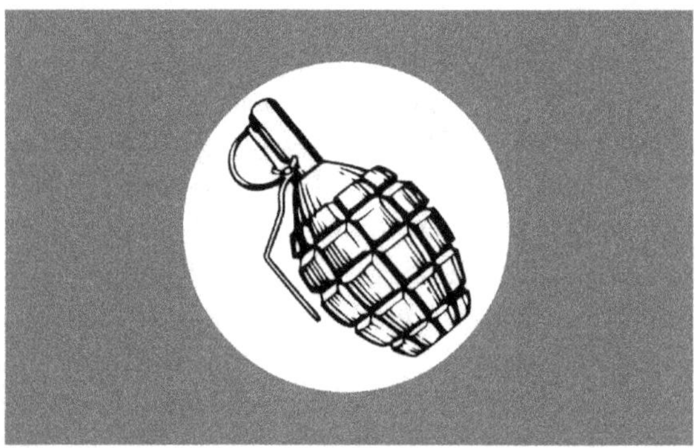

Figure 5. Symbol of the NBP/Drugaia Rossiia (grenade).

In creating *Limonka*'s distinct graphic style, Chuvashev was inspired by various forms of political art, including Soviet constructivism and the Dutch school of graphic design of the 1920s and 1930s. When I interviewed him, Chuvashev claimed that, political convictions aside, at the time he was very enthusiastic about participating in the creation of *Limonka* as this experience gave him the opportunity to experiment very early with a wide range of styles and political symbols.[25]

In its graphics and content alike, from the large squared print of the masthead to the front-page photomontages by John Heartfield and Aleksandr Rodchenko appearing on the cover of many of its issues, as well as in the selection of its historical role models, *Limonka* reproduced the aggressive and direct style of the Soviet propaganda of the 1920s and 1930s (referred to in Russian as *plakatnaia estetika*).[26] Party slogans—provocative, politically incorrect, sometimes ironic—were printed vertically in big letters on the right side of the first page of each issue, creating a visual history of the party line through the covers of its newspaper (see fig. 6). Every issue contained one of Limonov's now famous

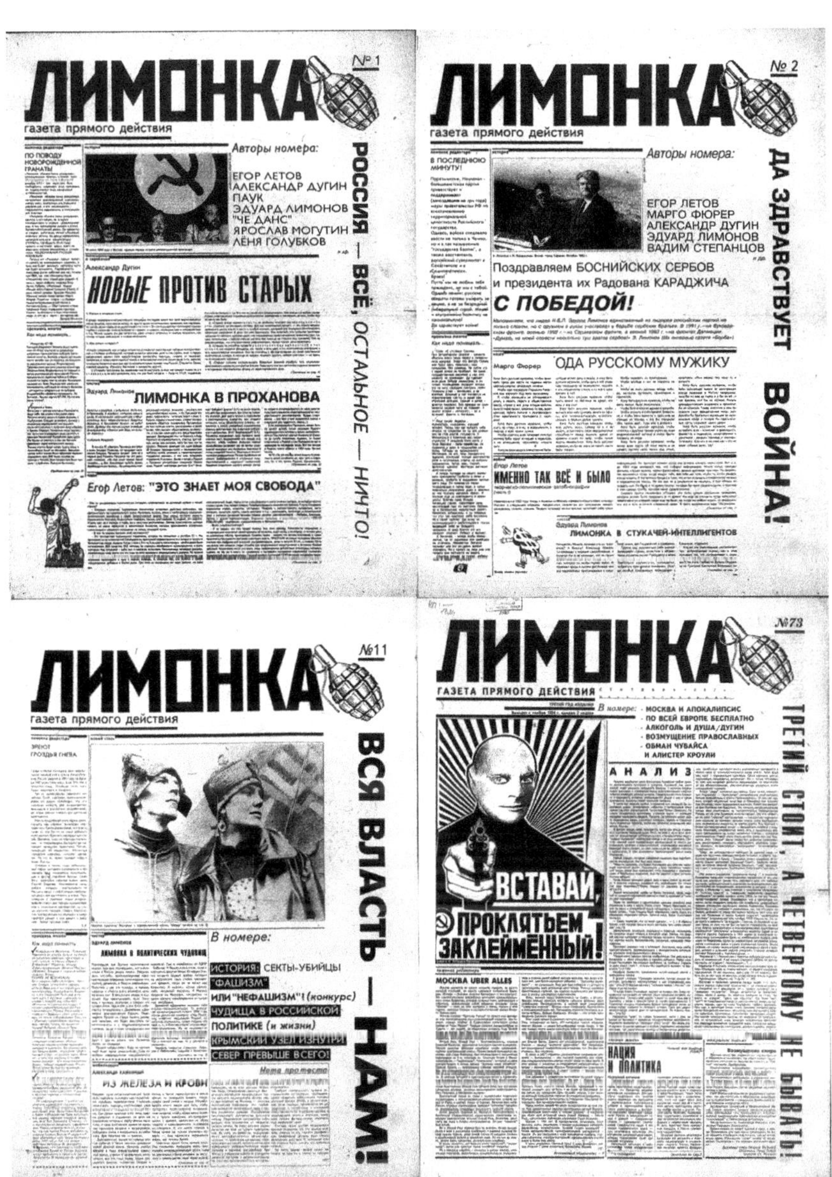

ЛИМОНКА
№ 1
газета прямого действия

По поводу новорожденной гранаты

Авторы номера:
Егор Летов
Александр Дугин
Паук
Эдуард Лимонов
"Че Данс"
Ярослав Могутин
Лёня Голубков

РОССИЯ — ВСЁ, ОСТАЛЬНОЕ — НИЧТО!

Александр Дугин
НОВЫЕ ПРОТИВ СТАРЫХ

Эдуард Лимонов
ЛИМОНКА В ПРОХАНОВА

Егор Летов: "ЭТО ЗНАЕТ МОЯ СВОБОДА"

ЛИМОНКА
№ 2
газета прямого действия

В последнюю минуту!

Авторы номера:
Егор Летов
Марго Фюрер
Александр Дугин
Эдуард Лимонов
Вадим Степанцов

Поздравляем БОСНИЙСКИХ СЕРБОВ
и президента их Радована КАРАДЖИЧА
С ПОБЕДОЙ!

Марго Фюрер
ОДА РУССКОМУ МУЖИКУ

Егор Летов
ИМЕННО ТАК ВСЁ И БЫЛО

Эдуард Лимонов
ЛИМОНКА В СТУКАЧЕЙ-ИНТЕЛЛИГЕНТОВ

ДА ЗДРАВСТВУЕТ ВОЙНА!

ЛИМОНКА
№11
газета прямого действия

ВСЯ ВЛАСТЬ — НАМ!

В номере:
ИСТОРИЯ: СЕКТЫ-УБИЙЦЫ
"ФАШИЗМ"
ИЛИ "НЕФАШИЗМ"! (конкурс)
ЧУДИЩА В РОССИЙСКОЙ
ПОЛИТИКЕ (и жизни)
КРЫМСКИЙ УЗЕЛ ИЗНУТРИ
СЕВЕР ПРЕВЫШЕ ВСЕГО!

Эдуард Лимонов
ЛИМОНКА В ПОЛИТИЧЕСКИХ ЧУДОВИЩ

Александр Дугин
ИЗ ЖЕЛЕЗА И КРОВИ

Нота протеста

ЛИМОНКА
№73
ГАЗЕТА ПРЯМОГО ДЕЙСТВИЯ

В номере:
- МОСКВА И АПОКАЛИПСИС
- ПО ВСЕЙ ЕВРОПЕ БЕСПЛАТНО
- АЛКОГОЛЬ И ДУША/ДУГИН
- ВОЗМУЩЕНИЕ ПРАВОСЛАВНЫХ
- ОБМАН ЧУБАЙСА
- И АЛИСТЕР КРОУЛИ

ТРЕТИЙ СТОИТ, А ЧЕТВЕРТОМУ НЕ БЫВАТЬ!

ВСТАВАЙ,
ПРОКЛЯТЬЕМ ЗАКЛЕЙМЁННЫЙ!

АНАЛИЗ

МОСКВА UBER ALLES

НАЦИЯ И ПОЛИТИКА

Figure 6. Covers of *Limonka*, the National Bolshevik Party's newspaper, 1994–97.

political articles, or *limonki*: verbal grenades aimed at political opponents, government leaders, and even the Russian intelligentsia in its entirety.[27]

Limonov contributed significantly to the creation of the political and literary canon of the newspaper, and also to its conception of history, by authoring, under the pseudonym of Polkovnik Ivan Chernyi (Colonel Ivan Chernyi), a series of articles about a diverse range of historical topics. These included the Beer Hall Putsch and the rise of Hitler in Germany; Italian radical right- and left-wing terrorist groups from the 1970s, and the Red Brigades in particular; the rise of Italian Fascism; Stalin's youth; and Lenin's ideas about nationalism.[28]

The cultural topics addressed in *Limonka*'s editorials in its first years of existence reflected a similarly eclectic mix by featuring such diverse heroes and role models as Louis Ferdinand Céline, William Burroughs, Jean Genet, Herbert Marcuse, Ernesto Che Guevara, and Guy Debord. Articles about even more extravagant "rebels" and "anti-systemic" figures, like Arnold Schwarzenegger and Charles Manson, also made their appearance in the newspaper.[29] Some of the texts that appeared in the newspaper, including fragments and translations from Burroughs and Genet and excerpts from some of Marcuse's books, were being published in Russian for the first time. In this respect, many *natsboly* referred to *Limonka* as a pre-internet source of information about a diverse range of countercultural authors, both on the right and the left of the political spectrum.

Generally, *Limonka* followed the principle of collective authorship. Many of its authors published under a pseudonym, and in certain cases the same pseudonym was used to sign articles by different authors, so that the authorship of certain pieces could become difficult, if not impossible, to establish.[30] This also guaranteed the possibility of anonymity for writing about controversial topics, or topics that could attract negative attention from the authorities. The collective principle also governed the editing and production of the newspaper, which was a group effort, realized entirely on a volunteer basis and financed at various stages by Limonov's income from his books (like the party itself, according to many of the *natsboly* I interviewed.)

One of the very first articles published in *Limonka*, Aleksandr Dugin's "Novye protiv starykh" (The new against the old), while mainly referring to recent developments in the Russian nationalist camp, echoed the style and cultural stance of Russian or Italian futurist manifestos. According to Dugin, a "schism on matters of style" had occurred within the patriotic opposition. For him, much more important than the distinction between left and right, or between communists and monarchists, was the distinction between the old and the new opposition, or between old and new patriots. The "old" were fundamentally oriented toward the past. They were reactionary and always supported maintaining the status quo or restoring a past system or regime—whether this regime was embodied by the USSR, socialism, or the Russian empire. The old respected power, but, Dugin wrote, "more than anything they keep in high consideration the 'mechanism of power,' a structure, organization, or system . . . because in their spirit they are bureaucrats . . . they are not revolutionary, but 'conservative reformers,' or, more simply put, just conservatives." The "new," on the other hand, were revolutionaries, and "regardless of their political view, be it communism, monarchism, or Russian fascism, they conceive the rise of a new society as a deeply revolutionary process, as a new creative construction, as a dangerous and dramatic genesis. Their aim is to build something new, and it doesn't matter if this is going to be a 'new communism' or a 'new Empire.'"[31]

The representatives of this new form of opposition were to be found, Dugin concluded, among outcasts, radicals, and passionate extremists. These included volunteers fighting in Transnistria, Abkhazia, and Serbia, members of radical right-wing and left-wing groups who participated in violent confrontations with the authorities, nonconformist artists, "anarchist rockers and nihilist punks," "fanatical idealists and crazy romantics," and, finally, mystics and "seekers of religious truth through radical experience." In his view, among these marginal groups one would find the future members of a new intellectual "counter-elite," which would be able to lead Russia out of its current ideological and spiritual crisis.[32] Such ideas about radicalism and marginality were in part connected to Dugin's discovery of some of the writings of the French New Right, which advocated for a right-wing, "conservative revolutionary" appropriation of the rebellious and creative spirit of May 1968.[33]

Through the establishment of a new historical, political, and literary canon, Dugin, Limonov, and the other "founding fathers" of the NBP aimed at creating a new intelligentsia that could somehow resist and propose alternatives to what they considered to be the dominant neoliberal and blindly pro-Western rhetoric of Russian mainstream culture. The "style" of this new radical intellectual elite was also reflected in the way in which NBP activists were supposed to dress, combining Soviet military clothing and accessories, allusions to Nazi and neo-Nazi aesthetics, and various Western punk movements. Suggestions about fashion, drawings, collages, and photographs displaying the ideal National Bolshevik dress code appeared in the pages of *Limonka* in the mid-1990s. This "new style" was closely linked to the beginnings of Russian alternative fashion and club culture during the late 1980s and early 1990s. Some of the early issues of *Limonka*, for instance, published a series of photographs of boys and girls in an urban setting wearing military boots and hats and black clothing, followed by somewhat ironic and provocative captions such as "A healthy fashion for a healthy idea!" and "Strength and sophistication, fury and a prayer for mercy: the new fashion starts here" (see figs. 7 and 8).

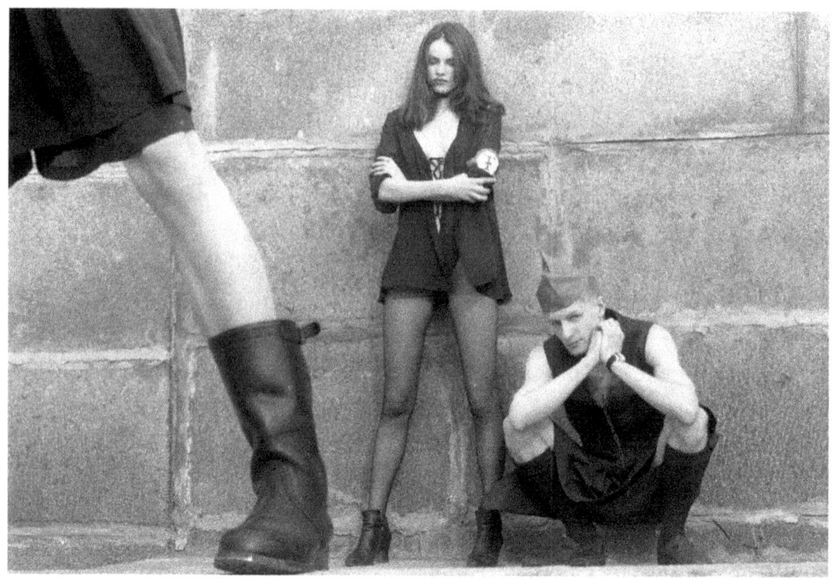

Figure 7. "The New Style," *Limonka* 4 (Dec. 1994). Photo by Laura Ilina.

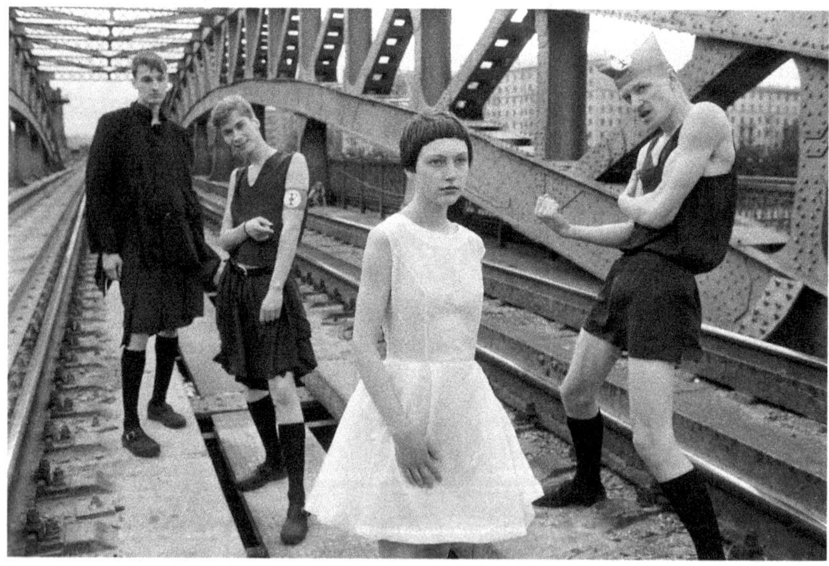

Figure 8. "Strength and sophistication, fury and a prayer for mercy: the new fashion starts here," *Limonka* 5 (Jan. 1995). Photo by Laura Ilina.

These images were part of a photo session of the last collections by the Polushkin Brothers, who were among the pioneers of Russian alternative fashion. The Polushkins' collection, called *Fash-Fashion* (that is, Fascist-Fashion), was supposed to reflect the apocalyptic atmosphere of the first post-Soviet years and Nikolai Polushkin's own "presentment of a dictatorship." The photographer was Laura Ilina, who was close to Limonov and other National Bolshevik leaders:

> We did the shoots on that bridge and somewhere else, with those Dr. Martens boots. Dr. Martens were, you know, they used to wear them in Germany, and they are made in the style of fascist, of Nazi uniforms; while the clothes were . . . On the one hand men wore silk skirts . . . It was a sort of mix of toughness and tenderness, and the idea was that, well, that "soon the fascists will come!" [*laughs*]. Intuitively I kind of understood him [Nikolai Polushkin]. He wanted to shoot a sort of fantasy on the theme of the future, in the style of [George Orwell's] *1984*, a totalitarian fantasy of sorts. This wasn't in any way related to the party. Limonov just really liked the photos, and he asked to get some copies for *Limonka*.[34]

In the beginning, the party fashion was largely determined by Limonov's own tastes, and it was closely linked with the emergence of Russian urban subcultures. At this early stage, no more than ten people were involved in the publication of *Limonka*. Limonov, as the founder and editor in chief, was still completely in charge of the editorial line, and he authored most of the collective articles, announcements, political programs, and declarations published in the newspaper.[35] The National Bolshevik aesthetics was at this point still largely the product of Limonov's, and partly Dugin's, imagery. Later on, by the beginning of the 2000s, when the party became a real political entity with thousands of members in Moscow, St. Petersburg, and throughout Russia, the National Bolsheviks developed their own distinct style somewhat independently:

> They now look like the widespread type of the urban youngster-teenager: black jeans, boots, jacket, and a black hat. At the same time, they distinguish themselves by their extreme asceticism. Everything looks the same, but there's nothing rich or capricious in their clothes. This is the style of a postnuclear war, or an urban partisan war, when dressed just as you are you can fall on the city asphalt and crawl away from the deadly fire of bourgeois machine guns. This is how it was at Ostankino, as a matter of fact. And dressed just like that you can also go to some Guelman Gallery,

> and dressed just like that you can be taken to the police station, or to prison. . . . For more than five years now, receiving letters and photographs from new regional branches over and over again, I never stopped being amazed at how fast the new kids assimilate the style of the NBP.[36]

Here Limonov combines fashion, contemporary art, and radical politics in a way that is typical of his own work and of the culture of the NBP as a community. The Marat Guelman Gallery, which Limonov mentions in this passage, was one of Moscow's main contemporary art galleries and is used here, somewhat sarcastically, as a symbol of refined urban culture. The Guelman Gallery was also for many years one of the few spaces in post-Soviet Russia where, through the filter of art and critical theory, political conversations could take place, although of course these conversations were for Limonov far too bookish and limited in scope. In contrast, Ostankino stands in for the radical "Red-Brown" rebellion against both the pettiness of modern life and the deception produced by mass media and television. Conflating these two images—the Ostankino TV tower and the Guelman Gallery—is a way to symbolically bring the raw violence of the revolution into the protected and civilized domesticity that characterizes the life of the liberal intelligentsia. As is clear from these materials, from the very beginning politics for the *natsboly* was first and foremost a matter of style.

Post-Soviet Utopianism and the Legacy of the Russian Avant-Gardes

Through Dugin's programmatic article, and consistently throughout the pages of *Limonka* in its first years of existence, the National Bolshevik Party was conceived as an artistic and political avant-garde, which could be described, borrowing Mike Sell's definition, as "a minoritarian formation that challenges power in subversive, illegal or alternative ways, usually by challenging the routines, assumptions, hierarchies and/or legitimacy of political and/or cultural institutions."[37] This was a conscious choice, as is manifested by a call for submissions published in *Limonka* in August 1995 that was laconically titled "Action": "Each revolution needs its independent and aggressive visual space: the Italian 'fasci' had futurism; the French leftists had the Dada movement; the Bolsheviks had the great posters of Mayakovsky and the daring constructions of Tatlin. *Limonka* calls for submissions by Russian art-revolutionaries who wish to participate in the creation of a new, invincible art."[38]

The NBP returned to the aggressive, provocative, and shocking gestures of the avant-gardes by appropriating, readapting, and combining symbols, aesthetics, and ideas belonging to Soviet culture (mainly of the 1920s and 1930s) as well as German Fascism and radical European terrorist movements of the 1970s. At the same time, they invoked various Western countercultural movements, ranging from the student protests of the 1960s and 1970s to various punk groups of the 1980s. From the point of view of Russian society and intelligentsia of the mid-1990s, it is hard to imagine a more unacceptable and morally unjustifiable combination of cultural categories.

Such a provocative selection of radical role models should not be interpreted literally (or not exclusively literally) but as part of a new post-Soviet performative mode of political dissent. The style of *Limonka* was mostly paradoxical and sarcastic. An explicit example of this was the satirical column of the paper, which was titled "Smachno pomer"—"he died in a vivid way," or, literally, "he died in a juicy way"—and which included such news as: "Underage Girl Rapes Retired Old Man"; "He Ran into Yeltsin and Got Scared"; "A Foreign Person Was Eaten by the Mafia"; "Solzhenitsyn Will Die from a Snake Bite at the Zoo (the One at the Year 1905 Metro Station)"; and, with a certain tragic irony, the following "recipe" to solve the problem of unemployment, titled "Those Who Do Not Work Shall Be Eaten" (*Kto ne rabotaet—togo ediat*):[39]

> Canned unemployed. The unemployed person is a parasite, a completely inept member of society: he is not able to open his own business, and he can't work for somebody else. One would think that the unemployed is just a waste, a defective piece. But even these individuals can serve capitalist society. In the form of food. The preparation is simple. Cut off the heads, wash, gut, and boil for a couple of hours, so that all the meat separates from the bones, and let cool down. Add nitrates, salt, calcium bicarbonate. . . . Wonderful colored labels can be ordered from Austria. How should we call it? Here are a few possibilities: "Humanitarians"; "Humanitarian Breakfast"; "Humanitarian Aid."[40]

The passage was a harsh and dark satire of the capitalist system and its periodic crises, which during the 1990s left behind and condemned entire sections of the Russian population to poverty and horrible deprivations. The proposed names for the labels polemically alluded to the food parcels marked "humanitarian aid" that invaded Moscow markets after the fall of the Soviet Union and that soon came to be perceived as a gloomy symbol of the "collateral damage" produced by the adoption of an unregulated capitalist system. Incidentally, the style of *Limonka*'s satirical section evoked that of another nonconformist author that had recently been published and rediscovered in Russia—Daniil Kharms, whose famous sketches reflected with similar tragic irony on the absurdity and brutality of everyday life during the Stalin period. Kharms, whose fiction and diaries were published by Shatalov's publishing house Glagol soon after *Eto ia—Edichka*, was also an important literary model for Limonov's poetry and was soon included in *Limonka*'s literary canon.[41]

For the old guard of the NBP, *stiob* and performativity, along with a return to the provocative stance of the historical avant-gardes, were at the same time part of an artistic strategy and a form of political action. One of the early issues of *Limonka* contained, almost as an homage or declaration of kinship, an interview with the members of the Slovenian experimental rock band Laibach, who were among the first to combine and manipulate ambiguous and multifaceted allusions to various forms of totalitarianism as part of a project that existed (and still does) fully at the intersection of contemporary art and popular culture.[42] The performances of Laibach, which started in the 1980s as part of the art project NSK (Neue Slowenische Kunst), feature strong allusions to both Nazi and socialist aesthetics and are known to produce in their audiences a unique combination of attraction, repulsion, and ironic detachment. The members of the band wear military uniforms strongly resembling those of the SS, with familiar but unrecognizable emblems that could be easily confused with those used by the military in communist countries. The band's name, Laibach, the Slovenian capital Ljubljana's German name, produced immediate negative associations with the Nazi invasion of the country, and with the Habsburg yoke. The band's repertoire, on the other hand, includes a mix of military marches, hard rock, disco music, and covers of international pop hits and catchy tunes sounding very off because of the deep and immediately recognizable hoarse voice of its lead singer.

As in the case of AVIA, a Soviet independent rock band that produced faithful imitations of military marches and patriotic songs, Laibach's concerts elicit diametrically opposed reactions in their audiences. Some applaud the performances as fierce parodies of totalitarianism. Others accuse Laibach's members of being horrible fascists and demand that their concerts be prohibited.[43] This disorienting effect is enhanced by the fact that Laibach's performances extend to the everyday life and behavior of its members. Band members often wear uniforms and remain in character even when they are not performing, thus failing to maintain a clear distinction between artistic provocations and actual political convictions.[44] According to Slavoj Žižek, the point of Laibach's performances is to *actually* experience the "jouissance" produced by the totalitarian ritual without any form of irony or critical distance. Laibach's performances, in Žižek's view, reveal the underlying totalitarian essence of any form of political power, as well as the fact that in the context of a post-ideological age, irony and critical distance are actually "the highest form of conformism."[45]

The complex form of overidentification that is typical of Laibach's performances can help explain the emergence of the NBP's ambiguous appropriation of totalitarianism in the context of early post-Soviet society, which in reaction to the empty rhetoric of Soviet official culture was pervaded by cynicism, disbelief, and a categorical denial of any form of political conviction. Even more important for understanding the artistic and political strategy of the NBP is the role that Kurekhin himself—widely known in Russia for having proven to TV audiences that Lenin was a mushroom (!)—played in the development of the movement's identity.[46] Kurekhin was an early supporter of the NBP. Before dying prematurely of a rare heart disease, he endorsed Dugin's campaign for a parliamentary seat in one of Saint Petersburg's districts, writing a musical piece for the occasion and organizing his campaign under the enigmatic and quasi-mystical slogan "What is concealed will be revealed" (*Tainoe stanet iavnym*).[47]

Kurekhin was one of the leaders of Leningrad's art and music scenes. His main project, Pop-mekhanika—in which he fulfilled the roles of orchestra director, musician, producer, and performer—freely combined free jazz, classical music, independent rock, industrial music, and traditional religious chants. Kurekhin gathered some of the most influential independent classical, jazz, and rock musicians of the time, involving them in a project in which "everyone just played the exact same music that they usually played."[48] As a result, the performances of Pop-mekhanika constituted, according to many of those who witnessed them as spectators or participants, absolutely chaotic, overwhelming, and confusing experiences. Kurekhin did not mind the perplexity and shock he produced in his audiences, and throughout the years the performances of Pop-mekhanika acquired an increasingly carnivalesque character. On various occasions, Kurekhin let animals (chickens, cows, or geese) on stage, ate flowers, licked his microphone, and copulated with his piano.[49] By the early 1990s, the grandiosity of Pop-mekhanika had become "completely absurd, with trucks, military equipment, huge orchestras, almost helicopters . . . maybe one could have gotten to airplanes and space shuttles, but this would have been a purely quantitative growth, which would have not translated into new quality."[50]

Pop-mekhanika was indeed a "total work of art" (*Gesamtkunstwerk*) in the Wagnerian sense of the word. In his project, Kurekhin mixed together media, musical genres, people, and cultural movements.[51] However, the "absolutist" character of his approach to art was not limited to the grandiosity of his performances. In addition to musical virtuosity and erudition, Kurekhin cultivated a vast knowledge of mystical authors like Pavel Florensky, Vasily Rozanov, and Nikolay Berdiaev, and was known for entertaining endless conversations about literature, philosophy, history, and natural sciences that verged on visionary storytelling.[52] In the late 1980s and early 1990s, he was also one of those who contributed to bringing Soviet underground culture into the mainstream, first by staging a shocking performance of Pop-mekhanika on Soviet TV, and second, by bringing to those same TV screens his taste for mystification, psychedelic intellectual meandering, and conspiracy theories.[53] At this stage, Kurekhin claimed, paraphrasing Lenin, that for him "of all forms of contemporary art, television is the most important."[54] Most famously, in May 1991, only a few months before the end of the Soviet Union, he argued for over an hour on a Leningrad-based TV program that the main motivation of the Russian Revolution was Lenin's and the Bolsheviks' massive consumption of hallucinogenic mushrooms and that, ultimately, Lenin and his comrades had themselves turned into mushrooms. The program included interviews with actual scientists from reputable academic institutions and a creative combination of historical facts and scholarly references. As a result of Kurekhin's ability to imitate the tone and register of Soviet "authoritative speech," many viewers actually believed him, or at least wondered if it could possibly be true that Lenin was in fact a mushroom. In reality, the elaborate prank had originated in a long, drunken conversation between Kurekhin and the artists Timur Novikov and Sergey "Afrika" Bugaev.[55]

Kurekhin's participation in the NBP was the last, and perhaps the most controversial, of his public performances. This time, he declared that "politics is the only relevant form of art, and this is what I'm going to do now, on the side of the National Bolshevik Party." During Dugin's electoral campaign in 1995, he invited Dugin and Limonov to participate in what turned out to be the last performance of Pop-mekhanika, dedicated to the memory of English occultist Aleister Crowley. During the show, Limonov read a text about "fallen angels" and sang with Kurekhin, a bit awkwardly, Bulat Okudzhava's popular song "Nam nuzhna odna pobeda" (All we need is victory, 1970). Dugin read excerpts of Crowley's books in French and Russian translations, while Kurekhin performed some pseudo-ritualistic and seemingly mocking gestures behind him. Half-naked men in Roman and Egyptian costumes danced on stage, the Necrorealists (a famous Leningrad art collective) spun two crosses with two men nailed to them (a reference to a Satanic symbol), and Kurekhin played the piano dressed as the Indian god Shiva, overlapping with dissonant, ominous-sounding electronic music that played in the background throughout the show.[56] During the campaign, Dugin and Kurekhin were interviewed on a political TV show wearing the masks of the Egyptian gods Ibis and Anubis and argued that voters should simply assign a *p* or *kh* (to stand for *plokho* and *khorosho*—good and bad) to such concepts as "capitalism," "socialism," "Russia," and "the West," deciding on that basis how to vote.[57]

Kurekhin's involvement in the NBP was a strange, complex mix of absolute *stiob* and authentic commitment, of radical cynicism and childish playfulness, and a romantic, uncompromising ingenuity. Kurekhin was indeed truly disappointed in the consequences of the liberal reforms and the widespread vulgarization of post-Soviet culture and everyday life. According to his wife, Anastasiia, in Dugin Kurekhin "had finally found a person who was intellectually equal to him."[58] Kurekhin and Dugin evidently shared a strong interest in conspiracy theories, mass manipulation, and storytelling. During Dugin's campaign, Kurekhin fully devoted himself to promoting his candidacy and introduced him to most of his friends, including underground artists and intellectuals like the members of Timur Novikov's New Academy, the Mit'ki (a group of alternative poets), and people close to the Leningrad Rock Club. Later, he found the location and paid the rent for the first NBP Saint Petersburg headquarters.[59]

Kurekhin's absolutely radical and uncompromising approach to art and politics, as well as his ironic and provocative stance, made him a model for several generations of NBP activists, and some of his statements were in fact even more radical and reactionary than those of Limonov or Dugin. In an interview, he claimed that the logical consequence of romanticism is fascism, and that "if you have a romantic sensibility, you should immediately stop, because otherwise you will become a fascist."[60] He declared himself a supporter of any "totalitarian regime," and even the kind they had in the Soviet Union in the 1980s, because that "would still be better than what's happening now." When some of the artists and intellectuals in his circle criticized his quasi-Satanist production of Pop-mekhanika and accused him of "fascist propaganda," he yelled that they would be "the first in the list of those who will be executed . . . today I have my hands in blood up to my elbows!"[61] Finally, when the disastrous results of the election were announced, and Dugin ended up being the sixteenth candidate out of the seventeen in his district, he told journalists that it would be necessary to "repress all dickheads . . . dickheads are the main enemies of our cause."[62]

Kurekhin's involvement with the NBP produced mixed reactions among the Petersburg intelligentsia. Some interpreted it as another one of his pranks, not different from his "Lenin is a mushroom" (*Lenin—grib*) hoax. Others took him seriously and expressed outrage at his support of "the fascists." At one point Dugin himself denied that Kurekhin's support of the NBP was sincere and claimed that his participation in the election had been indeed just a prank.[63]

In and of itself, the fact that Kurekhin's last political performance was taken, at the same time, as a prank and an irresponsible but sincere gesture, tells us something important about the complexity of his art project and his influence on the identity of the NBP as a political community. After his death, Kurekhin became a symbol of a heroic, desperate, and somewhat childish protest against the lowness, vulgarity, and materialism of post-Soviet reality. On the other hand, quite paradoxically, Kurekhin is also widely seen, to this day, as a pioneer in the art of mystification and even mass manipulation. This unique combination of radical, uncompromising romanticism and a taste for provocation also became an important component of the "political style" of the NBP. Mass manipulation was even more important for what later became the reactionary, pro-Putin branch of National Bolshevism, Dugin's Eurasia Movement.

Dugin was also clearly conscious of the ironic, ambiguous, and provocative side of this political project, for he also had a similar countercultural and unconventional background.[64] In the spirit of the French situationists, Dugin (and the other founders of the NBP) called for an alliance between radical politics and certain forms of art and art performance. In an enthusiastic review of a performance by the punk art collective Sever (the North), for instance, Dugin hailed the foundation of what he considered a genuinely Eurasian art through the combination of contemporary forms (such as techno music, body art, and postmodern ballet) with a return to, and creation of, Aryan myths, mystical rituals, and religious cults. The purpose of the National Bolsheviks' political struggle, Dugin wrote in this article, was to create a world in the image and likeness of a performance by the art collective Sever.[65] In a later article devoted to Guy Debord's suicide, which he interpreted as marking the final triumph of the society of the spectacle in the Western capitalist world, Dugin called even more explicitly for the creation of a post-Soviet situationism, metaphorically embodied in an "eternal return" to the siege of the Ostankino TV tower: "We have to go back to Ostankino, again and again. With those who are alive and those who died. With Guy Debord. That sinister tower—that Satan's phallus, generating the poisonous hypnosis of the 'society of the spectacle.' Blowing it up, we castrate the demon of violence hiding behind the decrepit masks of the brezhnevs, the gorbachevs, the gaidars, the yeltsins, the ziuganovs [*sic*], and the other puppets of the systems. And the eternal spectacle will finally end."[66]

The presence of Grazhdanskaia oborona's lead singer, Egor Letov, among the "founding fathers" of the NBP marked symbolically the continuity between the anti-liberal National Bolshevik agenda and the late Soviet underground, rock, and anarchist movements. In 1994–95, during his Russian Breakthrough (Russkii proryv) tour, Letov famously performed on the background of a gigantic NBP flag. Since then, the history of the NBP has remained closely linked with that of the post-Soviet punk, rock, heavy metal, noise, and industrial scenes.[67]

In *Limonka*, Letov contributed to the definition of the party line by publishing an interview and a long, two-part "creative-political autobiography." Here he described his career as an underground artist, his struggle against Soviet authorities, and his subsequent forced internment in a psychiatric institution. He then related how he had decided to get involved in politics as a consequence of the political stagnation that followed the coup of 1991 and the siege of the White House of 1993. According to Letov, during the 1980s the artistic method of Grazhdanskaia oborona, based on futurist shock tactics and "the absurd," conceived as "the principle of maximal rebellion against logical reality," had quite naturally turned into political activity in the form of criticism of Soviet institutions. Referring to the alliance between the punk movement and radical right- and left-wing groups, Letov now imagined the creation of a new utopian civilization of artists, poets, and heroes—a "young force" that would be able to deliver the final blow to a dying Western civilization.[68]

Sexuality and the body also played a crucial role in the NBP's aesthetics and ideology. Throughout the years, *Limonka* published both provocative and overtly macho calls for promiscuity and an end to monogamous relationships among party members (at times verging on the absurd), along with articles promoting the return to patriarchy and traditional values.[69] As in the ideological realm, so in the sphere of social politics the NBP developed what might be seen as a fluid position or identity. In the early issues of *Limonka*, this stance was mirrored in an ironic play on gender roles and identities that one would certainly not expect from a nationalist publication. For instance, the openly gay artist-cum-provocateur Mogutin authored in the paper's first issue a ferocious indictment of Russian intellectuals, significantly titled "Without Intellectuals. Utopia." In the article, Mogutin defines Russian intellectuals as "flabby and childish beings, with greasy hair and rotten teeth, who inhabit dark, smoky, and moldy lodgings, are absolutely useless and meaningless, but have an opinion about everything," and claimed that a situation in which intellectuals occupy positions of power was to be considered "dangerous" and "unacceptable."[70] As a solution to this problem, he advances a number of "theses," prescribing that Russian intellectuals "should live in perpetual fear," that they should not be allowed to have a family or publish, and that, finally, they should be "assimilated and destroyed as a class."[71] Here Mogutin's language echoes that of the Soviet propaganda of the 1920s and 1930s. The expression *unichtozhit' kak klass* (to destroy as a class) is borrowed directly from early Soviet slogans calling for the destruction of the kulaks (small landowners) as a class, or "dekulakization"—as in the famous slogan, *Unichtozhim kulaka kak klass!* (We will destroy the kulak as a class!).

The shocking, uncategorizable stance of Mogutin's article became a trademark of *Limonka*, and, in turn, of the *natsboly*'s "style of behavior." In his indictment of the Russian intelligentsia and, indirectly, in his call to create a new alternative community of radical intellectuals, Mogutin introduced two fundamental elements or themes that the National Bolshevik aesthetics and ideology partly inherited from Limonov's work: the juxtaposition of periphery (or marginality) and the center (of power, the country, or the cultural or literary system); and the crucial role played by the body in determining aesthetic and moral categories. Mogutin's hatred toward Russian intellectuals, as he himself explained in the article, came from his belonging to another class, and from the fact that he grew up in a family of workers from the Russian province. Furthermore, his critique is primarily physical and aesthetic—that is, the passivity and backwardness of the *intelligent* is mirrored by his/her physical weakness and repulsiveness. Finally, Mogutin's cult of youth, masculinity, working class values, and political violence against what is described as a conformist, stereotypical, and fundamentally powerless intelligentsia is even more difficult to define or classify according to traditional political categories if one considers that Mogutin was one of the first openly gay public figures in Russia.

The singer, writer, and model Natalya Medvedeva, Limonov's third wife and herself a cult figure for several generations of *natsboly*, authored a series of short and provocative articles that appeared to aim at producing in the reader a similar form of "estrangement."[72] In her "Ode to the Russian *muzhik*," also published in one of the first issues of *Limonka*, she wrote: "I want to be a Russian *muzhik*, to occupy two seats in the metro at the same time, spreading my legs very-very wide. . . . I want to be a Russian *muzhik*, in order to swear at everyone, pick on everyone, and just not do a damn thing, and drink away my underdeveloped skills in front of the TV. . . . I want to be a Russian *muzhik*, in order to wipe them all out—communists and democrats, fascists and faggots, prostitutes and racketeers—close the borders and finally live in peace."[73] Here Medvedeva "overidentifies" with, or performs, the Russian *muzhik* (the common man) producing a portrayal that challenges any patriotic idealization of Russian manhood. At the same time, this vivid, unflattering description conveys a certain closeness and sympathy toward its target. Between the lines, this short piece seems to suggest that the Russian *muzhik* is an arrogant, embittered, entitled, desperate, untalented, and useless being, who deserves our sympathy after all. Thus, by playing with gender categories and stereotypes, Medvedeva also produced an ironic and ambiguous message, through which she both endorsed and undermined some of the values that the newspaper was supposed to promote, namely nationalism and masculinity.

This way of embracing paradox in fact came to be a trademark, a philosophy of life, and a code of behavior of the NBP activist. As a sign of this, at the end of 1995 *Limonka* published a sort of handbook of the perfect National Bolshevik, which explicitly elevated this style and behavior to a moral ideal:

> The National Bolshevik is that person who will bring death to radical-right and radical left-wing ideologies. The National Bolshevik is their dialectic

> sublation, and negation. . . . The National Bolshevik is a person who hates the system and its lies, alienation, conformism, and stupidity, but he is able to immerse himself in it, to assimilate it, to then destroy it from the inside. This is a person who loves paradox and "sublation" [*preodolenie*]; discipline and freedom, spontaneity and calculation, erudition and inspiration. He is against dogma, but for authority; he is against external limitations, but he is capable of a strict self-control.[74]

This quotation captures what can be considered a fundamental duality in the aesthetics and ideology of *Limonka* and the NBP. On the one hand, we have the "avant-garde posture," the taste for the aggressive and shocking gesture, which often took the form of harsh attacks and derision of any cultural and political institution or hegemonic group. On the other hand, we see a return to utopian romantic ideals belonging, in very different forms, to both the Soviet system in various stages of its existence and to German Fascism (here embodied in the image of a new man). These romantic ideals were employed to call into question what during the 1990s the *natsboly* saw as a cultural and stylistic "liberal dictatorship." The totalitarian aesthetics adopted by *Limonka* and the NBP, and their celebration of war and world revolution (as well as a new conception of nationality), assumed very unexpected meanings and helped form a sense of community and collective identity in the midst of the cultural, moral, and ideological void left behind by the fall of the Soviet Union.

In her article "Fascinating Fascism," Susan Sontag explains the interest and fascination of American culture with Nazi aesthetics (both in New York high-brow intellectual circles and in gay subcultures) by laying bare some of the values that such aesthetics surreptitiously evoked: "It is generally thought that National Socialism stands only for brutishness and terror. But this is not true. National Socialism—or, more broadly, fascism—also stands for an ideal, and one that is also persistent today, under other banners: the ideal of life as art, the cult of beauty, the fetishism of courage, the dissolution of alienation in ecstatic feelings of community; the repudiation of the intellect; the family of man (under the parenthood of leaders)."[75] Sontag's words capture some of the fundamental elements of the revolutionary or subversive potential of fascism as a response to a utopian and romantic impulse aimed at a complete and quasi-mystical regeneration of society. In May 1995, *Limonka* asked its readers to send the newspaper their own personal definition of the word "fascism." Some of these definitions clearly resonate with Sontag's article, and they can help in understanding what the return to a totalitarian aesthetics could mean for the members of this radical community: "Fascism is active pessimism; fascism is leftist nationalism; fascism is social romanticism; the futuristic impulse; the will to die; the celebration of a heroic style; anarchism plus totalitarianism; loyalty to the sources, and the aspiration toward the future."[76] These definitions suggest that, in the early issues of *Limonka*, totalitarian symbols and ideas were used to signify both a radical form of protest against the current political system and the return to a romantic and utopian conception of art and politics.

In the pages of *Limonka*, and in general within the intellectual and political community built around the NBP, fascist and totalitarian aesthetics and ideas were used to produce a futurist-like "slap in the face of the public taste" (or a form of Shklovskian "estrangement"), calling into question mainstream cultural and political values. At the same time, these political symbols reflected a return to the romantic impulse (as well as to the artistic values) of the early Soviet period. The aesthetics of the early NBP, and the collective narrative produced by its official newspaper *Limonka*, should be considered the result of this complex and paradoxical combination of *stiob* and dark humor—as well as a return to what was seen as the original utopian spirit of the Russian Revolution.

From Avant-Garde Aesthetics to Radical Politics

In the second half of the 1990s, the NBP gradually turned into a more explicit experiment in mass mobilization. The anarchist, radical leftist journalist and political activist Aleksey Tsvetkov, who was associate editor of *Limonka* between 1996 and 1998, had a key role in this process. When I interviewed him in the spring of 2015, Tsvetkov explained that before joining the NBP he had an early career in journalism and radical politics. Still in his late teens, he became a regular contributor to the Soviet newspaper *Komsomol'skaia pravda*. At the same time, he founded and led several radical leftist and anarchist organizations, like the Purple International, the Committee for the Cultural Revolution, and Student Defense; he also self-published a few anarchist and punk fanzines. Student Defense achieved a certain notoriety, Tsvetkov explained, because of a series of violent disorders and clashes with the police that the group initiated in the center of Moscow in the early 1990s. The members of the group were regularly beaten by the police, arrested, and prosecuted. "I used to live like an American Yippie, like Abbie Hoffman—it was an easy way to become famous and attractive, although this involved a certain amount of risk—to regularly end up at the police station, get hit on the head with a baton, and so on and so forth," Tsvetkov commented, laughing.

The members of these groups were mostly "not very successful rockers," punks, and anarchists, who were against the Soviets (*protiv sovka*) and "stylistically absolutely pro-Western." They were attracted to Western music and counterculture, but diffident toward capitalism, the free market, and the

"Western political system." These "new leftists" were allied with groups that expressed a more straightforward nostalgia for the Soviet regime, who were "in the best case interested in Mao Tse-tung, and in the worst—in Stalin." Tsvetkov himself was at the time skeptical toward "Western liberalism," but drawn to Western critical theory and counterculture: "at the time we read Barthes, the Freudo-Marxists, the Frankfurt School, and all that stuff."[77]

During the parliamentary crisis of 1993, Tsvetkov was on the barricades with the defenders of the Russian parliament. As for many of the artists, intellectuals, and political activists with whom I talked, for him this was a turning point: "Of course, this was a shock, it was a very strange political alliance, a very strange political community which included some Cossacks, antisemites, neofascists, Stalinists, anarchists, and everyone who was against Yeltsin—each of them with their own barricade." The violent conclusion to the confrontation between Yeltsin and the parliament, as well as the subsequent ban on all nationalist and communist newspapers and organizations, made Tsvetkov reconsider his playful attitude toward Western counterculture and critical theory: "All of a sudden, I realized that this was much more serious. This was in fact a dictatorship, neoliberal from an economic standpoint, and absolutely authoritarian from the point of view of media, censorship, and culture." In 1994, he heard of Letov's and Limonov's declarations about the necessity of an alliance between communist and nationalist forces. Letov's statements, which were published in the ultrareactionary newspaper *Zavtra* (Tomorrow), were particularly significant for him. Letov was an immensely popular, absolutely unconventional, and incredibly charismatic figure. As Tsvetkov noted, "at the time we all talked through the lyrics of his songs—it was the language of the generation."

When the young Tsvetkov visited the Bunker of the NBP for the first time, it was the "crazy mystical philosopher Dugin" who made the strongest impression on him. Tsvetkov told me that at the time he was particularly fascinated by Dugin's "paradoxical thinking," by his ability to combine apparently incompatible ideas, and by his "dark pessimism": "what would win you was his paradoxical psychology—Dugin used to tell people: 'there is the mainstream, and this is capitalism, liberalism, the West—and then there is all of us: fascists, leftists, Marxists; and we have all been defeated, we have all been totally defeated.'" Everyone at the time would promise "money, career, stability": "the NBP was the only place where they just told you: 'you came here in order to die beautifully'—and this of course was deeply fascinating for us."

Tsvetkov immediately embraced the paradoxical aesthetics of the NBP and in part transformed it and made it his own. Between 1994 and 1998, when he left the party to follow Dugin and his group of Eurasianist "schismatics," he wrote regularly for *Limonka* and became one of its main contributors. In this period, he also helped shape and define the identity of the movement and its revolutionary strategy. Among his main sources of inspiration were the theories and tactics of the Situationist International of Guy Debord, an author that Dugin also actively promoted at the time. As if trying to multiply his authorial identities, for his articles in *Limonka* he used a number of different pseudonyms: Pavel Vlasov, Ian Geil, Fridmen, Gruppa kommunisticheskii realizm (Communist realism group), Sindikat nebezopasnogo iskusstva (Syndicate of unsafe art), and Doktor Zig Khailer.[78] In his articles, he promoted a creative approach to politics, which involved the invention of a "new revolutionary language":

> The so-called culture in the current media situation only fulfills the function of a condom that the system wears to protect itself from everything that is undesirable. . . . An artist, in order to win, needs to become the Stalin of his artistic Kremlin. Art needs to be cold, sharp, and smooth, like a bayonet. The inevitable civil war in the coming century requires art to be dangerous, but radical art can become truly dangerous only at the point of intersection with radical politics.[79]

Indeed, Tsvetkov approached political activism as a form of radical art. Especially considering the extensive reference to modernist culture and totalitarianism in *Limonka*, his programmatic text reminds one of the demiurgic dream of the historical avant-gardes, and of what Boris Groys has defined as Stalin's *Gesamtkunstwerk*, or "the total art of Stalinism": the complete socialist transformation of society according to aesthetic principles.[80] Given the NBP's flirtation with far right-wing and nationalist politics, Tsvetkov's idea of radicalism as a form of art could also be linked to Benjamin's famous definition of fascism as "aestheticization of politics."[81]

Perhaps even more significantly, Tsvetkov was at the time trying to initiate a dialogue with, and send a challenge to, the Moscow Actionists Anatoly Osmolovsky, Aleksandr Brener, and Oleg Kulik. The members of Moscow Actionism were at the time "bringing art to the street" by organizing provocative and politically charged performances. Among other things, Osmolovsky and his movement E.T.I (Ekspropriatsiia territorii iskusstva, or Expropriation of the Territory of Art) reenacted various forms of public protest. In one of E.T.I.'s most famous performances, the action Barricade from 1998, a group of more than three hundred artists and art students occupied a central street in Moscow for over two hours, replicating some of the classic slogans of the French May, such as "It's forbidden to forbid!" and "Power to creativity!" In 1995, in the middle of the Russian winter, Brener jumped, half-naked and with boxing

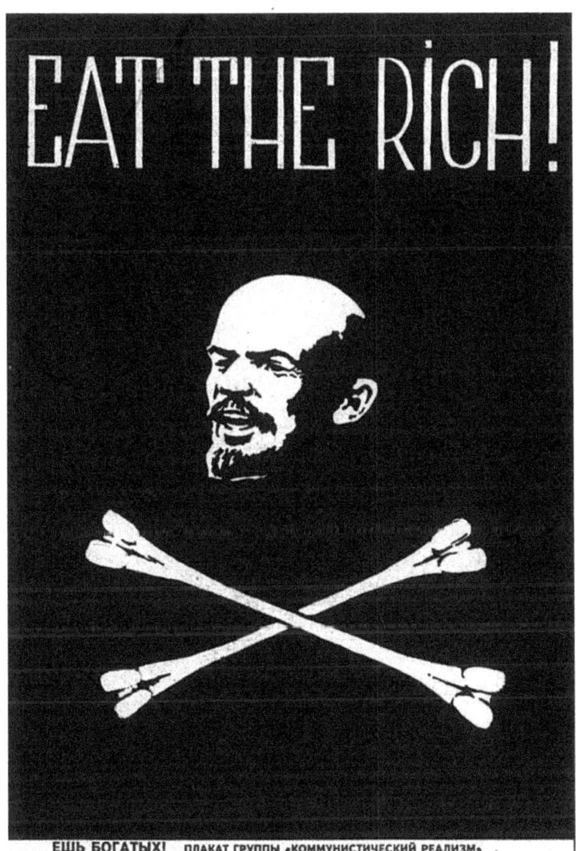

Figure 9. An example of NBP "situationism": Aleksey Tsvetkov's political poster *Eat the Rich!*, *Limonka* 59 (Feb. 1997).

gloves, onto the historic execution block on Red Square and challenged Yeltsin to a bout to protest the Russian invasion of Chechnya. In the fall of 1994, in his performance "The Mad Dog, or Last Taboo Guarded by Alone Cerberus," Kulik was led on leash through the streets of Moscow and performed "the dog," naked, barking and, at times, biting passersby. This was a "total performance" of sorts; Kulik actually lived as a dog for several days at a time, and in the mid-1990s he even founded a Party of Animals, within which he formally ran for elections. The performances of the Moscow Actionists, however, remained within the framework of contemporary art and never involved the creation of actual forms of political activism, although they did draw the attention of Russian mainstream media at various points.[82]

In contrast, Tsvetkov at the time claimed that radical art should go a step further, by directly dealing with, and being involved in, grassroots politics,

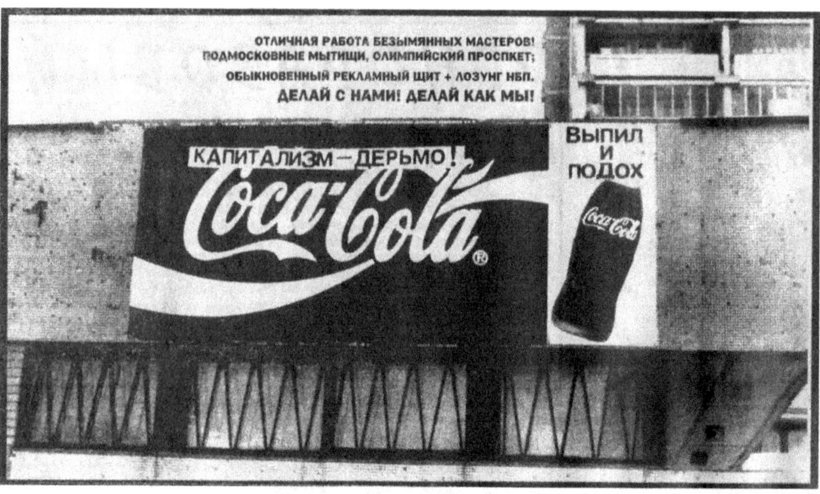

Figure 10. Another example of NBP "situationism": a Coca-Cola advertising board on the outskirts of Moscow modified by anonymous *natsboly*. The caption reads: "Capitalism is shit! Drink and die." *Limonka* 95 (July 1998).

mass mobilization, and political violence. On the basis of this idea, he tried to involve Osmolovsky, Brener, and Kulik "in the production of our newspaper [*Limonka*], in order to make it even crazier." Osmolovsky and Brener did publish a few pieces in *Limonka*, and some of their actions were featured in the newspaper. When, in 1997, Brener spray-painted a dollar sign on Malevich's painting *Suprematism* in the Stedelijk Museum in Amsterdam, and was prosecuted for vandalism in the Netherlands, Tsvetkov wrote about his performance as an example of "authentic art." However, a series of misunderstandings and disagreements between Limonov and the Moscow Actionists hindered this extravagant collaboration from succeeding. Although there are several examples of interaction and mutual influences between the two projects, the NBP and Moscow Actionism remained two parallel but separate experiments at the intersection of art and radical politics.[83]

In his political strategy, Tsvetkov explicitly drew on Guy Debord and the experience of the Situationist International. In his article "Spectacle—trap number one," he proposed to fight the illusion and habits of the society of the spectacle through a "game of revolution, that is, a creation of life." The emancipation from the system should occur, according to Tsvetkov, through a "new revolutionary design," which should produce a radical critique of the capitalist system based on the principles of "New Bolshevism, new esotericism, and new ecologism," all of which implied nationalism as a common ideological background. The fight against the spectacle involved the creation of an alternative material culture, including pins, clothes, posters, music, comics, literature, and independent fanzines, in order to attract the current "soldiers of the system" to the revolutionary cause.

The result of this form of emancipation from "the spectacle" was a return to the authenticity of bodily experience: "Learn everything you can about Paul Goodman, Guy Debord, Raoul Vaneigem . . . and in general about the Situationist International and what came out of it. Throw away your TV. This is not a metaphor, but a concrete order. Why would you need erotic programs that distract you from sex, or films about war that don't leave you any time to go to war?"[84] Tsvetkov's strategy consisted of turning critical theory into political action by combining it with the sheer brutality and aggressive masculinity of the periphery, the marginals, and the lumpen proletarians who represented the potential constituency of ultranationalist organizations:

> At some point we buried the charismatic image of the dissident—the Jesus-like asthenic PhD student, cackling about his rights while in the pigs' clutches, and his place was taken by the extremist—the energetic guy in black leather, who liked and knew how to fight . . . in '91 we built the barricades in front of the White House, each with one's own flag, not out of love of the bureaucrat Yeltsin, but because we wanted to continue the revolution. . . . In '93 we built barricades in the same spot not out of love for the general Rutskoy or the speaker Khasbulatov [the leaders of the opposition against Yeltsin], but because this was the rehearsal of our own revolution, when the young member of Russian National Unity, the young Bolshevik, the young anarchist, and the punk with a swastika in his ear warmed up by one and the same fire.[85]

In his writing, Tsvetkov absorbed everything that could be used for the purpose of provoking political violence. He combined references to global anarchist, ecologist, and radical leftist movements, the American militia movement, and the Tupaç Amaru.[86] He envisioned an "armed paradise" where a young National Bolshevik activist at his first direct action would end up shooting at BMWs from a Kalashnikov, and join the heroes and "immortal brothers" from the posters on the walls of his bedroom: Charles Manson, the leader of the German Red Army Faction Andreas Baader, Che Guevara, and Malcolm X.[87] He wrote a semifictional biography of the "romantic hero" and "superagent" anarchist philosopher Mikhail Bakunin, whom he defined as "one of the absolute embodiments of the Hollywood heroic myth."[88] In his column *Natural Born Killers*, he wrote about the most successful serial murderers in world history and eventually invited his readers to send real stories of their own violent crimes.[89] Finally, he proposed to create a new kind of Russian skinheads, who should have an ironic attitude toward Adolf Hitler and Mao Tse-tung and find inspiration in their own national version of "fantasy literature": Aleksandr Dugin's *Mysteries of Eurasia* and *Conspirology* (*Misterii Evrazii* and *Konspirologiia*).[90] In order to create the style of the Russian skinhead, Tsvetkov proposed to dig up, like "revolutionary archaeologists," the most successful elements of Soviet aesthetics. He imagined that one could shoot a homemade sequel to the famous Soviet TV series *Seventeen Moments of Spring* (1973), in which the protagonist Stierlitz would change sides and, after the war, organize a "world conservative revolution" in collaboration with Chilean conspiracy theorist and mystical neo-Nazi thinker Miguel Serrano, a few former SS generals, and extraterrestrial forces.[91] Stierlitz would then sponsor Jean Thiriart's far-right organization Young Europe (which was sympathetic toward the National Bolshevik cause) and would reinvent the style of the Russian skinheads, which would include "switchblade, baseball bat, purple bomber jacket, military boots in the Dr. Martens style with red and brown laces, tattoos of a grenade or a hammer and sickle in the shape of a snake biting its own tail." The gendered nature of the new revolutionary subculture was beyond any possible doubt: "we will have to cultivate the masculine idealism (totalitarianism), despite the feminine cynicism (democracy), that is in the air."

Tsvetkov's writing in *Limonka* was so visionary, provocative, and voluntarily excessive that the sociologist Aleksandr Tarasov (himself a political activist and a leftist) argued in a report about the Russian new left that Tsvetkov had "in fact turned *Limonka* into the object of an aesthetic game. Tsvetkov did not just fill *Limonka* with the fruits of his psychedelic literary creations, but also turned the [newspaper's] political texts into psychedelic-artistic ones."[92] Indeed, under Tsvetkov's editorial control, the ideology of *Limonka* became even more eclectic than it used to be and even harder to pin down. Articles denouncing the conspiracy behind the murder of the Italian leftist and openly gay poet, film director, and public intellectual Pier Paolo Pasolini could appear almost side by side with revisionist comments about the Holocaust, including references to British Holocaust denier David Irving.[93]

The editorial line of *Limonka* seemed to follow the principle of "the more provocative, the more outrageous, the more shocking, the better." For instance, in 1997 *Limonka* published two handbook-like lists of rules that were supposed to regulate the social life and the relationships between the sexes within the movement: "The Sex Trainer of the Elite Party Member" and "The Sex Trainer of the Elite Party Woman." These two short pieces produced something of a scandal, and they are sometimes quoted as proof of a fundamental male chauvinism and machismo in the NBP. However, these texts, like Tsvetkov's, shared in the early NBP's taste for "paradoxical thinking":

> 1. A member of the party has the right not to know the program of the party. . . . 4. A member of the party has the obligation to harass all women, because tomorrow he could be killed on the front line. . . . 6. If the encounters between a member of the party and a woman occur two or more times, the party member is supposed to beat her up. Ideally—one beating for every ten sexual encounters. . . . 8. The member of the party has the right not to work and to be financially dependent on a woman. 9. If a member of the party lives with a woman who has children, he has the right to eat the food that she has prepared for her children. . . . 11. A member of the party is required to demand depraved behavior on the part of a woman in relation to his party comrades. . . . 16. A member of the party has the right to wear red underwear with a swastika.[94]

Nobody in the party took these instructions seriously, and different generations of *natsboly* with whom I talked, both men and women, referred to them jokingly, as a consciously excessive, provocative, and "punk-like" display of bad taste and political incorrectness. The fundamental downside of this type of dark irony or *stiob* is, of course, that it allows one to avoid any kind of political responsibility. This is a fundamental issue related to the paradoxical aesthetics and ideology of the NBP. By promoting and trying to co-opt any kind of rebellious, violent, or revolutionary impulse, the NBP and *Limonka* gave space to almost any sort of speech, and at times even hate speech. This was in part connected with the groups that constituted the party's potential "target audience" and its "foot soldiers": marginalized youth, anarchist rockers, *and* members of far-right and ultranationalist organizations. This applied to the treatment of both gender and racial issues. From the point of view of gender politics, the history and culture of the NBP in general, and the editorial line of *Limonka* in particular, included all sorts of ideological positions. The issue of *Limonka* in which the aforementioned "handbooks" were published also contained an announcement about the party's attitude toward issues of gender and sexuality declaring that the NBP was against any form of "sexual segregation . . . and sexual exploitation of women (sexism)."[95] A member of the party, the piece continued, "should exclude any poeticization or romanticization of sex, and, after having freed himself from all feelings, direct all of his energy toward the pursuit of Revolution," and the party should promote full "collectivization" of men and

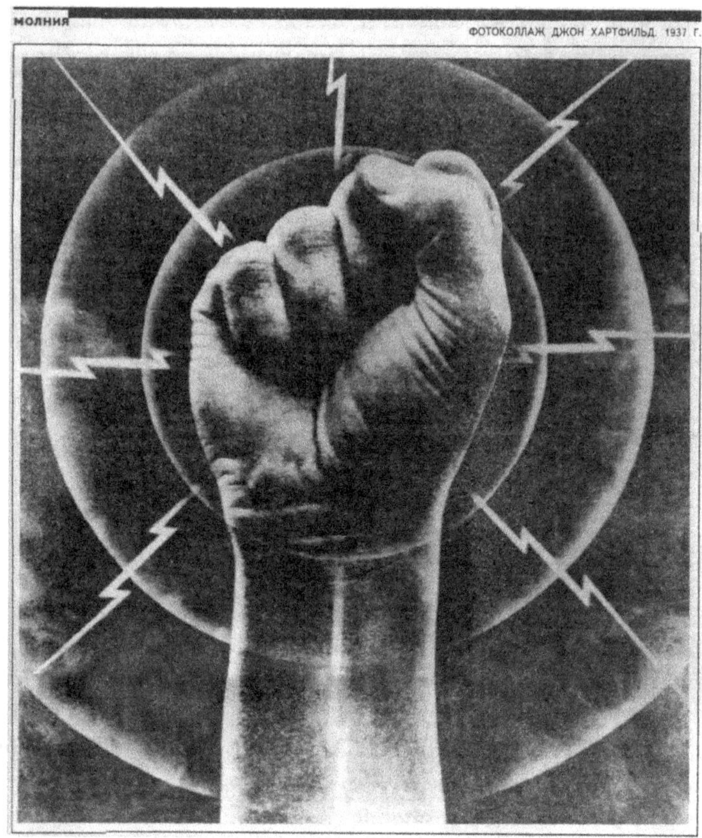

Figure 11. John Heartfield's collage *The Voice of Freedom in the German Night* (1937), a symbol of the communist resistance against German Nazism. Published on the cover of *Limonka* 10 (May 1995).

women and gender equality. Contradicting its own premises, the article concluded that the NBP was also in favor of the "sacred institution of marriage" and of the family as "the fundamental unit of society."

The position of the party leaders on issues of gender and sexuality could not be more ambiguous. The traditionalist Dugin wrote about a return to the patriarchal family and the "restoration of the social centrality of the Man, through the establishment of a masculinist society," while Limonov called for the destruction of the bourgeois monogamous family and for the creation of "sexual comfort" through communal living and widespread promiscuity.[96] From the point of view of racial issues, the party officially rejected any form of racism or antisemitism, and both Limonov and Dugin repeatedly stated that nationalist

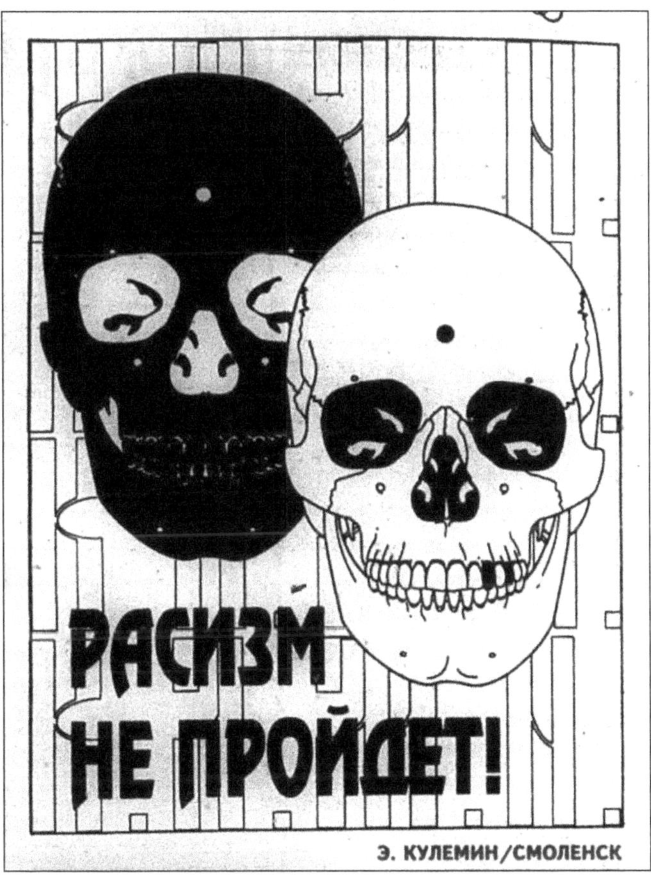

Figure 12. Eduard Kulemin, *Rasizm ne proidet!* (Racism shall not pass!), *Limonka* 88 (Jan. 1998).

and right-wing ideologies should be freed of any racial elements.[97] Occasionally, *Limonka* even displayed symbols of the struggle against racism and Nazism (see figs. 11 and 12). This was certainly unusual for a political organization that included nationalism in its ideology and positioned itself on the right side of the political spectrum. However, because of the presence in the organization of activists coming from the radical right, it was not uncommon to see explicitly racist or xenophobic articles published in *Limonka*. In such cases, the editorial board would often distance itself from the content of a given article, either by claiming that the piece in question was ironic or satirical, or by explicitly reminding the reader that the party did not support the opinions stated by the author.[98]

Anti-Fascism and Anti-Antifascism

In 1996, the rise of nationalism in general, and the activity of the NBP in particular, became the subject of an art exhibit that took place in Moscow, funded and organized by the international association Youth Against Racism in Europe and curated by Osmolovsky. The exhibition, titled *Anti-Fascism and Anti-Antifascism*, was conceived as an occasion to discuss and redefine the political and philosophical meaning of fascism and its role in contemporary Russian and European society. It included an art exhibition and a series of seminars and discussions specifically aimed at raising awareness about issues related to fascism and racism in contemporary society. Tsvetkov participated in the event with a series of "alternative street signs" that were originally part of a performance he had organized under the auspices of an invented radical art collective, the Communist Realism Group. In the performance, seemingly inspired by the Situationists' concept of *dérive*,[99] Tsvetkov covered ordinary street signs at an intersection in Moscow with made-up political symbols associated with different collective states of mind: "demonstration, divination, worshipping, annihilation, limitation." The signs were supposed to create (somewhat jokingly) a revolution in the consciousness of random passersby: "Revolution—this is when you cannot use your car to get to your money, because there are new unknown signs on the street. Other signs" (see fig. 13).[100]

In the exhibition catalog, drawing on Deleuze and Guattari, Osmolovsky defined Tsvetkov as an "accomplished schizophrenic" who "plays with politics, turning it into an irresponsible show . . . [and] demonstrating to the political milieu the experimental possibilities of communication." With his "street signs" Tsvetkov identified "fascism with any form of law-creation [*zakonotvorchestvo*] . . . [or] preestablished rules." Tsvetkov's own "involvement in fascism" would be in this context a form of protest against commonly accepted rules within the radical leftist milieu, or a form of "self-negation."[101]

The introductory notes to the exhibit addressed some important issues concerning the general political situation of the mid-1990s, and they are useful for gaining a better understanding of the role of the NBP in the shaping of post-Soviet political culture. In his introduction, the British activist Robert Jones, one of the organizers, looked at the danger produced by the emergence of neofascist, xenophobic, and ultranationalist organizations in Europe. Jones focused in particular on the question of widespread racism and discrimination against national minorities in Russian schools and workplaces, as well as on the part of the Russian police and other law enforcement agencies. He also highlighted the way in which the Russian government exploited nationalist discourses to distract the population from the pressing issues of corruption, deep economic

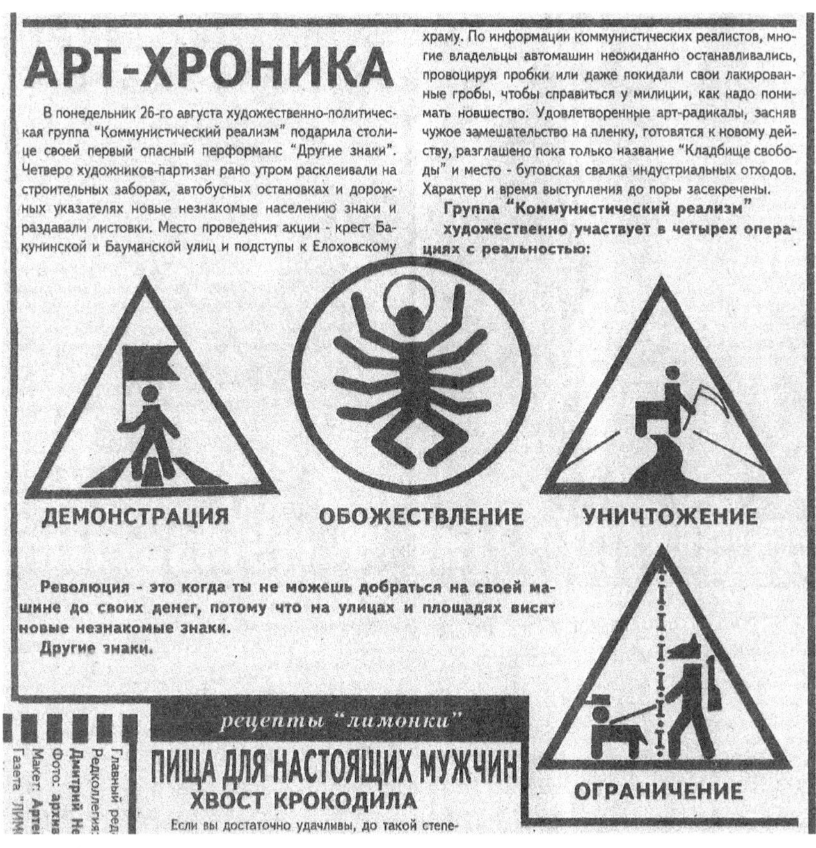

АРТ-ХРОНИКА

В понедельник 26-го августа художественно-политическая группа "Коммунистический реализм" подарила столице своей первый опасный перформанс "Другие знаки". Четверо художников-партизан рано утром расклеивали на строительных заборах, автобусных остановках и дорожных указателях новые незнакомые населению знаки и раздавали листовки. Место проведения акции - крест Бакунинской и Бауманской улиц и подступы к Елоховскому храму. По информации коммунистических реалистов, многие владельцы автомашин неожиданно останавливались, провоцируя пробки или даже покидали свои лакированные гробы, чтобы справиться у милиции, как надо понимать новшество. Удовлетворенные арт-радикалы, засняв чужое замешательство на пленку, готовятся к новому действу, разглашено пока только название "Кладбище свободы" и место - бутовская свалка индустриальных отходов. Характер и время выступления до поры засекречены.

Группа "Коммунистический реализм" художественно участвует в четырех операциях с реальностью:

ДЕМОНСТРАЦИЯ

ОБОЖЕСТВЛЕНИЕ

УНИЧТОЖЕНИЕ

Революция - это когда ты не можешь добраться на своей машине до своих денег, потому что на улицах и площадях висят новые незнакомые знаки.

Другие знаки.

ОГРАНИЧЕНИЕ

рецепты "лимонки"

ПИЩА ДЛЯ НАСТОЯЩИХ МУЖЧИН

ХВОСТ КРОКОДИЛА

Если вы достаточно удачливы, до такой степе-

Figure 13. Aleksey Tsvetkov, "Street signs," "Art-khronika," *Limonka* 47 (Sep. 1996).

crisis, and the drastic decline of the quality of life in Russia during the 1990s. The demagogical use of the term "fascism" by the Russian government and mainstream Russian media, Jones pointed out, was based on a "myth of totalitarianism," which was aimed at discrediting socialism (in part because of its inevitable connection with Stalinism), and which was used to "prove that democracy is only possible in a society based on a free market economy."[102]

This view disregarded, according to Jones, the fundamental financial and political support that Hitler received, despite his populist rhetoric, from Germany's largest corporations, as well as the fact that Stalinism was a bureaucratic and reactionary degeneration of the Russian Revolution that denied the fundamental principles of socialist internationalism.[103] Finally, Jones underscored the fact that because of rising poverty, instability, and social inequality, Russian youth, and former members of anarchist and leftist organizations

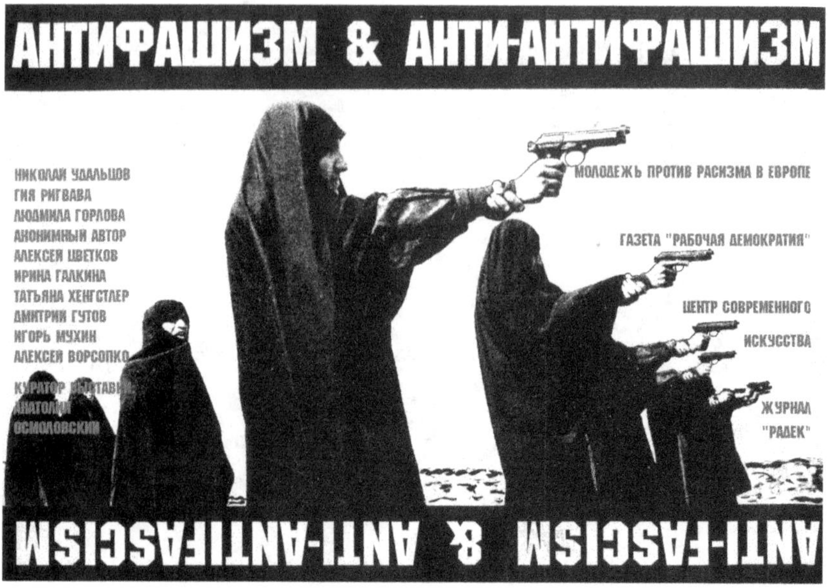

Figure 14. Cover of the catalog of the exhibition *Antifascism and Anti-antifascism*, 1996. Image courtesy of Gosudarstvennyi tsentr sovremennogo iskusstva, Moscow.

among them, more and more frequently joined right-wing organizations like the NBP and even the neo-Nazi Russian National Unity, which in turn could appropriate socialist symbols and discourses and present themselves as anti-capitalist forces. As a consequence, Jones concluded that in order to be successful the movement against fascism, racism, and xenophobia should openly address pressing social questions of unemployment, poverty, increased crime, and the lack of any form of state-supported social welfare.[104]

Osmolovsky focused more specifically on the philosophical definition of fascism, and on the way in which the blatant misuse of the term was having nefarious effects on early post-Soviet political culture. The term "fascism," Osmolovsky noted, had gradually degenerated into a "political insult" used to discredit political opponents. Leftist politicians would use the term "demofascism," while the government and the media commonly used the "idiotic term Red-Brown," to discredit both the leftist and the right-wing opposition to the government, as well as any possible critique to the new course of economic reforms. This improper and simplistic use of the term was particularly harmful, Osmolovsky continued, because it did not allow one to distinguish between authentic expressions of fascist or authoritarian ideology and the use of fascist symbols as a shock tactic among youth subcultures, as in the case of "Sid Vicious and his legendary T-shirt with a swastika," or to recognize fascist-like (*fashizoid-nye*) tendencies within nominally leftist political organizations.[105] Furthermore, this terminological confusion favored the misleading association of right-wing ideology and leftist radicalism, which was common both among mainstream journalists and "hopeless extremists."

Finally, and most importantly, in his explanation of the increasing popularity of various forms of fascism among youth, Osmolovsky pinpointed two fundamental issues connected to nationalism in general, and to the emergence of the NBP as a political movement and a social practice in particular. First, for Osmolovsky fascist ideology stood in sharp contrast to "the general political-economic tendency toward integration," something that one could define as the final global triumph of Western liberalism captured by Francis Fukuyama's famous catchphrase about "the end of history."[106] Fascism drew its "protest energy," Osmolovsky argued, from its clashing against the dominant political system—and this helped explain its strong appeal among rebellious Russian youth. Second, Osmolovsky claimed that the potential mass popular appeal of fascism was connected with its fundamental eroticism: "Undoubtedly, the ideology of the superman, of the Hero, is extremely sexual. It charms subjugated women and is flattering for dominating men."[107]

In his explanation, Osmolovsky connected fascism with an aggressive, all-encompassing sexuality. Sexuality in the "liberal-democratic model" is for Osmolovsky "segregational" (*segregativnaia*), because Western capitalist society provides "sexual ghettoes," red-light districts and swing clubs, and at the same time "de-sexualizes public life as much as possible." By contrast, fascism on the one hand relegates sexuality within the limits of the traditional family, and on the other "permeates with sexuality every aspect of the life of the individual." Western leftist intellectuals despise both "the passion for the uniform and the interest in porn production," and they consider them forms of bad taste. However, Osmolovsky noted, "the leftist movement will have to develop a new (different) strategy of sexual representation if it plans on being competitive in the twenty-first century."[108]

This commentary is particularly useful for understanding the culture of the NBP as a political community. Indeed, the aesthetics and culture of the NBP had a strong sexual or erotic component. Sexuality and physicality in general, in the form of an appeal to political violence, were crucial features of the type of mass mobilization that the leaders of the movement attempted to realize, through the promotion of a cult of war, heroism, and revolution. This was mirrored in the everyday life of the community, and in the lifestyle, personal motivations, and values of its members.

3

Bohemianism, Political Militancy, and Resistance to Modernity

The NBP as Social Practice

Mass politics in my opinion works on the distortion of meanings. And radical art destroys stereotypes. It destroys them and brings back public awareness.

Tanya, thirty-seven, political activist and former member of the NBP, April 2015

On November 7, 1997 [the anniversary of the October revolution], for the first time the *natsboly* went out into the street and started *shouting*. That was not considered acceptable in the Soviet Union. We used to march in silence during demonstrations. There was no such thing as chanting slogans. Limonov and his kids were the first to do this. And they showed it on television. This was absolutely shocking.

Anatoly Tishin, former leader of the NBP, May 2015

This is a world made of plastic [*U nas plastmassovyi mir*]. Since childhood, everyone is turned into a consumer. And all they care about is their comfort, their phones, their clothes, and their shoes. Armani is the only thing that matters to them. . . . And the problem is that Armani is unstoppable. . . . *You can't stop Armani with a punch.*

Misha, twenty-seven, National Bolshevik activist at a protest meeting in Moscow, April 2015

> The world made of plastic has won / The scale model turned out to be stronger / The last toy-ship has cooled off / The last small lamp is tired / But in my throat, lumps of memories are wheezing // My defense is / A speckle of sun on an eye made of glass / My defense is / The funereal little ball of a ridiculous world / The funereal little ball of a cheap world // The world made of plastic has won.
>
> Egor Letov, "Moia oborona" (My defense), 1989

Yes, Death! Radical Politics and the Authenticity of Physical Experience

My first visit to the current party headquarters of Drugaia Rossiia took place on March 13, 2015. After I called a phone number listed on the party website, somebody put me in touch with Pasha, a current activist, who proposed that we meet at the party headquarters, the Moscow "Bunker." Pasha gave me the address and directions, and he told me to wait for him in the backyard of a big Stalinist building close to the metro station Voykovskaya. At the time of our meeting, Pasha was thirty-three and the head of the Moscow branch of Drugaia Rossiia or, as the *natsboly* would say, the Moscow Gauleiter. For party ranks, members of the NBP use terms borrowed from the nomenclature of the German Nazi Party and from the Soviet military and bureaucracy. The leader of larger party branches is a Gauleiter. The person in charge of the Bunker, the party headquarters, is the Bunkerführer. The head of a regional or provincial section is a *komissar*. A senior member of the party is a *brigadir*, and the executive committee of the party is the *ispolkom* (*ispolnitel'nyi komitet*, the executive committee). A comrade is a Parteigenosse, or simply a Genosse. Limonov, the leader of the party, is commonly referred to as *vozhd'* (the leader), a term associated in Soviet popular culture and propaganda with Lenin and Stalin. Pasha was dressed in black, except for a small red party pin with a grenade, the party symbol of Drugaia Rossiia, and its main slogan: "Russia is everything—Everything else is nothing!" (*Rossiia—vse, ostal'noe—nichto!*). Underneath his winter jacket, he was wearing a Che Guevara T-shirt. In order to get into the Bunker, somebody had to let us in through a metal door locked from the inside.

The original NBP Bunker on 2-aya Frunzenskaya, as I learned from older activists, was a "huge underground labyrinth" of spaces and rooms merging one into the other, "where something would always be going on": a concert, an art exhibit or performance, or a lecture. The Bunker I visited was a smaller, more modest version of its predecessor. Its three main spacious rooms—an office, a bigger room where the weekly party meetings took place, and a third sleeping space—were located, along with a kitchen and restroom, in the basement of the building. The makeshift bedroom was kept hidden from me because it was technically illegal for party activists to be sleeping there. It was suffocatingly hot inside, because the building's boiler room was very close.

The main room was filled with boxes of humanitarian aid that were about to be shipped to the war in Donbass. Although most of the boxes were sealed, I could see some boots and warm clothes, diapers, sanitary pads, gauze, and several big bottles of iodine. The walls were covered with photos of old party demonstrations and meetings, political posters, a portrait of Stalin, and a series of posters portraying Russian oligarchs seen through a gunsight. While Pasha and I sat in the kitchen, a few activists came and went. They sat with us for a while, joining in the conversation. These were mostly volunteer soldiers who had just come back from Eastern Ukraine because they had been injured. A few of them were Latvian and had come to Moscow to renew their Russian visas, something very important considering that because of their participation in the war they would not be allowed back to Latvia or the EU.

After I told him about my project, Pasha started sharing some of his thoughts about the party: "Yes, it all started as an aesthetics, a *style*, but now as you can see it has all become *serious, this is all reality* [*eto vse—real'nost'*]. We used to have slogans like 'Love is War!' [*Liubov'—Voina!*] and 'Yes, death!' [*Da, smert'!*] . . . Well, now *it has all become a reality* [*vse stalo real'nost'iu*]. Our people are going to war. It all started as an aesthetics, a style, but now we are the only serious political force left in Russia." Pasha would have been ready to go to war himself, but, as he put it, "the party needed me here." He added that this was what he had signed up for when he joined the party. For him the party, he said, was not just a lifestyle but a "life path."

Pasha had moved to Moscow from a relatively large industrial city where he grew up at the beginning of the war, about a year before we met. Aside from his political activism he earned a living working as a programmer. He had learned about the NBP, he told me, at a concert of the punk band Grazhdanskaia oborona more than ten years earlier and decided to join the party because certain issues "fundamentally resonated" with him, in particular the ideas of "social justice and national justice": "during the 1990s we suddenly became a colonized country. We used to have a wonderful education, a wonderful health system, and all of this was destroyed in an instant." As I discovered later, Pasha was also one of the thirty-nine *natsboly* who were arrested for peacefully occupying the Presidential Reception Office on December 14, 2004, an action that at the time symbolically established the NBP as one of the main oppositional movements against Putin's government.

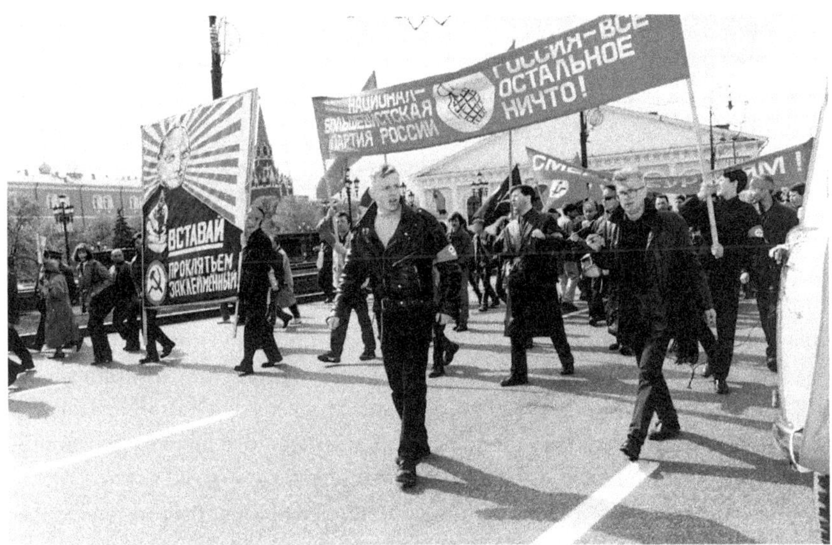

Figure 15. *Natsboly* marching through the center of Moscow, mid-1990s. Photo by Heidi Hollinger.

What Pasha told me during my first visit to the Bunker highlighted some important elements of the culture and activity of the political community built around the NBP. First, *natsboly* of different ages, ranks, social statuses, and cultural backgrounds consistently connected their nationalism, anti-liberalism, and "anti-Westernism" to Russia's abrupt and traumatic transition to capitalism. In addition, Pasha interpreted the "liberal reforms" of the 1990s, and the shift to an unbridled form of free market economy, "spatially"—that is, as a form of colonization of Russian culture by Western, and more specifically American, civilization. Also, in his narrative Pasha returned several times to the question of "authenticity" or "reality," which activists would achieve through personal sacrifice, total commitment to a collective cause, and proximity to or experience of violence and death. Finally, his responses highlighted two coexisting, although apparently mutually exclusive, aspects of the culture and history of the NBP as a cultural network and a political community: the group's bohemian, artistic form of protest against mainstream culture and society, and its grassroots, militant ethics and lifestyle.

In *The New Spirit of Capitalism*, Luc Boltanski and Ève Chiapello identify two fundamental types of critique that have been historically used against the capitalist system and its values: the "artistic critique, . . . based on the invention of a bohemian lifestyle," and a social critique.[1] According to Boltanski and Chiapello, these critiques draw on different "sources of indignation." The artistic critique is mainly based on the idea of "capitalism as a source of *disenchantment* and *inauthenticity* of objects, persons, emotions and, more generally, the kind of existence associated with it," and on the idea of "capitalism as a source of *oppression*" of individual freedom and creativity. The social critique, "inspired by socialists, and, later by Marxists," mainly relies on the idea of capitalism as a source of poverty and inequality and points to the "*opportunism* and *egoism* which, by exclusively encouraging private interests, prove destructive of social bonds and collective solidarity."[2] The artistic critique and the social critique are, to an extent, mutually exclusive, in that the social critique, being implicitly based on Christian ethics, is fundamentally opposed to the immorality and egotism linked with a dandy or bohemian lifestyle.[3] In addition, one might argue, while the Marxist idea of future social justice and equality shares with capitalism its fundamental faith in progress, the bohemian and artistic ideals of aristocraticism, "art for art's sake," and the rejection of work and productivity, are potentially much more in line with a conservative or elitist view of the world.

According to Boltanski and Chiapello, after the global protest movement of 1968, the "new spirit of capitalism" has gradually selectively absorbed and readapted, in its time management, employment, and marketing practices, many of the elements traditionally associated with an "artistic critique" of the capitalist system, such as flexibility, adaptability, individual freedom, and creativity. At the same time, however, this new corporate culture has also deprived individuals of security and stability and has produced new forms of indirect exploitation through exclusion. As a consequence, the artistic or bohemian form of anti-capitalist critique has generally become ineffective: "because the new spirit of capitalism incorporated much of the *artistic critique* that flourished at the end of the sixties, the accusations formerly levelled at capitalism out of a desire for liberation, autonomy, and authenticity no longer seemed to be soundly based."[4]

In this chapter, I argue that the culture of the NBP, which can be seen as an elaborate form of resistance to late capitalism, has combined bohemianism, radical militancy, and political activism, or, to borrow Boltanski and Chiapello's scheme, elements from both the "social critique" and the "artistic critique" of a capitalist worldview. I contend that the "search for authenticity," and the protest against capitalism, modernity, and mainstream politics that National Bolshevik activists have engaged in throughout the years, frequently occurred through forms of political activism, cultural production, and self-expression that are in different ways connected to the sphere of bodily or physical experience. In different stages of the history of the movement and for different activists, this way of experiencing political activism took the form of art and public performance, the personal sacrifice for a collective cause, and, in certain instances, the physical risk and closeness to death provided by the experience of war. These are all (at times extreme) bodily and spiritual conditions, or individual and collective forms of expression, that many National Bolshevik activists experienced as a way of establishing their values and identity, in opposition to mainstream culture and modern consumerist society.

For many young men and women coming from a condition of disadvantage and marginality, the NBP offered an opportunity for self-expression and belonging to a community, as well as a platform for political discussion. Because of the fundamentally eclectic nature of the organization, many of its members appropriated, reinterpreted, and transformed the ideology of the movement for their own purposes. Starting from similar sociopolitical premises, participation in the life of the community frequently resulted, for different National Bolshevik activists, in opposite experiences and opposite life choices.

A good example of this is the story of two young activists with whom I interacted during my research in Moscow: Misha and Aleksey. Misha, twenty-seven, was a current activist with Drugaia Rossiia. I met him for the first time at a party demonstration in Moscow in spring 2015 and later interacted with him a few times at the party headquarters, usually after the weekly party meetings, when it was common for activists to gather informally and have a drink in a courtyard or a park close to the Bunker. When I met him for the first time, Misha had just come back from Donbass, where he had fought as a volunteer on the side of the pro-Russian separatists. His partner, Nastya, was also at the demonstration, and she had also been in Donbass with Misha. Misha and Nastya had moved back to Moscow because Nastya had become pregnant. At the demonstration they were both taking care of the daughter of two other party members who were in prison for political reasons.

In addition to being a *natsbol*, Misha was a *futbol'nyi fanat* (soccer hooligan), a member of a soccer team's supporters' organized group. This is not unusual among the NBP common activists or "foot soldiers" (*riadovye aktivisty*). Before joining the NBP ten years earlier, Misha had been "a nationalist, and for the rebirth of the empire," by which he meant that at that time he used to be closer to more overtly ultranationalist or neofascist groups or positions. Although he now took the side of the pro-Russia separatists in Ukraine, Misha did not support Putin's government because "contemporary Russian power is anti-popular [*antinarodnaia*], and this is why it persecutes us [the *natsboly*]." Before leaving for Donbass, Misha, like many other party members, spent several years in prison because of his political activities. Leading Russian human rights organizations, such as Memorial and the movement Solidarnost', included him (along with several of his party comrades) in a list of Russian political prisoners, arguing that his was one of the many cases fabricated in order to crack down on groups opposing Putin.

Because of its focus on human rights and freedom of expression, during the first decade of the 2000s many Russian journalists and political commentators have at various points described Drugaia Rossiia as a de facto leftist organization.[5] Yet Misha did not really conform to the classic image of a civil rights activist. He was obviously not a pacifist. Because of his current affiliation with an organization of soccer ultras, and the fact that he had formerly belonged to a hard-core ultranationalist group, he had clearly been exposed to violence and did not refrain from it. Most recently, of course, he had also voluntarily participated in a civil war, an experience that he, like most *natsboly*, considered fulfilling, enriching, and honorable. In fact, Misha justified violence as an instrument of political struggle and even appreciated its formative and "spiritual" value.

Misha's account of both his political biography and his experience with violence was inextricably intertwined with the evolution of his religious views and his interest in mysticism. When he became a member of the NBP, Misha told me, he "took off his cross" (*snial krest*), meaning that he left the Orthodox Church. After that, he first became a Buddhist and then a Shivaist. In our conversations, he frequently mentioned Italian conservative thinker Julius Evola and his cult of heroism, tradition, and mystical experience.[6]

The first time we talked, I asked Misha why he had decided to go to war and whether he was at all afraid of losing his life (or a limb, like some of his fellow party members I had seen returning from the conflict). He answered that he considered death to be something unavoidable and natural, and an important part of everyone's life experience. "Contemporary society," he continued, "is repressive toward *men*—because if a cop brings you to the police station and he beats you up, you can't fight back, because if you punch him you end up in prison." "Kids nowadays," he continued, "are raised to become consumers from the time they are little, even through games and cartoons. At least in the Soviet Union they cultivated the image of the hero, but it's not like that anymore." In describing the decadence of contemporary society, Misha used the lyrics of one of Egor Letov's most famous songs, "Moia oborona" (My defense, 1989): "The world made of plastic has won" (*Plastmassovyi mir pobedil*). This was a recurring motif of my interactions with NBP activists. Although Letov's lyrics are fundamentally cryptic and could be interpreted as an expression of general disillusionment with reality, the *natsboly* frequently used these words to describe the post-Soviet triumph of Western materialist culture.

I interviewed Aleksey, the second activist, in a café in the center of Moscow on April 8, 2015. Aleksey was a young artist and political activist. Like Misha, he was in his mid-twenties. For many years, he had also been a very committed member of the NBP/Drugaia Rossiia, participating in numerous protest actions and spending several months in prison for political reasons. At the time of our interview, Aleksey was regularly collaborating with several liberal media outlets and leftist art groups and was an active member of Moscow cultural and political life. He considered himself a leftist. He was openly anti-fascist and anti-racist, and he embraced straight edge, a current of hardcore punk subculture that promotes veganism and abstinence from drugs, alcohol, and tobacco. For several years, he had been actively campaigning against homophobia in Russia, promoting the creation of a map of gay-friendly cafés and public spaces in Moscow.

Aleksey grew up in a small provincial town. As a young adolescent, he hung out with "punks, skinheads, provincial thugs [*gopniki*], and soccer hooligans" and became addicted to drugs and alcohol. When he was thirteen, he learned about the NBP through a copy of the party newspaper *Limonka* that a friend had bought, along with a few punk audio cassettes, at a local record store. He soon became an active member of the party and later participated in several demonstrations and "direct actions." His political activism deeply changed his social life and habits: "If before my friends had been punks and skinheads, now they were all *natsboly*," he told me. Because of the Russian authorities' strong hostility toward the NBP, he was expelled from school: "they said that I was immoral and that I drew swastikas on my notebooks." After traveling around Russia for a while, Aleksey moved to Moscow, and for several years he lived in a "conspiratorial apartment" with twenty other committed activists who "shared food and bunks, and were involved in political and agitational activities on a day-to-day basis." As with many other activists that I met in the course of my research, for Aleksey, *Limonka* and the NBP had fulfilled the function of an informal social and cultural network.

> I quit school and started hitchhiking around Russia. On the fourth page of the newspaper *Limonka* one could find all the addresses of the regional sections. There were more or less ninety cities with phone numbers, and you could go to any city, call, and someone would come and pick you up, they would let you stay at their place, they would feed you and give you something to drink, and gave you some money for the road. That is, it was a sort of family. . . . So I hitchhiked around Russia and expanded my . . . Because you read an article, and every article was signed. . . . And you liked this article and you went to Saratov for instance, and you met with this guy, and then you met someone else, and they introduced you to artists, poets, musicians. This was very interesting because at the time the internet was not that developed . . . only personal relationships. At the beginning of the 2000s, or in 2005—when you were interested you needed to *go after* information . . . you couldn't just open your laptop and find what you needed, but you had to perform some actions [*sovershit' kakie-to deistviia*] to

> learn something. Even just go to the store and buy a book. And this is how I met a huge amount of very committed and loyal friends.

When I interviewed him, Aleksey had mixed feelings about the organization. On the one hand, he explained, by becoming involved in the NBP many people "got off the streets." Although it was true, as many detractors of Limonov argued, that some of the members of the NBP were ultranationalists and neo-Nazis, according to Aleksey, "one should be thankful to Limonov for the fact that these people got off the streets," that they did not kill anyone and instead "devoted themselves to a political struggle." For him, too, the NBP had been a school of politics, art, and life. When members of the NBP/Drugaia Rossiia started Strategy-31, which took place in Triumfalnaya Square in Moscow, where a famous statue of Soviet poet Vladimir Mayakovsky is located, Limonov told Aleksey about the tradition of the Maiakovskie chteniia (Mayakovskian readings). These were spontaneous poetry readings that took place in front of the monument to Mayakovsky in the early 1960s and were regularly dispersed by the Soviet authorities.[7] Aleksey was inspired by Limonov's story and thought that this was a "very relevant idea, because everyone was tired of poets in taverns and night clubs [who read] poems about Putin and the revolution . . . it just looked a little absurd." With a group of friends, he then organized a new version of the Maiakovskie chteniia, which starting in 2010 took place regularly on the last Sunday of every month. The participants had to fight for their right to be there: the police would often try to disperse them and complain when the participants used profanities in their poems. However, after a few years, the poets were able to "conquer the square," and the new post-Soviet version of the Maiakovskie chteniia became an unofficial ritual of sorts for many young Muscovites.

Although he acknowledged that his experience in the NBP had greatly influenced his development as an artist, a political activist, and an individual, Aleksey explained that he had eventually decided to leave the party because of some "fundamental disagreements" with some of its members in relation to his anti-fascist, anti-racist, and anti-homophobic positions. In doing so, he described certain aspects of the everyday life and culture of the NBP that I had not been fully exposed to. Racism, antisemitism, and homophobia were not officially part of the ideology of the NBP, and Limonov and other party leaders repeatedly declared themselves in favor of a form of "cultural nationalism," devoid of any form of racism or antisemitism.[8] However, among common NBP activists, who were often recruited among former skinheads, members of ultranationalist organizations, and groups of fanatical soccer fans, racism, antisemitism, and homophobia—at least "in words"—were part of the everyday life of the movement. Hate speech, Aleksey told me, was not uncommon among NBP activists, and certain members of the party would regularly make violently racist and antisemitic remarks. According to Aleksey, nationalism was not the dominant ideology of the NBP, and "people of leftist views, Marxists, Trotskyists, and anarchists" coexisted with nationalist and right-wing activists within the organization. At the same time, he continued, the issue of gay rights "was not under discussion" and homosexuality was generally stigmatized. Limonov, he said, promoted this policy mostly for practical reasons; although in principle he would have been in favor of promoting gay rights in Russia, Limonov understood that his main electorate, the "Russian *muzhik*," would have never understood him if he had done so.[9]

Misha's and Aleksey's stories highlight certain important and interconnected aspects of the culture and identity of the political and intellectual communities built around the NBP. In Misha's account, the "search for authenticity" and the protest against mainstream culture and politics took the form of aggressive masculinity, and of a cult of war, death, and heroism, seen as liminal states in which the values of modern ordinary life are systematically called into question. In Aleksey's case, the resistance to—and protest against—capitalism, inequality, and modernity occurred through the creative combination of art and social protest, and through the participation in unstructured, utopian, and nonhierarchical forms of socialization, similar to what Victor Turner has described in his definition of *Communitas*.[10]

Combinations of the aforementioned models and cultural paradigms played an important role in determining the identity and culture of the NBP as a political and intellectual community in different stages of its existence. In the first, "bohemian" period of the NBP, war, heroism, and political militancy, as well as the references to fascist and early Soviet symbols and ideas, were still part of an aesthetic posture, and of a way of creating spaces "outside" or "beyond" early post-Soviet society and everyday life. Calling themselves "Red-Brown" (*krasnokorichnevye*), the early *natsboly* were also reclaiming a derogatory term that the Yeltsin government and the Russian mainstream media had used to dismiss any form of opposition to the economic "shock therapy." Anton, the early member of the NBP introduced in chapter 2, described how back in the 1990s the party had served as an escape from the bleakness of post-Soviet everyday reality, which was dominated by vulgar gangsters, Soviet-era corrupted bureaucrats, and former Komsomol members turned wealthy arrogant oligarchs.

> At the time Moscow was a kind of chaos, where one could find certain oases, where normal people would gather . . . Because it was a very tense city. And there were such oases where people could relax, rest, and laugh.

> And well . . . This is what our NBP (or what people later started calling the NBP) was. Our company was just such a "salon." And we regarded all of this—all of these scary symbols—absolutely as a Dadaist way to deliver a blow to this aggressive early capitalism that we found so unpleasant . . . [as if with those symbols we were saying] "you took from us our city, our motherland, our country—and we respond with Limonov, and an article about Mussolini!"

Throughout the years, this peculiar search for "safe spaces" and "scary symbols" turned to different art forms that, for one reason or another, could not be accepted into traditional cultural venues and institutions. All the artists and poets who ended up reflecting in their work the strange combination of paradoxical irony, taste for the absurd, and childish romanticism, which characterized the political style of the NBP, occupied a liminal position within the art and literary worlds. Although not all of these artists and poets were active members or supporters of the party, at one or another moment in their career their work ended up resonating with the multifaceted identity of the NBP.

In the sphere of visual arts, the names that became most commonly associated with the NBP were those of Aleksandr Lebedev-Frontov, Pavel Losev, and Eduard Kulemin. These artists' styles were connected with the aesthetics of different youth subcultures, and all of them were interested in the possibility of blurring the boundaries between art, propaganda, and political action in their work. Aside from his collaboration with the NBP, Losev worked in the sphere of book illustration, where his work centered mostly on mystical and decadent subjects; his drawing style was most reminiscent of that of early twentieth-century Russian symbolism. For the NBP, he produced aggressive and dynamic images that provided an original take on Limonov's and Dugin's Russian and European avant-garde references, making them closer to the angry style of punk and hard rock subcultures that the younger generations of *natsboly* belonged to (see fig. 16). When I interviewed him, Losev said that he was very proud of his collaboration with the NBP, which allowed him "to reach thousands of people" and use "the streets of Saint Petersburg [where many of the flyers and posters he authored were displayed] as my own art gallery."[11]

Kulemin, who worked with different media, including visual poetry, installations, and performances, used his "agitational" work for the NBP to play ironically with the party's tough image and paradoxical death cult. His skeleton in an NBP uniform, quite absurdly inviting the viewers to "not piss their pants" and join the NBP, became one of the most iconic images commonly associated with the movement (see fig. 17).

Lebedev-Frontov was perhaps the artist who most clearly embodied the ironic radicalism of the NBP. He was a pioneer of Russian noise and industrial

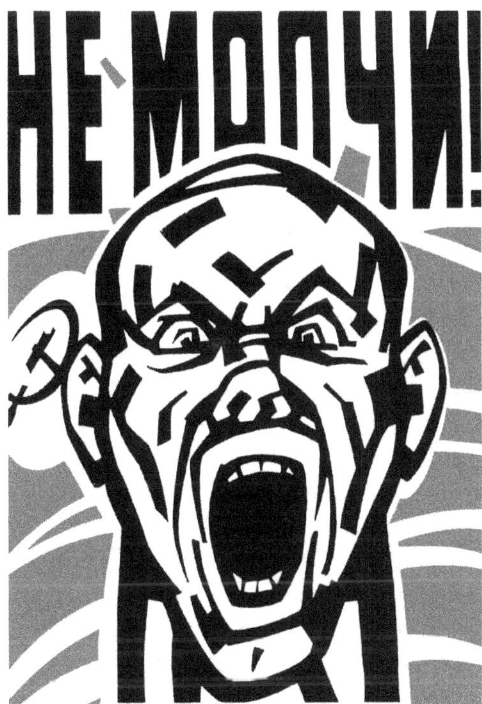

Figure 16. Pavel Losev, *Ne molchi!* (Speak up!). Political poster, n.d.

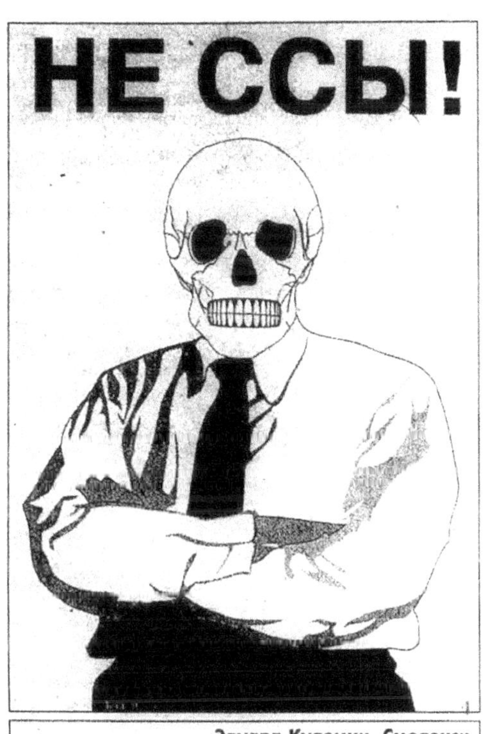

Figure 17. Eduard Kulemin, *Ne ssy!* (Don't piss your pants! Join the NBP!). Political poster, n.d.

music based in Saint Petersburg, with a keen interest in the futurist experimental composer Luigi Russolo, Italian Fascism, and, more generally, early twentieth-century European culture. A larger-than-life figure, he was the only one among my informants with no internet connection, which is in itself significant, considering that he was a pioneer of electronic music. His concerts were legendary for being absolutely extreme and uncompromising. For instance, Dmitry Zhvanya, the anarchist who led the Saint Petersburg branch of the NBP for a few years in the 1990s, in his memoirs remembers that at one of these concerts the music was so loud and overwhelming that he lost consciousness and had to be taken away in an ambulance.[12] In the last year of his life, Kurekhin, who was interested in exploring "the most extreme, most radical, and wildest" forms of music, became very close to Lebedev-Frontov and made him the secret legendary hero of his last radio program, "The Russian Cannibal" (*Russkii liudoed*).[13]

In his collages, Lebedev-Frontov used techniques inspired by the work of the Soviet avant-garde artist Aleksandr Rodchenko and produced a totalitarian or retro-futurist surrealism of sorts, combining motifs such as the death of God, a horrifying mechanization of the flesh, early modernist decadence and sexuality, and a meticulous reconstruction of historical details (e.g., uniforms, emblems, and family mottoes; see fig. 18).[14] The NBP organized various exhibits of Lebedev-Frontov's work, and his collages appeared on several issues of *Limonka*. His most famous work, which Limonov proudly hung as a poster in the NBP Moscow headquarters, displayed the French crime novel super-villain and ruthless murderer Fantômas pointing a gun in the direction of the viewer. The writing on the poster reproduced the first line of the Russian version of "The Internationale": "Stand up, you branded by a curse!" (The first two lines of the song in Russian are "Stand up, you branded by a curse, / The whole world of starving people and slaves!" [*Vstavai, prokliat'em zakleimennyi, / Ves' mir golodnykh i rabov*]) The words evoked the communist hymn, which every Russian of that generation would immediately recognize. At the same time, if taken out of context, they could also be perceived as an allusion to a satanic or mystical brand of bolshevism, an ambiguity that well reflected the provocative irony of the early NBP (see fig. 19).

The kind of poetry that attracted the young and angry members of the NBP was one that had to be performed publicly and loudly. Andrey Rodionov and Vsevolod Emelin, for instance, who worked within the emerging genres of "lyrical rap" and poetry slams, and whose poems focused on surreal and alcohol-ridden stories about Moscow's working-class "neighborhood dormitories," started performing in the Moscow Bunker very early in their careers. Later on, Rodionov became an accepted and even celebrated figure within the

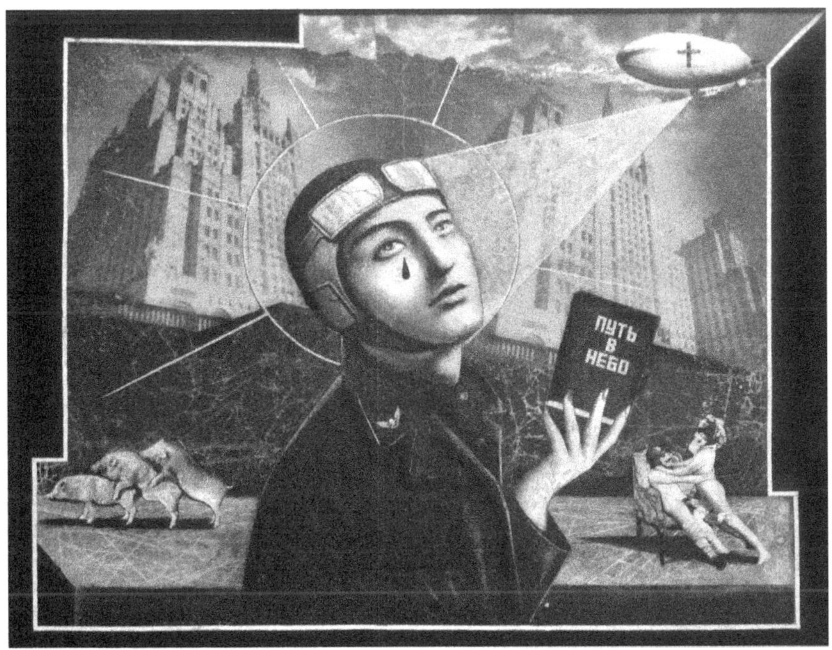

Figure 18. Aleksandr Lebedev-Frontov, *Put' v nebo* (The path to the sky). Collage, 1995. Photo by author.

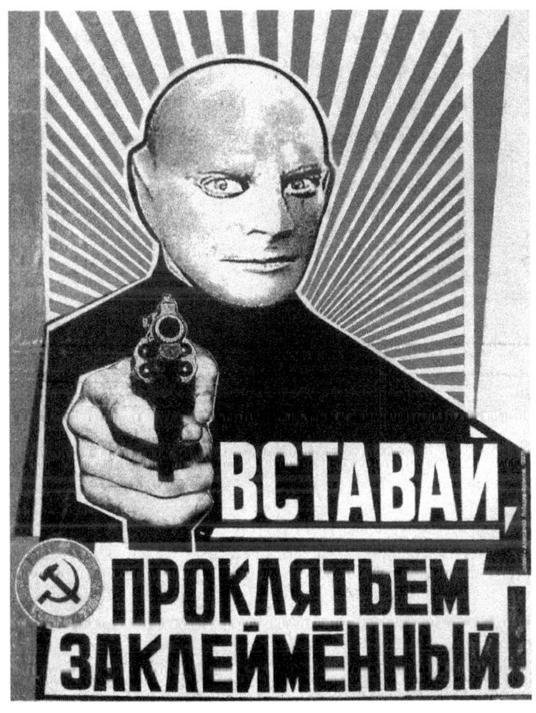

Figure 19. Aleksandr Lebedev-Frontov, *Vstavai, prokliat'em zakleimennyi!* (Stand up, you branded by a curse!) Poster, n.d.

Moscow literary scene, and Emelin a widely read poet writing satirical verses, both online and in print, in response to topical news and events. At the beginning of the 2000s, however, when they had not yet found a venue for their writing styles, both poets found in the young *natsboly* the ideal audience for their work.[15]

The poetry that the young NBP activists most openly identified with was that of Alina Vitukhnovskaya. Even if now, being a strong supporter of libertarianism, Vitukhnovskaya denies any association with the NBP, both her writings and her personal history resonated deeply with the experience and sensibility of the *natsboly*. After a successful debut as a poet in the early 1990s, Vitukhnovskaya became famous as one of the first victims of the absurdity and arbitrariness of the post-Soviet judiciary system. At that time, she was a talented young writer and a member of the Moscow beau monde, and of its clubbing scene. At a time in which everything seemed to be allowed, she wrote an article about her experiences with the emerging post-Soviet drug culture that was used by the authorities as evidence against her, and she ended up facing an unexpectedly harsh and clearly unfair punishment for writing it. Russian intelligence agents planted some drugs in her apartment and framed her for possession and dealing, possibly to set an example and send a message to some of her peers from wealthier and more influential families. Before being escorted out of her home, she wrote on the wall of her childhood bedroom the following sentence: "make me the hero of your comic strip." Still only a little over twenty years old, she was imprisoned and prosecuted for no apparent reason. The case drew immediate attention from the media. Leading Russian intellectuals and international human rights organizations signed petitions on her behalf, but sluggish bureaucratic procedures caused her trial to last for five years, one and a half of which Vitukhnovskaya ended up spending in prison.[16]

The *natsboly* were among those who vehemently protested her incarceration. In the late 1990s, she was invited to the Bunker by someone within Dugin's "mystical-philosophical" circle and started performing there frequently. Her poetry was characterized by dark and "goth" atmospheres, quasi-satanic nihilism, apocalyptic overtones, and a decadent taste for the macabre. They were filled with sex, violence, and references to both Soviet and Nazi iconography. In one of her poems, she described the poet Vladimir Mayakovsky as a "poetic skinhead / killed by second-hand politics" (*Skinkhed poeticheskii / Ubit politicheskim second-khendom*) and a "London dandy . . . dressed in vivid propaganda" (*dendi londonskii . . . odet v nagliadnuiu agitatsiiu*).[17] In "To Love the Cruiser Aurora and the Reichstag" ("Liubit' Avroru i Reichstag"), a poem that many *natsboly* could recite by heart, she celebrated the love for "The hatchet, the blade cutting cocaine, / Both the swastika, and the red flag, / Both Hitler and Mussolini"

(*Topor, i britvu v kokaine, / I svastiku, i krasnyi flag, / I Gitlera, i Mussolini*), for "The reliable rhythm of the execution lists" (*Rastrel'nykh spiskov vernyi ritm*), the "Empire of Voids" (*Imperiiu Pustot*) and "the metaphysical morgues" (*metafizicheskie morgi*).[18] As in the case of Lebedev-Frontov, the twentieth-century totalitarian imagery here mirrors the apocalyptic moods of the early post-Soviet period. Vitukhnovskaya's dark nihilism and fascination with death echoed the *natsboly*'s adolescent angst and radical, uncompromising rejection of post-Soviet materialism. Her poetry involved a total performance of sorts. Like many *natsboly*, Vitukhnovskaya had become an involuntary victim of the new system. The mystical and decadent mood of her poetry was based on the actual physical experience of injustice and deprivation at the hand of the Russian state.

The physical, firsthand experience of collective performances and rituals was an important component of the life and culture of the NBP from its beginnings. Indeed, the foundation of the party coincided with, and was marked by, a forbidden public performance. On November 7, 1994, on the anniversary of the October Revolution, Limonov and Dugin—along with a diverse group of visual artists, musicians, and performers—organized the *First Moscow Festival of Performance*, which was supposed to take place in the Feniks Art Gallery in Moscow. On the day of the opening, the authorities chained the entrance to the gallery and prevented the event from taking place. In reaction to this, the exhibition organizers raised a barricade in front of the art space, which they also saw as a symbolic reference to the October Revolution. They placed a rusty machine gun, which they claimed to have found in a nearby dumpster, at the entrance of the art gallery. Limonov and the two curators of the exhibition, Dugin and the art critic Sergey Kuskov, delivered inflammatory speeches from the podium, and the Moscow Actionists Oleg Kulik and Aleksandr Brener joined them in the protest. While wearing golden horns on his head, Kulik railed loudly against a repressive state power that "once more humiliates Russian artists." Brener threw a cobblestone and shattered a window of the building, shouting that talking was useless, and that this was the only possible way to interact with the authorities.[19]

The actual *Moscow Festival of Performance* took place two weeks later. It was then followed, a year later, by the "exhibition—project" *Extremism and Erotica*, organized by the artist Mikhail Roshniak and the art critic Sergey Kuskov at the newly built Bunker of the NBP at 2-aia Frunzenskaia Street in Moscow (see fig. 20). During the opening event, as if enacting a ritual of death and rebirth, Roshniak first wrapped in bandages, and then unveiled, the "mummies" of the leader Limonov and of one of his young female followers, both dressed in black leather with steel studs and handcuffs. The performance was accompanied by the music of Aleksey Tegin, a mix of industrial, minimalist electronic music

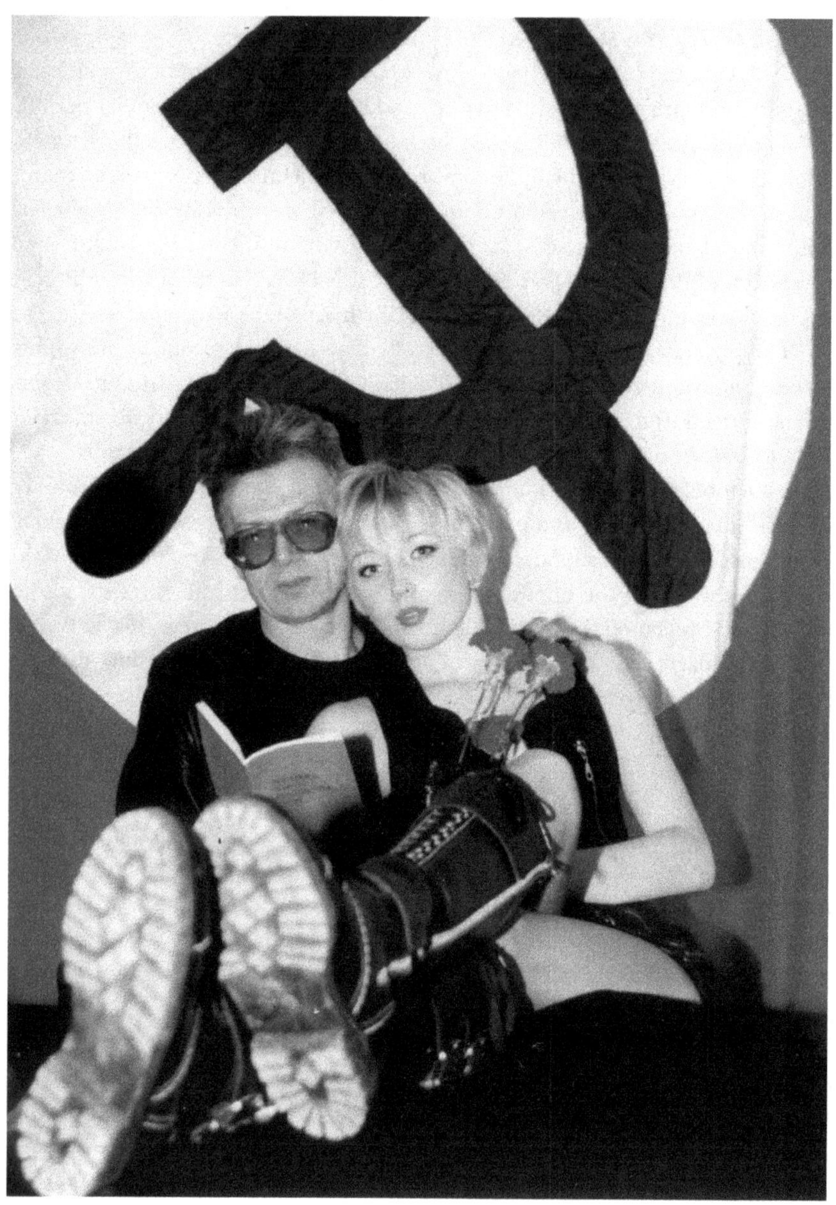

Figure 20. *Ekstremizm i erotika*, performance at the "Bunker," Moscow, Nov. 24, 1995. Photo by Mikhail Roshniak.

and Tibetan sacred chants.[20] Interviewed after the performance, Limonov stated that if "law and order" were supposed to rule society, then culture had to "grow absolutely freely, like a wild plant": "I believe in the revolution as purification, regeneration, and beginning. The satiated, dull democracy does not produce culture, it produces the average person, whereas culture is produced by the elites."[21]

Death, sexuality, and the return to the authenticity of experience were important themes in the art performances that symbolically inaugurated the political activity of the NBP. In his introduction to the performance of the art group Sever, which took place at the Feniks Gallery, Dugin focused on the "experience of the swastika," which he took as a symbol of the circular movement of time and the return to an original abstract concept of tradition. According to Dugin, the "ritual of the swastika" was part of most religious and cultural traditions. The participants of this ritual, depending on the different traditions, would stand in circles and rotate fast and repeatedly, consume alcohol and narcotics, or (in its tantric version) have sexual encounters with "specially trained women," in order to achieve an altered state of consciousness and experience a form of ritualistic death. Dugin saw contemporary art performance as a way to achieve "authentic experience" through a return to sacred archaic rituals: "Avant-garde art in its most essential core gravitates toward *pure experience*, not toward the creation of valuables or products, but toward personal and collective transmutation. . . . This becomes apparent in the most striking way in the genre of the performance, the abstract action, summoned 'here and now' to reveal some hidden side of the human fact."[22] Sergey Kuskov identified the "mysticism of the action" with the traditional ancient Greek pair of Eros and Thanatos, Love and Death, which he saw as inherent to the concept of revolution.[23] Both in Dugin's and Kuskov's pieces, the authentic experiences achieved through art performance, ritualistic death, and sex were set against the commodified and materialistic nature of "Western" capitalist society, and the "sellability" of the contemporary art market and the "sex-industry." In addition, Dugin considered performance, by virtue of the fact that it did not produce an object that could be turned into a commodity, the anti-capitalist form of art par excellence.

Most of the participants in these first art experiments did not actually contemplate the possibility of turning these forms of countercultural production into political action. In fact, many of the first wave of *natsboly* that I interviewed, most of whom were at the time university students from educated families, acted surprised that the party *actually* ended up drawing to its ranks aggressive punks and "provincial thugs" (*gopniki*). Some of them displayed an explicitly elitist attitude, saying that that they would have never personally hung out with such "trash" (*bydlo*, literally: cattle), and that they left the party as soon as it turned into a radical political organization. Others stated that they even found the radicalism and fanaticism of the younger generations of *natsboly* somewhat scary, comparing these young radicals to late nineteenth-century Russian revolutionaries like the terrorist-nihilist Sergey Nechaev.[24]

Eroticism remained an important component of the aesthetics of the NBP and its "propaganda strategies." A few years after its foundation, the party started regularly posting online erotic pictures of "Our Militant Girlfriends" (*Nashi boevye podrugi*), young female activists portrayed in more or less provocative and revealing attire and poses, displaying political banners and symbols. Thinking about the ways in which official state culture appropriated the aesthetics and political strategies of the NBP, one could see these displays of sexualized female bodies, along with the general cult of aggressive masculinity that characterized the movement, as something that preannounced the machismo surrounding Putin's "personality cult," the "displays of erotic attachment to the leader," and the promotion of traditional gender roles and family values that has become increasingly widespread in Russian public culture and official discourses.[25] As mentioned, the NBP took a fluid and paradoxical approach to gender issues, publishing articles that promoted a range of positions from conservative values and the establishment of a patriarchal society to calls for overcoming the bourgeois family and monogamous relationships in general, or establishing complete equality between the sexes.[26] When I visited the Bunker, the practical organization of everyday life seemed indeed to reflect a certain acceptance, and even promotion, of traditional gender roles, in part connected with the party's recent involvement with the war in Eastern Ukraine. Women in the organization (generally, a minority), mostly took care of "housekeeping" and food supplies, and they looked after comrades suffering from war injuries. Most of the female party members who left for the war as volunteers worked on the "home front" or as nurses, although some of them did join one of the battalions as simple soldiers, like their male counterparts.

However, I would also argue that the models of femininity promoted by the party were not really in line with the traditional gender roles of mainstream Russian culture, and that in many cases they actually went strongly against them. Most of my female informants confirmed that the NBP was, by and large, a male-dominated organization (although many also added that the life of the party simply reflected the general situation of contemporary Russian society), but they also added that the relationships between party members were generally characterized by a higher degree of equality and independence than traditional ones. A few of them were also proud to have independently reached leadership roles within the movement. Finally, the promotion of a militant or

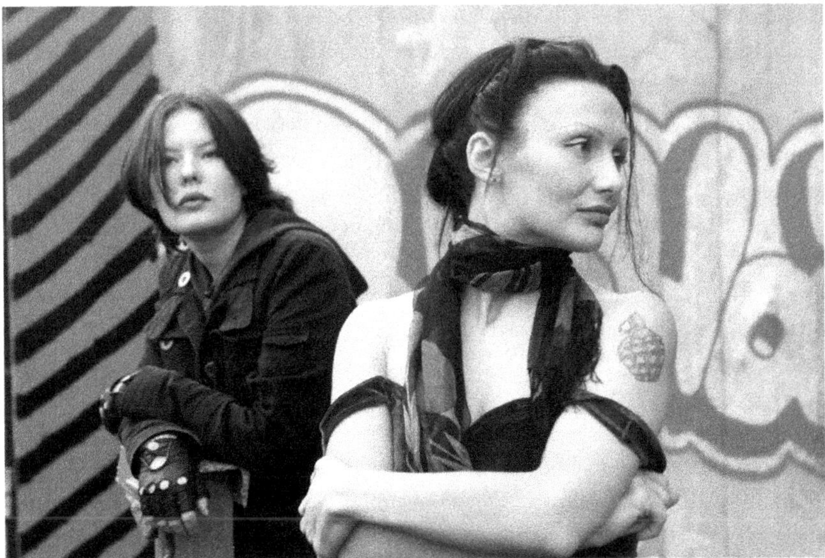

Figure 21. *Devushki partii* (The girls of the party). Published in *Devushki partii*. S.ART Gallery, Moscow, 2011. Photo by Sergey Belyak.

revolutionary lifestyle within the NBP also resulted in alternative gender roles and the support of strong and independent models of femininity. As mentioned, homophobia, in relation to male homosexuality, was not uncommon among the *natsboly*, most likely because it could threaten the ideal of aggressive masculinity that the party embraced; however, this did not apply to women, who could be openly gay, wear male clothes, and have masculine haircuts (in fact, buzzcuts, military clothes, and combat boots were quite common among female activists). Furthermore, the fact that, for instance, the adventurous life of the Bolshevik leader Larisa Reisner could be used as a model of strength and independence for the NBP female activists also corroborates the idea that the movement could incorporate a diverse range of narratives about gender and sexuality.[27]

A certain sexual liberty and promiscuity was also what attracted some of the party's constituency. As Irina, one of my informants, put it, Limonov himself cultivated an image based on "brutality" and "aggressive sexuality," which young activists were drawn to, as they were drawn to a "certain free love that was common at the Bunker among party members . . . and the liberation from certain taboos." During our conversation, Irina also connected this "sexual energy" with the activists' quasi-religious involvement in the party and their participation in dangerous protest actions, which they often paid for with several months, if not years, of prison. At the beginning, she said, the NBP was a "party of intellectuals," but things changed when people from the provinces (*iz regionov*) joined the organization. Then, Irina explained, for young people coming from disadvantaged families, who "would have not been able to accomplish anything in life through the path of normal *socialization*," the NBP represented an opportunity to realize themselves. Young people, and especially young men, would follow the "promise to become a hero" and have "all the girls at their feet," either by participating in dangerous actions of protest or, most recently, by fighting as volunteers in Eastern Ukraine.

"An Armed Paradise": From War to Political Militancy

Between the late 1990s and the beginning of the 2000s, the party grew exponentially. Although it is hard to have a precise estimate because of the semi-informal structure of the organization, it is reasonable to assume that at its peak NBP membership amounted to two to three hundred committed activists in Moscow and one to five thousand activists throughout Russia, while between the years 2000 and 2005 *Limonka* reached a print run of fourteen thousand.[28] In 1998, Dugin left the party, followed by a group of activists who joined him at the New University, and later helped found the Eurasia Movement and the Eurasianist Youth Union. Although my informants provided different explanations for why Dugin decided to leave the organization (e.g., jealousy toward Limonov over a woman or the fact that Limonov had protected certain activists who had been accused of stealing from Dugin), the vast majority agreed that the schism occurred because of Limonov's and Dugin's opposite (although, up until that moment, complementary) political styles. While Dugin and his followers were mostly interested in pursuing cultural and quasi-academic activities, such as lectures, seminars, and journal and book publishing, Limonov wanted the party to become a "real political force," with activists who were directly involved in various forms of propaganda and mass mobilization.[29]

In the late 1990s, the NBP turned all at once into a punk subculture, a grassroots political movement, and a radical revolutionary organization. The Bunker at 2-aia Frunzenskaia Street became an important center for the development of the emergent Moscow underground punk subculture and the regular stage for several self-organized punk concerts. Banda chetyrekh (Gang of Four), which combined existentialist lyrics, aggressive calls for indiscriminate vandalism and destruction, and clear allusions to English post-punk music, became one of the most popular bands among the *natsboly*. The band, whose members were mostly "children from well-off families, who consciously go and sing for the dregs of society, bring themselves down to their level, drink heavily, and mess up everything in the world," drew to the party headquarters their main fan base, entire crowds of violent soccer hooligans.[30] The refrain of one of the most popular songs of Banda chetyrekh—"in Moscow there is not enough blood, in Moscow there is not enough fire"—aptly summarizes the nihilistic and rebellious spirit of the NBP of this period.[31]

The beginning of "direct actions" (*aktsii priamogo deistviia*) as a political strategy within the NBP is closely connected with this type of punk culture and lifestyle. The first-wave "NBP actionists" I talked to connected their political engagement to their alternative lifestyle, which included communal living and hitchhiking through Russia, and they compared their participation in political actions (which often ended with their imprisonment) to the thrill and excitement of performing on stage.

Dima, one of my informants, was the organizer of one of the early NBP direct actions. When I met him, Dima, who was in his late thirties, had recently gone back to college to pursue a degree in the sciences. As we walked around the building where the original Bunker was located, he explained that back in the 1990s he had fully embraced the National Bolshevik alternative lifestyle. Still a teenager, he had dropped out of school to become a full-time revolutionary. While the party grew in popularity and the number of active members increased, he had moved to the party headquarters—the Bunker—and lived there with a few other activists. During our conversation, he was candid about the activities, political and otherwise, that he engaged in as a member of the organization: "as we used to say, we drank, we had sex, we took drugs, and all of this we called 'honorable service in defense of the motherland.'"[32] An important turning point in the political strategy of the NBP, Dima explained, occurred in 1999, when a group of *natsboly* interrupted a speech by Yegor Gaidar, one of the architects of the controversial "shock therapy." When Gaidar made a predictable allusion to the united "communist-fascist" threat looming over Russia, the *natsboly* stood up and started shouting the slogan "This is how we will implement reforms: Stalin, Beria, Gulag!" Following this protest action, which created a scandal and received wide media coverage, the *natsboly* understood the importance of attracting the attention of mainstream media.[33]

As part of their next direct action, Dima and another party member threw eggs at the film director Nikita Mikhalkov in a sign of protest against his public support for the regime of Nursultan Nazarbaev in Kazakhstan, which the *natsboly* considered guilty of discriminations and persecutions against the Russian minority in the country. Before being arrested, Dima and his party comrade were brutally beaten by Mikhalkov's bodyguards. Mikhalkov himself kicked Dima in the head several times, while his bodyguards held him to the ground, causing him to suffer a skull fracture and a traumatic brain injury, and the scene was captured by one of the cameras in the room. Because of this violent reaction on the part of Mikhalkov and his bodyguards, and because of the disproportionate sentence that the two *natsboly* received (two and a half years in prison for "hooliganism"), the media that covered the event displayed a sympathetic attitude toward the protesters. This is how the *natsboly* understood how an excessive reaction on the part of the authorities could at the same time help discredit the government in the eyes of the public, draw attention to the party agenda, and increase the popularity of the movement.

In this sense, a form of political martyrdom helped shape the identity of the NBP as a movement. As Mikhail Sokolov pointed out, the NBP's specific approach to violence distinguished it from other nationalist political movements that emerged from the anti-Yeltsin "national-patriotic opposition," such as the mass neo-Nazi organization Russian National Unity (Russkoe natsional'noe edinstvo, or RNE).[34] While not being particularly vocal about its intentions and ideological positions, the RNE was regularly involved in violent attacks against immigrants and political opponents and in other forms of vigilante-like activities, aimed at "reestablishing order" within Russian society. By contrast, despite their frequent calls for terrorism and revolutionary violence and the fact that they cultivated an aggressive military aesthetics, members of the NBP were usually the victims and not the perpetrators of political violence.

In the late 1990s, direct actions became increasingly staged in order to produce the strongest media response while also having an impact from a legal and "military" standpoint. To this end, a former member of the Russian intelligence trained future direct action participants so that they would be able to evade security and carry out the protests without breaking the law. The goal of this training was twofold. On the one hand, by staging a peaceful and legal protest, and by being, almost without fail, harshly persecuted by the authorities, the *natsboly* intended to make themselves a living proof of the repressive and corrupt nature of the Russian judicial system. On the other hand, NBP activists conceived the direct actions as a rehearsal and training for the actual armed revolution that they envisioned as the true final goal of their political activism.

A fundamental turning point was the first real (albeit unsuccessful) attempt at making the party's celebration of war, heroism, and the revolution a political reality. In 1999, when the NBP had grown to about fifty chapters around Russia, Limonov and the Moscow leadership produced a series of confidential "closed bulletins" called "NBP-INFO," which were used as a safe way of communicating with a few selected regional leaders. The bulletins were handed to the members of the regional chapters with the latest issue of the party newspaper.

A section of one of these documents, which was later extensively discussed as evidence in the trial against Limonov and five other *natsboly*, provided a detailed explanation of the so-called Second Russia project (Proekt Vtoraia Rossiia).[35] This section contained detailed instructions on how to organize a partisan war in Kazakhstan. It explained that, since an armed revolution in Russia in the current situation would most likely be unsuccessful because of the strength of the army and the scarce support from the general public, the most promising strategy for the party, which had recently been denied official registration, was to start a partisan war in one of the former Soviet republics with a numerous Russian minority. After seizing power in such a bordering territory, the National Bolshevik Army would have been in a more advantageous position to spread revolutionary ideas and effect an actual regime change in Russia.

The cause of the defense of a Russian minority in a country of the former Soviet Bloc, and the promotion of a socialist ideology, the author explained, was more likely to attract sympathy from the Russian media and public opinion. By starting the war in a foreign country, the *natsboly* would have avoided a direct confrontation with the Russian army, and technically they would have not broken any Russian law. The document concluded that Kazakhstan was the ideal place for such a partisan war because of its potentially advantageous ratio of Russians to the rest of the population, its relatively weak army, its vast, not easily defensible border, and its mountainous territory, which would favor "guerrilla warfare.

In March 2001, four members of the NBP were arrested in Saratov and Ufa for illegal possession of arms and explosives. According to the investigation records, the activists had a total of six Kalashnikovs, one hundred and fifty units of ammunition, approximately one kilogram of plastic explosives, and two detonators. Allegedly, Limonov had ordered the activists to purchase the weapons, which were supposed to be delivered and stored in the Altai Republic with the aim of creating an illegal paramilitary formation. On April 7, 2001, Limonov was arrested in Altai. As it was later revealed, one of the activists involved in the operation had been collaborating with the Russian intelligence for some time. During the trial, which lasted almost two years, the prosecution invoked articles 205 and 208 of the Russian criminal code (terrorism and organization of illegal armed groups), which would have resulted in sentences of up to fourteen years for Limonov and his followers. Vladimir Linderman, one of the leaders of the NBP at the time, managed to get the accusations of terrorism removed by testifying that he, and not Limonov, was the author of the text "Second Russia," which had been printed in the secret bulletin NBP INFO, no. 3. Linderman and Limonov claimed that the text had been written for a party members' open "contest for the best revolutionary project." The best piece, which was allegedly supposed to be purely fictional, was supposed to be awarded publication in *Limonka*.[36]

The arrest of Limonov and the failed attempt at transforming the party into an unlawful paramilitary organization marked a turning point in the history of the movement. After Putin's rise to power and the establishment of what the *natsboly* defined as a "police state," the NBP abandoned its anti-Western, anti-capitalist rhetoric in favor of a struggle for human rights and freedom of expression. Because Putin appropriated the patriotic discourse and aggressive masculinity of the NBP and other nationalist organizations, the NBP consciously renounced its totalitarian aesthetics and slogans and generally adhered to a more straightforwardly leftist political line.[37]

The main enemies of the organization became the corrupt Russian bureaucrats and the *siloviki*, members of the security and military services who constituted the core of Putin's political entourage. The *natsboly* abandoned their infamous catchphrase "Stalin, Beria, Gulag" and instead began chanting such slogans as "No to the police state!," "We need Another Russia!," and "Russia without Putin!" (*Rossiia bez Putina!*). During the first decade of the 2000s, the NBP struggled for the "widening of the political space," to borrow an expression that many of my informants used to describe their political goals. The party became part of, and had a key role in, the large anti-Putin coalition Drugaia Rossiia, which included liberal, nationalist, and leftist organizations and organized the Dissenters' Marches, the first series of large protests against the Putin regime. The activity of the NBP was crucial for the emergence of a liberal opposition movement in Russia. In a time of widespread political apathy, the NBP was the only organization with grassroots activists and the ability to effectively organize and participate in public protests. After the NBP was legally banned in 2007, the *natsboly* claimed for themselves the name Drugaia Rossiia. In 2009, they returned to the streets and organized Strategy-31, which constituted one of the few forms of expression of dissent in the years leading up to the mass movement "for fair elections" of 2011–12.[38]

■

In this period, the *natsboly*'s main sphere of activity became public performance in the form of peaceful direct actions. Although, as opposed to the organization of a partisan war in the mountains of Kazakhstan, direct actions constituted a peaceful and democratic form of protest, activists who participated in these actions were inspired by a form of radical utopianism not dissimilar from the potentially suicidal project "Second Russia." Tanya, who was an active member of the NBP for more than ten years, helped me navigate and better understand these different aspects of the identity and culture of the NBP through an account of her own experience in the organization. At the time of our meeting, Tanya was working for a liberal news outlet, and she was completely at odds with Limonov's support of Putin's policy in Ukraine. Like most *natsboly*, she considered the NBP the first organization that actively protested against Putin's authoritarianism, and she was very proud of having been a part of it. This is why she was absolutely appalled and felt deeply disappointed when she heard Limonov praising the Berkut (the Ukrainian special police force) for violently repressing the protests against Yanukovich's corrupt government in Maidan square in Kiev in 2013. For Tanya, these statements in support of a repressive and corrupt government betrayed the fundamental anti-systemic and revolutionary spirit of the NBP.

Tanya had become acquainted with the NBP through a heavy metal subculture when still teenager. In a few years she had become a very committed member of the organization and had eventually assumed a leading role in the party. Like many other *natsboly* who were active after Putin's rise to power, she had been unjustly prosecuted and had spent several years in prison because of her political activism. Like many other activists that I interviewed, she considered the NBP to be a radical "political art project," aimed at raising awareness in the population about the mechanisms of power and challenging accepted notions and common opinions.[39] At the same time, it was evident that Tanya was extremely devoted to the "collective cause" of the party and that she highly valued the NBP as a political community. On the one hand, Tanya described the cult of heroism that was such an important element in the culture of the NBP with a certain dose of irony. Her main inspiration for becoming a political activist, she claimed, were the popular Soviet children's books about the *pionery-geroi* (pioneers-heroes). Although they were very receptive toward international culture, the early *natsboly*, all members of the "last Soviet generation," were mostly inspired by the Soviet heroes of their childhood: "some of us wanted to become cosmonauts, others 'pioneers-heroes,'" Tanya said jokingly. On the other hand, as opposed to most early NBP activists, who described their ideological stance as an aesthetic posture, she called herself an extremist. In the party she saw something that she could finally "be ready to sacrifice her life for."

Tanya had decided to join the NBP soon after hearing about the project "Second Russia." I was somewhat surprised by this comment, because many considered the whole operation to be fundamentally quixotic and cobbled together, and asked her whether the *natsboly* really thought that they were going to be able to seize power in Kazakhstan and start a revolution in Russia from there. Tanya replied that for her and the other party members the goal of the revolt had never been political. In fact, the *natsboly* would often openly say that they did not have any particular political goals but were instead interested in the process of the revolution itself. Many activists clearly had no interest in surviving the revolution: "This was a wonderful epic story. This Altai story was kind of like Yukio Mishima's last action. It was never seen as a ticket to power, but as a *ticket to eternity*."[40] With a combination of self-irony and nostalgic romanticism, Tanya described the "Altai project" (and the activity of the NBP) as "an attempt to go back to the world of modernity from the world of postmodernity." For her, if postmodernity was "the world of simulacra," modernity was the time when "everything happened *in reality* . . . and when a person had the possibility of becoming a hero—not to live the existence of a slave, but to become a hero, and to be an active character in the historical arena." Tanya clearly connected postmodernity to political passivity, whereas she saw modernity—in her view, the violent, tumultuous first half of the twentieth century and, in general, any revolutionary time—as the time in which common people are actually given the opportunity to participate in the political process.

During the first decade of the 2000s, the "actionist period" of the NBP, this cult of heroism was associated with the attempt at "conquering" public spaces for the expression of political dissent. In a period of widespread political passivity, the *natsboly* paid for their active opposition to Putin's government with unjust prison sentences, beatings, and in certain instances with their own lives.[41] In this period, NBP activists were frequently attacked and brutally beaten by violent groups of soccer ultras hired by pro-government youth organizations like Nashi, and the party headquarters were raided several times. Isolated *natsboly* were regularly ambushed and beaten to death, with serious allegations that undercover members of the police were actually directly involved in these attacks.[42] A cult of heroism and martyrdom also informed the type of public performances and political activism that the *natsboly* practiced, with a deep impact on the later wave of Russian "art-activism," exemplified by the art collectives Voina and Pussy Riot.

The Invention of Post-Soviet Protest Culture

Some of the earliest direct actions organized by the NBP, like the "Sevastopol operation" and the "Riga operation," focused on defending the rights of the Russian minorities in former Soviet republics, a cause that played an important role in the agenda of the NBP since its foundation. Later, the actions addressed more specifically questions of social justice and freedom of speech. These direct actions were very carefully staged and organized. During the action in Sevastopol, the *natsboly* occupied the top of a thirty-six-meter tower overlooking the

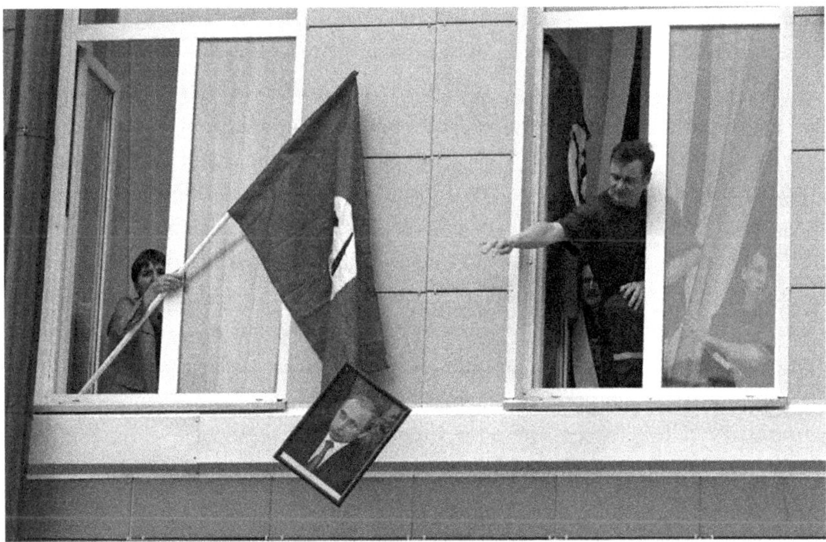

Figure 22. A famous example of a direct action organized by the NBP in Moscow in 2004: the occupation of the Ministry of Health featuring a symbolic "defenestration" of Putin.

town. From there, they dropped copies of *Limonka* and flyers calling for a return of the city to the Russian territory, all while playing Bach from a speaker. During the occupation of the Ministry of Health in Moscow, one of the activists threw a portrait of Putin out of the window while surrounded by NBP flags hanging from the governmental building. The resulting photograph became a sort of icon of the resistance against Putin's corrupt and repressive regime and, although it looks perfectly natural, was actually staged: the activist himself brought the portrait to the building to enact Putin's symbolic defenestration (see fig. 22).[43]

The capture (*zakhvat*) of the Ministry of Health in Moscow—organized to protest drastic cuts to benefits for veterans and people with disabilities—and the occupation of the Presidential Reception Office in 2004 were the two actions that established the reputation of the NBP as a leading oppositional force in Russian society. The action at the Presidential Reception Office, in particular, played a crucial role in establishing the image of the young *natsboly* as political martyrs and heroic victims of Putin's repressive regime, and it contributed to the public's understanding of political and personal freedom (or lack thereof) in Putin's Russia.

On December 14, 2004, the *natsboly* occupied the Presidential Reception Office for forty minutes, all the while shouting the slogan "Putin, get out yourself!" (*Putin, uidi sam!*), before being forcefully dragged out of the building and arrested. Holding copies of the Russian constitution and a list of complaints, they demanded a meeting with the president. In the list, the *natsboly* indicated the main reasons Putin should resign: the falsification of both parliamentary and presidential elections; the governmental ban on or acquisition of most independent media in Russia; the casualties suffered in the terrorist attacks at the Nord-Ost Theater in Moscow and the elementary school in Beslan—for which the *natsboly* blamed Putin's disastrous politics in Chechnya; Putin's interference in the elections in Abkhazia and Ukraine; and his systematic repression of political opponents. The action took place on the anniversary of the famous Decembrist uprising of 1825, when a group of Russian officers led a protest against the newly crowned Tsar Nikolai I, challenging the legitimacy of his succession to the throne. Like the original Decembrists, the *natsboly* accused Putin, whom they called "successor to the throne" (*naslednik prestola*), of having been unlawfully handed the Russian presidency by Yeltsin, depriving the Russian people of the right to choose their president. The *natsboly* who participated in the action were arrested, brutally beaten by the police, and condemned to one and a half to three and a half years in prison. The sentences of thirty-one out of forty participants were suspended; the remaining activists had to serve their sentences in a penal colony.

During the long trial against the "Decembrists," the famous journalist and writer Anna Politkovskaya had a key role in drawing the public's attention to the unjust persecution of the *natsboly*. Politkovskaya herself fought relentlessly against the injustices and abuses that Putin routinely committed while consolidating his power. Her investigative journalism exposed the widespread corruption and political repression perpetrated by Russian officials and the systematic violation of human rights in Chechnya.

In her coverage of the trial against the *natsboly*, Politkovskaya underscored that the harsh punishments and methodical persecution of the young activists signaled the establishment of an authoritarian system of government in Russia. Like the trial against Mikhail Khodorkovsky, the prosecution of the *natsboly* was a symptom of the arbitrary and repressive nature of the Russian legal system, which clearly could be used to stifle political opponents.[44] Politkovskaya also pointed out that the case of Khodorkovsky constituted an example of the persecution of the financial and political elites, whereas in the case of the NBP the government was persecuting "poor and disenfranchised students." Because of this, she accused independent media of not devoting enough attention to the case.[45]

The protests organized by the NBP were particularly important public statements in the otherwise politically stagnant climate of Putin's first two terms in office. It was at this time that the Russian leader, in part thanks to the wealth granted by the rise of oil and gas prices, and in part because of the "political apathy" inherited from the 1990s, was able to dismantle civil society and democratic institutions and establish a form of capitalist authoritarianism in the country. This system was authoritarian from the point of view of civil rights and freedom of expression and neoliberal in terms of economic policies. At the time, the mainstream media, which were gradually being taken over by the state, disseminated the idea of a gradual "stabilization" and normalization of life according to a Western standard under Putin's strong and decisive leadership. In continuity with the culture of the Yeltsin period, the transition to neoliberalism and, implicitly, to Putin's authoritarian rule, was also commonly accepted as a "natural," nonideological process that did not require public discussion or debate.[46] In opposition to this dominant view, NBP activists proposed the return to "old-fashioned," and at times extreme, ideological narratives, and they produced new creative ways of aggressively "conquering" the Russian public sphere and political arena. Although they always defined themselves as an anti-liberal and antidemocratic movement, the *natsboly* by and large ended up promoting "the broadening of the political space," and the production of alternative discourses and historical narratives.

In this sense, the history of NBP direct actions is closely connected with the tradition of Russian art actionism and, in general, with the post-Soviet tendency to use performance and visual art for political contestation and debate as a way to compensate for the generally scarce opportunities for public discussion and political participation in contemporary Russian society.[47] In particular, the history of the NBP is closely linked with the tradition of Moscow Actionism, from Osmolovsky's art collective E.T.I. to the actions of the art collective Voina and the now internationally renowned Pussy Riot, which was founded by former members of Voina and could be considered, to a certain extent, its continuation. Voina was a leftist art collective that continued the legacy and radicalized the strategies of Moscow Conceptualism, combining art performance with political protest and vandalism. Although it had started as a largely marginal anarchist group of young artists living in a commune, practicing ethical shoplifting and tipping over police cars as a form of protest against global capital, in 2008 Voina began to draw attention from the media and the art world with their provocative political art performances. Their increasing recognition culminated in them being awarded the prestigious Innovation Prize for art in 2011.[48]

Several examples illustrate the close connections and mutual influences characterizing these different cultural and political formations. In one of their very first actions in Moscow, realized in collaboration with the radical performance artist Oleg Mavromatti, the *natsboly* staged a mutiny at a local McDonald's for the artist's video art project *Tainaia estetika marsianskikh shpionov* (The mysterious aesthetics of the Martian spies, 1997–99). As a signal to start the action, one of the activists shouted "Bratsy, chervi!" (Brothers, worms!) a reference to the beginning of the mutiny on the battleship *Potemkin*, which inspired Eisenstein's homonymous film (1925). The *natsboly* then proceeded to vandalize the premises, while Mavromatti shot the sequence from the outside.

When the organization of direct actions became one of the NBP's main activities, Osmolovsky, a veteran of political performance, taught several classes about the history of art actionism at the Bunker so that the *natsboly* could stage their actions in an effective way from the standpoint of both aesthetics and media coverage.[49] When the art collective Voina, and later Pussy Riot, decided to bring art back to the streets and started the most recent wave of "art-activism," they took the NBP as a fundamental source of inspiration.[50] In fact, one might argue that the new radical aesthetics of Voina started as a combination of the tradition of Moscow Conceptualism and the uncompromising radicalism of the NBP.

Voina was formed in 2007, the same year NBP was banned. The art collective clearly took its inspiration not only from the Moscow Conceptualists but also from Limonov and the NBP. Nadia Tolokonnikova, one of the founders of Voina and Pussy Riot, once stated that the first political performance that she organized as a teenager was inspired by the NBP's occupation of the Presidential Reception Office in 2004 and conceived as an expression of solidarity with the *natsboly* who had been unjustly arrested.[51] Refusing to define themselves as "contemporary artists," the members of Voina preferred instead to be identified as "real political activists": "we had a common background: an obvious sympathy for the culture of rebellion, and the reluctance to find our place on the map of existing art and political systems. In addition, we all shared a list of key-figures: these were Andrey Monastyrsky, Dmitry Aleksandrovich Prigov, Aleksandr Brener, Eduard Limonadze."[52] The strong link with radical politics, and with the NBP in particular, was also reflected in the structure and organization of Voina, which its members saw as a "group of pioneers" and a "sect-like art-group" that at least theoretically followed collectivist and egalitarian principles. Like a political organization, Voina was supposed to be open to anyone who was interested in joining.[53]

Another political action by Voina that illustrates its collaborative ties with the NBP was a public performance in which Anton Nikolaev, one of the group's cofounders, demonstratively joined the party in sign of protest against its legal ban. With the help of a member of the NBP, Nikolaev signed the application, was handed the party membership card, and recited "the prayer of the *natsbol*" in front of the flag of the party: "I, warrior of the NBP, greet the new day. / And at this time of unity with the party I am with my brothers! / I feel the powerful strength of all the brothers of the party, / No matter where they are now. / Let my blood flow into the blood of the party, / Let us become one body. Yes, Death!"[54] Nikolaev explained that "the fact that they banned the NBP is already a good enough reason to join. However, I also happen to be in many ways close to the ideas of the National Bolsheviks." The idea for the performance was inspired by a conversation between Nikolaev and another member of the collective, Oleg Vorotnikov, during which Nikolaev concluded that to prove his commitment to radical art he needed to become part of a radical organization. Nikolaev never actually became an activist of the NBP, but after joining he did participate in some of the party's activities and discussions and regularly attended the weekly party meetings for some time.[55]

Despite the radical differences between NBP actionism and the wave of art performances by Voina and Pussy Riot (and, most recently, Petr Pavlensky), there are nevertheless important similarities and examples of mutual influence between these two movements. Like the NBP (although in a different way) Voina and Pussy Riot systematically crossed the boundaries between art production and political activism and were created in reaction to a period of drastic limitations to freedom of expression and political dissent. Also, like the direct actions organized by the NBP, the radical performances of Voina and Pussy Riot pushed the limits of what is socially, morally, and legally accepted in order to create new spaces for public debate and political contestation.

■

In terms of its political actions and influence on other cultural and political movements, the NBP played a crucial role in the shaping of post-Soviet protest culture. In the long period of fundamental "political apathy" that pervaded Russian society between the parliamentary crisis of 1993 and the 2011–12 wave of protests "for fair elections," the NBP functioned as an artistic and political avant-garde, producing new forms of counterculture and experimentations in radical politics and mass mobilization.[56] As a cultural and political movement that fundamentally opposed Russia's abrupt transition to capitalism, the NBP combined elements of "the artistic critique" and "the social critique" of the capitalist system. Within this political community, the "search for authenticity" and the protest against late capitalism occurred through forms of political militancy, connected in different ways with the sphere of physical experience, including art performance, protest actions, and war.

The NBP started as a bohemian art project that by and large took the form of a provocative intellectual game involving the appropriation and reinvention of radical political symbols and ideas. Over the years, new generations of *natsboly* embraced a revolutionary lifestyle and system of values based on a utopian cult of heroism, death, and personal sacrifice for the collective cause of the party. The ideology of the NBP was generally inconsistent, and the community tried to co-opt aggressive and violent impulses in Russian society through various forms of cultural and political radicalism. By drawing in people from all kinds of radical movements and subcultures, including ultranationalists, radical leftists and anarchists, punks, members of heavy metal subcultures, and soccer hooligans, the NBP became associated with rhetoric that included a diverse range of discourses and ideological positions: some of these were subversive and emancipatory, some were apolitical or detached, and still others could have strong sexist or xenophobic overtones. In general, a form of aggressive sexuality and aggressive masculinity played an important role in determining the identity of the movement.

Violence and aggression within the NBP, however, were generally channeled against the state and its repressive apparatuses. After Putin's rise to power, this collective rebellion primarily took the form of peaceful direct actions aimed at drawing attention to the authoritarian nature of Putin's regime. Despite their aggressive rhetoric, the *natsboly* were seldom the perpetrators of violence; they more often became the victims of violence, and of state violence in particular. In fact, the *natsboly* cultivated a form of political martyrdom; their direct actions were designed to cause a violent reaction from the authorities in order to draw the public's attention to the fundamentally authoritarian nature of the Russian political system.

As a political and intellectual community, the NBP contributed to the creation of new forms of political dissent, and it challenged common assumptions about power and the post-Soviet transition to capitalism. It produced alternative forms of cultural production and alternative lifestyles, which resisted mainstream politics and culture. Particularly for young men and women coming from a position of socioeconomic disadvantage, the NBP provided an opportunity for self-realization and a platform for political discussion and contestation, something extremely rare in the context of post-Soviet culture and society. In the following chapters, we will see how certain elements of the culture of this organization, through the public activity of Aleksandr Dugin and the Eurasia Movement, also paradoxically contributed to the formation of state ideology and the circulation of conservative discourses during the Putin era.

4

Aleksandr Dugin's Conservative Postmodernism

> The postmodern intellectual . . . does not look for meaning, he operates with meanings. He is free of ethical and aesthetic connotations [*sic*]. Like a DJ, he brings together different semantic systems into the general intellectual rhythm. . . . He is informed rather than engaged, he is "up to date" but he does not "believe." . . . [He] considers "truth" as something superfluous, he factors it out. . . . The intellectual is indifferent to scientific truth. He turns to it only "ironically." Nietzsche wrote that "the last people," when they hear the word "truth," will blink and say: "what is truth?" This is about the intellectuals. More likely, they will yawn.
>
> Aleksandr Dugin, *Geopolitika postmoderna*

Aleksandr Dugin's excerpt about the typical "postmodern intellectual," quoted in the epigraph above, could be seen, with a certain amount of (self-)irony, as an effective parody of Western academia in a post-ideological age. The image of the cultural "DJ" who freely "brings together different semantic systems into the general intellectual rhythm" aptly captures the condition of contemporary highly professionalized scholars and public intellectuals, who, instead of following or believing in a higher national, religious, or scientific truth, or in a scholarly mission, freely combine theories and political trends in order to produce educational "services" and forms of cultural entertainment.[1] At the same time, one could also turn the parody against its creator. It is easy to see the archetype of the cynical conservative thinker, which Dugin himself embodies and aspires to, as a radicalized version of the bored "intellectual DJ" at the brink of the apocalypse whom he parodies in this passage.

Dugin, the Russian fringe nationalist philosopher who cofounded the NBP, widely known today as the leader of the Eurasia Movement, has acted, both in Russia and on the international stage, as the second-world ultranationalist version of the postmodern intellectual, combining the latest and most fashionable philosophical ideas with the thrill of street politics, counterculture, media manipulation, trolling, and political violence. Soon after leaving the NBP, Dugin became a vocal supporter of the Putin administration and founded the Eurasia Movement and the Eurasian Youth Union (Evraziiskii soiuz molodezhi, or ESM), two pro-government organizations that actively promoted repressive measures against the liberal opposition. He also started exerting an influence on Russian foreign policy through connections in the Russian military, while at the same time developing an international network of far-right organizations in Western Europe, the United States, and South America.[2] In 2008, he managed to achieve academic recognition, becoming a professor in the very corrupt and politically conservative Department of Sociology at Moscow State University, only to be removed from the position in the summer of 2014 after a public call to "kill, kill, kill" in response to the Odessa clashes of May 2, 2014, when forty-two pro-Russian activists died while trapped inside a burning building.[3]

Dugin's scholarly output verges on graphomania, with more than fifty-four published books and a myriad of articles on topics ranging from Russian history, literature, and geopolitics to art performance, alternative rock, and pop culture.[4] In recent years, he has been regularly invited to wear the hat of "the political expert" or "the sociology professor" to speak about the latest news on Russian mainstream television, without any reference to his political background. His political organizations, the Eurasia Movement and the Eurasian Youth Union, have a massive presence on the Russian internet, with several websites, online TV channels, journals, bookstores, and publishing houses. Through this network, these movements have actively contributed to the circulation of conspiracy theories about the existence of a Western plot aimed at destroying Russian culture and civilization and about the presence of a "fifth column" within Russian society, made up of the Russian liberal intelligentsia, independent media, and Western NGOs.[5] As radical representatives of the conservative camp, Dugin and the Eurasia Movement have actively contributed to the shaping of a mainstream official public discourse during the Putin era. They have cooperated with the Russian government at the levels of propaganda, repression of the political opposition, street and grassroots politics, and, to an extent, military strategy. Just to mention a few examples, Dugin influenced Russian media portrayals of the Russo-Georgian war in 2008, and he was one of the conservative leaders supporting the repression of the 2011–12 movement "for fair elections." He also had an important role in the recent Ukrainian crisis, giving ideological and logistical support to the annexation of Crimea, calling for a full-force Russian invasion of the country, and maintaining contact with separatist movements in Eastern Ukraine.[6] In part because of Dugin's own aggressive rhetoric, his self-promoting tactics, and the Eurasianists' massive presence on the Russian media and blogosphere, Western commentators have often described him, wildly exaggerating his political role, as the Kremlin's chief ideologue and the mastermind behind Putin's regime.[7] Dugin's influence on Russian politics is real, but it mainly operates at the level of language and public culture rather than at the policymaking level, and his ideology can hardly be identified with that of Putin's government.

Rather than in the original Eurasianists of the 1920s and 1930s, the main sources of Dugin's ideology are to be found in the writings of such representatives of the French and European New Right as Alain de Benoist and Jean Thiriart, and in the works of classic traditionalist thinkers René Guénon and Julius Evola.[8] This connection, among other things (including Dugin's weakness for various forms of "mystical Nazism"), has motivated scholars to debate the possibility of classifying Dugin's ideology as fascist or neofascist, seeing it as a possible symptom of the imminent rise of a violent totalitarian regime in post-Soviet Russia.[9] However, the list of Dugin's cultural references, spanning from Martin Heidegger to Guy Debord, is so long, and his public statements so contradictory, that it is hard to pinpoint his exact political views. To borrow Limonov's own words, Dugin should be seen primarily as a "storyteller," with a great memory for scholarly ideas and the ability to present topics to his audience in a "poetic and inspired way."[10] The "originality" of Dugin's work, and its influence on the development of contemporary Russian politics and public culture, lies in the ways in which this fringe political thinker has appropriated and combined a multiplicity of (often apparently incompatible) ideas and has made them part of a specific cultural strategy and political practice. It is not possible to fully understand Dugin's work and public activity without looking at the "conditions of its production," and at its position in relation to power structures, larger socioeconomic trends, and global and local value systems. As Marlène Laruelle points out, "historically, the study of Russian nationalism has been part of the field of political philosophy, with the focus on ideas and concepts, their intellectual legacies and logical order. We are thus still lacking a sociology of intellectual life in Russia and an 'ecology' of the places of its production."[11]

Indeed, Dugin's work should be primarily seen as a form of public performance or "story-telling." In this regard, the connection between his politics and ideas surrounding the concepts of postmodernism, globalization, and the postindustrial society is particularly revealing. Dugin's neo-Eurasianism represents in fact a specific form of conservative or reactionary postmodernism, which manifests itself, first and foremost, as a method informing both the writing style and the public performances of this self-taught conservative thinker, countercultural figure, and media personality. Throughout his career, Dugin has literally (and quite consciously) treated politics as a form of postmodern performance, carefully choosing and combining "the most dangerous" ideas and political movements, and those capable of producing the most violent and radical forms of social change.

In the aftermath of the fall of the Soviet Union, Dugin appropriated, through the mediation of the French *Nouvelle Droite*, the ideas and methods of critical theory, using them as a tool in a cultural and geopolitical struggle against capitalism and Western liberalism. Later, his specific form of neo-Eurasianism turned into an experiment in political technology that involved supporting Putin's regime through mass media and pro-government grassroots organizations.[12] In this period, Dugin also formulated his own radical conservative vision of the postmodern project. Dugin sees in postmodernity and "the end of history" an opportunity to accelerate an allegedly already imminent apocalypse through a global revolution fought under the banners of hierarchy, collectivism, and mystical socialism. The development of this specifically Russian version of a conservative postmodern political project follows an intellectual trajectory from West to East and back. In the 1990s, Dugin assimilated and produced a collage of ideas from Western political philosophy and critical theory, contributing to the circulation of these ideas among the Russian public. More recently, his own conservative revolutionary postmodernism has influenced international politics in unexpected ways. It has contributed, among other things, to the emergence of the so-called American alt-right and to the widespread paradoxical vision of Russia as a stronghold of conservative values and a last line of resistance against the triumph of consumer culture and globalization. In the process, Dugin's neo-imperialist project has subversively co-opted ideas and values belonging to the radical left and the anti-globalization movement.[13]

Postmodernism and Its Double

The idea of a close, ambiguous connection between the postmodern condition and cultural and political conservatism is not new. In the sphere of architecture, for instance, postmodernism emerges as a "reaction" to the utopian—and, potentially, totalitarian—impulse of high modernism. The language of postmodern architecture is closely connected with the ideas of historicism and neoclassicism, and is identified with the style and methods of "actually existing" public and commercial spaces. On the one hand, in part as a consequence to the failure of modern mass housing, postmodern architecture reacts against modernism's elitism and disregard for the collective experience of existing communities in favor of more sustainable forms of living. On the other hand, it negates the revolutionary spirit of modernist architecture, making a conscious effort to return to more traditional, populist, and conventional forms.[14]

A similar ambiguity informs the relationship between postmodernism and conservatism in the spheres of art and politics. Some of the leading theoreticians of postmodernity grappled with this fundamental contradiction. On the one hand, postmodern art forms emerged as a reaction to the elitism of the historical avant-gardes—which by the second half of the twentieth century had become fully canonized within academic culture—and favored more accessible and democratic aesthetic principles. On the other hand, the emergence of postmodern culture has been frequently associated with a turn toward populism and the complete and final commodification of Western culture and society.

Many identify this late capitalist turn with a new subtle form of totalitarian rule. For Fredric Jameson, the postmodern embodies the highest stage of the "culture industry," which Adorno and Horkheimer saw as fulfilling a function of totalitarian control over the population within capitalist relations of production. Significantly, Jameson compares the postmodern "immense dilation" of the sphere of culture, and its commodification, to the "aestheticization of politics" (or "aestheticization of reality"), which Walter Benjamin saw (with reference to the rise of Mussolini in Italy and Hitler in Germany) as the main feature of fascism.[15]

The postmodern condition is also generally associated with the end of history and ideology, and the beginning of a postindustrial, hyperrationalized technocratic age.[16] On a local and global scale, this coincides with prophecies about the triumph and "normalization" of liberalism and the free market. At this point, capitalism and Western democracy become cultural mythologies; they are "naturalized."[17] In the 1950s, the sociologist Daniel Bell famously saw the sphere of culture, and counterculture in particular, as the only obstacle to the full development of a technocratic, post-ideological rule in the United States.[18] At the level of foreign policy, this translated into Francis Fukuyama's later prophecy about the final global victory of capitalism and liberal democracy over any other political system after 1989.

If the emergence of a postindustrial society is seen as coinciding with the global victory of a postmodern, subtly repressive, and ideologically conservative capitalist rule, then the resistance to this state of affairs is connected with both leftist and localist, identitarian, or traditional communities and modes of expression. This is reflected in Samuel Huntington's oft-cited definition of the

New World Order as a "clash of civilizations" but also, in a different way, in David Harvey's vision of the postmodern condition as a dialectic of space, in which global capital is "continually reterritorializing with one hand what it was deterritorializing with the other."[19]

> Movements of all sorts—religious, mystical, social, communitarian, humanitarian, etc.—define themselves directly in terms of antagonism to the power of money and of rationalized conceptions of space and time over daily life. . . . Much of the color and ferment of social movements . . . as well as of artistic and other cultural practices . . . derives precisely from the infinitely varied texture of oppositions to the materialization of money, space, and time, under conditions of capitalist hegemony.[20]

Postmodernism (as the cultural embodiment of a "global capitalist hegemony," if we are to accept such a definition) emerges as a force that is both emancipatory and repressive and that challenges traditional hierarchies, values, and beliefs. It creates opportunities for new forms of individual and collective freedom and at the same time deprives local communities of their identities through the imposition of a global, standardized worldview and way of life. However, while functioning as an instrument of global capitalist hegemony, one might argue, postmodern culture (in all of its forms) also challenges the foundations of the Enlightenment, of Western civilization, and of global consumerist culture itself, by reducing all grand narratives to pure signifiers within particular "language-games."[21]

Herein lies a fundamental contradiction within late capitalist culture, which swallows, reappropriates, and "de-ideologizes" any form of political conviction or belief and, as a consequence, any opposition to the status quo. Over the past few decades, corporate culture has seemingly assimilated the values of the 1968 revolutions—and their bohemianism and revolutionary appeal—by paradoxically and perversely promoting individual freedom, creativity, mobility, *and* precarity as instruments of social, economic, and political control.[22] In a similar vein, Michael Hardt and Antonio Negri argue that in the context of the new globalized system of production, direct control over labor has been replaced by a more subtle and fragmentary form of capitalist control over sheer life and desire.[23] Under these circumstances, revolutionary practice cannot involve resisting or challenging the globalizing process of postmodernity but embracing it and bringing it to its most extreme consequences.[24] Realizing a "counter-Empire" and "counter-globalization" is only possible by strategically appropriating and exploiting the atomism, fragmentariness, and "de-territorialization" of global capitalism against global capitalism itself. The "multitude" generated by the new global system of production would accomplish this "nomadism," "barbarianism," and "miscegenation" by freely crossing spatial boundaries and boundaries of gender, race, and social class.[25]

This same issue—that of the ambiguous connections between postmodern culture, populism, the emergence of a postindustrial society, and the growing power of global capital—affects all major theorists of postmodernity dealing with the political consequences of scholarship and cultural production. Hal Foster famously argued for the creation of a "postmodernism of resistance," in contrast with, and opposition to, a "postmodernism of reaction." Jürgen Habermas advocated for a return to the values of the Enlightenment and for a recuperation of the "unfinished project of modernity."[26]

Today, with the rise of explicitly illiberal, nationalistic, authoritarian, and anti-global political projects across Europe and the United States, the call to create a "postmodernism of resistance" but also to elaborate an understanding of the postmodern condition that goes beyond the boundaries of Western culture and society appears to be even more relevant. In the United States, in particular, the so-called alt-right, the fringe reactionary movement that became unexpectedly part of the mainstream during Donald Trump's presidential campaign in 2016, has clearly proven to Western audiences that postmodern irony, critical theory, and protest culture can be co-opted even by the extreme right, often in the distorted and perverted form of trolling and publicity stunts. Dugin had a significant role in the emergence and popularization of this new form of "postmodernism of reaction."

The "Establishment Conservative's Guide to the Alt-Right," the unofficial manifesto of this largely virtual movement, co-authored by Allum Bokhari and Milo Yiannopoulos and published by Breitbart News (at that time under the direction of Stephen Bannon—Donald Trump's former "chief strategist"), illustrates how the American alt-right's "postmodernism of reaction" embraces similarly contradictory positions: racial and gender diversity and gay culture, along with anti-egalitarian and reactionary ideologies, white masculinity, libertarianism, anti-political correctness (including jokes and internet memes about the Holocaust), and anti-feminism.[27] The authors clearly aim at promoting radical conservatism as a new form of counterculture and postmodern provocation, by identifying themselves with "young rebels . . . [who are] drawn to the alt-right for the same reason that young Baby Boomers were drawn to the New Left in the 1960s: because it promises fun, transgression, and a challenge to social norms they just don't understand."[28]

Breitbart News itself, defined by Bannon as a platform for the alt-right—and frequently accused (not without reason) of promoting racism and antisemitism—started out as a Zionist, "unapologetically pro-freedom and pro-Israel" news platform.[29] Bannon has called himself a "Leninist," determined to "destroy the state" and "all of today's establishment."[30] In 2016, Milo Yiannopoulos, a self-proclaimed internet troll and member of the alt-right, was popularizing a new form of queer nationalism based on internet memes, trolling, and uber-camp performances. These included a "Dangerous Faggot Tour" of lectures organized by conservative student organizations across American colleges, which pushed and broke the boundaries of free speech on campuses in a way that was often offensive, particularly to female, minority, gay, and transgender students.[31] In certain cases—most famously at UC Berkeley—Yiannopoulos's scandalous lectures had to be canceled because of violent student demonstrations.[32] Incidentally, Bannon, along with many other leaders of the alt-right, sees Dugin, along with Julius Evola and other more recent neoreactionary authors, as a source of inspiration.[33]

However, beyond a shared passion for fringe right-wing mystical writers and conspiracy theories, it is in the fields of postmodern provocation and political technology that American right-wingers learned their most important lessons from Dugin and his radical neo-conservative crowd.

Postmodernism, or, the Cultural Logic of Late Socialism?

Dugin's theorizing about postmodern culture and his political strategy cannot be fully understood without taking into consideration the specific meanings that postmodernism and postmodernity assume in the context of contemporary Russian culture and society, and, in particular, the close connection between postmodernism and the post-Soviet experience. Russia was seemingly excluded from Western theorizing on the postmodern condition, late capitalism, and postindustrial economies until the fall of the Soviet Union. However, at the same time, during the late Soviet and post-Soviet period, postmodern art and literary forms (or what came to be so defined) became predominant, first within the underground circles of Moscow and Saint Petersburg, and later in the context of the newly born post-Soviet art and literary market. A postmodern sensibility appeared to be the most apt to capture and conceptualize the skepticism, dark ironic detachment, and ideological disengagement that characterized the decline and fall of the socialist project.[34]

According to many, postmodern art also represented a form of resistance against the repressive and monolithic Soviet state apparatus and propaganda. Boris Groys argues that Sots Art and Moscow Conceptualism—two late Soviet literary and art movements whose members produced ironic deconstructions of Soviet visual and linguistic mythologemes—should be seen as examples of "postutopian art." According to Groys, in contrast to the demiurgic impulse of the historical avant-gardes and Stalinism's totalitarian transformation of reality "on the basis of a unitary artistic plan," artists and poets like Dmitry Prigov, Lev Rubinstein, Ilya Kabakov, Vitaly Komar and Aleksandr Melamid, and Erik Bulatov consciously avoided reproducing or assimilating any kind of hegemonic discourse. Instead, being aware that any form of oppositional art is potentially totalitarian in nature, these artists produced a form of "postutopian," or fully de-ideologized art, based on a reflection about the artistic will to power itself, and, as a consequence, about the experience and failure of the Stalinist project.[35]

The absolute predominance in every sphere of Soviet culture and reality of a socialist realist aesthetics, which had little or no connection to the everyday experience of Soviet individuals, also perfectly coincided with Western conceptions about late capitalism as an "immense accumulation of spectacles" or a "reign of simulacra."[36] Stalin's "lacquering of reality" appeared to be surprisingly similar to Horkheimer and Adorno's "culture industry."[37] This is why Mikhail Epstein, a prominent theoretician of Russian postmodernism, provocatively defines postmodernism as an inherently Russian phenomenon. According to Epstein—who "essentializes" postmodernism, identifying it, in fact, with the Russian national identity—postmodern hyperreality is a fundamental component of the Russian cultural tradition that preceded Baudrillard's ideas on the postindustrial society by several centuries. Because of its unique position between West and East, Russia absorbed elements of both the Western spiritual system, which "originates from empirical reality and explains all apparent illusions as its own handiwork," and the Eastern spiritual system, where "all reality is illusory, a product interwoven of the many-colored veil of Maya, which must be cast off to reveal Absolute Nothingness."[38] Because of this, Epstein argues, Western symbols and beliefs manifested themselves in Russia in the form of pure simulacra, whose existence was perpetually questioned and denied. These simulacra included Christianity, a religion imported from abroad and imposed on the Russian people, even though it had no connection with their traditions and reality; Peter the Great's Westernization of Russian society; the myth of Saint Petersburg, which Pushkin, Gogol, and Dostoevsky depicted as a fundamentally artificial, ghostly, and "unreal" city; and Marxism, which, as "the only theoretical viewpoint to be sanctioned by the Soviet regime," came to "incorporate all other types of discourses. Internationalists and patriots, liberals and conservatives, existentialists and structuralists, technocrats and ecologists all pretended to be genuine Marxists."[39] The Russian postmodern tradition culminated with Socialist Realism, the Soviet official artistic norm that created a "hyperreality that is neither truthful nor false, but *becomes* reality for millions of people" and which produced a "pastiche of many ideologies and philosophies," the combination of "classicist, romantic, realist and futuristic models," the "erasure of the opposition between elitist and mass culture," and the "attempt to construct a posthistorical space where all great discourses of the past should find their ultimate resolution."[40]

During the post-Soviet period, Russian postmodern literature became canonized. The two authors who came to embody the post-Soviet transition, the two "monuments" of post-Soviet literature, are Vladimir Sorokin and Viktor Pelevin, writers who brought the aesthetics of the late Soviet underground into the mainstream by producing ironic stylistic patchworks of Soviet propaganda, pop culture, Eastern philosophy, and the classics of Russian literature. The protagonists of Sorokin's and Pelevin's novels mostly experience reality as a consumeristic semiotic overload that degenerates into cognitive dissonance and a complete loss of identity.[41]

With Putin's rise to power at the beginning of the 2000s, the Russian postmodern sensibility seemed to extend from the sphere of art and literature to that of politics and public life.[42] Because of the lack of transparency, manipulation of public opinion through state-owned mass media, and increased government control over civil society and political parties, scholars and pundits have often described Russian society and public life under Putin as the reign of virtual politics and triumphant postmodernism.[43] In Russia, postmodernism has gradually turned into a cultural paradigm encompassing both oppositional culture and state ideology, both progressive and reactionary tendencies within society.

In part because of Russia's historical logocentrism, literature took the lead in this popularization of right-wing postmodernism. Patriotic and conservative artists drawing on the tradition of Russian postmodern fiction and ironically exploiting its themes and devices entered the Russian literary mainstream. The "Red-Brown" novelist and publicist Aleksandr Prokhanov, the longtime editor in chief of the far-right publication *Zavtra* (Tomorrow), published the bestseller *Mr. Hexogen*, which combined feuilleton, dystopian spy fiction, nationalist conspiracy theories, Soviet communism, and Russian orthodoxy and messianism.[44] Pavel Krusanov, a former member of the Leningrad art and music subcultures, drawing on Dugin's own neo-Eurasianist conceptions and on Pelevin's and Sorokin's alternative histories, began publishing successful neo-imperialist fantasies. These typically depicted future geopolitical conflicts between American Atlanticist and Russian Eurasianist forces with a strong parodic flavor and references to the Saint Petersburg countercultural scene. Krusanov also became the leader of a group of writers and intellectuals named the Petersburg Fundamentalists, which fought against political correctness and advocated for Russia's return to its past imperial glory.[45] A few years later, in 2008, Mikhail Elizarov, a young writer who expressed publicly his sympathy toward Stalinism and other illiberal and totalitarian ideologies, was awarded the Russian Booker Prize for another dystopian account of Russian politics, *The Librarian*, which depicted a secret ongoing war to achieve control over original copies of socialist realist novels, endowed in the novel with supernatural powers.[46] Finally, even Vladislav Surkov, arguably the true "mastermind" behind Putin's brand of authoritarian neoliberalism, and the inventor of the famous slogan "sovereign democracy," made his own contribution to the Russian postmodern canon, publishing (under a pseudonym) the novel *Okolonolia* (*Almost Zero*), a similar logocentric dystopian conspiracy, or a parody of a parody, portraying Russian politics and mass media as a bloody war between "bookkeepers," "speechwriters," and "cinephiles."[47]

In relation to the "conservative turn" in (late) Russian postmodern culture and society, Mark Lipovetsky distinguishes between, on the one hand, an "authentic postmodernism," which challenges and reveals the contradictions of "revolutionary and conservative utopias, of Stalinist 'archaic modernity,' and of the liberalism of the 1960s," and, on the other hand, a postmodernism of pretense, which turns into a form of "*pseudo-deideologization*" and uses the "postmodern mask of irony" to promote and legitimize neotraditionalist, premodern, authoritarian, and xenophobic discourses.[48] In fact, far from "hiding behind the postmodern mask," many Russian conservative artists and intellectuals fully embraced postmodern contradictions and paradoxes and made them an essential component of their lifestyle and ideological vocabulary. Most of the writers, artists, and public figures who wore "the postmodern mask of irony" to promote various forms of anti-Western or neotraditionalist discourses started doing so in the wake of the neoliberal reforms of the 1990s. Their "postmodern conservatism" was therefore conceived as a discourse of resistance, not as an official, institutional one. Even now, as Laruelle points out, not all actors in the nationalist or conservative camp are fully aligned with Russian pro-government positions, but they are instead divided into "nonstate actors, whose agenda is anti-Putin; parastate actors, who have their own ideological niche, not always in tune with the presidential administration's narrative, but who operate under the state umbrella; and state actors, in particular, the presidential administration."[49] Such subdivisions can be applied to political leaders and movements and to conservative artists and public intellectuals.

From the perspective of global sociopolitical trends, it is also clear that most of these artists and thinkers conceived the promotion of anti-Western and imperialist aesthetics and ideologies in their work as a specific form of counterculture. "De-ideologization" is also, in and of itself, a slippery concept, and one that can be used to promote surreptitious forms of exclusion, injustice, and political repression. While the concept did inform some specific forms of resistance to the hyper-ideologized Soviet state, Putin's government also presents itself as "de-ideologized" or "unideological," in the sense that it aspires to embody a specific model of Western managerial efficiency. The eclectic combination of corporate and patriotic rhetoric in Surkov's pro-government movement Nashi is a very good example of this.[50] Dugin, one of the main ideologists and inspirators of this "conservative postmodern turn" in Russian culture and politics, who planned to "defeat postmodernism" and ended up being one of the most perfect incarnations of postmodern politics, represents one of the most revealing examples of this larger trend.

Conservative Postmodernism as a Method

Following Benedict Anderson, one might argue that nationalism and national identity are more about the production of collective narratives than about political theory. Dugin's work and public activity, in particular, are based on an eclectic combination of symbols and ideas aimed at producing an alternative version of Russian national or imperial identity. His brand of conservative postmodernism should be considered, first and foremost, a "method" that has largely informed his writing, public performances, and political strategy. Through this method, Dugin has created a particular countercultural paradigm that has contributed to the circulation of an image and idea of Putin's Russia as an "anti-imperialist empire," to borrow Nancy Condee's definition of the Soviet paradoxical position as both subject and object of Orientalism and colonization.[51]

Dugin's conservative postmodernism cannot be fully appreciated without considering his key role as a popularizer of radical political ideas that could advocate for the most violent forms of political repression and at the same time call for a global anti-capitalist revolution. As the poet and left-wing political activist Kirill Medvedev puts it:

> [During the 1990s] politics became a giant blanket onto which Dugin tossed all sort of interesting stuff, from the far right to the far left . . . [creating] a paradigm that incorporated many different tendencies and people in the Russian cultural and political space. . . . This was in sharp, visceral contrast to the liberal paradigm, where anything dangerous or incomprehensible . . . either could not exist, or could exist only formally, not as itself, but . . . as an example of the liberalism and tolerance of the liberals.[52]

Dugin's nickname among the old guard of the NBP and the Eurasia Movement was "Merlin" because of his almost bewitching manner of writing and lecturing about political and mystical topics, often interspersed with digressions on literature and pop culture. Allegedly, Dugin chose this nickname for himself when he asked Limonov to cofound the NBP. In Dugin's vision, Limonov was to be the leader, the man of action, while Dugin would be the ideologist of the party, like "Merlin at the court of King Arthur." [53] Dugin has frequently combined political theory with art and public performance, which has often involved the use of his very hypnotic and distinct voice. Starting in the 1980s, he wrote and recorded several songs under the pseudonym of Hans Sievers, which

> was not just a stage name: it was a complete persona and alter ego. This was painstakingly composed of as many antisocial elements as its creator could find—a total and malevolent rebellion not just against the Soviet Union, but against convention and public taste as a whole: his namesake, Wolfram Sievers, had been the *Reichsgeschäftsführer*, or director, of the Ahnenerbe, a Nazi organization set up by Heinrich Himmler to study esoteric and paranormal phenomena. . . . The lyrics composed by Dugin/Sievers were both clever and composed to achieve maximum shock value. They were mainly inspired by nineteenth-century author Isidore-Lucien Ducasse, aka the Comte the Lautréamont, whose "Maldoror verses" were taken up by twentieth-century surrealists. Maldoror was the chronicle of an eponymous outcast monster who embarks on a surreal binge of torture, cannibalism and general malevolence—a vicious being in total revolt against any form of moral authority and every convention.[54]

In 1992, Dugin hosted a program on Russian television titled "the mysteries of the centuries" in which he talked about the mystical undercurrents of the Nazi regime. In the mid-1990s, he participated (along with Limonov) in the last performance of Kurekhin's Pop-mekhanika, dedicated to the memory of the English occultist Aleister Crowley.[55] Later, he hosted a radio "musical-philosophical program" called *FINIS MUNDI*. During each episode, he lectured on the life of intellectuals and historical figures like René Guénon, Guy Debord, and the terrorist and adventurer Boris Savinkov, while the cult DJ and musician Garik Osipov, also known as Graf Khortitsa, played mixes of rock and electronic music. In this period, he participated in the punk art collective Sever, organizing, among other things, a performance and video installation titled Bogema protiv NATO (Bohemia against NATO). At this stage, Dugin was a cult underground figure who was able to attract numerous young radical intellectuals to the cause of the anti-capitalist revolution. He was frequently described as "an artist philosopher" and a "dark romantic."[56]

At the beginning of the 2000s, Dugin's "hypnotism" turned into an experiment in political technology and mass manipulation. Soon before leaving the

NBP, he published *Foundations of Geopolitics*, which was adopted as a textbook for the General Staff of the Armed Forces of the Russian Federation. The publication of this volume marked a turning point in his career and his entrance into official politics.[57] In this period, he became closer to the Russian political establishment and, in particular, to the Russian "power ministries." He taught classes at the Ministry of Defense and other law enforcement agencies, and for a period, he was also appointed special adviser to the then speaker of the Duma Gennady Seleznev.

Dugin's influence on Russian public culture functioned on two levels. On one level, because of the success of *Foundations of Geopolitics* and its influence on the higher spheres of the Russian military, elements of his version of neo-Eurasianism were assimilated by the Russian leadership, and Dugin's buzzwords and slogans even gradually became part of Putin's official vocabulary. On another level, Dugin was invited to collaborate with Gleb Pavlovsky's Foundation for Effective Politics—an organization that was largely in charge of a radical transformation of Russian mass media aimed at supporting the solidification of Putin's power through mass political campaigns. Along with the gallerist Marat Guelman, a (politically very liberal) pioneer collector and promoter of contemporary art in post-Soviet Russia, Dugin curated a series of virtual "political art projects" designed to weaken the Communist Party and attract conservative votes to Putin's newly created party United Russia.[58]

Dugin's political organizations turned out to be similar experiments in political manipulation. Soon after Putin's rise to power, Dugin made a conscious decision to abandon the political underground and become actively involved in mainstream politics on the side of the Kremlin. The Eurasia Party and International Eurasia Movement (founded in 2002 and 2003, respectively) were the first institutional steps in this direction. Both organizations were largely based on the Gramscian idea of cultural hegemony, which came to Dugin through the mediation of the theorist of the French New Right Alain de Benoist.[59] As Dugin said in a frequently quoted passage from his initiation speech for the Eurasia Party in 2001, "Our aim is not to reach power and not to fight for power; our aim is to fight for influence over the regime."[60]

The main tool that Dugin used to achieve this influence was the internet, which he saw as a "geopolitical weapon" that non-Western countries can use to appropriate meanings and concepts that the West imposes on the rest of the world, and use them against Western domination itself. For him, the World Wide Web creates the possibility of challenging accepted values and bringing counterhegemonic meanings to the forefront: "for instance, it is worth looking at the quantity of online links to the words 'anarchy,' 'drugs,' 'fascism,' 'maniacs,' 'bomb,' 'nationalism,' 'extremism,' which leaves far behind the pacific politically correct 'market,' 'human rights,' 'Soros,' 'open society.'"[61]

Conservative postmodernism as a method and a political vision also applies to Dugin's writing, which is largely based on the appropriation and subversion of discourses that the author perceives as ideologically opposite to his own. In their 1995 "Manifesto of the New Wizards," Dugin and Kurekhin declare: "The new wizards establish their art and realize social upheavals. They specialize in geopolitics, mass science, and they subjugate the elements; they tame the Atlanticist Leviathan, and they fatten up the continental Behemoth."[62] Dugin and Kurekhin's provocative statements clearly evoke, in part ironically, the idea of *Gesamtkunstwerk*, and of a "total work of art" through which to realize a complete mystical transformation of society "on the basis of a unitary artistic plan."[63] According to Groys, this idea belongs to Malevich and the Russian avant-gardes, who dreamed to produce a similar mystical regeneration of reality through art, and was fully realized in Stalinist Russia, when "the dream of the avant-garde was in fact fulfilled and the life of society was organized in monolithic artistic forms, though of course not those that the avant-garde itself had favored."[64] Of course, the concept of *Gesamtkunstwerk* is primarily associated with Wagner and German Romanticism and, by extension, with the utopian impulse of Nazism that one can see mirrored, for instance, in Hitler's architect Albert Speer's visionary projects.

A similar creative (or, better, demiurgic) approach to politics informs Dugin's writing style. In one of his earliest books, Dugin defined conspirology as the "method of historical insanity." Conspirologists, he wrote, should be seen as visionary writers who live as outcasts and are recognized only postmortem as geniuses ahead of their time, in that "the bourgeois and positivist dogma about the fundamental randomness of all historical processes is as grotesque and absurd as the artistic method of 'socialist realism.'"[65] Dugin linked his approach to history and political theory to the creative process usually associated with art and literature, as opposed to what he deemed to be the dry scientific approach promoted by "Western positivism." At the level of national culture and politics, Dugin's work aimed at creating a cultural paradigm that radically opposed capitalism, (neo-)liberalism, globalization, and ultimately modernity in its entirety. On a geopolitical level, this resulted in a vision of Russia as an "anti-imperialist empire," or a countercultural empire, seen as a stronghold of conservative values and resistance against Western cultural and political hegemony.[66] Drawing on the traditionalist thinker Guénon, Dugin rejected the modern linear conception of time and any teleological faith in progress. He instead supported a circular conception of time (based on traditional Hinduism) and the idea that history moves in a progression toward decadence, from a past ideal golden age to a bronze age, or Kali Yuga, the time of maximum materialism and detachment from any form of spirituality in which we are supposedly currently living.[67]

Dugin's arguments often took the form of a subversive appropriation of liberal authors and philosophers. In one of his essays, for instance, he takes as the starting point for his reconceptualization of Russian history a classic of liberal thought, Karl Popper's *The Open Society and Its Enemies*. For him, the pillars of National Bolshevism are supposed to be the "enemies of open society," thinkers who "promote against the individual and his central position different models based on the idea of the Absolute . . . [like] Plato, Schlegel, Schelling, Hegel, Marx, and Spengler."[68] In his view, National Bolshevism is supposed to produce an unexpected synthesis between right-wing and left-wing ideologies under the banner of ideocracy and "objectivism." This would result in a cultural paradigm favoring the collective over the individual, the rights of the nation/people (*narod*) over the rights of the citizen, the spiritual over the material, and tradition over progress and modernity. As part of this strategy, Dugin formulates an alternative narrative of Russian and Soviet history that mainly focuses on the mystical and messianic undercurrents of the Bolshevik revolution and its fundamental continuity with Russia's spiritual and imperial mission.[69] Marxism itself is for Dugin the product of a philosophical lineage—from Hegel to the utopian socialists Saint-Simon and Fourier—that privileged mystical experience over rational thought.

As far as the Russian cultural context goes, Dugin's main scholarly sources were the works of Mikhail Agursky and Aleksandr Etkind.[70] From these scholars he borrowed the idea of a fundamental link between the Russian revolution and various forms of sectarian mysticism. Agursky and Etkind underlined for Dugin the crucial importance of patriotic and messianic currents in the Russian revolutionary movements of the nineteenth and twentieth centuries as well as in early Soviet culture and society. Following their ideas, he created an alternative historical narrative, which included such phenomena as *smenovekhovstvo*, Scythianism, the poetry of Aleksandr Blok and Nikolay Kliuev (with his idea of a Krasnaia Rus', or Red Rus'), as well as ethnographic research about communities of religious dissenters conducted by Lenin's personal secretary, Vladimir Bonch-Bruyevich.[71] Through these examples, he tried to prove the affinity of the Bolshevik revolution with nationalist, spiritual, and traditional religious values it formally opposed.[72]

In so doing, during the 1990s Dugin produced a cultural paradigm based on various conceptions of what can be defined as the "aesthetic state" and on a romanticized vision of totalitarianism as the last stronghold against what he saw as the spiritual degeneration of Western culture and society.[73] At the same time, he saw Russian history as a process of permanent "colonization," resistance, and "recolonization" of physical, cultural, and political space.[74] National Bolshevism constituted the ultimate form of intellectual and political resistance through the combination of the only political doctrines that could "achieve a temporary victory over liberalism, that is, Soviet (and Chinese) communism and Central European fascism." In 1997, Dugin summarized this ideology through the uncanny slogan "Third Rome—Third Reich—Third International."[75] As is clear from his description of an ideal National Bolshevik empire, and from his frequent references to the myth of Moscow as the third Rome, Dugin's thought is fundamentally utopian and apocalyptic in nature, and the triumph against Western liberalism for him is closely linked with the end of history and linear progress. Such an eschatological vision of a global "conservative revolution" is also at the basis of Dugin's specific theory of postmodernity.

Postmodern Geopolitics and the Fourth Political Theory

Drawing on such classics of geopolitics and military strategy as Halford Mackinder, Alfred Thayer Mahan, and Karl Haushofer, in *Foundation of Geopolitics* Dugin divides global political agents into "Land Powers" and "Sea Powers" struggling for world domination through military, diplomatic, and cultural means. This strategic partition of the world formed the basis for Dugin's essentialist interpretation of history and contemporary politics. For Dugin, "space determines everything": culture, beliefs, religion, and way of life. In his theoretical model, Sea Powers (Carthage, England, and the United States) are characterized by mobility, technological progress, materialism, liberalism, and the primacy of the individual over the collective. On the other hand, Land Powers (Rome, the Austro-Hungarian Empire, Russia and the Soviet Union) are dominated by the observance of tradition, hierarchy, and the primacy of collective over individual values. When applied to the contemporary geopolitical situation, this scheme allows Dugin to reconsider Russia's messianic role as the leading nation in a revolt of the Second and the Third World against the "New World Order," identified with Western (and, specifically, American) economic, political, and cultural hegemony. The idea of space as a determinant component of a nation's political fate allows Dugin to apply his syncretic ideology to contemporary Russia as the center of a future post-historical Eurasian Empire.[76] Dugin also applies this geopolitical approach to his vision of postmodernity, which he sees as an era in which faith in progress has been replaced by a dialectic of spaces, allowing for the coexistence of a plurality of identities and historical visions.

Postmodernism became a crucial element of Dugin's political theories at the beginning of the 2000s. At this point, Dugin had left the NBP with a small group of "Eurasianist secessionists" and was still divided between his former bohemian life and new, more institutional collaborations with the Russian military. With the help of a few young radical intellectuals, he organized the New University, a cycle of lectures on topics ranging from alchemy and neotraditionalism to information wars and the economy of postindustrial societies. Among the ranks of the lecturers were most members of the Iuzhinskii "metaphysical" circle, an underground bohemian group to which Dugin belonged in the late Soviet period. These included the postmodern (or, more accurately, "metaphysical realist") writer Yuri Mamleev; the ideologue of Russian Islamic Marxism Geydar Dzhemal; and Evgeny Golovin, a cult figure in Moscow alternative culture who, among other things, produced samizdat translations of Baudelaire's and Rimbaud's poems, wrote the lyrics for a pioneer Soviet alternative rock band (Vasia Shumov's Center), and introduced Dugin and other members of the Moscow bohemia to traditionalist philosophy.[77]

The early Eurasianist debates about postmodernism and postmodernity are still largely affected by Dugin's "leftist turn," by his days as a member of bohemian circles and revolutionary organizations, and by his interest in counterculture and critical theory.[78] At the same time, in elaborating his specific conception of "reactionary postmodernism," Dugin largely draws on the theorists of the French and Belgian New Right Alain de Benoist and Robert Steuckers, who themselves appropriated the ideas of the New Left and the experience of May 1968, and who first theorized about the possibility of co-opting postmodern culture as an instrument in their struggle against liberalism and modernity.[79]

The ninth issue of *Elementy*, a journal that Dugin had conceived as a platform for the Russian New Right, was entirely dedicated to the concepts of the "postmodern," "post-history," and the postindustrial society.[80] Dugin's editorial, by his own admission, was largely based on an essay by Robert Steuckers that was first published in the Belgian far-right journal *Vouloir* in 1989.[81] Steuckers's article contained a few main ideas that remained central in Dugin's own reflection on postmodernism throughout the years. First, Steuckers pointed out how the main theorists of postmodernity—Lyotard, Deleuze, Foucault, and Derrida—shared with the intellectual leaders of the French New Right a common vision of postmodernism as a critique of the "mechanicist/rationalist humanism" of Cartesianism, Newtonism, and the philosophy of the Enlightenment. Next, he argued that both the French New Left and the French New Right belonged to a longer tradition of "counter-modernity," or *Gegen-Neuzeit*. This tradition, according to Steuckers, included philosophers like Giambattista Vico, who promoted a "cyclical conception of history"; Jean-Jacques Rousseau, who criticized Descartes's project of a *mathesis universalis* (a universal science); and Alexander Gottlieb Baumgarten, who "reclaimed an 'aesthetic compensation' to the rationalist dryness" of modernity. "Counter-modernity" culminated with German and European romanticism and the emergence of "an organic vision of politics and history." Finally, for Steuckers, modern art was also part of this struggle against progress and rationalism: "Schlegel calls for an aesthetic revolution; Baudelaire, Nietzsche and Gottfried Benn, each in their own way, celebrate art as a 'space of survival within unlivable conditions.'" Steuckers seemed to implicitly draw a parallel between the postmodern "sphere of culture," which Daniel Bell saw as "subversive" in relation with the final triumph of technocracy and rationalism within postindustrial society and an artistic "anti-modern" struggle. At the same time, he identified the identitarian philosophy of the French New Right and the Conservative Revolution with what could be seen as a similar "aesthetic rejection of modernity," described as "the interest in history, narrative, aesthetics, and the productive nostalgia of the origins and the archetypes."

Drawing on Steuckers's exposition, Dugin distinguished between a "passive" and an "active" kind of postmodernism. Dugin's "passive postmodernism" coincides with Baudrillard's "pessimistic" conception of "post-history," with Bell's "optimistic" conception of a "postindustrial" society, and with Fukuyama's "end of history." It is "the historical existential and cultural background of the postmodern," characterized by the loss of any utopian or ideological impulses, the resolution "of all socioeconomic contradictions . . . due to technological development," and by the transformation of liberalism into the only "social and technological reality available."[82] "Passive postmodernism," or "the postindustrial society," or "the ultramodern" are, for Dugin as for Baudrillard, an "objective reality," the realization of all historical possibilities that results in a widespread indifference and mechanization of life, and in a hypertrophy or "obesity" of information.[83]

The "active," "optimistic," or "revolutionary" form of postmodern is, on the other hand, a cultural and political project aimed at resisting and overcoming the advancement of post-history and post-ideology.[84] For the New Left, this project takes the form of "a liberation from the 'terror of rationality,'" of "the orgiastic feast of the revolution, the performance [*sic*] of the displacement of meanings, the dissolution of hierarchies, saturnalia and 'potlatch.'" For the New Right, the victory against the "ultramodern" postindustrial technocracy results in a "constructive stage, the creation of a 'new order,' 'the return of the sacred,'" which is possible only after a radical dismissal of 'classic rationality' and its social products."[85] Such theoretical affinity for Dugin could turn into a "fusion of the extremes," aimed at bringing the "postmodern illusion" to an end.[86]

While largely borrowing from the leaders of the French New Right and their theories about postmodernism and conservative revolution, Dugin and the neo-Eurasianists took these theories one step further, by turning them into a countercultural practice. The issue of the journal *Elementy*, in which Dugin's editorial was published, reflected such a "fusion of the extremes," presenting articles and ideas belonging to the extreme left and the extreme right of the political spectrum.

Dugin's editorial was followed by the translation of an article by Alain de Benoist about the "French intellectual landscape." De Benoist focused on the hegemonic status of Marxism among French intellectual elites, along with the "institutionalization" of the French left. He argued that belonging to the academic and financial establishment had caused the left to lose its oppositional edge and tacitly accept the status quo. He called for the alliance of the ideological "peripheries" against the "center" of the "dominant ideology," that of Fukuyama's "End of History," and of Western liberalism and global capitalism.[87]

The Duginites tried to accomplish a similar convergence by producing forms of revolutionary culture in the context of post-Soviet society. De Benoist's article was preceded by an interview with Viktor Misiano, a leftist art critic who talked about the necessity to produce politically engaged art forms that would bridge elite and mass culture on the model on the Soviet avant-gardes.[88] The section "classics of postmodernism" included translations of an essay by Deleuze about the "societies of control" and an essay by Baudrillard about "aesthetic disillusion" and the impossibility of a utopian art within the conditions of postmodernity.[89] Finally, in addition to articles about the original émigré theories of Eurasian statehood and world conspiracies, the issue also contained articles by a range of leftist and anarchist intellectuals. In his article "Godard as Voltaire," the anarchist Aleksandr Tarasov claimed that Godard's aesthetics had preannounced and implicitly provided an ideology for the 1968 protest movement.[90] Tsvetkov, the former chief editor of *Limonka*, compared two approaches to anarchism in the works of French utopian socialist political thinker and forefather of nihilism Max Stirner.[91] The independent music producer, blogger, and mathematician Misha Verbitsky, who had spent several years in the United States to get his PhD from Harvard, provided an overview of Adam Parfrey's underground collection *Apocalypse Culture*, a survey of all things countercultural and extreme, from necrophilia, Eugenetics, and self-castration to Satanism, red terrorism, and schizophrenia.[92] Finally, the DJ and musician Garik Osipov (the one who had co-hosted with Dugin the radio program *FINIS MUNDI*) combined Western and Soviet subcultures by providing a comparative analysis of the figure of the "Nasty Nazi" in European, Soviet, and Soviet Ukrainian cinema.[93]

Dugin's reflection on postmodernity has later evolved in close connection with the development of his "fourth political theory."[94] Referring specifically to post-Soviet culture and economic relations of production, Dugin argues that three cultural paradigms, corresponding to three stages of economic development, coexist in contemporary Russian society: the premodern/preindustrial; the modern/industrial; and the postmodern/postindustrial. While manifestations of the postmodern paradigm in Russian art and literature mark for Dugin the invasion of Western, Atlanticist, or American values in Russian society, the postmodern paradigm can also be reappropriated and used as part of the Eurasianists' revolt against the modern world. Applying Steuckers's and de Benoist's right-wing co-opting of postmodern discourses to the Russian situation, Dugin claims that if postmodernism is aimed at destroying the values and traditions of modernity in order to challenge any form of hierarchy or canon, the Eurasian, conservative, and traditionalist form of postmodernism is supposed to challenge the status quo to establish a new hierarchy and a new tradition from the ashes of modern culture.[95]

Broadening the scope of his reflection, Dugin then applies his ideas about the reactionary nature of postmodernity to political theory and recent geopolitical trends. Whereas earlier he explicitly and uncompromisingly supported radicalism in all of its forms, and even called for the creation of a Russian "boundless and red fascism," later Dugin promoted the idea of overcoming all of the main political theories of modernity—liberalism, communism, and fascism—in order to produce a system of government that would be fitting for the current historical situation (i.e., a "fourth political theory").[96] The fourth political theory also appears to be a fundamentally postmodern project, presented as a synthesis of all previous ideologies and a political system that embodies and resolves all past ideological contradictions.[97]

From communism, Dugin borrows the critique of the capitalist system. From fascism, he "saves" the focus on "ethnos," thought of as collective identity and shared culture, history, and way of life. This takes the form of "ethnopluralism" (also a concept borrowed from de Benoist), conceived as the coexistence of a plurality of separate ethnicities and cultures, which would supposedly preserve, in contrast with multiculturalism, local identities and historical roots. From liberalism, Dugin values the idea of freedom, but he rejects the liberal idea of a "freedom from" (hierarchies, tradition, collective values, etc.) and proposes instead to promote a "freedom for," supposedly aimed at creatively realizing human potential.

Dugin sees the fourth political theory as a way to overcome post-liberalism and post-ideology. He accuses the West of a form of "cultural racism," grounded on the widespread assumption that modern society represents the peak of human civilization. Drawing on postcolonial theory, and on such classic anthropologists as Franz Boas and Claude Lévi-Strauss, he questions and relativizes

Western faith in progress as a form of social Darwinism and a justification of colonialism and cultural and economic globalization.[98] Drawing on Bruno Latour, he advances the idea of considering modernity as one specific narrative or myth among a wide range of historical, collective, or national narratives, presently coexisting in different regions of the world.[99] As a result, in a way not dissimilar from David Harvey, Dugin sees postmodernity as replacing the historical dialectic of modernity with a "dialectic of space," reflected in a synchronic global polylogue among a plurality of historical visions governing the life of different communities throughout the world. At the same time, he insists frequently on the idea that the fourth political theory should not be considered a closed system but a creative exercise in political imagination based on the production of new narratives, myths, and rituals that are in direct contrast to the narratives, myths, and rituals of (post)modernity.[100] This approach implicitly follows Steuckers's idea of an "aesthetic revolution" against progress and modernity.

The fourth political theory is therefore conceived as a humanistic revolution against the hegemony of global technocracy, as theorized by such authors as Daniel Bell and the military strategist Thomas Barnett.[101] Like the neo-Marxists Negri and Hardt, Dugin and other Eurasianists see geopolitics as a creative process aimed at consciously producing a narrative alternative to that of a "unipolar world," marked by Western undisputed cultural, political, and economic domination.[102] Like Negri and Hardt, Dugin conceives his own "counter-Empire," or his specific form of anti-globalism, as an ongoing, unfinished collective project. However, according to him, Deleuze's, Derrida's, Foucault's, and Negri and Hardt's versions of postmodernism are nothing but a pale shadow of his own forthcoming neotraditionalist pastiche.[103]

Dugin's narrative takes as a starting point a "search for the subject" of the fourth political theory, which begins, again, as a survey of previous existing ideologies. If "the subject" of liberalism is the individual, "the subject" of communism is class, and "the subject" of fascism is the state (in the case of Italian Fascism) or race (in the case of German Fascism), then "the subject" of the fourth political theory could be a compendium or synthesis of all of these concepts, or "imagination" itself.[104] The other main hypothesis is that the subject of the fourth political theory should be found in the Heideggerian concept of *Dasein*, or "being-there," conceived as "the human experience of being in the world."[105]

Heidegger's philosophy becomes in fact the foundation for Dugin's approach to postmodernity. In particular, a crucial role in Dugin's strategy is played by Heidegger's concept of *Ereignis*, or "event." According to Heidegger, the pre-Socratics' reflection on the question of Being, and later, Plato's theory of forms, marked the separation between subject and object within the Western philosophical tradition and, as a consequence, the beginning of a process of alienation from pure Being and existence, which culminated in "calculating thinking" (*das rechnende Denken*), technology (*Gestell*, or "enframing"), and ultimately the triumph of nihilism and "nothingness." *Ereignis* is, in Dugin's exposition of Heidegger, a "sudden return of being" that occurs at "the darkest moment in history" and at the height of danger, when, through "nothingness" itself, "pure Being . . . in such a paradoxical way!—reminds mankind of its existence." For Heidegger, the source of "nothingness" and "calculative thinking" was modernity and "Western nihilism." For Dugin, it is postmodernity: "postmodernity . . . is, in every sense, the ultimate oblivion of being: it is that 'midnight,' when nothingness (nihilism), begins to seep from all the cracks."[106]

This kind of eschatological conception of postmodernity is what allows Dugin to see it both as the source of all evils, the neo-Eurasianist nemesis, and its "dark inspiration," or an opportunity to realize his own post-historical traditionalist fantasy.[107] The fourth political theory is defined as a "crusade" against "postmodernity, the postindustrial society, liberal thought, and globalization, as well as its logistical and technological bases."[108] It is, at the same time, a technological "battle for postmodernity" that can be realized through hacking and terrorism (as in the case of the attacks on September 11, 2001).[109] The Eurasianists are supposed to both fight against "the society of the spectacle" and fight for the control over the spectacle, or for the creation of a spectacle of their own.[110] In fact, Dugin sees the actually existing late capitalist "society of the spectacle" as a parody of Eurasianist postmodernism, in eschatological terms a kingdom of the Antichrist preceding the new coming of Christ. Deleuze's rhizome, and his "body without organs," are a parody of the Heideggerian *Dasein*.[111] At the same time, the neo-Eurasianist ideal of the fourth political theory, which is identified with the Heideggerian overcoming of the subject-object duality, is in fact an analogue of the existing postmodern virtual reality.[112]

This is a mirroring game of sorts, which takes the form of an elusive dialectic between reality and appearance, pretense and physical experience, superficiality and depth. Dugin's appropriation and use of postmodern performance best summarizes this ambiguity. For him, as for Kurekhin, there is a strong distinction between an "elitist" highbrow postmodernism, in which performance realizes a return to archaic rituals of initiation, and the vulgar postmodernism of pop and mass culture and illusion.[113] Such "Eurasianist" performances include those staged by Kurekhin's Pop-Mekhanika and the art collective Sever, in which Dugin himself took part.

For Dugin, these happenings become a way of preparing for an epiphanic return to reality that occurs through the experience of violence and death. To express this idea, he uses the vivid metaphors of the Dadaists' ritual suicide, of Dostoevsky's character Kirillov's philosophical proof of God's nonexistence, and of terrorism. The most horrifying example of such a "return to reality" and experience is indeed that of the terrorist attack at the Dubrovka theater in Moscow, when, during the performance of the musical *Nord-Ost*, Chechen terrorists stormed the stage and barricaded themselves inside the theater with 850 hostages, and when, after four days of unsuccessful negotiations, Russian special forces pumped poison gas into the theater's ventilation system, killing all the terrorists along with many of the hostages. Allegedly, when the terrorists entered the stage, many in the audience thought that the attack was part of the performance.

> The disgusting sleazy comedian Sasha Tsekalo puts on a show attended by a noteworthy Moscow audience. Then the Chechen terrorists arrive, and at first people think that this is part of the play. Only later they understand with horror that something is not right on the stage, and then the real horrible tragedy begins. The Conservative Revolutionaries have something fairly similar in mind: let the buffoonery of the Postmodern have its turn; let it erode fixed paradigms, the ego, super-ego and logos; let the rhizome, the schizomasses and the splintered consciousness do their job; let nothingness swallow and carry away all the content of the world. Then the secret doors will open, and the ancient, eternal, ontological archetypes will come to the surface and, in a horrifying way, will put an end to the game.[114]

Dugin's struggle against (post)modernity, progress, and a linear conception of time results, paradoxically, in a return to the teleological conception of history of the historical avant-gardes—and Dugin's reference to the Dadaists here is particularly significant. The neo-Eurasianist, conservative revolutionary struggle ends with a return to modernism, seen as a time in which reality, experience, and political engagement are still possible. The return of "pure Being" is identified in his argument with the utterly physical experiences of death and the apocalypse.

In elaborating his own "post-humanism" and "post-anthropology" (clearly conceived on the model of—and, at the same time, in opposition to—Negri and Hardt's post-humanism and Donna Haraway's "Cyborg Manifesto"), Dugin summons the figures of the "political soldier" and of the "angels," both closely related to the concepts of death, faith, and ideology. The "political soldier," a term that he borrows directly from Nazi ideology and European neo-fascist movements of the 1960s and 1970s, is, according to him, the "romantic figure" of an individual who "kills and dies for politics." It is the pure incarnation of militancy, political commitment, and ideology, and the exact opposite of the postmodern disengaged "intellectual DJ" from the epigraph to this chapter. It is the embodiment of the ideological struggles of the twentieth century.[115]

Dugin takes his postapocalyptic pastiche even further with his idea of post-humanism and post-politics as "angelopolis," a vision of postmodern ideology as the struggle between superhuman beings.[116] The idea of "angelopolis" also allows Dugin to propose a surprisingly unconventional, for a self-proclaimed conservative and traditionalist, theory of gender in the context of neo-Eurasianism. Whereas Dugin has not infrequently celebrated aggressive masculinity and traditional gender roles and family values, and has criticized the LGBT movement and the recognition of rights for gay, queer, and transgender people as a sign of the global triumph of Western consumerism and moral degradation, in his discussion of gender in the fourth political theory he actually criticizes Western patriarchy and proposes to overcome traditional gender roles.[117] He argues that all political theories, in different ways, have chosen the "Western white man" as the ideal subject of ideology and the ideal "political gender." He criticizes Western feminism because, he argues, it conforms to the ideal of white masculinity: "a businesswoman is one who manifests male qualities: white females become 'citizens.'"[118] However, he also criticizes Western conservatives for advocating for a "return of masculinity," embodied in the figure of a "white wealthy person," and argues that such white patriarchal ideals only perpetuate the ideology of "modernity through gender reconstructions."[119]

Starting from these assumptions, Dugin argues that gender in the fourth political theory should not be fixed, and that the "sex of *Dasein*" "cannot be either male or female." The ideal sexuality of the fourth political theory is therefore the playful sexuality of the "non-adult male," or "androgyny": "we suggest taking a step towards gender as *Dasein*, despite the notorious representations and opprobrium that we will cause. By going beyond the limits of gender which we know, we get to the domain of uncertainty, androgyny, and sex as practiced by the angels."[120]

The definition of neo-Eurasianist androgyny extends to that of neo-Eurasianist subjectivity, which is supposed to be decisively "non-White/European, insane, non-urban or defined by a constructed landscape. For example, the ecologist or aboriginal: that is, the person who did not break with nature."[121] Interestingly, the "mirroring game" with Western postmodern and critical theory also applies to Dugin's premodern, anti-bourgeois, non-white and non-European definition of gender in that his theory of androgyny and childish playful sexuality is built in direct comparison and opposition with that of "cyborg feminism."[122]

Beyond his flirting with fascism, the calls for violence, the collaborations with ultranationalist organizations in Russia, Europe, and the United States, and the open support of Putin's authoritarian regime, there is something interesting, and even perversely and paradoxically appealing, in Dugin's "conservative postmodernism." This is probably why his ideology has been, in a way, so effective from the standpoint of PR and political technology. Dugin's neo-Eurasianism provides a surprisingly powerful critique of late capitalism, postmodernity, and globalization, in a way not dissimilar from Marxism in connection to nineteenth-century capitalism. Dugin himself significantly defines Eurasianism as "a planetary . . . revolutionary doctrine, the Marxism of the twenty-first century."[123]

Dugin's extreme and convoluted philosophical provocations have the merit of challenging and revealing the internal contradictions of commonly accepted and, to borrow Barthes's formulation, fully "naturalized" mythologies of progress and modernity, providing a fundamentally different perspective on recent global historical processes.[124] Trying to fully understand even such an extreme perspective can be a fruitful exercise in "radical relativism" that allows one to shed a clearer light on Western ideology in relation to a multiplicity of global historical narratives and value systems. In addition, Dugin's countercultural fantasies can be surprisingly thought-provoking. If taken with a grain of salt, they can allow one to productively call into question hegemonic discourses and ideological commonplaces.

At the same time, of course, Dugin's traditionalist critique of modernity is potentially dangerous in its radicalism. His theorizing is characterized by a completely unrestrained and amoral ideological freedom and creativity (at times verging on ideological stream of consciousness), which in fact unleashes the possibility for political violence and wipes out the positive values and the *minima moralia* guaranteed by the legacy of the Enlightenment. Although it is presented as a way to preserve and support local identities, cultural traditions, and forms of sustainable development, the concept of "ethnopluralism," for instance, could potentially turn out to be, and is seen by many as, blatantly racist. It is a kind of postcolonialism that fully disregards the fundamental interdependence between the colonizer and the colonized.[125]

Perhaps because of this, Dugin's "conservative postmodernism" could also be seen, paradoxically (and of course against Dugin's own intentions), as an admonition to rethink, reformulate, and consciously and selectively recuperate the values of modernity and the Enlightenment. In addition, as we have seen, the ideology of neo-Eurasianism is presented as formally subversive and emancipatory at a global level but absolutely reactionary and repressive at the level of internal Russian politics. Drawing on the idea of a "countercultural empire," the ideology of neo-Eurasianism embodies, at the same time, revolutionary and authoritarian impulses in Russian society and identity.

Most importantly, Dugin's neo-Eurasianism should be seen, first and foremost, as a strategy and a political practice. Dugin's "conservative postmodernism" is aimed at co-opting the logic of postmodern culture for revolutionary purposes. For Dugin, postmodern culture can be destabilized from the inside, by exploiting its own widespread moral and ideological indifference. Radicalism can, at first, return in the apparently innocuous and more acceptable form of simulacra, only to be later unleashed in all of its revolutionary potential to destroy modern society from its foundations. Communism can reemerge through the iconic portrait of Che Guevara on a cell phone ad, or on the "shirts of idle and comfortable petty bourgeois youth."[126] Religious fundamentalism and premodern morality are already slipping through the cracks of the postmodern spectacles through the ominous figure of Osama Bin Laden on Western TV screens, as well as through American ultraconservative Christian sects and televangelists.[127]

Dugin sees the internet as the fundamental weak spot of Western capitalism and globalization. In order to take advantage of the counterhegemonic and fragmentary nature of the web, he believes that it is necessary to create a global network of like-minded revolutionary Eurasianist intellectuals who would function as a counterpart to the Western "cultural DJs" and who would produce an alternative, conservative, and continental "society of the spectacle," based on Eurasianist websites, domains, online journals, and TV channels.[128] In addition to fostering such an international community through seminars, conferences, and alternative academic groups, Dugin and his followers have created an online network of Eurasianist websites within the Russian blogosphere with the goal of promoting the most destructive and inflammatory ideas, ostensibly to accelerate a postmodern neoconservative end of times.

Dugin's own mediatic image has reflected over the years the neo-Eurasianist specific conception of postmodernity. Like the protagonist of Viktor Pelevin's iconic postmodernist novel *Generation P*, Dugin has disseminated avatars of himself over the media, playing different roles and wearing disorientingly different masks.[129] He has been portrayed wearing an Old Believer's monastic garb with an ominous look on his face and holding a grenade launcher during a "Eurasianist summer camp" in South Ossetia before the beginning of the Russo-Georgian conflict in 2008. On February 4, 2012, during the "anti orange" meeting organized by the Russian government in the midst of the wave of protests for fair elections, he went on stage and screamed with a possessed look on

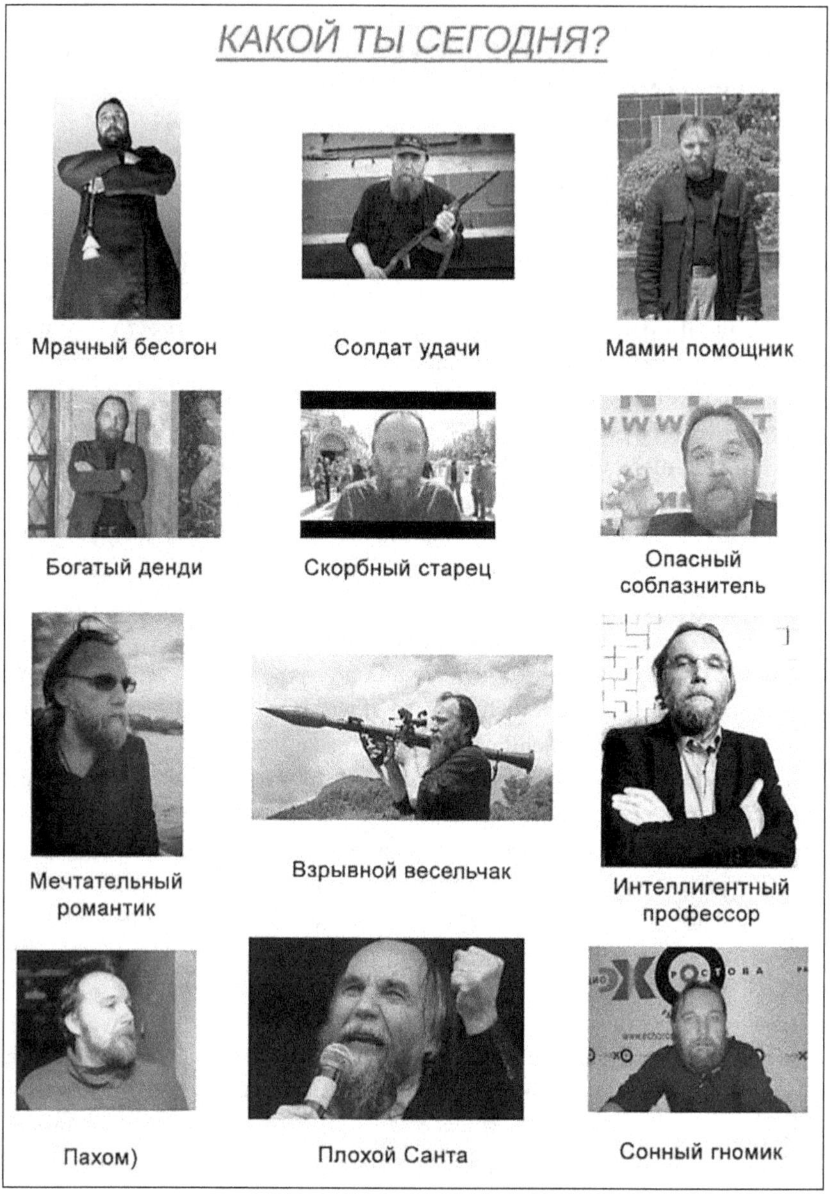

Figure 23. "Kakoi ty segodnia?" internet meme about Dugin, n.d.: "Which One Are You Today? Demon Chaser, Soldier of Fortune, Mother's Helper, Rich Dandy, Sorrowful Elder, Dangerous Tempter, Romantic Dreamer, Explosive Funnyman, Educated Prof, Pakhom [a famous comic actor], Bad Santa, Sleepy Gnome."

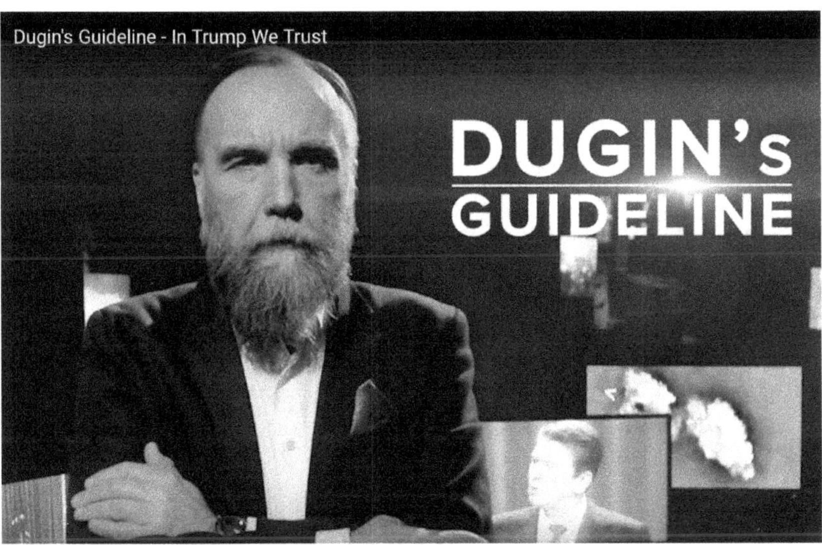

Figure 24. Dugin's Guideline: "In Trump We Trust!" YouTube video, March 4, 2016.

his face that Russia "either will be great, or it won't be at all"—an implicit reference to his eschatological convictions about Russia's geopolitical mission. Dugin's transformism and paradoxical thinking has become so proverbial that parodies of him have also started appearing in Russian media. An ironic collage of his extravagant disguises, titled "Which one are you today?," has circulated in the Russian internet; in it, each one of Dugin's portraits is followed by an ironic caption: "Dark exorcist," "Rich dandy," "Soldier of fortune," "Bad Santa," etc. (see fig. 23).

In recent years, Dugin has started to address a more international audience. For instance, in one of his online political shows, "Dugin's Guidelines," this time performing the role of the polished and freshly groomed anchorman, he provides regular commentaries, in Russian and English, to the latest national and global political news (see fig. 24). In one of the episodes of the show, broadcast during the 2016 American primaries ("In Trump We Trust!"), Dugin voiced his full support for Trump's candidacy: "Trump is the voice of the real right-wing America, which, in fact . . . only cares about the Second Amendment and the good old tradition of the single-storied or, at least, two-storied America, a predictable way of life on the ranch and expressing freedom wherever they like, but not how the liberals prescribe it."[130] Dugin's show was widely seen as proof of the Russian far-right endorsement of Trump, which in fact it is, but only if one sees it as a parody of a parody, and as part of Dugin's nihilistic and apocalyptic postmodern provocation. The rationale behind such a statement is that Donald Trump being elected president of the United States is a cheerful sign of an imminent apocalypse, which for Dugin is a good thing. In fact, I argue that all of Dugin's statements, theories, and political performances should be read through the prism of this dark twisted double irony—which is a reflection of what Dugin himself theorized through his idea of a "Russian conservative postmodernism."

5

A Conservative Bohemia

The Eurasia Movement as an Aesthetic-Political Project

At the beginning of the twenty-first century we, for the sake of a joke, designated me as the "stylist" of the International Eurasia Movement, and somebody picked up on that. But the movement is so great and boundless, and it includes in itself on the whole everything. . . . How could I be its stylist? It's as if I were the stylist of the sky, or the stylist of the earth. It is categorically impossible. . . . In a sense, I illustrate . . . and I hope that my inner vibrations will coincide in the representation of plastic forms with the Eurasia Movement, which in different moments formulates itself differently. In one of the readings, this is a group of intellectuals of the terrestrial globe, united by a common code, a common protocol. In another possible reading, for example as a section of Moscow University, it is a scientific-educational structure, which, in laboratory silence, is giving sense to a gigantic continental project, its philosophy, its metaphysics, its scientific foundations. Third, it is a hot-tempered group of street fighters who react immediately to everything that happens in the country and change its agenda.

Aleksey Beliaev-Gintovt, visual artist, Moscow, 2015

This is the disease of all intellectuals. They all see themselves in the role of Merlin in the court of King Arthur. [They think] that King Arthur without Merlin doesn't go anywhere. [But] isn't it possible that Merlin in the court of King

> Arthur is just a variety performer, just a designer? [This] would just deeply offend Dugin. If someone just told him: "Sasha, you are just getting carried away by this . . . It's just that the things you say are so cool . . . We could do just everything that we are doing without all of this—sell gas and other things . . . steal . . . our secret services. [*laughs*] It's just that it's so cool when you come and talk about Genghis Khan, about Behemoth, and Leviathan. It's just so crazy to think about . . . So, that's what we are doing! The cosmic war! Mysticism! And we thought that we were just embezzling money!" [*laughs*]
>
> Aleksey Tsvetkov, writer and political activist, Moscow, 2015

> Those who go against the day should not fear the night.
>
> Evgeny Golovin, leader of the Moscow mystical underground, n.d.

My first encounter with the Eurasianist community took place in the studio of the contemporary artist Aleksey Beliaev-Gintovt in Moscow. I visited Gintovt's studio for the first time at the end of March 2015. Earlier that month I had tried, unsuccessfully, to make contact with some Eurasianist activists. The "headquarters" of the Eurasian Youth Union, which also functions as a distribution point for Dugin's online bookstore, was revealed to be an empty office with a few desks, several bookshelves filled with Dugin's books, and a huge black-and-gold painting of the Kremlin skyline (as I later discovered, one of Gintovt's works). The room was part of a gated, corporate-looking office building attached to a mall. After passing security and having my passport dutifully scanned, I managed to get only a few contacts from the lone employee in the room, who did not really seem to have a clear understanding of the nature of the organization. Before leaving, I had also run into two other customers of the bookstore. These were two very muscular and fairly aggressive-looking men wearing Lonsdale clothes (a fashion brand popular among skinheads and soccer fans). They claimed to be part of Aleksey Kochetkov's ultranationalist organization Narodnaia diplomatiia (popular diplomacy) and were eager to hear my opinion about the moral decadence of Western Europe and the fact that, as they claimed, "Norway had recently legalized incest and pedophilia."[1] The question was, I believe, a way to verify my ideological position. In order to avoid any unnecessary conflicts, I acted vague and surprised and left the building quickly.

This first missed encounter with the Eurasia Movement had left me with the impression that Dugin's organization could, in fact, be a virtual or "imagined" community. Somewhat puzzled and a little distressed by this experience, I had also decided that it was probably wiser to ask a friend to introduce me to somebody in Dugin's organization. Irina, an old friend, agreed to help me. A singer and a musician with no political affiliation, Irina had met Gintovt years ago at a party organized by the late video and performance artist Aleksandr Lungin, the founder, along with his partner Katya Ryzhikova, of the punk art group Sever (the North). As mentioned, Aleksandr Dugin had also been involved in Lungin's art collective, writing texts for it and participating in Lungin's and Ryzhikova's psychedelic performances and mystical rituals. Irina told Gintovt about my project and my interest in talking to him and other members of Dugin's organization. Before inviting us over, in a secretive and quasi-military tone (as Irina told me was typical of him, laughing), Gintovt asked: "Is he a verified person?" (*A on proverennyi chelovek?*).

Gintovt's studio, which, as I later discovered, was often informally (and half-jokingly) referred to by its regular guests as the "Eurasianist salon," was filled with symbols, visual references, and "sacred objects" connected, in one way or the other, to the aesthetics and ideology of Eurasianism. When we arrived, Gintovt had just finished working on one of his red-and-gold canvases, which portrayed a post-human gigantic birdman holding a globe and displaying the Eurasianist rose of the winds, the emblem of Dugin's movement and a symbol of Russia's future territorial expansion. Gintovt had just washed his hands, and he was rehydrating them with lotion. As he explained, his trademark technique consisted of applying paint to the canvas, frequently through a computer-generated stencil, with his bare hands. For him, this gesture represented a form of performance through which he left a physical trace of himself on the canvas. His handprints on the canvas, Gintovt told us laughing, were also an allusion to the many times he had to have his fingerprints taken at the Lubyanka (the KGB headquarters) because of his association with various late-Soviet underground subcultures.

In addition to his new painting, Gintovt showed us a few small oval portraits from his series *People of Long Will* (*Liudi dlinnoi voli*), portraying what amounts to a hall of fame of Eurasianist role models.[2] We immediately recognized Friedrich Nietzsche, the Russian poet Nikolay Gumilev, and Yukio Mishima, but we had some trouble with the last portrait, displaying a curly-haired, Medusa-like woman. That one, Gintovt told us, is "Lenochka"—Leni Riefenstahl, the German propaganda director whose semi documentary films *Triumph of the Will* (1935) and *Olympia* (1938) established the dominant aesthetics of the Nazi regime (see fig. 25).

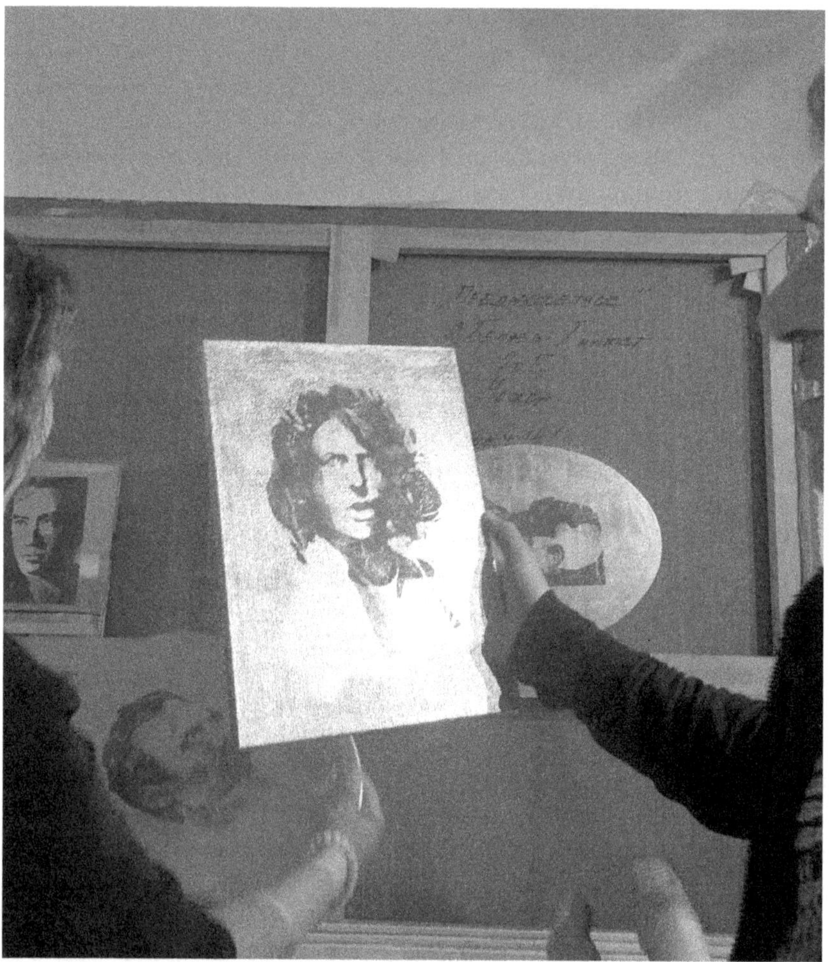

Figure 25. Gintovt showing his guests some portraits from his series *Liudi dlinnoi voli*: Leni Riefenstahl ("Lenochka"), Friedrich Nietzsche, Yukio Mishima, Nikolay Gumilev. Moscow, April 2015. Photo by author.

The studio contained other "props" that Gintovt gradually unveiled to his guests in a playful manner during their stay: several replicas of Kalashnikovs (which looked very convincing, especially considering that Gintovt had been posting on Facebook several photos of himself in front of heavily armed soldiers in Eastern Ukraine); the replica of a Soviet pistol; and an axe covered in gold leaves and topped with a gunsight symbolizing the combination of tradition and technological progress that would characterize the Eurasianist ideal of

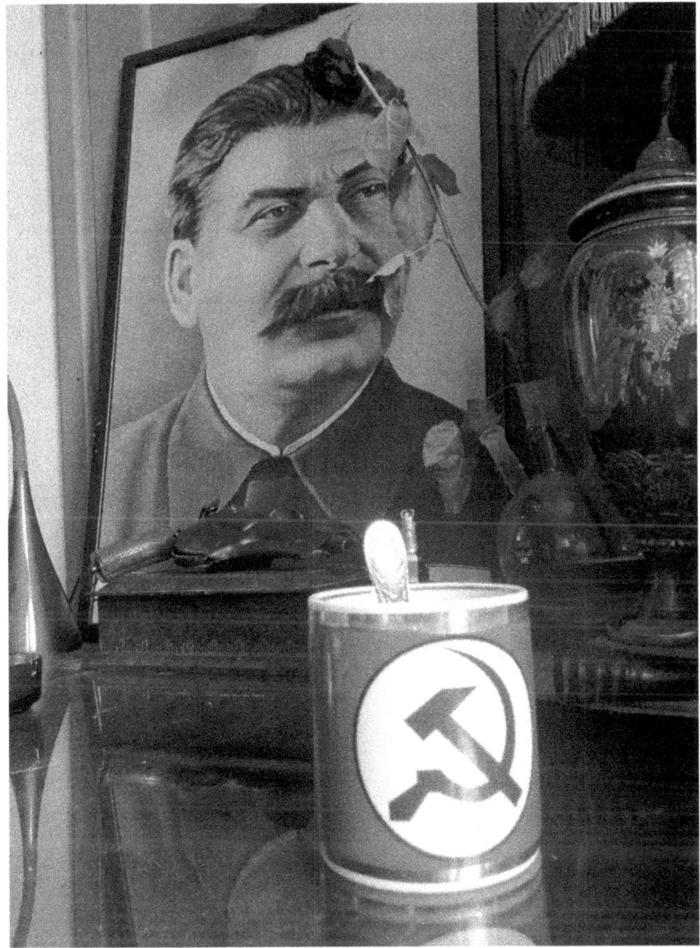

Figure 26. Objects from Gintovt's "Eurasianist salon": a woven portrait of Stalin (a gift to the Soviet Union from the People's Republic of China), a grenade, a pistol, a wilted rose. Moscow, June 2015. Photo by author.

statehood. The living room was decorated with a vintage Soviet velvet flag and a black-and-white woven portrait of Stalin, originally a present to the Soviet Union from the People's Republic of China (see fig. 26). We drank tea out of souvenir mugs decorated with a hammer and sickle, very similar to the original NBP flag, and each room had a flat, muted TV screen broadcasting LifeNews, a pro-Kremlin news channel. Finally, to add to the somewhat curious atmosphere, we were introduced to a bearded Orthodox priest who was staying at Gintovt's place for Easter.

Gintovt himself had a highly theatrical appearance and demeanor. On the several occasions when I met him, he often wore black military clothes and sniper pants reinforced at the knees. He had a deep voice and would often use an artificially old-fashioned diction and pronunciation. He used *vy* (plural "you," like *vous* in French), the formal form of address, even with old acquaintances. In the manner of Old Church Slavonic, he often did not turn the -g between vowels into -v, as it is common in modern Russian, and avoided turning the unaccented -o into an -a (as in "father"), as is also common in modern Russian, and especially Muscovite, pronunciation. He was often ironic and hyperbolic in his statements, laughed loudly, and did not seem to take himself too seriously. On the other hand, his words and actions conveyed an unconditional, quasi-religious commitment to the political cause of Eurasianism. As he told us, lately he had been trying to find an aesthetics and a set of symbols that could unite Russian conservative and leftist forces involved in the war in Eastern Ukraine. He had recently visited the war zones in Donbass, and had close friends who were working with Igor Strelkov, one of the main pro-Russian separatist military commanders in Eastern Ukraine until the fall of 2014.

When I later interviewed him, always in his studio, Gintovt told me more about his past and his career. He told me that in the mid-1980s he had become part of the late Soviet "underground." He was a member of *Sistema*, a Russian community of hippies and hitchhikers, and lived in a squat.

> In 1988, I dropped out of the architectural school, I burned my passport, and, from then on, I found myself in the situation of the so-called underground, although we always insisted on the fact that we were the "obergraund": not the basement, but the attic—that we were not worse, but better. I was always interested in this part of subcultures. Perhaps because of my architectural training, I was always interested in "constructive processes" [*sozidatel'nye*—that is, "constructive" or creative]. I was deadly bored by the numerous "decadents" that I saw every day. I witnessed numerous "punk-excesses" . . . [of people] drinking urine and eating feces . . . literally. [*laughs*] A limit had been reached. This is why I always looked for people who could have a "constructive" program. And since none of the existing parties which started to appear at the beginning of the 1990s inspired either interest or trust, I programmatically didn't take any interest in politics. . . . [For years] I didn't even own a TV. I couldn't distinguish Gorbachev from Yeltsin. [For me] they were both representatives of the most miserable party-bureaucratic trash.[3]

Because he didn't have any affinity with the "democratic" and "overly familiar" style of Moscow Conceptualism, Gintovt said, his squat remained fundamentally isolated, and he and his alternative community supported a "spirit of closeness, secrecy, and inaccessibility." The style of Leningrad's nonconformist circles, where people lived in huge prerevolutionary apartments and cultivated the "nineteenth-century, military-aristocratic spirit of Tsarist Russia," was much closer to his own: "Petersburg is distance, cold, verticality, . . . and there I finally found my new friends [smiles]." While he considered the Moscow Conceptualists "anti-Soviets and Russophobes" and "vulgar and foolish people," he continued, "Petersburg emphasized individuality, the grand style . . . eventually, Timur [Novikov] formulated this inclination toward hierarchy, toward meaning, toward a new figurativeness, in the form of the movement New Russian Classicism [Novyi russkii klassitsizm]."

Although in other circumstances Gintovt told me that before joining the Eurasia Movement at the beginning of the 2000s he had never been actively involved in politics, during this interview he defined the origins of his political stance as an "initiation to red" that occurred soon after the fall of the Soviet Union. In Gintovt's account, this "initiation ritual" took place during the Russian parliamentary crisis of October 1993, when, as a consequence of the violent confrontation between Yeltsin and the resistance led by vice president Aleksandr Rutskoy and Ruslan Khasbulatov, Moscow was on the verge of a civil war. Strikingly, Gintovt does not describe the origins of his political convictions as part of a rational decision but instead conveys those political stirrings through vivid images (and colors) and associations of ideas. In October 1993, under the Red Army's fire, Gintovt told me, he "fell in love with 'red'":

> Absolutely by chance, on October 3 and 4, 1993, I found myself first in Ostankino and then at the White House. This was absolutely inconceivable. For the first time, Red Army soldiers were shooting at me. My own (*rodnaia*, that is, "native" or "dear") Soviet army was shooting at me unarmed, and, for me like for many others, this was the turning point, it was an initiation, an initiation *through war*. And if before I had been more inclined toward the "white version," I was a monarchist, I even shot the film *Nikolay II* in 1989 [*laughs*] . . . I was a vague intuitive monarchist. Well, in 1993, once and for all, I was initiated to "red" "red." . . . For me, this was the beginning of a "red mega-project."

Gintovt's words, and the way in which he interpreted and provided me with an account of his biography, bring up two important aspects of the culture and language of the Eurasia Movement. First, in relating the beginnings of his intellectual and artistic trajectory, Gintovt participates in a sort of cult of the late-Soviet underground, seen as a secluded, inaccessible, and secret space that resists mainstream culture and production of meaning. The "underground," at the same time, stands for an intellectual community supposedly destined to produce a social and political revolution, with which Gintovt and other Eurasianists, in different ways, identify. Second, Gintovt describes his "conversion to politics" as an initiation ritual, in which the "red" of the Soviet project is confused with the "red" of the blood embodying the direct experience of violence and war—in this case, the Moscow civil war of 1993.

Paradoxically, Gintovt "fell in love" with the Soviet project after becoming the victim of its violence. Interestingly, in his narrative, he also set his near-death experience against the virtual nature of postmodern culture. As he recalled, "out of pure coincidence," straight before being shot at "by his own compatriots," he was working with a friend on the layout of a translation of Jean Baudrillard's essay "The Gulf War Did Not Take Place" for the *Moscow Art Journal* (*Khudozhestvennyi zhurnal*). In this article, Gintovt reminded me, Baudrillard "demonstrates the postmodern character of the wars of new generation, and the fact that there will be no more real wars." As soon as they arrived in Ostankino looking for weapons (and snipers started shooting at them from inside the building), Gintovt continued, "Baudrillard's argument was immediately disproven." In Gintovt's account, death and violence are celebrated as traditional forms of initiation, and as a way to overcome the virtual nature of the postmodern condition.[4]

Many of the members of the Eurasia Movement I met and interviewed during my fieldwork described their fascination with Dugin's ideas as a visionary or psychedelic experience, as a way to achieve an altered state of consciousness, or even as a door to the afterlife. A former member of the Eurasian Youth Union told me that, when the organization was created, the Eurasianists considered themselves part of a "conservative bohemia," and that they somehow lived and experienced reality through Dugin's ideas. At the time, he continued, Dugin's followers considered themselves destined to infiltrate power and state apparatuses and to revolutionize Russia and the world from within the system.

Others I interviewed described the "hallucinogenic" or otherworldly nature of Dugin's Eurasianism in even more explicit terms. The blogger and mathematician Misha Verbitsky, who is ideologically on the far left, claimed that he decided to collaborate with Dugin because he saw Eurasianism as a way of achieving "dreamtime," a concept linked to Australian Aboriginal mythology, in which one exists outside of the linear progression of time. At the time, Verbitsky told me, this was a very popular idea among Dugin's followers.[5] Valery Korovin, at the time of our conversation Dugin's right hand and a member of the Civic Chamber of the Russian Federation (Obshchestvennaia palata Rossiiskoi Federatsii), compared the intellectual transformation produced by his first reading of Dugin's book *Foundations of Geopolitics* to the discovery of LSD for American hippies during the 1960s.[6] Vladimir, an artist and early supporter of the Eurasia movement and, like Gintovt, a proponent of imperial art, defined Dugin's "alternative history" as a "myth about the afterlife."

Anatoly, another visual artist close to Gintovt's inner circle, defined his political position as a form of "faith in a higher truth [*istina*]." He described the Eurasianist empire as a dream-like vision of an "absolute fatherland, which never existed, and for which we long . . . a heavenly, eternal empire, which is hidden in the past and belongs, paradoxically, to the future." When I asked him, Anatoly confirmed that what he was talking about was an imagined, reinvented past and tradition, and that the "Aleksander Nevsky we know and imagine is the beautiful actor Nikolay Cherkasov from Eisenstein's 1930s film." Gintovt himself talked about the importance of the "post-apocalyptic aesthetics" and the mystical laughter produced by the newspaper *Limonka*, which he used to read regularly well before becoming a member of the Eurasia Movement. Interestingly, Gintovt spoke in an analogous way about his fascination with the 1990s, a similarly apocalyptic time, when "one knew that the world might end tomorrow, and when therefore everything was allowed."

Many other members of Dugin's "conservative bohemia" also had a similar paradoxical attitude toward the chaos and *bespredel* (literally, "absence of limits") of the post-Soviet 1990s, which they saw as the beginning of the ultimate ruin and defeat for Russia and at the same time, nostalgically, as a time of incredible adventures and intellectual discoveries, or, as my other informant Vladimir often put it, "the youth of our freedom."[7] Like their predecessors, the dandies, bohemians, and *flâneurs* who inhabited the Parisian Left Bank, they both rejected and embraced the modern (or late capitalist) condition, which was inextricably connected with the shaping of their culture and identity.

As is clear from these responses, for Dugin's "conservative bohemia" neo-Eurasianism is a means to produce an alternative collective identity and an alternative intellectual community, resisting mainstream culture and values. In a way not dissimilar from the late-Soviet "metaphysical underground" to which Dugin originally belonged, for this intellectual community neo-Eurasianism is a way to escape and produce an alternative to what they see as the post-Soviet mainstream culture, reality, and ideology. In a way, the Eurasianists replicate and attempt to realize Dugin's myth about a sectarian, metaphysical underground, which would supposedly grant access to higher spheres of knowledge and alternative interpretations of history and reality. Many of the members of this community, and especially those who do not have an active official involvement in the political or financial side of the project, consider Dugin's political project "an intellectual game" in which they decided to participate.

The association of conservative ideology and a bohemian life style could seem surprising at first; however, bohemianism has often overlapped with traditionalism, the rejection of progress and modernity, and a profoundly aristocratic (and therefore anti-egalitarian) outlook. Some of the first subcultures that emerged during the French Revolution, for instance, were formed by groups of aristocrats and "monarchists and had as their purpose the terrorizing of their radical counterparts of the Jacobin Club."[8] Charles Baudelaire, one of the main incarnations of bohemianism, and of the decadence of nineteenth-century urban life, had notoriously reactionary political views, and he defined dandyism, a very close relative of bohemianism, as a liminal condition, primarily characterized by nostalgia for a disappearing world. For Baudelaire, dandyism coincides with the creation of a "new aristocracy" against the "levelling" of modern democracy.[9] Like the ultrareactionary Baudelaire, Walter Benjamin's *flâneurs* were irresistibly drawn to the hectic movement of the city and to its crowds and at the same time they were repulsed by them. They distinguished themselves from the masses through their ability to enjoy leisure, and they provocatively demonstrated their hostility toward progress and modernity by taking "turtles for a walk in the arcades. The *flâneurs* liked to have the turtles set their pace for them. If they had had their way, progress would have been obliged to accommodate itself to this pace. But this attitude did not prevail; Taylor, who popularized the watchword 'Down with the dawdling!,' carried the day."[10]

Neo-Eurasianism shares with other forms of bohemianism the simultaneous attraction and repulsion toward (post)modernity and the attempt at creating an alternative reality and lifestyle, as well as, at least in some of its forms, an aristocratic, "anti-egalitarian," and anti-democratic worldview, but it is quite unique in its radicalism and its involvement with politics and mass culture. As opposed to other forms of bohemianism, neo-Eurasianism is hyper-ideological and militant, and it aims at producing actual political change through mass manipulation. In fact, one might argue that Eurasianism as a social practice exists on two levels, that of an "invention of a bohemian lifestyle" and that of mass mobilization and "political technology."

This final chapter studies the ways in which Dugin's ideas inspired, or translated into, specific social practices, and how such practices affected the shaping of public culture and state ideology during the Putin era. The vision of a "conservative bohemia," based on a cult of the late Soviet underground, is the main defining feature of the identity of most intellectual and political communities surrounding the Eurasia Movement. The main aesthetic sources of this "neo-Eurasianist bohemianism" can be retraced to the late Soviet "metaphysical underground" of Yuri Mamleev's Iuzhunskii Circle, where Dugin's intellectual and political trajectory began, and to Timur Novikov's New Academy. In the case of the latter, it is appropriate to talk about mutual influence, in that Dugin had a role in the conservative turn toward a so-called new seriousness within the New Academy. On the basis of these specific cultural references, neo-Eurasianism evolved as a vision of an imagined closed world and reality built on alternative historical narratives, as well as on a paradoxical nostalgia for late Soviet unofficial culture. The neo-Eurasianists' "golden age" is that of a largely reimagined and reinvented Soviet underground, opposing both Soviet socialism and Western capitalism as two different incarnations of the modern project.

Next, the chapter moves to the social life and culture of the artistic and intellectual communities built around Moscow's Eurasianist intellectual circles, with a focus on Gintovt's art project. Gintovt's art involves, among other things, an unconditional commitment to Dugin's ideology and the attempt at creating an alternative community of neo-Eurasianist artists, sharing a common aesthetics, ideology, and sensibility. Starting with the example of Gintovt's art project, this section investigates the ways in which the members of Dugin's inner circle consider themselves part of a conservative bohemia and, at the same time, an alternative intellectual and academic network aimed at covertly influencing Russia's policymaking and global political processes. Eurasianists paradoxically consider themselves both a reactionary and a revolutionary force within Russian society, and they have actively contributed to the circulation of a vision of Russia as the site of a post-historical imperial modernity.

The final section discusses different examples of the impact of Dugin's thought on contemporary Russian public culture and mainstream media. These include the activity of the Eurasian Youth Union (Evraziiskii soiuz molodezhi, ESM) and the recent collaboration between the Eurasianists and the Russian government in the annexation of Crimea and the creation of a separatist movement in Eastern Ukraine. On the basis of Dugin's anti-globalist and "countercultural" vision of Russian national identity, the neo-Eurasianists have contributed to the widespread circulation of a vision of the Russian public sphere as a territory of continuous violent struggle, conquest, colonization, and recolonization of cultural and political space.

A Metaphysical Underground

Both the cult of death and the cult of the underground as an alternative sphere of cultural production are important elements in the social life and culture of the Eurasia Movement. Both of these elements resonate with Dugin's own writing and intellectual background, which goes back to late Soviet unofficial culture. During the 1980s, Dugin was a member of the Iuzhinskii Circle, whose leader, Mamleev, one of the forefathers of Russian postmodern literature, had a deep influence on several generations of Moscow writers, intellectuals, and political dissidents. The activities of his "metaphysical circle," named after Mamleev's small apartment in Iuzhinskii Lane, allegedly included philosophical discussions, literary readings, magic rituals, copious amounts of alcohol, and sex.[11] These gatherings offered opportunities for transgression and experimentation and, starting in the 1960s, they were attended by prominent writers and intellectuals, including the writer Venedikt Erofeev, the poet Leonid Gubanov, and the dissident leader Vladimir Bukovsky.[12]

Dugin joined the circle in the 1980s, well after Mamleev's emigration to the United States in 1974. At this point, the charismatic leader of the group was Evgeny Golovin, an almost legendary figure within the Moscow underground. Golovin was a man of many talents and diverse interests, such as decadent poetry, alternative rock, and occultism. He translated Baudelaire and Rimbaud into Russian, was a prolific songwriter, and was the author of the lyrics of many of the songs performed by Vasily Shumov's popular alternative rock band Tsentr. He was also the one who introduced the other members of the Iuzhinskii Circle to traditionalist authors René Guénon and Julius Evola, while the Islamic activist and philosopher Geydar Dzhemal gave them access to the rich library of German philosophers he had inherited from his grandfather, a professor of philosophy at Moscow State University.[13] While Guénon's traditionalism was purely philosophical, the "Sicilian baron" Julius Evola was an ultrareactionary writer, philosopher, expert in different forms of mysticism, and former Dadaist painter, who had supported, at different times, both Italian Fascism and German Nazism. Both Guénon and Evola had been models and sources of inspiration for the European far right during the postwar period.[14] Not surprisingly, the works of these authors were not easily accessible in the Soviet Union. Allegedly, members of the group mostly read them in French and German editions held in a special section of the Lenin Library in Moscow, to which Golovin had access thanks to his work as a translator.

Under the influence of Golovin and Dzhemal, Dugin first discovered these traditionalist authors and became fascinated with mysticism, conspirology, esotericism, and the occult undercurrents of the Nazi regime, which later became the main sources of inspiration for his specific conception of neo-Eurasianism.[15]

The young Golovin was, in Dzhemal's words, sarcastic and aggressive "like a young dark Socrates-provocateur." He had incredible charisma and was deeply admired and even envied because of his prodigious erudition.[16] Golovin was also the one who introduced explicit references to Nazi aesthetics and symbols into this community. In addition to the discussions about the classics of traditionalism, which carried a quasi-fascist subtext, he renamed his close group of friends and acolytes the "Black Order of the SS" (Chernyi orden SS), a name that could not but produce horror and outrage, and introduced various more or less ironic rituals connected to the "occult undercurrents" of the Nazi regime.[17]

The group's "Nazi mysticism," among other things, represented a way of rejecting and living "beyond" the dull and arid late Soviet reality, and of challenging its hypocrisy. The circle's rituals and behaviors were highly performative and intentionally transgressive and defiant. They were marked by dark irony and bad taste, and by a paradoxical desire to be "on the wrong side" and systematically nonaligned. Golovin adopted the nickname "Sternberg," after Baron von Ungern-Sternberg, a general of the White Army who fought in the Far East during the Russian Civil War, converted to Buddhism, advocated for reestablishing the empire of Genghis Khan, and was known for his incredible cruelty and penchant for violence.[18] As a challenge, Dzhemal would walk around Moscow wearing an SS officer's hat.[19] As mentioned, Dugin followed his mentor in choosing the most outrageous name possible, Hans Sievers (after the head of Ahnenerbe, a quasi-mystical, pseudo-scientific society established in Nazi Germany to study the origins of the Aryan race), and wrote songs inspired by Maldoror, the absurd character from a nineteenth-century French poem whose gruesome adventures had been a source of inspiration for the Dadaists. Dugin's singing style went from pseudo-romantic and sappy to overtly cheerful and childish. His lyrics and references to fascism were comically irreverent, as in the song "Cadillac."

> In a wonderful morning mood, / In a celestial-blue Cadillac / We drive through the roads of Europe / Where the morning light is so wonderful. // Celestial-blue fascists / Greet us with their right hand, / You give them some cunning looks / And cheerfully laugh in response. // Celestial-blue fascists / In a celestial-blue Cadillac, / They have scary symbols on their armbands, / They have enormous cats in their arms.[20]

In addition to the surreal settings, the comical effect of the song is enhanced by the fact that "blue" (*goluboĭ*) in Russian is a slang word for gay, which conjures up the quite absurd image of "celestial-queer fascists" wearing Nazi uniforms and holding "enormous cats in their arms." A good American parallel of this kind of comedy, based on the systematic transgression of all the most deep-seated taboos, is Mel Brooks's film *The Producers* (1967), in which a failing Broadway impresario, in order to scam his insurance company, decides to produce a supposedly sure flop, *Springtime for Hitler: A Gay Romp with Adolf and Eva at Berchtesgaden*, by piling up an improbable mix of the most offensive stereotypes imaginable and by alienating all possible ethnicities and cultural groups. The Iuzhinskii Circle's "Nazism" originated in a similar form of dark irony and attraction for everything that went against Soviet "political correctness."

At the same time, this taste for transgression and desire to *épater les bourgeois* also ended up, in certain instances, determining moral values and political convictions. During an interview, pointing to an episode from his adolescence that marked the beginning of his interest in politics, Dzhemal recalled how he heard on the radio a series of clichés about "peace" ("peaceful coexistence"; "the Soviet government's struggle for peace," all of which were omnipresent ready-made formulas of late Soviet propaganda) and experienced "the most acute zoological hatred against these words, the person who was pronouncing them, and everything they represented."[21] In reaction to this kind of well-intentioned hypocrisy, Dzhemal became attracted to "the most extreme, romantic forms of anti-humanism," which for him came to be embodied by "social Darwinism," Hegel's objective idealism, and, ultimately, Guénon's traditionalism. Interestingly, in the post-Soviet period Dzhemal related this "romantic anti-humanism" to Islamic socialism, which, he argues, is the only political system that could counteract Western and American global political hegemony over the rest of the world.

In order to understand the mythology built around the Iuzhinskii Circle and the type of sensibility it came to embody in the post-Soviet period, consider Dugin's reading of Mamleev's most famous novel, *Shatuny*, which first appeared in samizdat in 1966 and is still a cult book among neo-Eurasianist circles. The title of the book (literally, "the roamers") metaphorically refers to the bears who wake up from their hibernation by accident and wander through the forest in a stupor. In the novel, Mamleev describes the encounter between the protagonist, Fedor Sonnov, an illiterate man from the deep Russian countryside who murders random people in order to experience personally the soul's transition to the afterlife, and a circle of Moscow metaphysical poets and philosophers, followers of the "religion of the higher I."[22] According to Dugin, Mamleev's novel should be interpreted as a metaphor for the Moscow underground:

> *Shatuny* is the mysterious core of the 1960s. In the nonconformist underground there was a hierarchy, too. Liberally inclined functionaries and intellectuals, who didn't break with the system, occupied the outermost part [of this structure]. These were in general very boring people, they lived on leftovers, mostly old stuff that everyone knew. Next, one would find political anti-Soviets . . . and the artistic bohemia. These were people who lived outside society, under control, but still in-between: they read bad samizdat and snatched the crumbs of the inner circle. At the center of

> the inner circle, that is, of the "schizoids," sat a solemn Yuri Vitalevich Mamleev himself, and a few more "superior unidentified persons," the "metaphysicians."[23]

The target of Mamleev's "destructive influence," Dugin continues, could not be just the Soviet system but needed to be "the foundation of the contemporary world, and maybe humanity in its entirety."[24] Here Dugin produces a sort of gnostic romantic myth of the late Soviet underground, seen as the site of an alternative experience, which granted access to a superior mystical knowledge. His vision is that of an "ontological otherness" or marginality, based on the idea of being "on the wrong side," and on the idea of protest as a source of collective and, ultimately, national identity. Through narratives connected with Mamleev's "metaphysical circle" (which is largely reimagined and reinvented, as Dugin had experienced firsthand only a later version of it), the image of a Eurasianist "conservative bohemia" overlaps with that of the religious sect or the secret lodge, founded on absolute marginality and exclusivity: in Dugin's reading of Mamleev the "schizoids" are a group of chosen people, who are at the same time absolute outcasts.[25] Most obviously, the image of the "chosen" or "saintly" outcasts reminds one of the figure, traditional in Russian culture, of the *iurodivyi*, the "fool for Christ" who adopts immoral, indecent, and blasphemous behavior as a way to escape vainglory. Even more aptly, because of the political nature of Dugin's conservative bohemia, the image of the "schizoid" evokes the mythology surrounding the figure of Oedipus, who embodies, at the same time, the "excluded" or the "wild beast" who violates the norms and taboos of the community, the scapegoat who is sacrificed to expiate its sins, and the "exceptional man" or the tyrant who acts beyond the boundaries of the law in order to reach power and impose an authoritarian rule.[26]

Timur Novikov's New Academy: Totalitarian Queerness and Intimate Monumentalism

The second source of inspiration for neo-Eurasianist bohemianism is the aesthetics of Timur Novikov's New Academy of Decorative Arts (Novaia Akademiia Iziashchnykh Iskusstv). The artist Novikov, along with Sergey Kurekhin, formed the hub of the Leningrad underground art and music scene, which included such phenomena as the Leningrad Rock Club, Viktor Tsoy's legendary rock band Kino, the New Artists movement, Kurekhin's own Pop-mekhanika, the late Soviet cult movies *ASSA* (1987) and *The Needle* (*Igla*, 1988), the poetry collective of the Mit'ki, as well as some of the first examples of post-Soviet club culture in Saint Petersburg and Moscow.[27]

After promoting and establishing himself as one of the main representatives of Soviet nonconformist art, in the early 1990s Novikov founded the New Academy and started advocating for the return to a classical ideal of beauty, figurativeness, and a traditional conception of art as craft. Novikov's "neo-academism" was the result of a curious combination of classicism, dandyism, and hedonism, which involved the rejection of both modernism and the international language of the contemporary art market in favor of more accessible artforms. In the late 1990s (before Novikov died prematurely), and in part under the influence of Dugin, the New Academy turned to the idea of a "new seriousness," which involved references to conservative ideology and a tongue-in-cheek, overtly moralizing attitude toward the decadence of contemporary art and society. The New Academy's "conservative turn" was in part the result of the neo-academists' rivalry with the other leading post-Soviet art group, the Moscow actionists. However, a group of neo-academists, including Gintovt, carried on, appropriated, and in part reinvented Novikov's legacy after his death, becoming involved in art-political projects even more explicitly connected to the idea of a "new seriousness," and to an overtly imperial, totalitarian, or "neo-Eurasian" aesthetics.[28]

Novikov was gay, as were several other prominent members of the New Academy, and the New Academy constitutes one of the earliest, and a deeply fascinating, examples of a specifically post-Soviet queer culture and aesthetics. It is crucial to highlight this aspect of the art and cultural production of the New Academy, because a queer sensibility, in the sense of a fluid sexuality but also in the sense of a refusal to be confined to a specific ideology, aesthetic norm, or cultural convention, was largely what defined the identity of the New Academy. A fundamentally fluid gender and sexual identity was something that the New Academy had in common with other early post-Soviet examples of gay and lesbian culture.[29] At the same time, "queerness," in the sense of a fundamental otherness, is also what determined the cultural (and to some extent political) strategy of the New Academy. This artistic community defined its identity in contrast with, and opposition to, what they saw as "mainstream" or institutionalized culture: Soviet official culture but also, after the fall of the Soviet Union, neoliberalism and even the Moscow Conceptualists and Moscow Actionists, who had become their main competitors on the international art market.[30]

In addition, the culture of this group participated in what has been defined, primarily in the context of Moscow Conceptualism, as a late Soviet "shimmering" or "flickering" aesthetics, marked by a fundamental tension between postmodern irony and a form of "new sincerity" on the part of the artistic or lyric subject.[31] The fundamental feature of this shimmering aesthetics within the

New Academy, in a way that is even more radical and disorienting than in the case of Moscow Conceptualism, is its positioning itself in-between, constantly oscillating between these two opposite poles. This shimmering aesthetics characterizes both the queer identity and the "traditionalist" or "neoclassical" turn of the New Academy, which defines itself, in a way not dissimilar from the Iuzhinskii Circle or the Eurasia Movement, through a condition of perpetual "otherness" or liminality.

Novikov's neoclassicism and the aesthetics of artists close to the New Academy had a very pronounced camp and queer dimension, but neither Novikov nor the other neo-academicians spoke openly about their sexuality or the role it played in their art. When they did talk about sexuality, they did so in an excessive, provocative, or even shockingly vulgar way. For instance, Novikov once described the "dropping" or "lowering" (*opuskanie*) of the avant-garde as follows: "So, the camera shows a new convict—acting all important and stuff, well . . . a former journal editor etc. All of a sudden, some real gangsters approach him, they drop his pants, they fuck him and force him to suck their cocks. This is what 'dropping' (*opuskanie*) means, for instance." Sergey "Afrika" Bugaev, another prominent representative of the New Academy, claimed that Novikov was acquainted with New York gay culture "by 20 centimeters or so." Both Novikov and Bugaev declared that they were "faggots" (*pederasty*), and they contrasted the fundamental "femininity" of the New Academy with the "masculinity" of Moscow Conceptualists, their main rival in the field of contemporary Russian art.[32] Queerness remained hidden and at the same time it largely determined the artistic position of the New Academy.

Taking as a starting point Jencks's ideas on postmodern architecture, Novikov identified postmodern art with a return to classic imperial forms and to the idea of art as a service to the state.[33] "Classical beauty," in Novikov's conception, is supposed to be figurative and accessible. It represents a rejection of the abstract, complex, and ultimately elitist language of modernism (hence, the "dropping" of the avant-gardes from the quoted passage). At the same time, paradoxically, neo-academism is supposed to produce a new hierarchy and canon of "objective beauty."[34]

A similar tension informs Novikov's vision of (Western) mass culture. On the one hand, neo-academism is deeply involved with various forms of mass culture, including fashion, club and rock culture, film, photography, video art, and various kinds of camp performances. Photography is for Novikov the medium through which a cult of unmediated beauty has survived in the modern world, and the images "of beautiful men and women from *Vogue*" preserve the signs of the ancient "cult of Apollo."[35] All of the modern archetypes of beauty for the New Academy belong to popular (or populist) and widely accessible artforms—Western mass culture and totalitarian art (Nazi art or socialist realism). Ultimately the main goal of the New Academy is to bring the classical cult of unmediated physical beauty back from the sphere of mass culture (embodied in the beauty of "the Coca-Cola bottle" and "Mr. Olympia competition") to the museums and art academies.[36]

On the other hand, neo-academism represented a form of "ethical and aesthetic ecology" against the decadence of both Western mass culture and the international language of modern art, and an attempt at creating national, specifically Russian and post-Soviet, art forms. According to Novikov, because of its specific geopolitical position, Russia had become the last shrine of European culture; the dusty Soviet academies of art (which were producing highly repetitive propaganda canvases and sculptures) had continued training their artists in the traditional techniques of figurative art, as opposed to their European counterparts, where abstractionism had become predominant. For seventy years, the Soviet Union had created a hermetically closed space, excluded from the flood of images of commercial advertising; in the case of Saint Petersburg, this situation had produced an aesthetically consistent environment dominated by imperial and neoclassical forms.[37]

For Novikov, neo-academism originated in the everyday experience of being part of the late Soviet underground while at the same time being surrounded, and inspired, by the neoclassical, perfectly symmetrical architecture of Saint Petersburg, which, because of its peripheral position within the Soviet system, remained largely unchanged throughout the twentieth century. The cult of Saint Petersburg as a neoclassical phantasmagorical space existing outside of modernity was a fundamental feature of neo-academism. The poet Iosif Brodsky saw Petersburg in a similar way and argued that Novikov's art reflected neoclassical tendencies in the city's cultural tradition extending from Evgeny Baratynsky's poetry to Anna Akhmatova's.[38] Incidentally, Novikov shared with Brodsky (as well as, in a different way, with Dugin) not only the interest in neoclassical forms but also the desire to be fully immersed in a (partly imagined) world of cultural references and allusions.

The eclectic and paradoxical nature of Novikov's "neoclassical postmodernism" cannot be fully understood without referring to the concrete art and social practices that it produced. Novikov's career symbolically starts in 1982 with the provocative action *Nol' ob"ekt* (Zero object): during one of the earliest semi-official exhibits of nonconformist art in Leningrad, Novikov and Ivan Sotnikov, in part as a parody of Andrey Monastyrsky's Collective Actions, cut a small square in one of the few empty spaces on one of the walls in the exhibit space, showing their faces through it and recording the surprised reactions of the visitors.[39] Irony and a playful taste for provocation marked Novikov's work from the beginning of his career.

At the same time, the art of Timur Novikov and the other artists involved in the New Artists/New Academy movement—Georgy Gurianov, Sergey "Afrika" Bugaev, Vladislav Mamyshev-Monroe, Olga Tobreluts, and others—was deeply rooted in the language and rituals of Leningrad's underground communities. The beginnings of the New Artists movement in the early 1980s were inspired by the rediscovery of the Saint Petersburg avant-garde tradition, of the poetics of Daniil Kharms and Aleksandr Vvedensky, and by Mikhail Larionov's doctrine of *vsechestvo*, or "everythingism," according to which "everything can be art." This influenced the artistic practices and techniques of the New Artists, who began using everyday materials instead of paint and canvas (which were only available to members of the Soiuz khudozhnikov, the Artists' Union) to produce their art. Novikov, for instance, worked extensively with various forms of collage, including his trademark fabrics, which could be easily transported and displayed during unofficial exhibitions in apartments and were used as stage decorations for the early unofficial concerts of Viktor Tsoy's band Kino.

Perhaps even more importantly, the idea of "everythingism" was closely connected with the Russian avant-gardes' concept of *zhiznetvorchestvo*, or life-creation, an artistic approach to everyday life and behavior that overlapped with the New Artists' discovery of new wave and post-punk fashion and music, which were then reaching the Soviet underground. This resulted in experiments in the field of video and especially photographic performance, and in the fact that a form of transformism was part of the New Artists' art project and their self-presentation. Novikov and other New Artists would pose in front of the camera with fashionable haircuts and outfits and in recognizably neoromantic poses (see fig. 27). In the 1990s, the style of the latest alternative subcultures was replaced by carefully staged photographs in overtly aristocratic poses, dressed as old-fashioned dandies or in campy, neoclassical outfits (see fig. 28). In the last years of his life, Novikov took on a severe, quasi-monastic look and a traditional orthodox long beard (see fig. 29).

The diverse styles and strategies of the New Academy artists included experiments with old painting and photographic techniques, collages, or more traditional oil painting techniques. Independently from the technique employed, the reference to antiquity remained playful and pervaded by a camp sensibility. Novikov was often portrayed in the role of the "spiritual leader" in various incarnations: wearing a tailcoat and acting as the role model of Petersburg's bohemianism or inspiring a neo-academist renaissance in the role of an unusually muscular Homer.

The New Academy is an artistic group too vast and multifaceted to do it justice in this short digression. However, a few examples of the art produced by some of its members, and of its reference to "neoconservative," totalitarian,

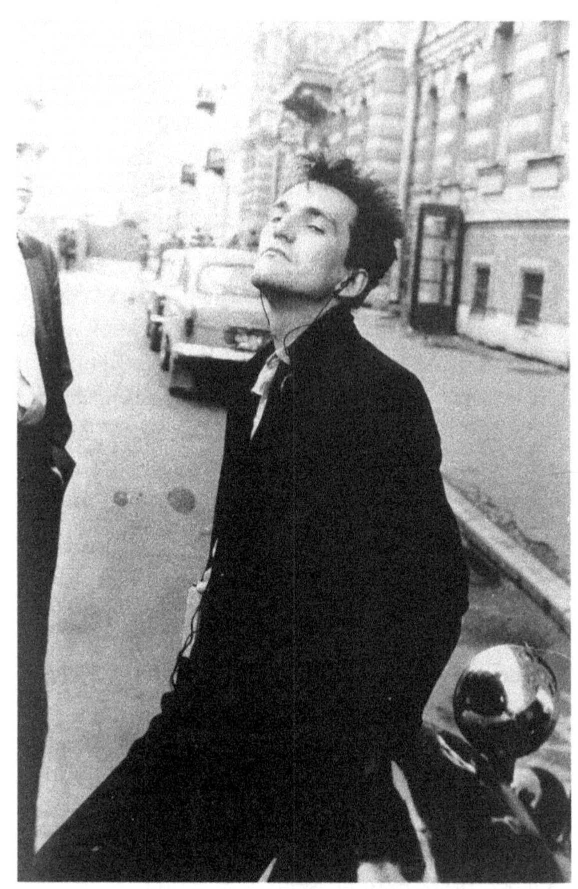

Right: figure 27. Timur Novikov in Leningrad, 1982. Reproduced from Andreeva, Chechot, and Novikova, *Timur.*

Below: figure 28. Novikov and other neo-academists (in very dandy outfits) posing in front of the painting *The Triumph of Homer* (by Oleg Maslov and Viktor Kuznetsov, with Timur Novikov in the role of Homer) as part of the performance *The Red Square, or, The Golden Section*, 1999. Reproduced from Ippolitov and Kharitonov, *Novaia Akademiia.*

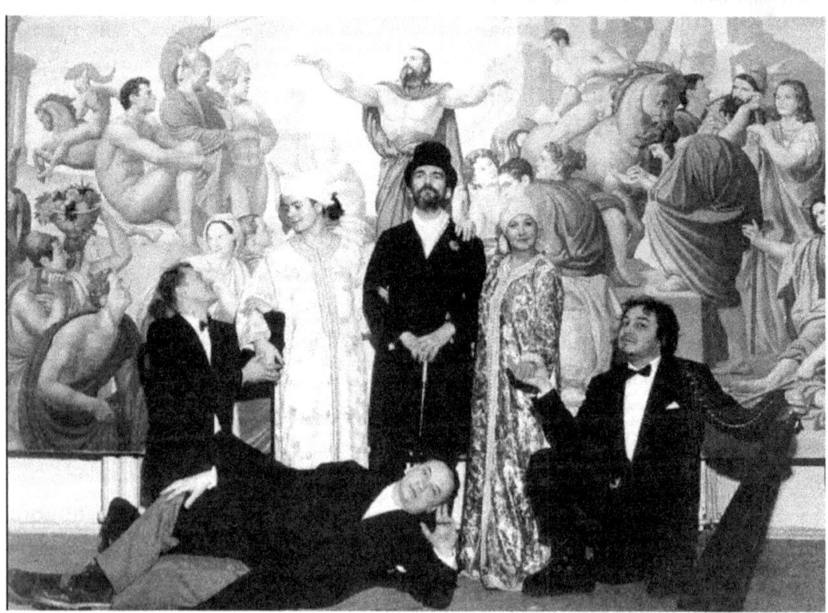

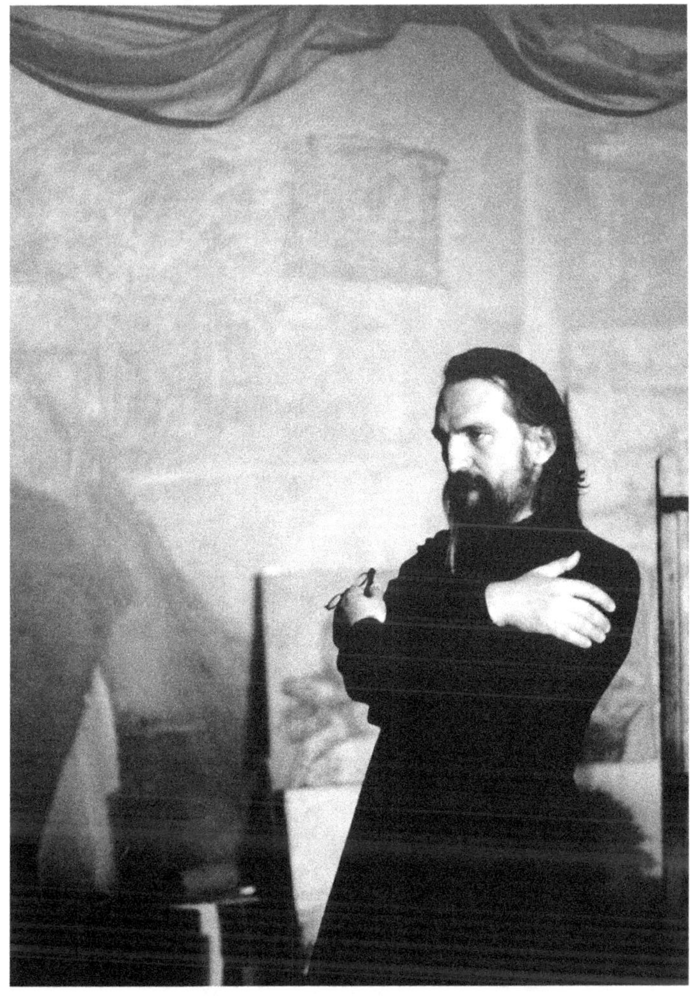

Figure 29. Novikov in 1998, after the "conservative turn" in the New Academy. Photo by Natalia Zhernovskaya. Reproduced from Andreeva, Chechot, and Novikova, *Timur*.

and socialist realist imageries, can help understand the way in which this art community affected the culture of the Eurasia Movement. Consider, for instance, the art of Georgy Gurianov, the drummer of the rock band Kino, who in the 1990s became one of the most prominent representatives of Novikov's neo-academism. Gurianov was one of the few artists in the group with a traditional fine arts training, and his art came to represent the perfect embodiment of Novikov's programmatic manifestos.[40]

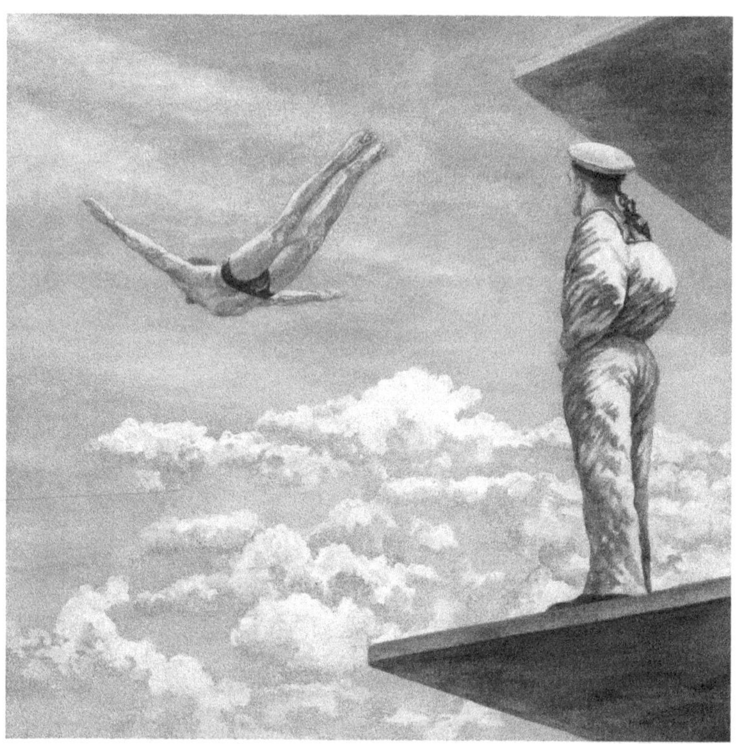

Figure 30. Georgy Gurianov, *Pryzhok v vodu* (The dive) (1995–2001). Acrylic on canvas, 150 × 150 cm.

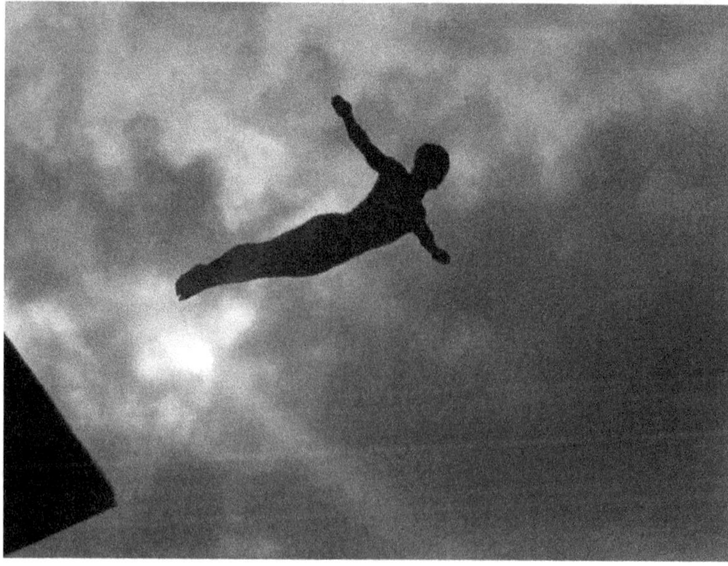

Figure 31. A diver from the documentary film *Olympia* (Leni Riefenstahl, Olympia-Film, 1938).

He mostly painted enormous traditional oil canvases combining homoerotic imagery, monumentalism, and explicit references to totalitarian art. The title of one of his exhibits, the *Strength of Will* (*Sila voli*, 1994), was an explicit tribute to Leni Riefenstahl, the director of *Triumph of the Will* (1935), one of the most infamous and iconic examples of Nazi propaganda. The subjects of Gurianov's paintings were mostly athletes, sailors, boxers, and wrestlers. Some of the images were almost exact replicas of still frames from Riefenstahl's other main documentary, *Olympia* (1938), which was produced to celebrate the 1936 Berlin Olympics and exemplifies the Nazi cult of the body and appropriation of neoclassical archetypes. The painting *The Dive* (1995–2001), for instance, replicated faithfully a shot from *Olympia*, although in this case Gurianov conflated Nazi and Soviet visual tropes: the canvas portrays a very Soviet-looking sailor observing the plastic pose of the perfectly executed dive (see figs. 30 and 31).

Many of Gurianov's paintings revealed the queer utopian subtext of different and apparently incompatible forms of totalitarian reinventions of antiquity. A series in Gurianov's exhibit, for instance, was made of painted adaptations of several shots of Abram Room's "shelved" feature film *A Strict Youth* (*Strogii iunosha*, 1935), with a screenplay by famous modernist writer Yuri Olesha. Shot in the midst of "high Stalinism," Room's film represented one of the numerous and diverse attempts at creating new socialist art forms, but it was never actually distributed in the Soviet Union because it was considered problematic from an ideological standpoint. *A Strict Youth* portrayed, and tried to find a solution for, the conflict between the old intelligentsia—scientists, medical doctors, and engineers involved in the "construction of socialism"—and a new generation of politically and socially engaged intellectuals. The film was quite visionary and very radical from a formal and narrative standpoint, and it depicted the communist future as a neoclassical utopia dominated by physical exercise (in fairly revealing outfits) and philosophical discussions about social equality and free love (two closely connected issues, according to the main characters). The film was censored, most likely, both for the fact that it did not fit well with Stalinist propaganda's focus on family values and for its aesthetic affinity with the "Olympic" models of beauty promoted by the Third Reich (see figs. 32 and 33).

Vladislav Mamyshev-Monroe, another member of Timur Novikov's group, played with some of the stereotypes of Soviet popular culture. Mamyshev-Monroe reached international notoriety in the early 1990s as "the first Soviet drag queen" when he appeared on the cover of numerous magazines in the guise of famous political leaders and other icons of pop culture. Throughout the years, he played the role of all the most recognizable media personalities: Marylin Monroe, Gorbachev, Hitler, Yeltsin, Putin, and Osama Bin Laden. At the beginning of the 2000s, he became particularly obsessed with Lyubov

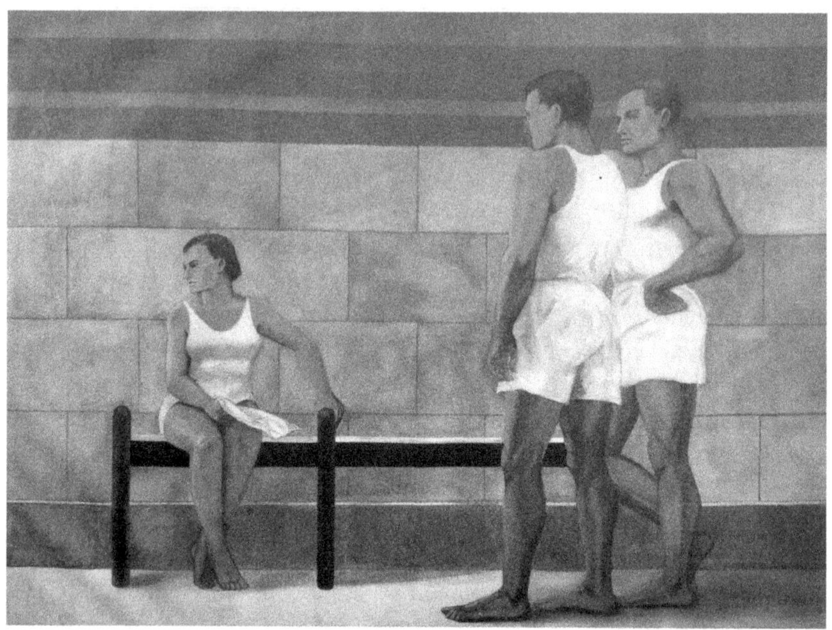

Figure 32. Georgy Gurianov, *Strogii iunosha* (A strict youth, 1994), right side of the triptych. Oil on canvas, 170 × 250 cm. Reproduced from Ippolitov and Kharitonov, *Novaia Akademiia*.

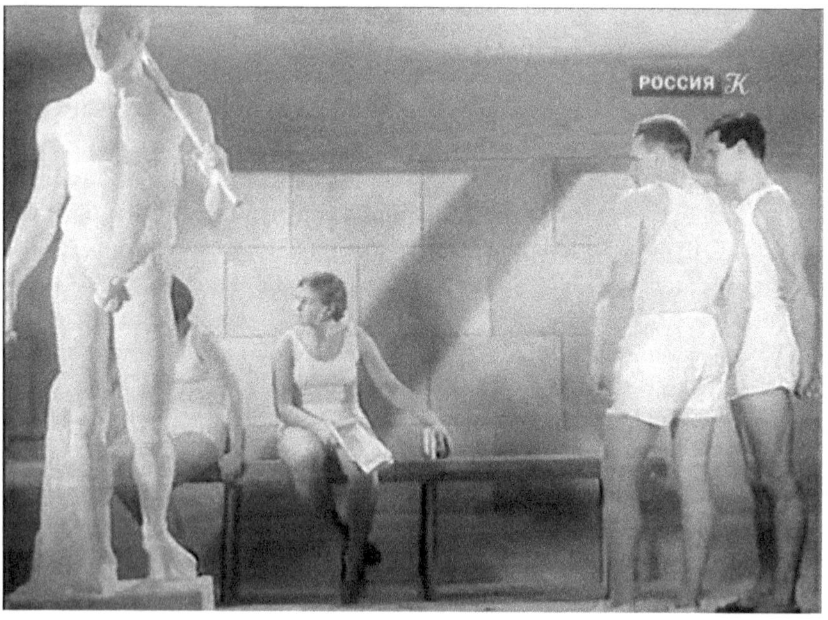

Figure 33. A screenshot from Abram Room's "shelved" film *Strogii iunosha* (Ukrainfil'm, 1935).

Orlova, the Soviet actress who had played the protagonist role in some of the most famous Stalinist musical comedies, and whose figure had come to embody the Soviet archetype of heroic, cheerful, and self-sacrificing femininity.

The Soviet star became the main alter ego of Mamyshev-Monroe, who in 2006 produced a video installation by superimposing his own face upon Orlova's in every single frame of the Stalinist musical *Volga-Volga* (1938) and reciting all her sung and spoken parts. In her films, Orlova was portrayed as an absolute model of Soviet chastity and pure dedication to the socialist cause. The romantic engagements of her characters were mostly a matter of mentorship and "reawakening" of class consciousness: in *Circus* (*Tsyrk*, 1936) she played an American artist who learns the Soviet values of color blindness and social equality from a very blond, immaculate Soviet aviator dressed in all white; in *Tanya* (*Svetlyi put'*, 1938), she played a village girl turning cinderella-cum-assault worker who becomes a weaver and eventually a Stakhanovite, breaking production records under the benevolent gaze of her suitor, the factory director.[41]

These relationships were not just platonic, but almost infantile, and they ended in the same predictable manner: with the two lovers barely touching shoulders while looking at the "bright future of humanity" (see fig. 34). Orlova's typical outfit, a very chaste and subdued Stalinist business suit, also highlighted the asexual nature of the characters she played. In contrast, in one of his early photographic impersonations of the actress, Mamyshev-Monroe chose to portray her as an aging star, sitting in her sumptuous and somewhat overcrowded Soviet apartment. His Orlova has in fact an almost predatory look: the photograph appears to catch her talking on the phone, possibly gossiping, and reacting to being photographed by gazing playfully and saucily at the camera (see fig. 35).

Novikov's own production during the 1990s was marked by what can be described as a form of intimate monumentalism. His fabrics took on very essential designs, like his signature "horizons" inscribed in the line dividing two colors, often with miniscule figures disappearing beyond them. In terms of his artworks, Novikov's "neoclassicist turn" was realized through a series of metaphoric allusions to symbols, ideals, and models of timeless beauty, spirituality, and bohemianism, which made their appearance in the form of miniature images and photographs at the center of several of his fabric or collages: "Apollo Trampling on the Red Square," "Oscar Wilde," "Ludwig of Bavaria," "Saint John of Kronstadt," and "Saint Martyr the Duchess Elizaveta Fedorovna." These figures created a very specific, and in part disorienting, cultural and moral canon. Most of them constituted examples of a more or less hidden homoerotic sensibility, along with an uncompromising dedication to artistic and aesthetic principles. They all shared a fundamental lack of faith or interest

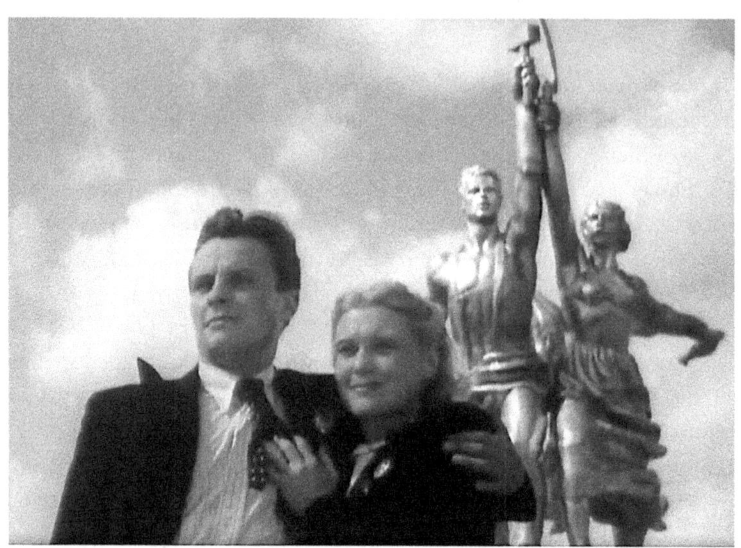

Figure 34. Lyubov Orlova in the final sequence of *Svetlyi put'* (The radiant path, released in English as *Tanya*, Mosfil'm, 1940).

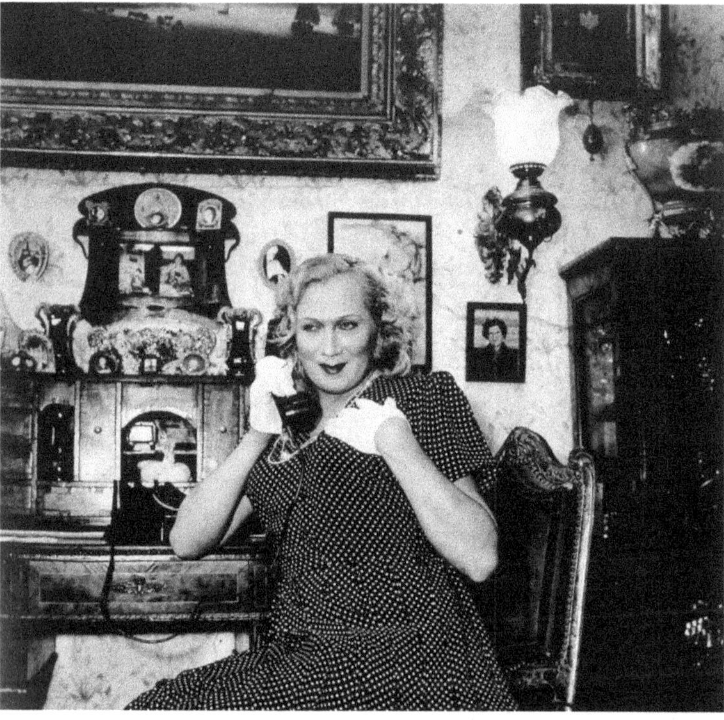

Figure 35. Vladislav Mamyshev-Monroe. From the series *Lyubov' Orlova*. Black-and-white photograph, 102 × 102.5 cm. Reproduced from Ippolitov and Kharitonov, *Novaia Akademiia.*

in progress or modernity and a strong sense of cultural identity and traditions. Some of the figures depicted, like Elizaveta Fedorovna, had been victims of the progress and historical change embodied by the Russian Revolution. These works look somewhat ironic and subdued in comparison to Novikov's daring and provocative manifestos. Consider, for instance, *Apollo Trampling on the Red Square* (1991), a work that became a symbol of the New Academy, and *Ludwig II of Bavaria* (2002).

In both cases the main subject almost disappears at the center of the piece, forcing the viewer to get close to the fabric to recognize it (in exhibit catalogs, the main subject usually needs to be magnified). As a result, the frame seems to take over, and the distinction between the subject of the painting and the surrounding decorations becomes blurred. In the case of *Apollo Trampling on the Red Square*, the archetype of classical beauty and proportions paradoxically appears to be reduced to one of its modern anonymous reproductions. At the same time, the miniature statue does not actually seem to triumph over the legacy of the avant-gardes; instead, the image seems to incorporate the formal experimentations of the historical avant-gardes (the miniature version of Malevich's *Red Square* within the golden geometric shape of the fabric) into newly rediscovered classical proportions (see figs. 36 and 37).

Ludwig II of Bavaria belongs to the series *The White Swan: King Ludwig II*, devoted to the Bavarian king and patron of the arts who discovered, promoted, and made possible the later works of Richard Wagner. Ludwig lived a secluded life, expressing little or no interest in the government of his country. He mostly dedicated himself to patronage, and to the building of sumptuous, fairy-tale castles replete with paintings and symbolic references to Wagner's operas. In the end he was dethroned and died under tragic and mysterious circumstances. The controversial king became a legendary figure during his lifetime, and his story also allegedly served as an inspiration for Tchaikovsky's *Swan Lake*. Novikov was deeply fascinated with Ludwig's story. He coauthored an essay about him and produced a series of collages portraying the king, Wagner, Tchaikovsky, and the white swan, the symbol Ludwig had been surrounded by throughout his childhood.[42]

In the collage *Ludwig of II Bavaria*, which Novikov realized a few months before he died, a small reproduction of the coronation portrait of the young king is surrounded by a soft white fabric covered with black feathers. In a mise en abyme of sorts, the fabric replicates the pattern of the ermine cape Ludwig is wearing in the portrait, a recognizable symbol of royalty, and a possible subtle allusion to the black and white swans of Tchaikovsky's ballet and the legend surrounding Ludwig's personality (see figs. 38 and 39). Through this series of references, Novikov's "conservatism" mostly appears to be realized in the form

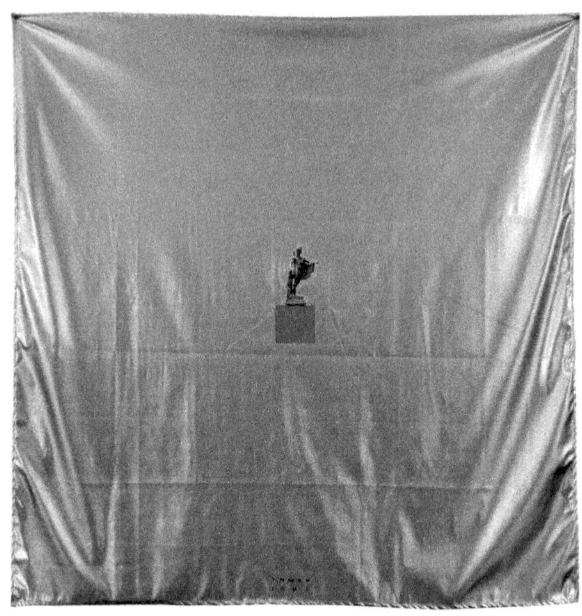

Figure 36. Timur Novikov, *Apollon, popiraiushchii krasnyi kvadrat* (*Apollo Trampling on the Red Square*), 1991. Acrylic and print on brocade and velvet, 141 × 137 cm. Reproduced from Ippolitov and Kharitonov, *Novaia Akademiia*.

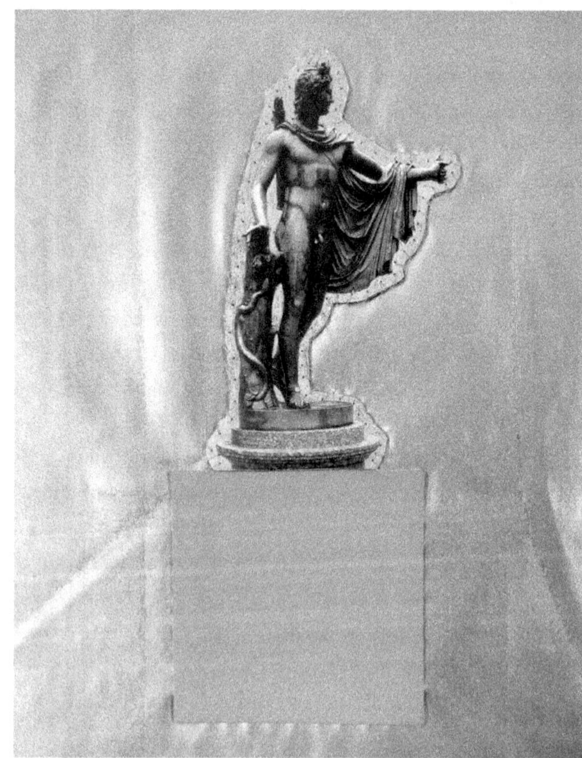

Figure 37. Timur Novikov, *Apollon, popiraiushchii krasnyi kvadrat* (*Apollo Trampling on the Red Square*), 1991 (detail). Acrylic and print on brocade and velvet, 141 × 137 cm. Reproduced from Ippolitov and Kharitonov, *Novaia Akademiia*.

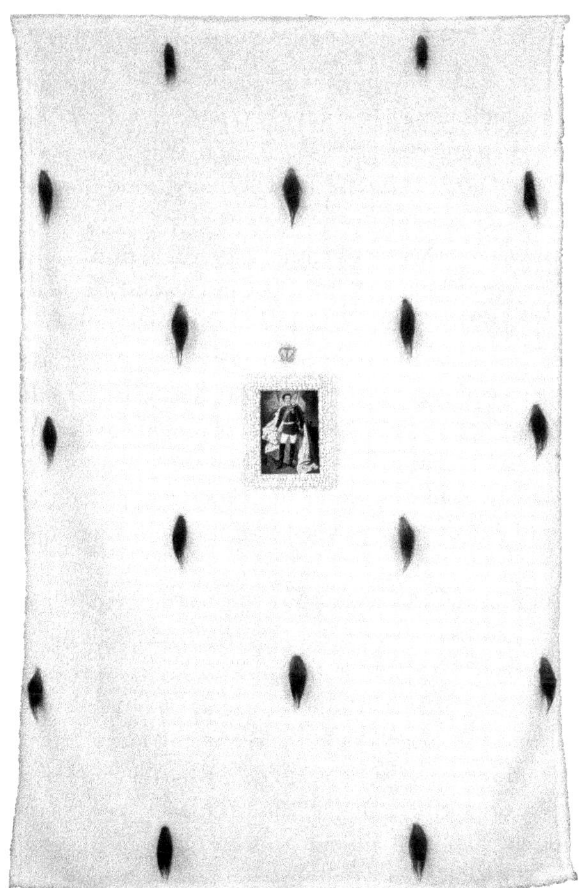

Figure 38. Timur Novikov, *Ludwig of Bavaria*, 2002. Fur, print, pearls, metal, 149 × 100 cm. Reproduced from Ippolitov and Kharitonov, *Novaia Akademiia*.

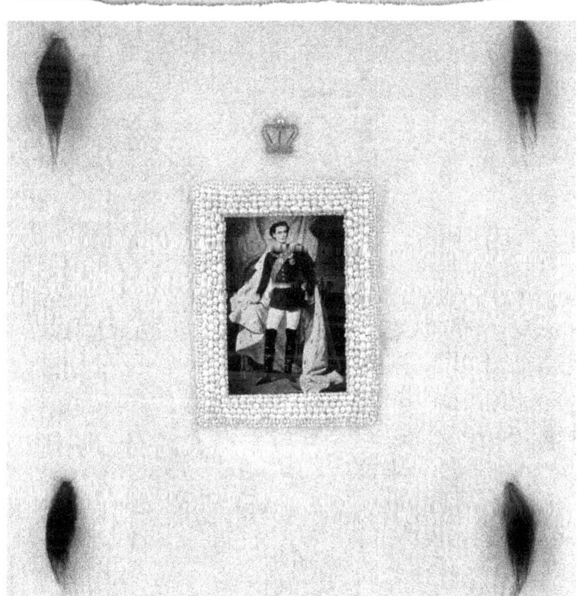

Figure 39. Timur Novikov, *Ludwig of Bavaria*, 2002 (detail). Fur, print, pearls, metal, 149 × 100 cm. Reproduced from Ippolitov and Kharitonov, *Novaia Akademiia*.

of a pure, hedonistic, and almost childlike pursuit of beauty and imagination. In a strange way, the Swan King's patronage of the arts and his romantic attempt at being fully immersed in a universe of artistic allusions reflect Novikov's own creation of an underground art community in the secluded atmosphere of late Soviet Leningrad.

Novikov and his acolytes were at their most carnivalesque and provocative in their performance and video installations. In the video installation *The Golden Section* (*Zolotoe sechenie*, 1999), Novikov, playing the role of the strict traditional art teacher, metaphorically enacted the neoclassicist struggle against modernism by adopting an expression of violent rage and using a wooden stick to spank the naked rear of Mamyshev-Monroe, who played the role of a naughty disciple failing to resist the lure of the avant-garde. Similarly, on one occasion some of the students of the New Academy comically declared to interviewers that they had to be periodically "punished" by their teachers, because sometimes they were "lazy" and did not practice enough.[43]

The conservative and moralizing performances of the neo-academists also appeared dominated by a playful and carnivalesque spirit. In the late 1990s, Novikov became religious; he grew a beard and adopted a stern and quasi-saintly look. He cofounded the movement Khudozhestvennaia volia (Artistic Will), which promoted a "cultural ecology" for Saint Petersburg and sought a unified artistic style that could serve as the expression of Russian statehood. The neo-academists' primary targets became the "sinful" mass culture of the 1990s and the art of the Moscow Actionists and the Moscow Conceptualists. As a form of ritual purification, in 1998 Khudozhestvennaia volia organized a performance in honor of the five hundredth anniversary of the death of the Florentine moralizer Girolamo Savonarola. As a demonstrative gesture, several members of the New Academy burned at the stake their own "shameless" (that is, overtly sexual) works, copies of popular magazines (like *Ptiuch'*, whose aesthetics they had helped to create), several issues of the art journals *Radek* and *Moscow Art Journal* (periodical associated with the New Academy's Moscow "competitors"), and piles of pornographic images. Petersburg *natsboly* expiated their own "sins" by throwing copies of *Limonka* into the fire (see fig. 40). In 2001, in collaboration with Gintovt and other Moscow sympathizers, the neo-academists replicated the action, which was renamed for the occasion *Khudozhestvennaia volia against Moscow Actionism*, in the courtyard of the Guelman Gallery in Moscow.

The traditionalism of the New Academy, its political and social conservatism, and focus on imperial and totalitarian art forms are usually seen as part of an ironic game, and part of the struggle between different art "cliques" (*tusovki*). According to many, Novikov's neoclassicism was largely motivated by his desire

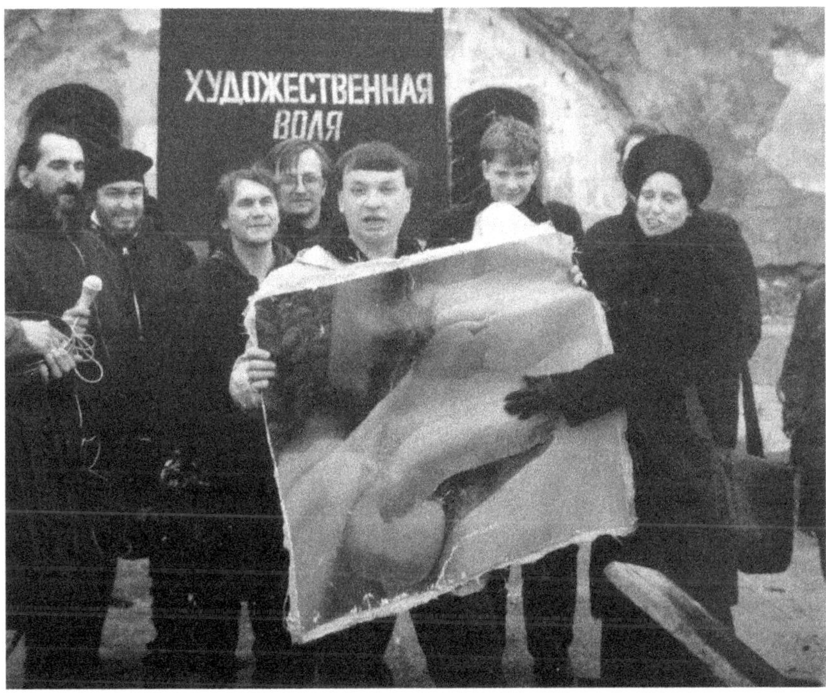

Figure 40. Novaia akademiia iziashchnykh iskusstv / Organization Khudozhestvennaia volia, *Sozhzhenie suet: K 500-letiiu sozhzheniia Savonaroly* (*The Bonfire of the Vanities: Performance in Honor of the 500th Anniversary of Savonarola's Bonfire*). St. Petersburg, May 23, 1998. Reproduced from Obukhova, *Performans v Rossii*.

to do "something new" and therefore, paradoxically (given the premises of his declarations), to produce the most innovative or "avant-garde" art forms at any given moment. Although they clearly evoked the ghost of Nazi book-burning (in a manner that some found distasteful), the neo-academists' "bonfires" and attacks on their Moscow rivals always maintained a fundamentally playful tone.[44]

Novikov's interest in various forms of neo imperialism, authoritarianism, and traditional religiosity—along with his provocative and inflammatory declarations—cannot be fully explained as a postmodern provocation or a PR move to gain ground against his competitors. Instead, his statements should be seen as continuously oscillating between irony and sincerity, between practice (or performance) and belief. Novikov was genuinely interested in these ideas, which overlapped with Dugin's own ideas about traditionalism and geopolitics. He was introduced to Dugin by Kurekhin in 1995, when he participated in a public meeting in support of Dugin's election campaign. Although, as opposed to Kurekhin, he was never actively involved in the political side of Dugin's project, clear references to Dugin's ideas can be found in Novikov's later articles and manifestos.[45] Novikov started using more and more frequently Gumilev's term "passionary" in his essays. He wrote an introduction to a collection of essays about the CIA's role in the promotion of modernism and contemporary art as part of a global struggle for cultural hegemony, with various allusions to Dugin's conspiracy theories about the "New World Order" and the infiltration of Atlanticist elements within Russian culture. In certain instances, he explicitly referred to some of Dugin's favorite authors and ideas in connection with various currents of traditionalism and "Nazi occultism," including Julius Evola, Herman Wirth (the author and cofounder of the Nazi archeological society Ahnenerbe), along with legends about the "Great North" and the existence of a "hyperborean civilization," which Novikov associated with the neo-imperial and neoclassical myth of St Petersburg.[46]

Furthermore, as another perfect example of the incredible overlap between art and fringe politics in post-Soviet Russia, the issue of the independent magazine *Khudozhestvennaia volia* that accompanied the neo-academists' bonfire action contained a "Contract," calling for the creation of a "Union on the Territory from the Baltic to the Adriatic Sea" aimed at "preserving the great traditions of authentic culture." The contract, which was provocatively written in the very stiff and pompous language of Soviet bureaucracy, was signed by Timur Novikov (as the representative of the New Academy), by Slovenian artist Milan Mohar (as the representative of Neue Slowenische Kunst [NSK]), and by Dugin (as the representative of the self-proclaimed "European Society for the Preservation of Classical Aesthetics").[47]

Novikov himself considered the emergence of a "new seriousness" in the visual arts as something that was taking place in close connection with politics. At the beginning of the 2000s, he argued that "postmodernism had died with Kurekhin," that Putin "was not joking," and that his rise to power had marked the end of Yeltsin's carnivalesque political spectacle. The New Academy, as a movement promoting aesthetic traditional values, according to Novikov, had intuited these broader cultural and political changes in the country.[48]

A radical fringe within the New Academy, headed by the artist Denis Egelsky and joined by Gintovt, Mikhail Rozanov, and others, had already founded a group that called itself New Serious and advocated for "stricter policies against cheap irony, cynicism, and dilettantism."[49] This group's actions at times verged on religious fundamentalism. Among other things, the New Serious, also known as "The Holy Inquisition," advocated a return to icon-painting and the destruction of neoclassical statues in Petersburg's Summer Garden. They also proposed that the city's premier art museums, the Russian Museum and the Hermitage, should close because they exhibited "disgraceful art."[50]

Be that as it may, in a very paradoxical way, considering that the New Serious claimed to be struggling against "postmodern irony" in favor of a return to straightforward figurative art forms, one might argue that their combination of art and reactionary politics pushed the New Academy's late Soviet "shimmering" further, producing an even more radical blurring of the boundaries between irony, performance, and political beliefs. This becomes even clearer in the context of neo-Eurasianist political art projects, in the context of which the sphere of politics and that of artistic creation become completely indistinguishable.

Gintovt's Art Project as a Form of "Radical Political Shimmering"

Dugin's Eurasia movement and Novikov's New Academy should be considered two interconnected cultural networks that shared people and ideas and influenced each other at various stages of their history. Dugin's ideas had a strong influence on the shaping of the aesthetics of the New Academy. At the same time, Dugin considers Novikov, along with Kurekhin, an important representative of the "elitist" highbrow postmodernism, which he sees as the preamble to a conservative revolution and the reemergence of a "premodern worldview." For Dugin, Novikov instinctively intuited the imminent return to a traditional hierarchy and system of values.[51] The work of Novikov and the New Academy also served as a fundamental source of inspiration for Gintovt's own politically engaged imperial art project.

However, neo-Eurasianism cannot be considered the natural continuation of the New Academy, just as it cannot be considered a continuation of the Iuzhinskii Circle. The Eurasianists appropriated the legacy and strategies of these communities in order to produce a very much reinvented myth about the late Soviet underground. Furthermore, even if the Eurasianists claim to be promoting a "new seriousness," I argue that their political project exists in between irony and belief.[52] In fact, the Eurasianists took late Soviet "shimmering" one step further, or "radicalized" it, by applying this artistic strategy to the sphere of grassroots politics. Gintovt's art project, which is based on such a form of "radical shimmering" between dark irony and blind faith in Dugin's ideology, can serve as a model to explain the culture of the Eurasia Movement as a whole and its impact on post-Soviet public culture.[53]

Some of Gintovt's artistic strategies resemble those of Novikov's postmodern neoclassicism, including the experimenting with unusual or old-fashioned

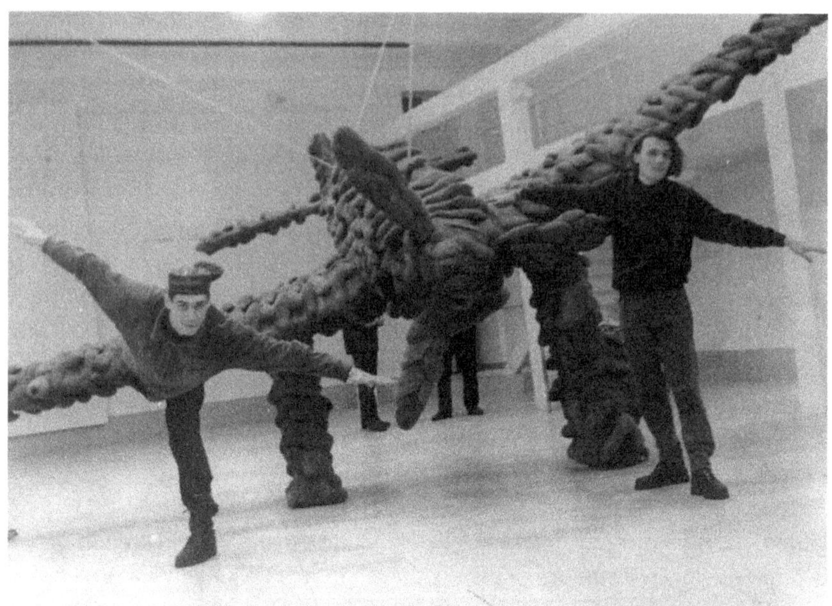

Figure 41. Aleksey Beliaev-Gintovt and Kirill Preobrazhenskii, *U-87*. Regina Gallery Moscow, 1994. Photo courtesy of Aleksey Beliaev-Gintovt.

materials and techniques, the reference to hierarchy and tradition, and a kind of bohemian resistance to modernity. As in the case of Timur Novikov and the neo-academists, Gintovt's art projects are fundamentally rooted in the materiality of the art object, and at the same time maintain a strong performative component. One of Gintovt's first works, realized in collaboration with artist Kirill Preobrazhensky in 1994, was the sculpture installation *U-87*, a tribute to the German sculptor and performance artist Joseph Beuys. In this project, Gintovt and Preobrazhensky created a faithful reproduction of the airplane on which Beuys crashed while fighting in World War II, all made of *valenki*, the Russian traditional felt boots. The installation, a reference to Beuys's partly invented "foundation myth," symbolically evoked concepts and questions that remained crucial in Gintovt's later career. These included Beuys's idea of social sculpture as *Gesamtkunstwerk*, able to shape and affect politics and society; the allegory of art as a form of myth-creation; and the conception of art performance as an archaic ritual of initiation, which Beuys promoted, as Dugin later did.[54] The sculpture also contained a more explicit ironic reference to historical memory and post-Soviet identity, through the combination of a classical Soviet and modern myth (the airplane) with a symbol of local folklore (the Russian felt boots) (see fig. 41).

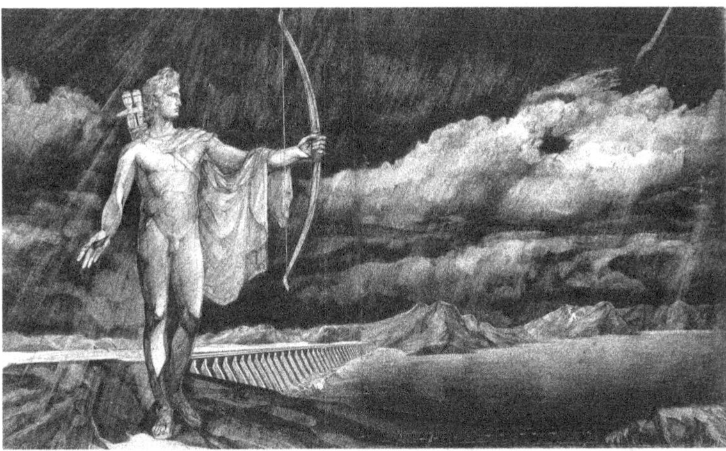

Figure 42. Aleksey Beliaev-Gintovt and Andrey Molodkin, *Plotina Apollona* (*Apollo's Dam*), 2001, from the series *Novonovosibirsk*. Ballpoint pen on canvas, 250 × 450 cm. Photo courtesy of Aleksey Beliaev-Gintovt.

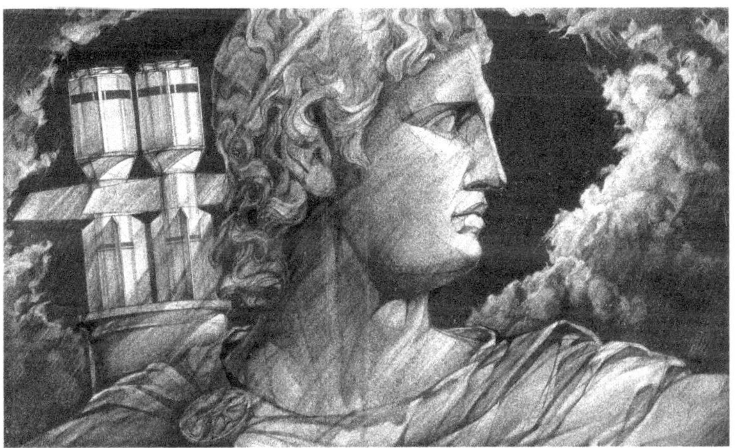

Figure 43. Aleksey Beliaev-Gintovt and Andrey Molodkin, *Apollon v silakh* (*Skillful Apollo*), 2001, from the series *Novonovosibirsk*. Ballpoint pen on canvas, 250 × 450 cm. Photo courtesy of Aleksey Beliaev-Gintovt.

At the beginning of the 2000s, when Gintovt became involved in radical politics, as well as in the conservative turn of the New Academy, this syncretic combination of modernity and tradition became inextricably intertwined with the vision of a postatomic utopian empire. In the 2001 project Novonovosibirsk, Gintovt, this time in collaboration with the artist Andrey Molodkin, depicted a postapocalyptic capital located at the center of Eurasia (see figs. 42 and 43).[55]

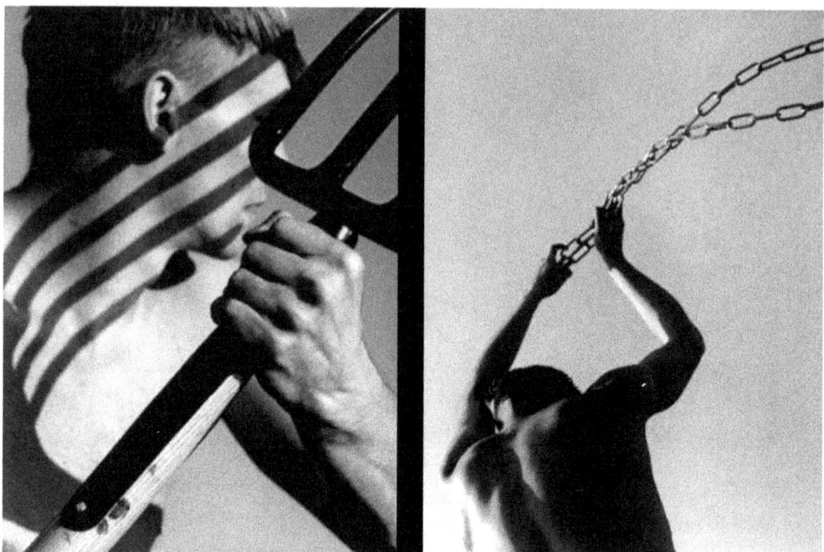

Figure 44. Andrey Molodkin, Gleb Kosorukov, and Aleksey Beliaev-Gintovt, *Monumenty* (*Monuments*), 2001, from the series *Novonovosibirsk*. Photo courtesy of Aleksey Beliaev-Gintovt.

The paintings in the series include classical and bucolic symbols (Apollo and a deer) combined with futuristic images, like the rocket-like arrows of Apollo and the atomic submarine emerging from the ice. This exhibition, too, had the character of an installation-performance. In addition to the large paintings, the exhibit included a series of photographs of Molodkin posing in pastoral-heroic poses, shot in a style reminiscent of Rodchenko's early experiments with photography (see fig. 44). Dmitry Shostakovich's Symphony No. 7, originally dedicated to Leningrad's heroic resistance to the Nazi siege during World War II, played in the background throughout the exhibition. As some of the commentators remarked at the time, the artists had appeared to express their devotion to their utopian vision through the physical effort and suffering involved in the execution of the large canvases (about 15 by 9 feet), which had been drawn using thousands of blue ballpoint Bic pens.[56] As in the choice of the subject, so in choosing the media and technique for these paintings the artists combined traditionalism, modern technology, and even marketing, as the technique was partly an attempt at gaining financial support from the powerful French corporation.

Through the years, Gintovt's art project gradually turned into an even more consistent embodiment of Dugin's neo-imperialist ideology and conception or vision of Russian statehood. The exhibitions *Rodina-doch'* (Motherland-daughter,

2007), *Parad pobedy 2937* (Victory Parade 2937, 2010), and *Sverkhnovaia Moskva* (Ultranew Moscow, 2012) combined imperial, Soviet, and orthodox symbols to reflect Dugin's metaphysics of the revolution in the form of a post-historical phantasmagoria and totalitarian utopia.

At first, Gintovt mainly decontextualized historical images of Stalinist mass spectacles and parades and transformed them into visions of a Eurasianist totalitarian future. Later, he combined images of post-human men-eagles, flying spaceships in the shape of red stars, high-tech guns in the shape of wheat sheaves, and hypermodern constructions with Russian churches and actual or unrealized monuments of Soviet architecture. The dominant red and gold in the paintings of this period evoked the reconciliation of Russian autocracy and socialism, but they also surreptitiously alluded to Dugin's Red-Brown ideology. The combination of imageries connected with space travel and agriculture was inspired by the sheaves and stars of the Exhibition of Achievements of the National Economy (VDNKh), a sacred space in the Stalinist universe that reflects, in Gintovt words, the paradoxical essence of the Soviet Union as an "agro-cosmic civilization."[57]

At the same time, these images clearly alluded to the fundamentally utopian nature of the Soviet project. They remind one of the Soviet "paper architecture" of the 1920s and the 1930s, and of the constructivist and socialist realist projects (like the Palace of the Soviets) that were not and could never have been realized. The critics who introduced these exhibitions wrote of a return to romantic childhood memories of the Soviet past and mentioned the Soviet sci-fi writers Aleksandr Kazantsev, Ivan Efremov, and Aleksandr Beliaev as possible sources of inspiration for Gintovt's imagery.[58]

Gintovt was inspired, among other things, by the sequence in Aleksandr Medvedkin's shelved 1938 comedy *The New Moscow* (*Novaia Moskva*, 1938). The reference to Medvedkin is in itself noteworthy. Like Room, Medvedkin was an innovative director who consistently tried to produce a new "socialist" cinematographic vocabulary and set of formal tools, and whose films ended up being shelved (i.e., were never distributed), because they were considered ideologically problematic. In particular, *The New Moscow* depicted the futuristic and fairy-tale nature of Moscow's reconstruction plan, which played a crucial role within the Stalinist cultural universe, in a way that could be easily misinterpreted.[59] In one of the final sequences of the movie, the protagonist, an architectural engineer-constructor from a Soviet province, displays a virtual "live" model (considered hypertechnological for the 1930s) of the reconstruction plan for the Soviet capital, which entailed destroying churches and old buildings to make space for the new socialist utopia. At the beginning of the demonstration, the mechanism malfunctions and shows the transformation in reverse:

the neoclassical, hyperrational, and hypertechnological socialist realist buildings disappear, and the recently demolished Orthodox churches are magically restored.

Both in Medvedkin and Gintovt, as in the case of Gurianov's art, the nostalgic reconstruction of the totalitarian Empire is not just "restorative" but reveals, while celebrating the past, its hidden subtext and repressed meanings. Gurianov's beautiful and athletic bodies revealed the queer subtext of the totalitarian cult of physical beauty; Gintovt's hypertechnological traditionalist utopia reveals the mystical and religious subtext of Stalinism, as well as the blood, repressions, and denial that creating this utopia would require. Significantly, when commenting on one of these exhibits, Gintovt stated, with the dark humor characteristic of his public declarations, that he "dreamt of a communism with an inhuman face."[60] His futuristic neoclassical spaces are in fact mostly empty or inhabited exclusively by supernatural zoomorphic creatures.

In his declarations and manifestos, Gintovt calls for the return to a concept of art as service to the state, to political authoritarianism, to imperial hierarchy, and to "verticality." However, as is the case with the art of Novikov's New Academy, Gintovt's work also contains significant pop-art and camp elements. His use of stencils of course evokes the legacy of Andy Warhol's silk-screen prints, but by manually adding gold to the canvas one leaf at a time and applying paint to the surface with his bare hands, he also adds an archaic, "analogic," and performance-like quality to his paintings. The subjects of his paintings also belong to popular culture. Their main source of inspiration is socialist realism, which can be considered the most common form of Soviet mass culture. Furthermore, the combination of Soviet mass culture, sci-fi, and propaganda—along with the overt, explicit ideological message in his works—also makes Gintovt's aesthetics potentially accessible to a broad public.

At the same time, the "physical trace" of the artist on the canvas suggests a camp appropriation of mass culture and propaganda with the purpose of returning to an (imagined) authenticity or ritual nature of the artistic experience, or, in other words, to simulate or recover the experience produced by the "aura" of the mechanically reproducible artwork.[61] The sheer proportions of the paintings and the depth produced by the golden leaves create a mesmerizing effect, as if drawing the viewer into the paintings or encouraging direct physical interaction with them. The canvases appear to be intended as scenic backdrops, and they are used for that purpose by Gintovt himself, who often poses in front of them, alone or in the company of political allies or fellow-travelers, as part of a public performance or political statement of sorts.

Indeed, here, too, as in the case of Novikov's New Academy, Gintovt's work is the result of a postmodern and technologically enhanced form of neoclassicism. His paintings usually re-create a retouched and modified version of one photographic image, or they combine several incongruous images together to produce phantasmagoric visions of a utopian future. The enormous stencils are cut from a computer-generated model, and so they are, in fact, "mechanically reproducible."

The results of this process are images that are at the same time appealing and horrible, or, to use the slogan of the NBP that Gintovt occasionally repeats when referring to the Eurasianist future that he dreams about, *fun and terrifying*. Consider, for instance, the painting *The Left March I* (*Levyi marsh I*, 2007).[62] This is a reproduction of a famous photograph portraying one of the parades of athletes in Red Square in 1937. As was true of many propaganda pictures of the time, the author of the photograph is unknown, although the original photograph is commonly attributed to Rodchenko. In this case, Gintovt's painting reproduces the photograph almost literally in the form of a painting. The only obvious change to the image is the addition of a political symbol in the background, the Eurasian Youth Union's acronym, ESM. The effect is somewhat uncanny. Because of the sheer proportions, the viewer is almost immersed in an ahistorical totalitarian reality. The mass of naked bodies and the display of aggressive masculinity is at the same time fascinating and distressing.

But the whole of Gintovt's art project cannot be grasped without reference to its performative aspects, its role in creating Gintovt's public persona, and Gintovt's own impact on the Moscow art world. Gintovt became widely known in 2008, when a scandal erupted after he was awarded the prestigious Kandinsky prize on the basis of two paintings, *Rodina-doch'* and *Brat'ia i sestry* (Brothers and sisters) (see figs. 45 and 46). Both paintings take as their subject matter key and problematic Soviet political and historical symbols. *Rodina-doch'* is a gigantic, hyperrealistic reproduction (about 10 × 15 feet) of a detail from Vera Mukhina's 1937 iconic socialist realist monument *Rabochii i kolkhoznitsa* (The worker and the kolkhoz girl). *Brat'ia i sestry* shows an anonymous Soviet crowd, supposedly listening to Stalin's historical speech of July 3, 1941, delivered after Germany invaded the Soviet Union. This painting is based on a blown-up detail from a photograph by the classic Soviet photographer Dmitry Bal'termants. Gintovt claims to have redrawn the details of each of the 418 faces in the crowd, calling attention to a number that ironically alludes to a mystical nature of the Soviet collective experience: 418 is a magical number associated with the occultist-Satanist Aleister Crowley. It is also the title of Kurekhin's final Popmekhanika performance (the one organized in support of Dugin's 1995 electoral campaign for the NBP).[63]

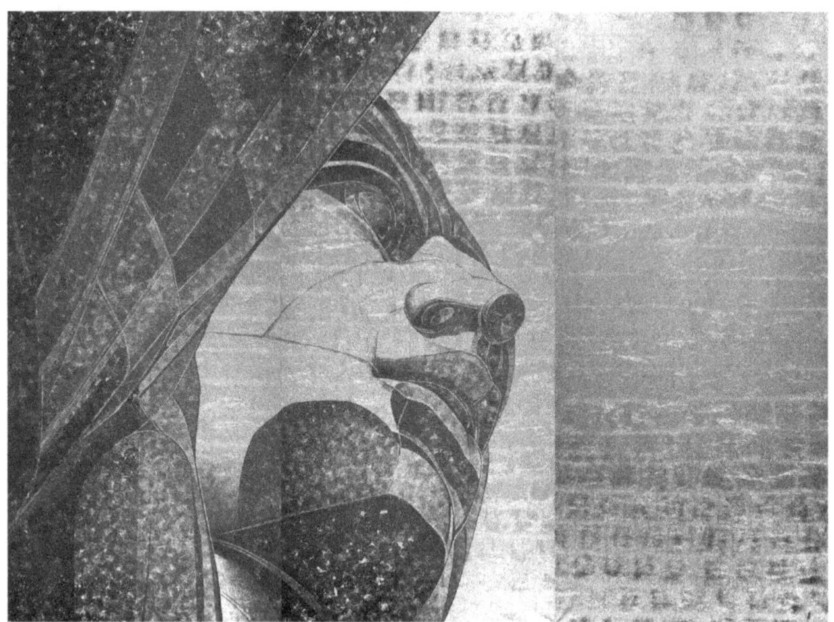

Figure 45. Aleksei Beliaev-Gintovt, *Rodina-doch'*, 2007. Gold leaf, red printing ink, hand-print on canvas, 300 × 450 cm. Photo courtesy of Aleksey Beliaev-Gintovt.

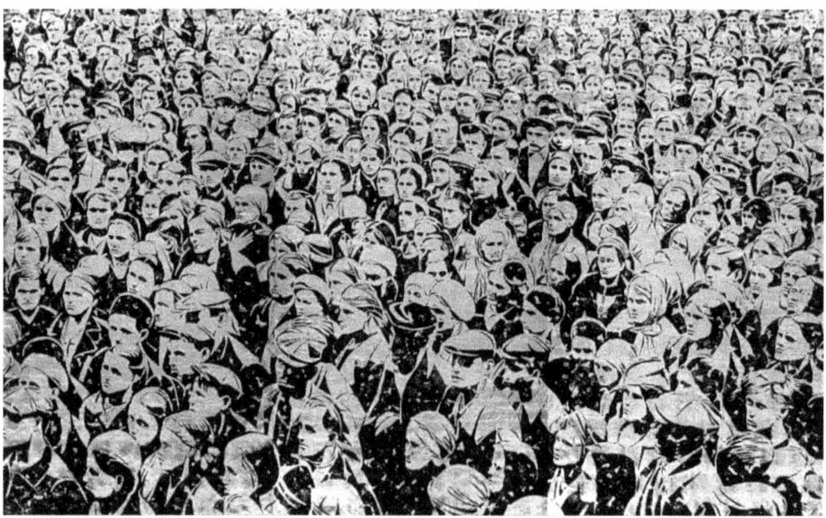

Figure 46. Aleksei Beliaev-Gintovt, *Brat'ia i sestry*, 2008. Gold leaf, black printing ink, handprint on canvas, 270 × 450 cm. Photo courtesy of Aleksey Beliaev-Gintovt.

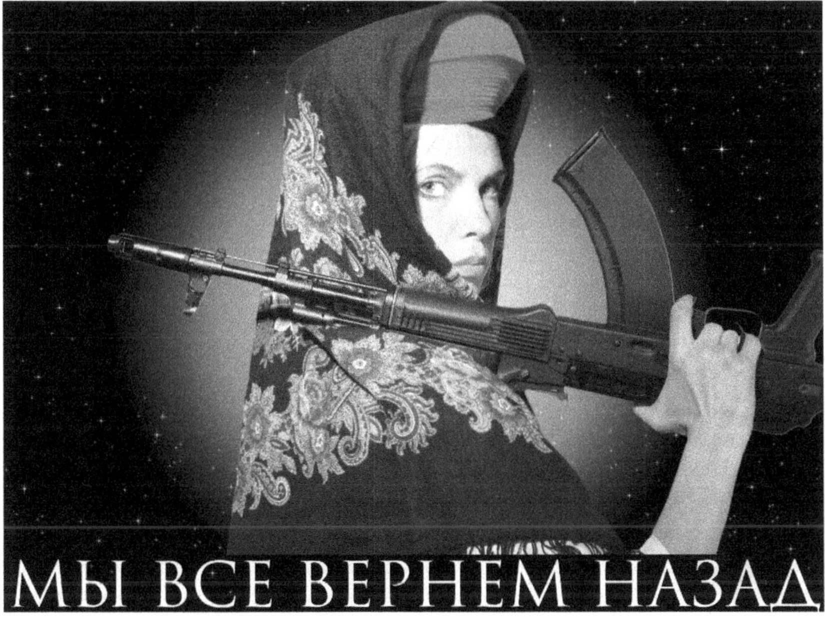

Figure 47. Aleksey Beliaev-Gintovt, *My vse vernem nazad* (We will bring everything back). Political poster for the Eurasianist Youth Union (ESM), n.d. Photo courtesy of Aleksey Beliaev-Gintovt.

As Il'ia Kukulin points out, both paintings produce an effect of "recognizability" by alluding to motifs from different photographs or film sequences that are part of the Russian collective unconscious.[64] The canvases also deprive these iconic images of their historical and ideological context, presenting them in their raw monumental essence, as pure embodiments of an imperial and totalitarian sublime.

The ceremony during which Gintovt was awarded the prize caused a stir in the Moscow art world, more motivated by Gintovt's direct involvement in Dugin's far-right Eurasia Movement than by the paintings themselves. Several commentators, in particular, expressed concern over a series of posters that Gintovt had designed for the organization portraying a woman wearing traditional Russian dress and holding a machine gun (see fig. 47). The posters featured such overtly nationalist slogans as "We will bring everything back"; "Sevastopol' is a Russian city"; and "One soul—one people" (*My vse vernem nazad*; *Sevastopol'—russkii gorod*; *odna dusha—odin narod*). During the ceremony, Anatoly Osmolovsky, one of the leading figures of Moscow actionism and a charismatic leader of the Moscow art community, yelled "shame" and "fascism" from the audience. In the following days, the socialist organization

Vpered! (Forward!) and the Saint Petersburg art collective Chto delat'? (What is to be done?) organized a protest in front of the art center Vinzavod, where the award ceremony had taken place. The art critic Ekaterina Degot' wrote that while she acknowledged Gintovt's talent, she interpreted the decision of the jury as a sign of the "fascistization" of the Russian economic and intellectual leadership.[65]

Osmolovsky then authored an open letter to the art community in which he criticized any form of politically engaged art, claiming that "the anti-aestheticism of [the art group] Voina . . . requires compensation in the glamorous fascism of Gintovt."[66] Gintovt's reaction to the public outrage seemed to confirm the concerns of Osmolovsky, Degot', and other critics about a "fascistization" of the Russian art scene. Gintovt publicly accused his critics of being "degenerates" and "the main enemies of the Russian people in the sphere of culture." The website of the Eurasian Youth Union accused Osmolovsky of producing "degenerate art" and even made an online announcement about a "March Against Degenerate Art."[67] Gintovt's language combined the two main nightmares of modernity: Stalinism, with its obsession with internal sabotage and the "enemies of the people"; and Nazism's famous "Degenerate Art Exhibition" and its tendency to pathologize subversive or simply different cultural forms and traditions.

The scandal surrounding the 2008 Kandinsky prize is revealing of the complex interconnections between the art world and the political sphere in contemporary Russian society. Beyond the provocative nature of Gintovt's imperialist art and right-wing affiliations, the harsh polemics surrounding the award mirrored conflicts and divisions among different art factions and *tusovki*. Osmolovsky, who had been one of the pioneers of Moscow Actionism during the 1990s, and who had been awarded the prestigious prize the year before, at this point had given up his more politically charged performances and decided to work within the limits of the Russian and international art markets and institutions. During the 1990s Osmolovsky had organized, and participated in, several provocative and politically charged art performances.[68] In the last public performance that he organized, in 2000, a group of his disciples displayed a banner with the slogan *Protiv vsekh* (Against all) on top of the Lenin Mausoleum. This action caused a harsh reaction from the authorities and marked a turning point in his career. Following the performance, all the participants, and Osmolovsky as the organizer, were summoned by the FSB (Federal'naia sluzhba bezopasnosti, the Russian intelligence service and the successor of the Soviet KGB) and warned that there would be serious consequences for the participants in these types of protests in the future. After this episode, Osmolovsky decided to devote himself to art exclusively, to limit his involvement in Russian politics to pedagogical work, and to work toward training a new generation of leftist and progressive artists. Understandably, because of this episode, and not just because of rivalries among different factions in the Moscow art world, Osmolovsky was particularly sensitive to Gintovt's anti-liberalism, his call for police violence and censorship, and, more generally, his unconditional support of Putin's authoritarianism.[69]

In his remarks, Osmolovsky sharply criticized the "anti-aestheticism" of both Gintovt and the members of the art collective Voina, which at the time was reaching notoriety within and outside the Russian art world with its provocative and politically charged (as well as often illegal) public performances. He therefore seemed to be attacking Gintovt not because of his ideology but because, exactly like the radical leftist-anarchist members of Voina, he had crossed the boundary between art production and political action. Like other leftist artists in Russia, Osmolovsky was critical of Voina's actions mostly because he considered them isolated radical gestures that did not produce long-term political results.

Osmolovsky's commentary in this context was rather surprising, especially coming from someone who had based his career on public performances at the intersection between art and political protest, and who could be considered one of the sources of inspiration for the second wave of post-Soviet art-activism that Voina represented. Indeed, his comments appeared to be at least in part motivated by the old rivalry between neo-academists and Moscow Conceptualists; Osmolovsky had also been the recipient of the first edition of the Kandinsky prize a year earlier and was in the process of becoming a Moscow art scene guru of sorts. In addition, the rivalry between neo-academists and conceptualists overlapped with the rivalry between Dugin and the Moscow gallerist and political technologist Marat Guelman, with whom Dugin had previously collaborated on several Kremlin-sponsored political and media projects.[70]

Although Osmolovsky's commentaries on Russian culture and society are usually uniquely insightful, in this case his attack against Voina's "anti-aestheticism" was questionable, especially in the quite unique context of post-Soviet society, where art appears to be the main channel for the expression of political dissent. Advocating for fully depoliticized art forms, existing exclusively within the boundaries of cultural institutions, can be a way of implicitly promoting a definitive commodification of the cultural sphere and "naturalizing" the absence of a political debate—something that ends up being paradoxically in line with the authoritarian-managerial rhetoric of Putin's government. As problematic as they might be, Gintovt's "glamorous" references to totalitarian symbols have at least the merit of provoking a discussion about ideology and the legacy of the Soviet project. Given the importance of radical political posturing for Gintovt's art project, the more or less outraged reactions to his institutional "canonization" become part of the art project itself. In this regard, it is interesting that the critic Aleksey Plutser-Sarno, the ideologist of the art group Voina who documented most of their actions online, expressed a more cautious opinion about Gintovt's work. Plutser-Sarno wrote that he was interested in Gintovt's work, but he was not able to express a definitive opinion about it and warned against taking Gintovt's ideology seriously even if Gintovt does so himself.[71] Degot' considered Gintovt's Eurasianism a kind of *stiob*. Guelman, also a target of Dugin's and Gintovt's attacks, considered the possibility that their whole political project could just be part of a postmodern provocation. Finally, Osmolovsky dismissed Gintovt as an untalented artist, claiming that there are criteria to judge, and, at the same time, that according to these criteria 90 percent of contemporary art does not in fact qualify as art. However, he added that Dugin's ideology and Gintovt's aesthetics should not be underestimated, especially given the wave of hate crimes, violence, and murders committed by ultranationalist groups in Russia since the beginning of this century.[72]

Maria Engström argues that Gintovt's return to imperial and Soviet imagery and grand style involves a form of romantic or postromantic irony—that is, a simultaneous identification with and detachment from these ideological constructs, in the spirit of what Yurchak has defined as "living *vnye*." Engström sees Gintovt's "Imper-Art" and "military dandyism" as a direct continuation of Novikov's "neo-neoclassicism," and of the posture and philosophy of such interwar conservative revolutionaries as Ernst Jünger and Julius Evola, who also displayed a weakness for authoritarian politics, masculinity, militarism, and a bohemian approach to life. She sees the emergence of an imperial or conservative aesthetics in contemporary Russian art as a form of resistance to the "mainstream," which she identifies with "the horizontal, shapeless and styleless Moscow postmodernism."[73] I agree with most of these statements, although I believe that they do not take into full account the ideological and political sides of Gintovt's project and the connection of his utopian aesthetics with Russian institutions and power structures. Gintovt, Dugin, and the intellectual community built around the Eurasia Movement do, in fact, see Moscow Conceptualism (broadly conceived) as the mainstream in contemporary Russian art, and they actively fight its cultural hegemony, as they fight the triumph of Western liberalism, mass culture, and globalization in Russian society. One of the most interesting aspects of Gintovt's art, of his "post-irony" (to borrow Engström's term) and of its impact on the art world, is its destabilizing or, better, de-realizing effect on viewers and critics, who are forced to abandon common assumptions and think critically about what they see.[74]

However, from a political standpoint, this form of "post-irony" remains trapped between a revolutionary and a reactionary stance. On the one hand it does represent, on the basis of Dugin's interpretation of postmodernity, a potentially effective critique and a form of resistance against the "New World Order"; on the other hand, at the level of internal politics, this discursive mode ends up promoting an authoritarian regime (Putin's), which is itself part of this same world order.

For instance, the fact that Gintovt declares himself against private funding of the arts and in favor of state-funded art that serves a national idea can be seen as his way of provoking reflection on the political role of art and the sources of its funding in modern societies.[75] At the same time, his support of Putin's regime raises fundamental questions about what happens when the sort of "counterdiscourses" that the Eurasianists promote are used to support repressive and authoritarian political structures, or when these power structures themselves are seen as an instrument of political resistance. Many elements of Gintovt's public activity seem to point indeed to a "total performance" of sorts: the all-black military clothes, the aphoristic and provocative statements, and the way in which he embraced the role of official artist for a post-historical Russian empire. At the same time, his commitment to Dugin's ideology, as well as his involvement with state power and leadership—including, most recently, contact with Russian military commanders in Eastern Ukraine—makes it morally problematic to define his activity solely as a form of performance art.

Gintovt's case raises crucial questions about performativity, performance, and political art, about the boundary between artistic production and political action, and between artistic, intellectual, and political responsibility. These questions also apply to the Eurasia Movement as a political project, and to its impact on contemporary Russian culture and politics.

Us and Them: A New Oprichnina

Eurasianism has been interpreted, by those who promoted it and participated in it, as an "intellectual game," a kind of "conservative bohemianism," and, in general, as a form of resistance to mainstream or official culture. The identity of the Eurasia Movement is defined by a cult and appropriation of the legacy of the late Soviet underground. Although their work is decisively oriented toward grassroots and mainstream politics, Dugin's neo-Eurasianists replicate some of the fundamental features of Mamleev's "mystical underground": the cultivation of paradoxical and esoteric thinking, bohemianism, and a cult of death as a source of mystical knowledge and experience. From the New Academy, the organization assimilates the imperial aesthetics, the fundamental queerness or "otherness," and the strategy of "radical political shimmering." A fundamental question to ask is: What happens when countercultural and subversive strategies of this kind become part of a political project aimed at supporting state power and ideology and justifying the repression of political dissent? In other words, what happens when a conservative bohemia goes public?

The former chief editor of *Limonka* Tsvetkov was a member of the Eurasia Movement for several years.[76] After leaving the NBP with Dugin and his group of "schismatics," he participated in the organization of the New University and lectured there along with Golovin, Dzhemal, Mamleev (who returned to Russia in the 1990s), and Dugin himself. Tsvetkov has always considered himself a leftist, but he never regretted his long association with Dugin, whom he considers a mentor and a deep thinker. He was interested in being part of Eurasianism, as he was interested in the NBP, because he considered it a radically subversive project, but he left when Dugin told him that he wanted to be more actively involved with government structures. He now looks at his participation in the movement with a certain amount of irony and self-awareness, and he describes Eurasianism as a form of "political mysticism following the Gnostic scheme of 'us' against 'them.'"

> This is Dugin's favorite idea—that a cosmic war is being fought. So all these things—fascism, communism, capitalism—they are all very relative. Behind them stand some superhuman beings, who are not good or evil. This is a pagan system, it is not morally determined. These are just different forces . . . and if you find yourself under the influence of one of these forces, you become its soldier—either a blind soldier, or a knowing soldier—that is, belonging to the minority. This is the Gnostic division of people into those who have heard nothing, those who have heard something . . . and those . . . hylics, pneumatics, psychotics [*sic*]. [And Dugin's] psychological strategy is based on the fact that no matter who he is talking to, he always says "we": "We are initiated, we know." [*laughs*] It's not them, it's us! As a matter of fact, somebody who can think critically, someone with an analytical mind, is perfectly able to understand how this works. But in fact, there are not that many people who can do that. That is, a huge amount of people ends up being intrigued by this. All of a sudden, you feel as if you were part of some sort of a lodge, of a sect, of some category of chosen people . . . After all, it's us, not them!

At the level of mainstream politics and discourses, this strongly polarized and essentialist scheme has been used to justify the neo-Eurasianist conception of the Russian public sphere as a territory of perpetual violent struggle, conquest, and colonization and recolonization of cultural and political space.

The Eurasian Youth Union was Dugin's first attempt at actively collaborating with the Putin administration at the level of grassroots politics. The organization was founded in 2005, the same year that the mass pro-government youth movement Nashi was founded.[77] Like Nashi, the ESM was officially created to counteract the possible emergence of a wave of liberal "orange" revolutions in Russia, on the model of Ukraine's 2004 street protests. As several former and present Eurasianist leaders and activists confirmed to me in the spring of 2015, the organization received governmental funding directly from Vladislav Surkov, one of the main ideologists of the Kremlin and the mastermind behind the foundation and activity of Nashi. This was in line with Surkov's (and Putin's) general strategy around the middle of the first decade of this century: repressing political opposition movements while appropriating the political space, rhetoric, and methods of right-wing nationalist organizations in order to capitalize on the potential popular appeal of these right-wing groupings.[78]

The Russian government commonly supported and financed organizations that were supposedly more moderate (and, most importantly, willing to prove their allegiance) while cracking down on more extremist (in fact all the anti-government) ones. At the same time, Russian courts systematically misused anti-extremism laws by banning oppositional parties and by arresting their leaders. In addition to the political issues connected with limiting freedom of speech and association, this system did not always work well in preventing terrorism and hate crimes and, in certain instances, it actually ended up favoring them. This has been the case, for instance, of the organization Russkii obraz (Russian Image), a pro-government group; the leaders of this organization used a good part of the funds they received from the state to secretly organize BORN (Boevaia organizatsiia russkikh natsionalistov, the Combat Organization of Russian Nationalists), an underground criminal group responsible for a long series of brutal murders of immigrants, human rights activists, and members of leftist and anti-fascist organizations.

As mentioned, one of the main targets of Surkov's strategy was the NBP.[79] The Russian government's support of the ESM was part of this strategy because the organization was ideologically close to the NBP but supportive of the government and opposed to any form of liberal or pro-Western opposition. At the same time, the Eurasianists contributed to the weakening of the NBP as a political force by supporting, sponsoring, and organizing the National Bolshevik Front, a movement that included former *natsboly* who disagreed with Limonov's recent alliance with the liberal opposition.

In this context, the activity of the Eurasian Youth Union has been aimed at "conquering" the Russian public sphere against a perceived hegemony of

Western agents in Russian culture and society. To this end, Dugin initially tried, unsuccessfully, to co-opt hardcore ultranationalist movements and was among the main organizers of the first "Russian March" in 2005. Beyond this first incursion into street politics, the Eurasianists' violent rhetoric and their attempt at "recolonizing" the Russian public sphere has remained for the most part virtual and performative, being limited to the dissemination of such ideas as the presence of a "fifth column" and the existence of Western, or American, agents in Russian culture and society through the Russian blogosphere, alternative academic networks, and mass media. The Eurasian Youth Union has mainly focused on the organization of Dugin's journals and publishing houses and on lectures and seminars on traditionalism and neo-Eurasianism. It also has a massive presence on the Russian internet, including numerous closely related websites linked to one another through a dense network of references.[80]

While formally supporting Putin's government, the members of this minoritarian organization, mostly Dugin's graduate students and quasi-sectarian followers, intellectuals, visual artists, and Old Believers, perceive themselves as an intellectual "counter-elite." Their main symbolic enemy is the United States, which they see as the embodiment of capitalism, consumerism, and multiculturalism, all values that they fundamentally oppose. At the same time, they criticize the current Russian leadership for its corruption and its lack of ideology. They believe that disseminating their ideas through alternative local and international networks within Russian academia and on the Russian blogosphere is an effective way to covertly influence current political processes. Finally, although they do not explain how this would happen, many leaders and activists within the Eurasia Movement are convinced that one day, according to the sociologist Vilfredo Pareto's theory of elite circulation, they will be able to replace the current leadership. As Korovin puts it:

> Today there are no political instruments. So, the only sphere through which one can operate is the sphere of meaning. With meanings, our establishment really seems to have a problem. So we create these concepts, we throw them in, and we promote them. And then somebody picks them up (and really there's nothing else to pick up, there aren't any other sources of meaning). So, if they need something, they look up on Yandex [the popular Russian search engine] "Eurasianism" or "ideology of Eurasianism"—and the first 100 links are to our resources. We write it, and they steal it and use it. And this actually works. Some bureaucrat calls his aide and says: "go and steal somewhere: 'what is Eurasianism?'" And that one goes and steals it from me, and I give it to him. And this is a form of influence.

On the basis of Dugin's vision, the Eurasianists see themselves, paradoxically, as both a reactionary and a revolutionary force within Russian society. On March 27, 2000, one day after the elections that resulted in Putin's first presidential term, Dugin published an article titled "Zaria v sapogakh" (The dawn wearing boots), in which he called for the creation of an "ideal secret service," a new caste or social stratum embodied in a "true KGB of divine continental scale, the ghost of which terrified the West . . . a heroic, Machiavellian, omnipotent, omniscient, and wise KGB, [which] in reality never existed, and [which, therefore] belongs to the future."[81] According to Dugin, this new aggressive intellectual military-trained elite should be conceived as a "New Oprichnina," modeled after Ivan the Terrible's ruthless secret army. In a somewhat surreal move, Dugin performatively realized this vision a few years later. The 2005 inaugural assembly of the Eurasian Youth Union took place in Alexandrov, where the original *oprichnina* was founded. Dugin's introductory address was significantly titled "The Metaphysics of the Oprichnina: The Symbolism of the Dog's Head and the Sociology of Repression." In it, Dugin combined the figures of Ivan the Terrible and Iosif Stalin as main role models for a Eurasianist Renaissance, and he argued that repressions and violence should be considered necessary measures to replace the old bureaucratic elites with new leaders to be chosen among the "best representatives of the nation."[82]

The program of ESM, and the "Catechism of the Member of the Eurasian Youth Union," which can be found on the official website of the movement, adopt a similar, overtly violent and aggressive rhetoric, calling for "bloody revolutions" and a "great purge" of the old corrupted elites. They combine a Nietzschean supermanism, a cult of masculinity and physical strength, and more straightforward echoes of tropes and language belonging to both Italian Fascism and German Nazism. The main enemy of the movement, the United States, for instance, is described as a country where "everything is upside down . . . [and] those who are weak and sick are kept in high esteem, and degenerates and monsters are at the center of attention, [where] it is allowed and required to be sickly, dishonest, and cowardly, while strength, will, and intelligence are prohibited." Furthermore, in keeping with Dugin's style, these documents are not ideologically coherent but rather based on an idiosyncratic collage of cultural and political symbols, and their form resembles more a manifesto than a political program. For instance, the main goal of the movement is identified with the constitution of a Great Eurasian Empire based on the principles of "tradition, of the avant-garde, of the conservative revolution, and of social justice."[83]

The concept of "Oprichnina" could be seen as a radical nationalist version of Mamleev's "metaphysical underground" or the late Soviet "living beyond" of Saint Petersburg's New Artists. It is an absolute "elsewhere." The Oprichnina (from *oprich*—"except"—so almost literally a "state of exception") was both Ivan the Terrible's guard and the separate territory that he created to impose his will over the boyars and literally conquer or "recolonize" the Russian territory.

As a matter of fact, death and the apocalypse are the concepts that best describe the condition of an "absolute elsewhere" in the neo-Eurasianist conception of political activism. Death, war, and the end of the world are recurring themes in Dugin's writing. Following the teaching of traditionalism, Dugin describes modern society as a world on the brink of apocalypse, a "bronze age" pervaded by moral and cultural decadence.[84] He once defined the future ideal Russia as "Motherland Death" (Rodina-Smert').[85] For him, fear of death is what makes individuals "slaves of the system": the new heroic elites will need to come "from the regions of death" to replace the current stagnant bureaucratic leadership. In line with the ideas of conservative revolutionaries like Evola and Jünger, he sees death and sacrifice as the measure of human value and commitment. Following this logic, Dugin also sees Stalinism as a tragic and heroic time, and he justifies its repressions as a way to continuously regenerate and recirculate the country's elite to achieve the socialist ideal. According to him, "dulce et decorum est pro Stalin mori."[86]

A decadent "dark romantic" taste for death and the apocalypse also characterizes the culture of the Eurasia Movement. In 2011, the Eurasian Youth Union organized a "summer eschatological camp," where activists were asked to perform different versions of the end of the world according to different religious and historical traditions. These amateur spectacles were conceived, according to Dugin, as a form of initiation and a preparation for the "real end of the world," and the performances included readings from Antonin Artaud and George Bataille.[87] Thus, the members of this organization appear to be truly preparing for the terrorist apocalypse that Dugin sees as the ideal culmination of his "conservative postmodernism."[88]

Eschatological and apocalyptic references feature prominently both in Gintovt's art and in the agitational materials of the Eurasian Youth Union. Yet such references also appear to be pervaded by a certain form of dark humor. When I visited Gintovt's studio for the first time he offered (of his own initiative) to pose in front of the painting he had just completed, a diptych portraying trunks of birches (an omnipresent folkloric symbol of Russian natural beauty) revealing shapes of skulls through their white-stained bark and a hammer and sickle. When I asked him to elaborate on the use of these symbols in the painting, Gintovt evaded the question, answering, in a somewhat playful tone, that these were just *berezki*, a classical symbol of *matushka Rossiia* (see fig. 48).[89]

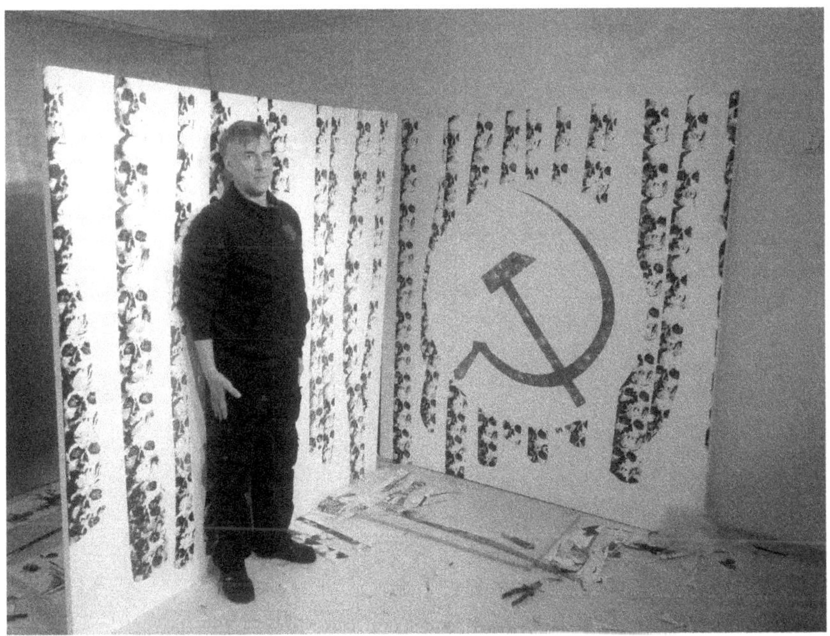

Figure 48. Aleksey Beliaev-Gintovt posing in front of his painting *The Revolution of Spaces*. Moscow, March 2015. Photo by author.

In a similarly ironic way, one of the flyers for the "Imperial March," organized by the ESM in Moscow in 2007, reproduces a classical illustration of an episode from the Sixth Canto of Dante's *Inferno* by Gustav Doré. The image is most likely an allusion to the fact that at the end of the canto Virgil explains how the souls of the dead will reunite with their bodies during the Universal Judgment; the slogan of the flyer reads "Glory to the Oprichnina! Arise from the dead!" The erudite reference to medieval poetry clashes with the enthusiastic tone of the slogan, and it looks almost surreal in the context of the promotion for a nationalist march (see fig. 49).

It is important to keep in mind that the Eurasia Movement, in contrast with the NBP, is by and large a virtual organization. Whereas the *natsboly* often sought firsthand experience of death, war, and sacrifice as forms of self-expression, the Eurasianists have tried to produce the preconditions for violence and conflict through their influence over mainstream media and discourses. On January 5, 2015, for example, two days before Orthodox Christmas, and still in the midst of the war in Eastern Ukraine, the Eurasianist Youth Union posted a short video on YouTube. In the video, a young, angelic-looking woman, bundled up in a white winter camouflage suit in the middle of a snow covered field

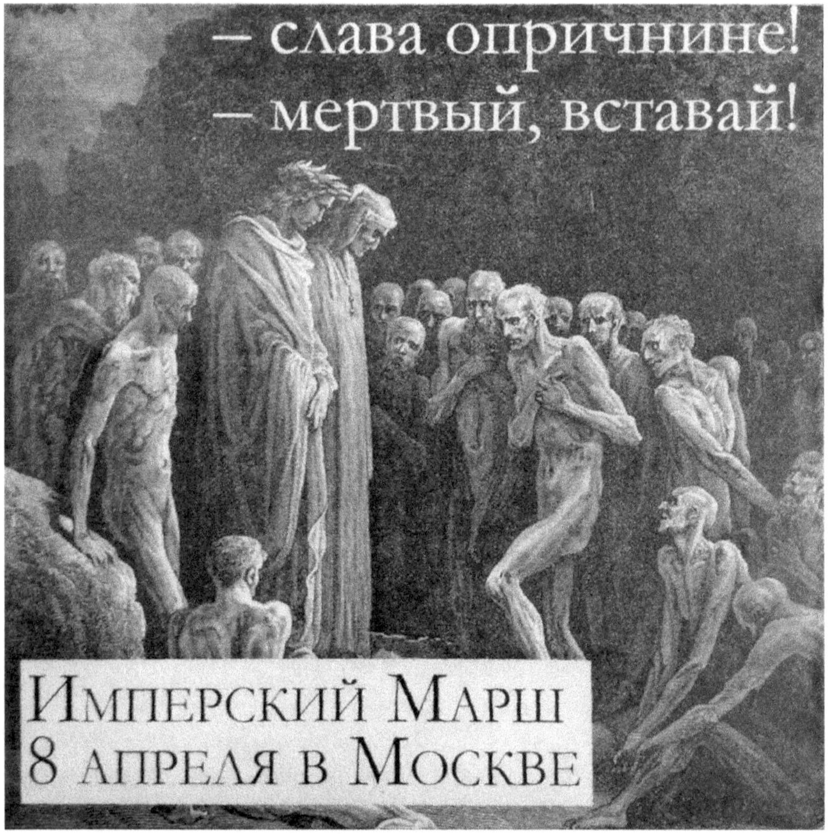

Figure 49. Eurasianist flyer for the Imperial March in St. Petersburg, April 8, 2007. From Tsentr sotsial'no-politicheskoi istorii: Gosudarstvennaia publichnaia istoricheskaia biblioteka Rossii.

with a Kalashnikov in her hands, wishes everyone a Merry Christmas in a somewhat unusual way: "Happiness to the people, death to the enemies! The enemy will be defeated. Victory will be ours. And, if we lose, we will annihilate the whole world!" After pronouncing these words, the woman moves her arm in a circle. The next scene shows a nuclear explosion (see fig. 50).

The authors of the video, which through the years has accumulated approximately 350,000 views and more than 2,000 (mostly derogatory) comments (as of August 2019), are Gintovt and another artist who embraced the philosophy of neo-Eurasianism. Gintovt showed me the video in his studio in the spring of 2015, laughing loudly while the nuclear mushroom filled the screen and the soothing notes of Soviet composer Georgii Sviridov's popular romance "Winter Path" played in the background. He said that this was an example of his most

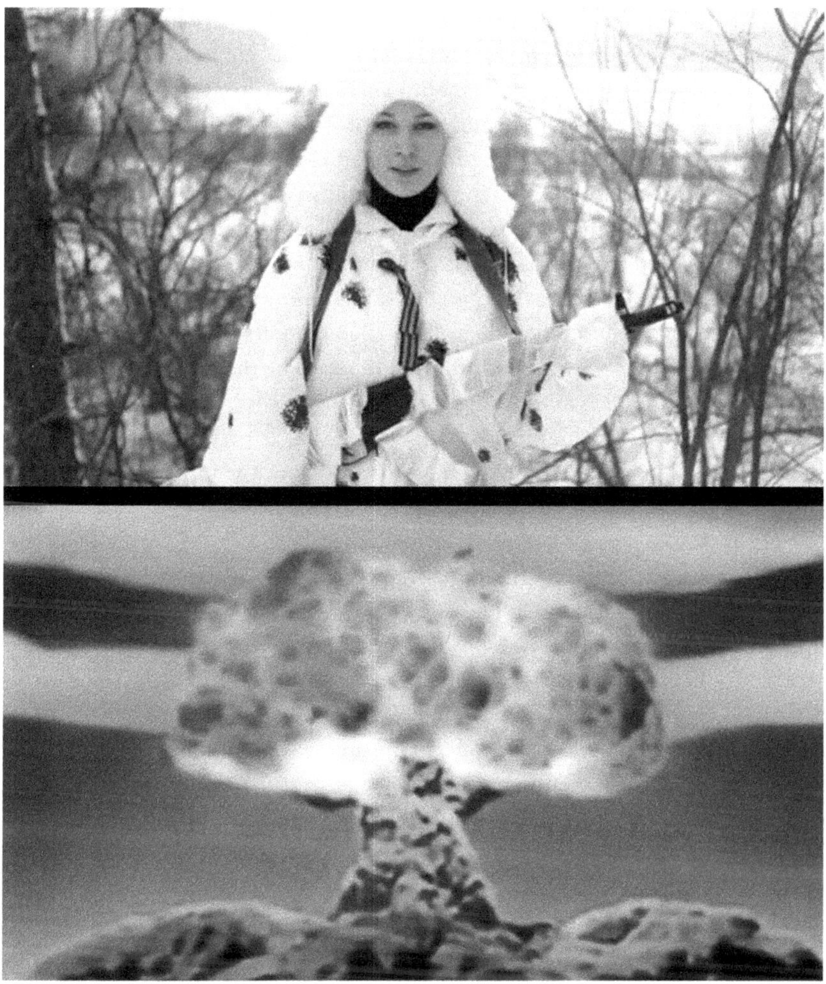

Figure 50. "Na radost' liudiam, na smert' vragam! S Rozhdestvom! S Novorossiei!" (Joy to the people, death to the enemies! Merry Christmas! Merry Novorussia!). YouTube video, January 6, 2015.

recent work. He described this genre as *video-plakat* (video propaganda poster). The phrase "If we lose, we will annihilate the whole world" was, according to Gintovt, Dugin's own.

This, of course, looks like a paradoxical, almost too straightforward, political statement, a sort of radical Dada gesture thrown into the Russian blogosphere. It is also one more step in the exercise of crossing any possible moral and aesthetic boundaries, in the style of Dugin's own overload of ideological backwardness. At the same time, this is a good example of how Gintovt's work, and that of Dugin's Eurasia movement in general, exists at the intersection of art, mass culture, propaganda, and grassroots politics. Gintovt's short "video poster" was part of a concerted effort to produce a pro-Russian propaganda campaign in Eastern Ukraine. During a meeting with members and sympathizers of the Eurasia movement that I attended at his studio, several activists of different ages and professions (students, artists, and government employees) discussed at length possible strategies to exploit more successfully youth culture and social media, spheres that, they claimed, so far had been mostly dominated by pro-Kiev and pro-Maidan cultural producers. The discussion involved possible slogans, colors, symbols, and musical genres that the activists thought could be successful for this purpose.

The model in the video, who also participated in the meeting, was Maria Katasonova, who was at the time the assistant to the deputy of the State Duma (the Russian Congress) Evgeny Fedorov, a member of Putin's United Russia party and the leader of the infamous NOD, the National Liberation Movement (Natsional'no-osvoboditel'noe dvizhenie). NOD is a pro-Putin organization, financed and supported by the Russian government (although formally created by Fedorov's initiative), which has been growing steadily since 2014, becoming de facto a direct (and even more radically nationalistic) successor of the youth movement Nashi. The official mission of this organization, according to its website and its members' public declarations, is to fight the "foreign forces" that are "actually ruling Russian society." According to Fedorov's and NOD's conspiracy theories, the representatives of these forces are to be found in the liberal opposition, the Russian intelligentsia, civil rights organizations and NGOs, international economic lobbies, but also among Russian politicians and members of the government and legal system, including Russian prime minister Dmitry Medvedev. In other words, everyone is involved in this foreign conspiracy but President Putin. In fact, Fedorov claimed (supposedly, as a sign of complete loyalty) that the only real leader of NOD is the Russian president.

In 2015–16, members of NOD organized patriotic marches and gathered humanitarian help and volunteers to be sent to Eastern Ukraine. They also attracted attention from the media for their violent attacks on defenseless civil rights activists, liberal intellectuals, and members of the opposition. They attacked, for instance, an elderly civil rights activist who was peacefully protesting at the entrance of Red Square, as well as Pussy Riot members Nadia Tolokonnikova and Maria Alyokhina in a McDonald's in Nizhny Novgorod.[90] In the summer of 2016, members of NOD attracted the attention of the Russian media for disrupting a competition rewarding the best school compositions on the theme of World War II, organized by the Russian civil rights organization Memorial with the participation of writer Liudmila Ulitskaya. During the ceremony, members of NOD covered Ulitskaya and other members of Memorial in green paint allegedly for not providing children a truthful account of Russian heroism.[91] In the spring of 2017, it was the turn of opposition leader Aleksei Navalny: members of NOD threw green paint in his face, too, and, as a consequence, he lost 80 percent of vision from his right eye.[92] As a political commentator pointed out, NOD borrowed the street direct-action tactics of the NBP, although the targets of the NBP were repressive power structures and institutions, and NBP activists paid for their actions with prison sentences and abuses. In contrast, some of NOD's victims are some of the most vulnerable elements of society, and NOD's aggressive actions have the support of the Russian authorities.[93]

In 2014–15, the Eurasianists were collaborating closely with NOD. After Dugin was removed from his position at Moscow State University, many of the seminars and meetings organized by his students and colleagues took place in NOD's general headquarters, a spacious office a few blocks from the Lubyanka, the headquarters of the FSB. Compared to the aesthetics and ideology of Nashi, which combined corporate rhetoric and entrepreneurial culture with aggressive patriotism and militarism, NOD's symbolism and ideas are based on a much more straightforward return to Cold War logic. The movement's flag is the ribbon of Saint George, a military decoration from the time of Catherine the Great that, starting around 2005, has been used to commemorate the Soviet defeat of Nazi Germany on Victory Day. When I visited NOD's headquarters, the doormat to the main entrance was an American flag. The central conference room (where, a few weeks earlier, an official meeting had taken place with Strelkov, one of the Russian generals who started the war in Eastern Ukraine) was decorated with a gigantic propaganda poster, somewhat rudimentary in its design.[94] The poster portrayed an American flag with an eagle on the left side and a Russian flag and a bear on the right, divided by a diagonal Saint George ribbon. The slogan was taken from a classic Soviet Cold War poster depicting a smiling blond Red Army hero who had just captured a rotten capitalist spy: "You forgot where the border is? We will help you land!"

In this spacious meeting room, I attended a "seminar on traditionalism," where several members of Dugin's organization delivered presentations on Guénon, Mircea Eliade, and various other aspects of traditionalist philosophy. The Q&A, which lasted for some time after the presentations, focused on the question of whether a "traditionalist form of progress" would be at all possible, or if the idea of progress should be simply excluded from the ideology of an authentically traditionalist society. This is also where Ivan, one of the leaders of the Eurasian Youth Union, agreed to meet me for an interview on May 1, 2015. Ivan was also working at that time on Fedorov's staff. On the day of our meeting, he was at the headquarters of the organization to pick up a few things for NOD's march at the International Workers' Day parade, a traditional Soviet festivity still widely celebrated in Russia. Ironically, he proposed that we talk at the Soviet Diner across the street, a flashy American-style diner displaying Soviet posters and slogans (instead of the classic pin-ups, greasers, and Cadillacs) and serving both cheeseburgers and traditional Russian food.

At the time of our meeting, Ivan was in his early thirties and had been active in the ESM for several years. In 2012, he was among the conservative groups who turned out to protest in front of the entrance of *Dukhovnaia bran'* (Spiritual struggle), a contemporary art exhibit organized in support of the members of Pussy Riot, who had been arrested for staging their "Punk Prayer" against Putin in the Church of Christ the Savior in Moscow. *Dukhovnaia bran'* displayed several works of contemporary artists painted in the style of Orthodox icons and featuring members of Pussy Riot in the role of saintly figures.[95] A photo from that time, of Ivan wearing a T-shirt with the symbol of the Eurasia movement and being dragged away by the police, has circulated widely among Russian and international news agencies in recent few years. Ivan was also a PhD student in the Department of Sociology at Moscow State University, where he was writing a dissertation on Euro-skepticism under Dugin's supervision. He grew up in a provincial mining town in southwestern Siberia, where he graduated with a degree in German literature and political science. His thesis was on Hitler's *Mein Kampf* and on Nazi propaganda and popular literature. While in college, Ivan developed an academic interest in questions of ideology and mass mobilization, and wrote a few articles that compared the themes of Soviet and Nazi propaganda posters. In college, he also studied the romantic poetry of Goethe, Heine, and Schiller.

Although he told me that he decided to study German in college because of an early interest in Nazi culture, Ivan claimed that he had no sympathies or inclinations toward the far right, but was only interested in learning "how the German people decided to support this idea." When I asked him about the links between political activism and cultural, artistic, or literary activities in his hometown, he scoffed and smiled, answering that among "the brutal miners of Kuzbass [the mining region where he was from]" there is not much space or interest for "countercultural activities."

During his school years, he continued, he became an active member of various leftist student organizations and workers' unions, created with the support and resources of KPRF, the Communist Party of the Russian Federation.

The primary motivation for his early involvement in politics, he said, was "the struggle against capital, the opposition of labor against capital, the oligarchs, and the bourgeoisie." This motivation had remained unchanged over the years, "initially on the side of the workers in Kuzbass, then already from somewhat different standpoints, on the side of traditionalism and the Eurasianist empire." Although he did not realize it at the time, he had always in fact been an "instinctive National Bolshevik." For him, National Bolshevism was "in just a few words, the sympathy toward a strong and social state . . . maximally strong and maximally social." The struggle between the working class and the ruling economic elite, which "quickly accumulated capital during the nineties" was particularly strongly felt in his hometown, where all of Ivan's friends and family members were miners or workers in metallurgic factories, and where financial and working conditions dramatically declined after the fall of the Soviet Union. Before becoming a member of Dugin's Eurasian Youth Union, when he was still in his hometown, the struggle against the bourgeoisie coincided with a struggle against power structures because in his provincial town "the bourgeoisie and the state officials [*chinovniki*] were the same thing."

Ivan's words can help highlight some important questions about the way in which Dugin's ideology circulates and is transformed in the context of grassroots politics, and about its impact on mainstream Russian culture and politics. First, in Ivan's account, Dugin's dark, postapocalyptic and paradoxical thinking is turned into a more or less presentable and simplified political program. The idea of a strong nation and a strong welfare state corresponds to the neo-Stalinist position of the Russian Communist Party, to which Dugin himself allegedly largely contributed.[96] Although this is an often overlooked issue, or one that is taken for granted and left in the background, Ivan's words remind one of the fact that disadvantaged educated youth from the province form the social basis for pro-government and nationalist organizations in Putin's Russia, and that class struggle and social inequality are crucial underlying issues of nationalist movements in general. Although the Eurasia movement, as opposed to mainstream pro-government organizations like Nashi or NOD, is a minoritarian intellectual formation, the disenfranchised lumpen proletariat and the impoverished Soviet intelligentsia are, along with conservative political leaders and members of the military, the ideal targets of Dugin's rhetoric.

In conservative circles, suspicion and resentment against capitalism, the "oligarchs," and multinational corporate power is also projected toward the Russian urban liberal intelligentsia, the culture and values that it promotes, and the private cultural and political institutions it is linked to; many of the artists and critics in Gintovt's and Dugin's circle saw Osmolovsky, Guelman, and the Soros Foundation, which was later banned in Russia, as their main political enemies. At the level of grassroots politics, Dugin's "countercultural paradigm" is employed as a mobilizing technique aimed at co-opting ideas on social conflicts and economic issues traditionally belonging to leftist discourses, and at producing a "common enemy" and "permanent state of emergency," to use the words of Carl Schmitt, a political thinker whom Dugin frequently quotes as a source of his own ideology.[97]

Ivan explained that he first learned about Eurasianism through a photocopy of *The Goals and Tasks of Our Revolution* (*Tseli i zadachi nashei revoliutsii*), a political manifesto for the National Bolshevik Party that Dugin authored in 1995. This thirty-page pamphlet is an excellent example of Dugin's "romantic prose," with a strong xenophobic and antisemitic subtext, in which, through vivid images and metaphors, Dugin turns the crisis following the fall of the Soviet Union into a national, religious, and class war, in order to attract to the party the ideal "common activists" that, at the time, he and Limonov believed would carry out their social and political revolution: war veterans, street fighters, skinheads, and angry young men from the slums of Russian cities.

Among Eurasianists today, the "image of the enemy" is projected onto social policies and values that are seen as closely connected with the Western (read: American) way of life in general and late capitalism in particular. In their vision, geopolitics and the struggle for human rights, multiculturalism, freedom of speech, and liberal values are interdependent issues that are interpreted through the spectrum of the global expansion of American cultural hegemony. For example, many Eurasianists considered multiculturalism not just a foreign concept but an oppressive form of cultural and economic colonization that actually destroys diversity rather than promoting it, because it effaces differences among cultural and historical traditions. Most neo-Eurasianist activists, when asked about racism, ethnic issues, and diversity, and about Dugin's own association with xenophobic movements throughout the world, referred very consistently to the nineteenth-century conservative thinker Konstantin Leontev's expression *tsvetushchaia slozhnost'* ("flourishing complexity"). As an alternative to the American melting pot, they referred to an idealized image of a future Eurasian empire, based on the peaceful coexistence of different peoples and communities maintaining separate historical and cultural traditions and identities.[98] Following a similar logic, when asked about the Eurasianists' position on gay rights in Russia, Nastya, one of my informants (and one of the few women in the organization, as the Eurasia Movement appears to be, even more than the NBP, male-dominated) explained that Eurasianists are not against homosexuality per se, but they see gay rights and gay marriage as expressions of the hedonistic-consumerist nature of Western society, where individual desire is the highest value, and "everything can be bought." The Eurasianists believe, she argued, that social rules and habits should be determined by cultural and historical traditions and develop with them "in a harmonious way."

When transferred to the sphere of grassroots politics, Dugin's "intellectual games" and "paradoxical thinking" are highly simplified and can quickly turn into cheap conspiracy theories, not dissimilar to the ones contained in mass paperback sci-fi and New Age books that overflow the shelves of post-Soviet bookstores. When I interviewed him, Korovin explained that the "revolution" that Dugin wants to accomplish is not a mere "revolt" (*bunt*) but a "paradigm shift" between the "paradigm of modernity"—marked by the direct relationship between subject and object—and the "premodern paradigm," where the relationship between subject and object is mediated by God. Playing the part of the good student of Eurasianism, I objected that according to the traditionalist Hindu philosophy that Guénon's ideas were based on, the only way to achieve such a paradigm shift would be through the apocalypse and the subsequent coming of a "new golden age." "That's absolutely right!" Korovin exclaimed with a professorial tone, "although according to the prophecy of Saint John the Apostle, the end of the world will be preceded by a one-thousand-year righteous empire; the Americans, the 'empire of the Antichrist,' think that they are the righteous empire, but as a matter of fact it is us!"

Yuri, another Moscow activist whom I interviewed, also mentioned the prophecy of Saint John the Apostle as proof of the forthcoming apocalypse. Credit card payments, current plans to implant chips into humans (as a first step toward turning them into cyborgs), and the presence of the number 666 in the barcode system were all, according to him, signs of the imminent end of the world and its connection with modern Western society.

These theories are not that far from the threatening remarks I heard from two skinheads upon my first visit to the ESM headquarters—alleging that Scandinavian countries had recently legalized incest and pedophilia. Korovin's claims notwithstanding, through the creation of a "common enemy," the Eurasian Youth Union has consistently functioned on behalf of the Putin administration as a technological instrument of repression working at the intersection of grassroots politics, academic culture, and mainstream media. The ESM's founding in 2005, a few months before the beginnings of Nashi, provided ideological justification for the existence of the latter group. The presence in the political spectrum of ESM, a radical (and minoritarian) anti-Western movement, made the apparently more moderate and mainstream Nashi more politically acceptable. According to an anonymous source, beginning in 2014 (with the approval and collaboration of the Russian authorities), members of the Eurasianist Youth Union also coordinated the gathering of volunteers, street fighters, and idealists from Russia to incite political unrest in Crimea and Donbass.

Throughout the years, Dugin's organization has consistently served as a political instrument in the hand of the Russian presidential administration. At the same time, this virtual, never fully realized grassroots movement has also fairly consistently replicated, on a mass scale, the romanticization of war, death, violence, and bohemianism that characterized the late Soviet "mythical underground" and Dugin's inner intellectual circle. The analysis offered in this chapter of the aesthetics, ideology, and social practices of Dugin's neo-Eurasianism, and the impact of Dugin's "countercultural paradigm" on various aspects of Russian public culture, can help explain Russia's recent self-positioning as the site of a possible alternative modernity, seen as both a stronghold of "traditional values" and a force resisting corporate power and globalization. This analysis sheds new light on the potential appeal of Dugin's ideology not only for Western conservative and far-right organizations but even, in certain cases, for radical left-wing and anti-global movements.

Conclusion

CREON: . . . Were you aware a decree had forbidden this?
ANTIGONE: Well aware. How could I avoid it? It was public.
CREON: And still you had the gall to break this law?
ANTIGONE: Of course I did. It wasn't Zeus, not in the least, / who made this proclamation—not to me. / Nor did that Justice, dwelling with the gods / beneath the earth, ordain such laws. Nor did I think your edict had such force / that you, a mere mortal, could override the gods, / the great unwritten, unshakeable traditions. / They are alive, not just today or yesterday; / they live forever, from the first of time, / and no one knows when they first saw the light.

Sophocles, *Antigone*

In a 1985 essay that produced fierce polemics in Italy at a time when the country was torn by radicalism and political violence, philosopher Massimo Cacciari used the character of Antigone, an archetypical rebel, as a metaphor for those comrades who chose "the critique of weapons" over the "weapons of critique." Alluding to the death toll that political terrorism had produced in the country, Cacciari wondered whether Antigone's radical gesture, and her rejection of "human laws," could become a "daydream," a utopian vision involving an actual political alternative, or if it belonged exclusively to "the time of the dead, the time that kills those who are alive."[1] The question has remained unanswered, and it is particularly relevant today, when all possibilities for contestation and political struggle appear to have been exhausted. By burying her brother Polynices, Antigone gives priority to her history, tradition, religious beliefs, and family ties—in a word, to her "identity"—over reason and the laws of the *polis*. Following a heroic impulse, she sacrifices her life for these values.

Her gesture is courageous, but fundamentally pointless, irrational, almost childish. Its consequences are absolutely disastrous for the community. Antigone would make for a terrible politician.

Present and former members of the NBP and the Eurasia Movement, in different ways, have a lot in common with Antigone and her unconditional radicalism. Both movements have given priority to historical and cultural traditions over the rule of law and the principles of the Enlightenment, although within both movements such traditions are very explicitly seen as "imagined" or creatively reinvented and combined. The NBP emerged as a form of radical rebellion against the crony capitalism of the mid-1990s, and it produced new forms of dissent, but not an actual political alternative. Street politics has been the only arena and stage the *natsboly* have actually been interested in. Dugin's Eurasia movement transferred this cult of the revolutionary process to a geopolitical struggle, seeking an alliance of convenience with the Russian government and far-right populist movements throughout the world. For better or worse, Dugin has produced a fairly effective critique of late capitalism and globalization, but this critique, like traditional Marxism, fails to produce actual instructions or ideas on "how to govern." Furthermore, even though it was conceived as a quintessentially radical system of thought, in terms of political practice, Dugin's provocative "intellectual game" has simply been used as one of the tools of repression in the hands of a fundamentally cynical, corrupt, and authoritarian ruling class. It has turned into a form of "trolling." In this sense, the history of the Eurasia Movement represents almost a parable about the "risks" of *stiob* and performativity: "we were pretending to be backward obscurantists, fascists, or postmodern cynical political technologists, and that's what we actually ended up being."

It would be easy to dismiss or label these forms of protest as "immature," ideologically inconsistent, or even primitive or "premodern." One could criticize Dugin for his graphomania and lack of academic rigor, Limonov for his narcissism and childishness, and their followers for being marginal and uneducated thugs. Yet doing so would mean to perpetuate the same precondition that motivated the emergence of these movements in the first place: a normative, unquestioning, and universalizing vision of Western political values and assumptions about culture and society. Although their approach to politics can be seen as irrational, uncompromising, or destructive, many of the critiques of late capitalism and (post)modernity that these movements have produced are valid, and many of the questions that they raised remain unanswered.

The goal of this book has been to produce, by looking closely at specific instances of post-Soviet political culture, something similar to what Bruno Latour describes as "an anthropology of the modern world," or what Dipesh

Chakrabarty sees as the "politics of despair," or a "history that deliberately makes visible, within the structure of its narrative forms, its own repressive strategies and practices, the part it plays in collusion with the narratives of citizenship in assimilating to the projects of the modern state all other possibilities of human solidarity."[2] The hope is that the in-depth study of Russian nationalism, radicalism, and political dissent offered in this book can serve as a way to challenge widespread notions and preconceptions about post-Soviet politics and public culture—and more broadly, to question and reelaborate common beliefs and assumptions about modern culture and society. This does not mean denying the values of modernity, liberal democracy, or the Enlightenment (as some have tried to do, misinterpreting Latour's project), but to reelaborate and rethink these concepts by looking at the meanings they acquired, and the way they were used in different places and different historical circumstances, or to accept the modern project, or liberal democracy, as one among many "metanarratives," and one that needs to be revisited and reformulated through an ideology (in the positive sense of the word).[3] Western concepts of modernity, liberal democracy, the "public sphere," and the value of the free market are too often presented, in a way analogous to science, as "facts speaking for themselves."[4] Being aware of the "repressive nature of history" means being aware of the fact that democracy and the free market cannot be presented as the only possible political and economic systems, or as Roland Barthes would put it, they cannot and should not be "naturalized."[5] Although this principle might appear obvious, it is in fact very commonly disregarded in the context of discussions and debates surrounding contemporary Russian culture and society.

This is a particularly difficult task from a political standpoint and from the standpoint of "cultural translation" in that many of the movements and ideologies discussed in this book are based on a radical rejection of "Western" or neoliberal cultural and political hegemony. Like the NBP, Latour's reflection about the "narrative" or ideological essence of science and modern democracy, and about the implicit connection between knowledge and power, was formulated in response to "the year of miracles," 1989, which marked the ostensible "triumph of liberalism, of capitalism, of the Western democracies over the vain hopes of Marxism," and when the utter failure of the socialist systems in Eastern Europe and Russia became finally explicit and undeniable. This resulted in what Latour aptly describes as a silent political tragedy.

> The perfect symmetry between the dismantling of the wall of shame and the end of limitless Nature is invisible only to the rich Western democracies. The various manifestations of socialism destroyed both their people and their ecosystems, whereas the powers of the North and the West have been

> able to save their people and some of their countryside by destroying the rest of the world and reducing its people to abject poverty. Hence a double tragedy: the former socialist societies think they can solve both [of] their problems by imitating the West; the West thinks it has escaped both problems and believes it has lessons for others even as it leaves the Earth and its people to die. The West thinks it is the sole possessor of the clever trick that will allow it to keep on winning indefinitely, whereas it has perhaps already lost everything.[6]

While embracing strongly anti-egalitarian and antidemocratic views, and while appropriating totalitarian symbols and ideas, the movements that populate the pages of this book have also given voice, or tried to give voice, to some of the victims of this neoliberal triumph. Their response to these forms of oppression was the most radical, and it involved, at least theoretically, the rejection and ultimate destruction of Western civilization. The goal of this book is not to find a solution to this predicament, let alone to support this revolutionary enterprise, but to study the reasons, meanings, and the significance of this protest.

In Russia, these political communities clearly had an important role in uncovering the risks connected with the widespread cultural and ideological conformism that took over after the fall of the Soviet Union. An example of this influence can be found in the writings of Kirill Medvedev, a poet and public intellectual who has made significant efforts to revive Russian political culture. In denouncing the self-proclaimed apolitical stance of the Moscow literary community and its implicit promotion of reactionary, anti-egalitarian, and conservative ideas, Medvedev referred explicitly to Dugin's and Limonov's "monopoly" over post-Soviet protest culture, and their paradoxical appropriation of "fascism," as what appeared to be the only possible form of political militancy in post-Soviet society. Interestingly, as was true in the case of Dugin and other members of the NBP and the Eurasia Movement, Medvedev's reflection about the alleged de-ideologization of Russian society also came as a criticism against "mainstream postmodernism," which had produced widespread cynicism and indifference both in mass culture and among the Russian intellectual elites. Even more interestingly, Medvedev's own personal solution to this political impasse involved a further appropriation of "fascism," or what he called "my fascism," as a way to reaffirm the value of ideology and political militancy.

> YES, WE'RE WITH THEM—with the young Arab men whom well-fed Saudi sheikhs tempt into blowing themselves up so as to get money for

> their families; with the young Chechen women who are sent to their deaths with promises of paradise by strong and clever men; and with their victims; and with the Palestinians in Israel, chased off their lands; with the Russians in the Baltics, where local authorities have erected a monument to the SS just around the corner from the EU; and with the Russians in Russia, who've been fucked over again by their recently elected officials; with Tajiks in Moscow who get attacked by skinheads and harassed by the police; with the "greens" who fight their doomed fight with those who refuse to give up even a bit of their newfound First World comforts; with the National Bolshevik Party, which plays out its cruel circus in the center of Moscow, and is beaten and jailed for it; with . . . with all of them, we're with all of them, and we feel no terror at the images of our civilization overrun with whoever it will be—Arabs, Africans, Chinese—because we don't have anything anyway, just the air, and that's how it will remain until we have nothing left to oppose it but our race and those things that are fundamentally unacceptable to us aesthetically: conservatism; nationalism; fundamentalism in all its forms, whether the conservative fetish for "fundamental ontological foundations" or the fascist fetish for "blood and soil," or the classical or modernist fetish for "high culture," or a positive identification with the "white" world elite, the "golden billion"—I'd like to oppose all of this with a conscious movement to the left, with a critically digested theory of democracy and internationalism, a reevaluation of many of the political ideas and sympathies we inherited from liberalism, including the idea that we could rationally understand and change the world; an understanding that politics is involved in every minute of our existence (I don't know what needs to happen before people finally understand this); and finally an understanding of the incredible hard work, the superhuman work of reason that will be required to oppose the waves of irrationalism and violence that are now engulfing the world, and those economic interests that often stand behind them.[7]

I quote this passage in its entirety because it accomplishes something quite remarkable; it manages to capture, at least in general terms, what a redefinition of leftist, progressive, and liberal politics could look like. Medvedev's reflections, and the study of the specific connection between post-Soviet nationalism and protest culture offered in this book, can also hopefully provide insights into Western and global politics more broadly, and the role that the more or less truthful image and perception of Russia as the site of an alternative form of modernity plays in it. Specifically, the recent emergence of populist movements throughout Europe and the United States, and the co-optation of leftist and anti-global values on the part of identitarian and nationalist movements throughout the world, indicate that today, more than ever, we really cannot rest on assumptions related to ideas about a global "end of history" or "end of ideology" that public intellectuals like Fukuyama and Bell have promoted in the past.

When I started my research on this project in 2013, the idea of a "Red-Brown" ideology as the ultimate form of resistance against late capitalism and Western liberalism was mostly relegated to distant memories of a political scandal produced by a few extravagant Parisian intellectuals in the early 1990s. In recent years, the term has become more and more common in the context of public discussions about populist, identitarian, and antidemocratic movements throughout the world, and the image of post-Soviet Russia as a metaphorical "other" has played an important role in this. In the United States, Richard Spencer, an advocate of white nationalism who is said to have coined the term "alt-right," defined Russia as "the sole white power in the world."[8] Spencer has collaborated closely with Jason Jorjani, the editor in chief of Arktos, the publishing house that curated and published English translations of some of Dugin's works. His ex-wife, Nina Kouprianova, has also translated some of Dugin's works into English, and, describing her political convictions in some interviews, she repeated almost verbatim some of the ideas traditionally associated with Dugin's Eurasianism, including the concept (borrowed from de Benoist) of "multipolarism."[9]

After the beginning of the war in Eastern Ukraine, members of radical political organizations on both the right and left sides of the political spectrum from Europe, South America, and the United States illegally joined the battalions in Donbass to fight on the side of the pro-Russian separatists. This is only an extreme example that reflects a more general tendency, among not only fringe organizations but also conservative and leftist European intellectual and political figures, to envision Putin's Russia both as a stronghold of traditional values and the site of an ultimate desperate resistance against late capitalism and globalization.[10]

One of the latest examples of this comes from my own homeland, Italy, where in the last year the term *rossobruni* (Red-Brown) has been more and more often associated with the coalition of the xenophobic, right-wing identitarian party Lega Nord and the populist (supposedly left-wing) Movimento 5 Stelle, which is currently governing the country. This coalition owes its success to a widespread disillusionment with the old and stale Italian political class and with the policies of the European government, compounded by frustration over decades-long economic and political stagnation. Discussions about a Red-Brown ideology in general have become more and more common in the Italian media. In the summer of 2017, Dugin himself was interviewed in the leading (and progressive) Italian newspaper *la Repubblica*, something truly unthinkable just a few years ago. In the interview, Dugin praised the emergence of Italy's "positively populist" coalition and argued that this political trend should be seen as proof of Italy's pioneering role in the context of international politics. Significantly, Dugin this time also reclaimed his countercultural past as a co-founder of the NBP, something that he had previously distanced himself from because of Limonov's and The Other Russia's vocal opposition to Putin's government.[11]

The culture of the NBP and the Eurasia Movement has also had a significant and ongoing impact on contemporary Russian art and literature. Most famously, the experience of marginality, rebellion, and desperate heroism of a typical National Bolshevik was at the center of Zakhar Prilepin's popular semi-fictional memoir *Sankya* (2006), a revolutionary fantasy based on the author's own active participation in the movement.[12] Prilepin's public persona (like Limonov's, mutatis mutandis) is also carefully crafted and largely determined by his unique biography and political views. Prilepin cultivated the image of the provincial, politically engaged writer, aggressively masculine and provocative in his demeanor, which he voluntarily used to cause a certain scandal among the Russian literary establishment.[13] His political militancy, his nationalist and socially conservative views, his past as a member of the special police unit OMON (which included periods of deployment in Chechen war zones), and even his participation in musical videos by popular Russian rappers—as well as his recent alleged participation in the war in Eastern Ukraine as a commander of one of the pro-Russian battalions—are some of the elements that have contributed to his persona and its complex interconnections with the fictional characters of his novels.

In the past, Prilepin has also tried to create a literary movement, the so-called New Realism, partly inspired by ideas that can be associated with a National Bolshevik aesthetics and worldview.[14] The movement, which included writers like Mikhail Elizarov, Sergey Shargunov, and German Sadulaev (who are, in Prilepin's own view, very different from the standpoint of style and imagination), was based on a few commonalities: the reelaboration of the memory and legacy of the Soviet past; the criticism of postmodern literature, which for Prilepin is in part responsible for the fundamental political passivity of the post-Soviet intelligentsia (and of post-Soviet society in general); and the fact that these writers identified, in different ways, with a Red-Brown ideology.

Other examples of the long-term influence of these movements include the works of "conservative postmodernist" writer Pavel Krusanov, who was also part of intellectual circles close to Timur Novikov's New Academy, and the recent canonization, at least at the level of official cultural institutions, of artists close to the New Serious and Gintovt's "conservative bohemia." In his novel *Amerikanskaia dyrka* (The American hole, 2005), for instance, Krusanov resuscitates a fictional version of Sergey Kurekhin, who specializes in the art of manipulating reality based on what could be seen as a combination of situationism and internet trolling. The fictional Kurekhin's secret "private company" struggles against "American mercantilism" in favor of a romantic cult of heroism and a pure, untainted pursuit of culture as an end in itself. Its activities include elaborate pranks against sexually predatory old professors, the terrorist attacks of September 11, and, most importantly, an incredible scam at the expense of the American government, ultimately aimed, according to convoluted and barely comprehensible conspiracy theories, at putting an end to the "New World Order."[15] The "canonization" of the New Serious and Gintovt's "conservative bohemia" included, beginning with the conservative turn of Putin's third term, a series of art exhibits devoted to new forms of "Russian patriotic art," some of which received significant promotion and funding from the Russian Ministry of Culture. The New Serious had already entered mainstream culture a few years earlier, and with great scandal with the famous case of the promotional campaign for the Sochi Olympic Games, organized by Dmitry Mishenin's Doping Pong, a group of artists and designers close to the New Academy that featured examples of "ironic totalitarianism" and explicit allusions to both Nazi and socialist realist celebrations of sports and physical beauty.[16]

All these topics deserve further analysis that lies beyond the scope of this project, but they represent important examples of the long-term impact that the cultural and ideological currents under study here had on Russian and global culture and politics. Some of the theoretical questions raised by this study also remain open. In the meantime, even if it could not fulfill the "daydream" of imagining a political alternative, this book has hopefully accomplished the task of opening new possible directions in the study of post-Soviet literature, art, and politics from a global perspective. Hopefully, it will also serve as a premise for further scholarly and political action.

Notes

Introduction

Epigraph: *Mal'chik, begi!*, 96: "Подростков затылки худые, / Костлявые их кулаки. / Березы. Собаки. Россия . . . / И вы — как худые щенки . . . // Пришли из вороньих слободок, / Из сумерек бледных столиц, / Паров валерьянок и водок, / От мам, от отцов и сестриц . . . / Я ряд героических лиц, // На нашем холме замечаю. / Христос им является, тих? / Я даже Христу пожелаю / Апостолов смелых таких! // Я поднял вас всех в ночь сырую, / России — страны ледяной, / Страны моей страшной, стальной. / — Следы ваших ног целую! // Вы — храбрые воины света, / Апостолы, дети, сынки, / Воители черного лета, / Худые и злые щенки . . ." Unless otherwise indicated, all translations are my own.

1. Kamardin, "Ubei menia, opolchenets!": "Убей меня, ополченец! / Ствол тебе купят менты из бюджетных денег. / Убей меня, ополченец! / Стань десницей карающей. / Я же не человек! Дерьмо течет в моих венах! / Убей меня, ополченец! / Будь бичом Божьим! / Ведь я не патриот . . . а может просто не вышел рожей. / Зачем тебе повод? Нах*й его! Не нужен! / Убей меня, ополченец! / Ну же! / Убей меня, ополченец! / Ты уже попробовал крови! / Ты видел, как братскому народу / Боевые братья братские могилы роют. / Ты включишь телевизор—тебя перекроет, / Самоконтроль никогда не был твоей сильной стороною. / Зато у тебя много других сильных сторон. / Убей меня, доброволец! / Отстреливай белых ворон. / Отомсти за распятого мальчика! / Спаси от меня Родину! / Стань героем! / Убей меня, доброволец! / Твой президент будет тобою очень доволен. / Разорви меня в клочья! / Втопчи в грязь! / Русской Весны распустились почки! / Не медли! Убей меня, мразь! / Ты же так этого хочешь . . . // Ведь пока ты воевал за Донбасс, / Я трахал твоих дочек, / А трехгодовалому сыну продавал спайс."

2. In post-Soviet Russia, the term "political technology" generally refers to the activity of Kremlin ideologists and media consultants who are seemingly in charge of manipulating the public opinion. The work of Russian "political technologists" includes controlling and manufacturing information on mainstream and independent media,

and the establishment of "virtual" political organizations. One of the most famous "political technologists" in Russia is Gleb Pavlovsky, the founder, along with the gallerist Marat Guelman, of the Foundation for Effective Politics (Fond effektivnoi politiki), an organization that allegedly was in charge of "staging" both Boris Yeltsin's 1996 reelection and Putin's succession to power in 1999. The other chief post-Soviet political technologist is Vladislav Surkov, Putin's main ideologue throughout the first decade of the 2000s, who coined the term *suverennaia demokratiia* (sovereign democracy), and who was behind the creation of Nashi, a state-funded youth movement more or less surreptitiously designed to prevent the emergence of independent forms of political protest in Russia. On political technology, see Wilson, *Virtual Politics*; Ostrovsky, *The Invention of Russia*; Clover, *Black Wind, White Snow*, 267–305. On Nashi, see Hemment, *Youth Politics in Putin's Russia*; Lassila *The Quest for an Ideal Youth.*

3. See Dunlop, "Aleksandr Dugin's Foundations of Geopolitics."

4. The term "anti-imperialist empire" is Nancy Condee's. See Condee, *The Imperial Trace*, 28.

5. On this very much prescriptive vision of an "imaginary Western democracy" in early post-Soviet culture, see Magun, *Negative Revolution*, 30.

6. See Ries, *Russian Talk.*

7. See Magun, *Negative Revolution*, 30–31.

8. Magun, *Negative Revolution*, 35.

9. See Magun, *Negative Revolution*, 1–72.

10. See Oushakine, "In the State of Post-Soviet Aphasia."

11. See Oushakine, *The Patriotism of Despair.*

12. Oushakine, *The Patriotism of Despair*, 1–14.

13. See Oushakine, 1–78; Hemment, *Youth Politics in Putin's Russia*, 1–104.

14. Sell, *The Avant-Garde*, 41. On the concept of "historical avant-gardes," see Poggioli, *The Theory of the Avant-Garde*; Bürger, *Theory of the Avant-Garde.*

15. For the distinction between "literary" and "political" public spheres, see Habermas, *The Structural Transformation of the Public Sphere.*

16. See Lotman, "Literatura v kontekste russkoi kul'tury."

17. See Lotman, "Dekabrist v povsednevnoi zhizni"; Lotman, "Poetika bytovogo povedeniia."

18. On this issue, see, among others, Groys, *The Total Art of Stalinism*; Clark, *The Soviet Novel*; Dobrenko, *The Making of the State Reader*; Paperny, *Architecture in the Age of Stalin.*

19. See Anderson, *Imagined Communities*, 21–38, here 25.

20. Anderson, *Imagined Communities*, 25.

21. Anderson, *Imagined Communities*, 34.

22. Shenfield, *Russian Fascism*, 17.

23. Griffin, *The Nature of Fascism*, 26. In their definition of the NBP as a "fascist" movement, Andreas Umland and Markus Mathyl also apply Griffin's concepts of "uncivil society" and "groupuscular new right." See Griffin, "From Slime Mould to Rhizome"; Umland, "Toward an Uncivil Society?"; Mathyl, "The National-Bolshevik Party and Arctogaia"; Mathyl, "Natsionalizm i kontrkul'tura"; Mathyl, "Nationalisme et contre-culture jeune."

24. See these works by Umland: "Toward an Uncivil Society?"; "'Konservativnaia revoliutsiia'"; "Post-Soviet 'Uncivil Society'"; "Pathological Tendencies in Russian 'Neo-Eurasianism'"; "Aleksandr Dugin's Transformation." See also Shekhovtsov,

"Aleksandr Dugin's Neo-Eurasianism"; Shekhovtsov, "The Palingenetic Thrust"; Shekhovtsov and Umland, "Is Aleksandr Dugin a Traditionalist?" For a discussion about the effectiveness and the heuristic value of this approach, see Gregor and Umland, "Dugin Not a Fascist?"; Gregor, *The Search for Neofascism.*

25. See Gregor, *The Search for Neofascism*, 111–65. A. James Gregor describes post-Maoist China as one of the most consistent applications of the ideology of Italian Fascism, using this as an example of how the "fascist" label can be quite slippery.

26. The full official name of Nashi was Molodezhnoe demokraticheskoe antifashistskoe dvizhenie "Nashi" (Democratic Antifascist Youth Movement "Nashi").

27. See Johnson, "The Putin Jugend."

28. See Yakemenko, *Limonov o Limonove*, and more on this in chapter 5.

29. See "Manifest molodezhnogo dvizheniia 'NASHI'"; "Vasilii Yakemenko: 'NASHI—dvizhenie oppozitsionnoe, deistvuiushchei elite'"; Hemment, *Youth Politics in Putin's Russia*, 70–103.

30. See "Misuse of Anti-extremism/SOVA."

31. As Marlène Laruelle points out, "scholarly works on the far right begin with terminological cautiousness. Academic use has to be dissociated from the general use of a terminology often brandished to denounce political enemies." Although the question is very complex, Laruelle's cautious decision to limit the use of the terms "fascist," "neofascist," and "neo-Nazi" to movements "that openly lay claim to historical Nazism or fascism and seek to reestablish it" seems the most reasonable. See Laruelle, "Dangerous Liaisons." On the indiscriminate use of the "fascist label" within American media in relation to the war in Eastern Ukraine (with a specific focus on the case of Timothy Snyder's public statements), see Laruelle, "Is Russia Really 'Fascist'?"; Pinkham, "Timothy Snyder's Bleak Vision."

32. Chabal and Daloz, *Culture Troubles*, 22.

33. See Yurchak, *Everything Was Forever, Until It Was No More*; Yurchak, "Post-Post Communist Sincerity"; Yurchak, "A Parasite from Outer Space"; Boyer and Yurchak, "AMERICAN STIOB."

34. See Groys, *The Total Art of Stalinism*; Lipovetsky, *Paralogii.*

35. See, for instance: Pomerantsev, *Nothing Is True and Everything Is Possible*; Wilson, *Virtual Politics*; Ostrovsky, *The Invention of Russia*; Masha Gessen, *The Future Is History.*

36. On Nashi's "cynicism" and the diverse range of social practices that the movement produced, see Hemment, *Youth Politics in Putin's Russia.*

37. On the possible connections and overlaps between "living beyond" and different forms of political militancy in late socialist societies, see also Fürst and McLellan, *Dropping out of Socialism.*

38. Epstein, *The Transformative Humanities*, 43–44.

39. Pilkington, *Russia's Youth and Its Culture*, 235.

40. Pilkington, *Russia's Youth and Its Culture*, 235.

41. See Gabowitsch, *Protest in Putin's Russia*, 1–43, 105–94; Lena Johnson, *Art and Protest in Putin's Russia*, 165–93. I am borrowing the terms "political grammars" (or "grammars of personal affinity") and "repertoires of contention" from Mischa Gabowitsch. See Gabowitsch, *Protest in Putin's Russia*, 12–27. On the history of Voina, see also Epshtein, *Total'naia voina.*

42. See Sperling, *Sex, Politics, and Putin*, 1–28, 80–124.

43. On this issue, see Rogers, "Postsocialisms Unbound"; Oushakine, *Patriotism of Despair*; Hemment, *Youth Politics in Putin's Russia*; Gabowitsch, *Protest in Putin's Russia*;

Verdery, *What Was Socialism, and What Comes Next?*; Burawoy and Verdery, *Uncertain Transition.*

44. On the political implications of ethnographic writing, see, among others, Clifford and Marcus, *Writing Culture.*

45. Geertz, *The Interpretation of Cultures*, 5. For an extensive discussion of the possibility and importance of a cultural approach to comparative politics, see, again, Chabal and Daloz, *Culture Troubles.*

46. Barthes, *The Rustle of Language*, 72.

Chapter 1. "The Power of the State Should Be in the Hands of the Punks"

1. Limonov, *It's Me, Eddie*, 3. For Limonov's novels *Eto ia—Edichka, Dnevnik neudachnika*, and *Podrostok Savenko* (*It's Me Eddie, Diary of a Loser*, and *Memoir of a Russian Punk*), I am using the existing English translations, modifying them where necessary. *Eto ia—Edichka* was written in the summer of 1976. According to Limonov's own account, in the following years the manuscript of the novel was submitted to and rejected by a total of thirty-six American publishers. A Russian edition of the novel was put out by the émigré publishing house Russica in New York in 1979, although Alexander Sumerkin, who was then in charge of Russica, decided to use the "made-up" name Index Publishers for the press in order to avoid possible attacks from the very socially conservative Russian émigré community. *Eto ia—Edichka* was then accepted by the French publishing house Éditions Ramsay and translated under the catchy title *Le poète russe préfère les grands nègres* (which Limonov himself claims to have come up with) in 1980. After the novel came out in French, Limonov moved to Paris. *Eto ia—Edichka* was then translated into most European languages. In 1990, the novel was published in Russia for the first time by the publishing house Glagol, with a total print run of 390,000. See Limonov, "The ABSOLUTE BEGINNER"; Limonov's full bibliography on his "unofficial" website, limonow.de (accessed April 19, 2016); and the website of the publishing house Glagol, old.russ.ru/info/GLAGOL/ (accessed April 19, 2016). See also "A Tribute to Alexander Sumerkin."

2. See Butler, *Gender Trouble*, 134–48.

3. See Butler, *Excitable Speech*, 159–62.

4. Butler, *Excitable Speech*, 160; Butler, *Gender Trouble*, 137.

5. See the following works by Lotman: "Poetika bytovogo povedeniia"; "Dekabrist v povsednevnoi zhizni"; "Literatura v kontekste russkoi kul'tury." I am grateful to Bella Grigoryan for pointing out the connection between Butler's discussion of gender performativity and Lotman's essays on the semiotics of Russian culture.

6. On *zhiznetvorchestvo* in the context of Russian modernism and early twentieth-century Russian culture more broadly, see Paperno and Grossman, *Creating Life*; Wachtel, "Zhiznetvorchestvo"; Ioffe, "Modernism in the context of Russian 'life-creation.'" On the theatricality of Stalinism, see also Averintsev, "Bakhtin, smekh, khristianskaia kul'tura."

7. Skidan, "Limonov, protivitel'nyi soiuz." On Limonov's *zhiznetvorchestvo*, see also Gol'dshtein, "Eduard velikolepnyi"; Matich, "Eduard Limonov"; Kukulin, "Prigov i Limonov." By retracing Limonov's influence on Prigov's early work, Il'ia Kukulin argues that Limonov and Prigov represent two different examples of "postmodern *zhiznetvorchestvo.*" The hidden connections and affinities between these two apparently very different authors that Kukulin's essay brings to light are very revealing, especially considering

the impact that both Limonov and Prigov had on more recent forms of art performance and protest culture. However, I would argue that Limonov's writing and politics are in fact closer to an avant-garde posture and sensibility, and that they ultimately represent a categorical rejection of postmodern culture broadly conceived.

8. On the complex relationship between Limonov's biography and his fiction, see Carden, "Limonov's Coming out"; Golynko-Vol'fson, "Chert s mladentsem"; Rogachevskii, *A Biographical and Critical Study*; Chantsev, *Bunt krasoty*; Wakamiya, *Locating Exiled Writers*; Skidan, "Limonov, protivitel'nyi soiuz"; Matich, "Eduard Limonov"; Kukulin, "Prigov i Limonov." Limonov's very eventful life has recently become the subject of Emmanuel Carrère's bestseller *Limonov*, published in France in 2011 and later translated into more than twenty languages. Interestingly, as the writer Zakhar Prilepin, who considers Limonov one of his mentors, pointed out, Carrère's "fictional biography" is mostly based on Limonov's own semi-autobiographical novels. See Carrère, *Limonov*; Prilepin, "Portret evropeitsa."

9. See Anderson, *Imagined Communities*.

10. Ong, "The Writer's Audience Is Always a Fiction," 11.

11. Ong, "The Writer's Audience Is Always a Fiction," 12.

12. These communities were portrayed, respectively, in Limonov's novels *Eto ia—Edichka*, *Podrostok Savenko*, and *Molodoi negodiai* (*It's Me Eddie*, *Memoir of a Russian Punk*, and The young scoundrel).

13. See Limonov's own discussion of the importance of futurist poet Velimir Khlebnikov and the poets of the group Oberiu in his work in Limonov, "Gruppa 'Konkret'"; Brodskii, "Posleslovie"; Zholkovskii, "Grafomanstvo kak priem" (both Brodsky and Zholkovsky point out the continuity between Limonov and the Russian avant-garde in general, and Khlebnikov and the Oberiuty in particular). Limonov is often compared by critics to leading avant-garde poet Mayakovsky. See, among others, Matich, "The Moral Immoralist"; Kron, "Pro babochku"; Rogachevskii, *A Biographical and Critical Study*, 73–118.

14. See Limonov, "My—natsional'nyi geroi," 57.

15. Limonov, "My—natsional'nyi geroi," 58.

16. Limonov, *Dnevnik neudachnika* (published in English as *Diary of a Loser*), 33–34.

17. Limonov, *It's Me, Eddie*, 5.

18. See Tynianov, "O literaturnoi evoliutsii."

19. See Ryan-Hayes, *Contemporary Russian Satire*, 132–33. On the reception of *Eto ia—Edichka* in the émigré community, and on the reactions to the inclusion of *mat* and explicit sexual descriptions in the book, see Simmons, *Their Fathers' Voice*, 91–125; Ryan-Hayes, *Contemporary Russian Satire*, 101–50; Rogachevskii, *A Biographical and Critical Study*. Simmons in particular sees *Eto ia—Edichka* as an example of "aberrant discourse" in post-Stalinist fiction. In his afterword to *U nas byla velikaia epokha* (We had a great epoch, first published in the Soviet Union in 1989), Mogutin discusses, among other things, how in the late 1980s and early 1990s Russian publishers still resisted the idea of publishing the type of "non-normative language" that appeared in Limonov's works. See Mogutin, "Vospominaniia russkogo panka."

20. Ryan-Hayes, *Contemporary Russian Satire*, 130.

21. Limonov, *It's Me, Eddie*, 48.

22. See note 1.

23. Limonov, *It's Me, Eddie*, 79.

24. Rogachevsky proposes this idea, suggesting that the homosexual experiences described in the novel are not autobiographical. See Rogachevskii, *A Biographical and Critical Study*, 30–31.

25. Limonov, *It's Me, Eddie*, 27.

26. Limonov, *It's Me, Eddie*, 83.

27. In relation to this issue, see the meticulous analysis of the correspondences and discrepancies between biographical and fictional events in Limonov's prose in Rogachevskii, *A Biographical and Critical Study*.

28. See Matich, "Eduard Limonov": "Эта сцена—самое грубое нарушение литературных табу в романе. . . . никогда прежде в русской литературе гомосексуальная связь не изображалась так откровенно и в таком положительном ключе."

29. Limonov, *It's Me, Eddie*, 81.

30. Limonov, *It's Me, Eddie*, 32. In connection with this passage, Ryan-Hayes remarks that "Edichka (perhaps ironically) reverses Freud." See Ryan-Hayes, "Limonov's *Eto Ia—Edichka*," 455. On the relationship between Edichka's femininity and his displaced émigré identity, see also Ryan-Hayes, *Contemporary Russian Satire*, 129–32.

31. Limonov, *It's Me, Eddie*, 71.

32. See Ryan-Hayes, *Contemporary Russian Satire*, 121, 128, 147.

33. See Simmons, *Their Fathers' Voice*, 103–6.

34. See Limonov, "Molodoi negodiai," 353–58.

35. Limonov, *Drugaia Rossiia*, 179–87.

36. Limonov, *It's Me, Eddie*, 91.

37. See Limonov's articles from *Novoe russkoe slovo*: "Zhit' ne po lzhi," "Russkaia oppozitsiia i zapad," "Razocharovanie," "Neterpimost'." See also the discussion of Limonov's articles in the Soviet press: Dzhalogoniia and Chekhonin, "Eto gor'koe slovo 'razocharovanie.'" On the reception of Limonov's articles in the Russian émigré community, see Ryan-Hayes, *Contemporary Russian Satire*, 102–4; Rogachevskii, *A Biographical and Critical Study*, 29–38.

38. Limonov, *It's Me, Eddie*, 71.

39. Limonov, *It's Me, Eddie*, 77–84.

40. Limonov, *It's Me, Eddie*, 71–72.

41. Limonov, *It's Me, Eddie*, 93.

42. Limonov, *It's Me, Eddie*, 86.

43. Ryan-Hayes, *Contemporary Russian Satire*, 144.

44. Limonov, *It's Me, Eddie*, 100.

45. In one of the first interviews he gave after returning to Russia in the early 1990s, discussing the inclusion of *mat* (uncensored language) in his work, Limonov provided the example of Henry Miller as one of his main predecessors. See Limonov, "Ne putaite menia s Limonovym."

46. "Roundtable with Edward Limonov"; Ryan-Hayes, "Limonov's *Eto Ia—Edichka*."

47. See "Roundtable with Edward Limonov"; Limonov, "Punk and National-Bolshevism." In his political manifesto *Drugaia Rossiia*, Limonov discusses the lack of countercultural literature as one of the main causes of Russian social and intellectual backwardness. See Limonov, *Drugaia Rossiia*, 85–109. On the NBP alternative fashion, see also Ferelov, "Moda NBP."

48. Marcuse, *Eros and Civilization*, 44.
49. Marcuse, *Eros and Civilization*, 184.
50. See notes 42 and 44.
51. Limonov, *It's Me, Eddie*, 230.
52. *Podrostok Savenko* and *Molodoi negodiai* were first published in the original Russian in Paris, in 1983 and 1986 respectively. *U nas byla velikaia epokha* was published by the Soviet journal *Znamia* in 1989 (the French translation was published in Paris in the same year). Later the three books were considered part of a cycle, the *Khar'kovskaia trilogiia* (see Mogutin, "Vospominaniia russkogo panka"). Here I will discuss the three parts of the trilogy following the chronological order of publication in order to respect the timing with which certain themes and motifs emerged in Limonov's fiction. In the case of *Podrostok Savenko*, when possible, I will be quoting from the available English translation: Limonov, *Memoir of a Russian Punk*. In all other cases, I will be quoting from a more recent edition of the trilogy: Limonov, *Russkoe*.
53. Limonov, *Memoir of a Russian Punk*, 3–4. Limonov gave his character his own real last name, "Savenko," which appears in the original title of the novel, *Podrostok Savenko* (The adolescent Savenko).
54. Limonov, *Memoir of a Russian Punk*, 4.
55. To this day, the term *gopnik* is commonly used to refer to destitute and aggressive petty criminals inhabiting the industrial peripheries of Russian and former Soviet cities.
56. See Mogutin, "Vospominaniia russkogo panka."
57. In this sense, as Matich points out, the book can be seen as a response to the Youth Prose. See Matich, "Eduard Limonov."
58. See "Eduard Limonov: Vstrecha v kontsertnoi studii Ostankino."
59. Limonov, *Podrostok Savenko*, 134: "По рыбам, по звездам / Проносит шаланду: / Три грека в Одессу / Везут контрабанду. . . . Чтоб звезды обрызгали / Груду наживы: / Коньяк, чулки / И презервативы."
60. Limonov, "U nas byla velikaia epokha," 29.
61. Quoted in Mogutin, "Vospominaniia russkogo panka," 162. The expression *zhestokii talant* (cruel talent) is a reference to the famous homonymous article by nineteenth-century populist critic Nikolay Mikhailovsky that criticized Dostoevsky for his "morbidity." Limonov's reference to Mikhailovsky's article here could be seen as a way to justify the inclusion of graphic descriptions of sex and violence in his own novels by comparing himself to one of the Russian classics. It can also be seen as a way for Limonov to dismiss his critics by comparing them to the somewhat ingenuous Mikhailovsky, who failed to distinguish between reality and literary invention by identifying Dostoevsky's personality with that of the characters in his novels.
62. On the "naïveté" of Limonov's lyric personas, see Kukulin, "Prigov i Limonov"; Kukulin, "Longing for Fear and Darkness."
63. Limonov, *Memoir of a Russian Punk*, 300 (modified translation); "Podrostok Savenko," 315: "Чистые листы кончились, и Эди, поразмыслив несколько секунд, решительно вырвал первый лист со стихами и поджег его. Скрючиваясь в огне, корежились строчки "Наташи"—"В белом платье / В белый день / Погулять ты вышла . . ."—В белом платье . . . —шепчет Эди горько. И швыряет «Наташу» в крыс.—В грязном платье . . . В сальном платье . . . В платье из сала . . . —шепчет он зло.— . . . В украинском национальном костюме, в платье из сала!—говорит Эди вслух и решительно спускается с двери."

64. See note 61.

65. Marijeta Bozovic suggested to me the idea that the image of Natasha "in a dress made of lard" in this passage could be seen as a form of displaced self-hatred.

66. Limonov, *Memoir of a Russian Punk*, 236–37. The term that Eddie-baby uses—*shpana*, here translated as "punks"—is a collective derogative word for "hooligans" or "petty criminals," the meaning and connotation of which is not far from that of the word "thugs" in the context of contemporary American media and mainstream culture (including the racist and/or classist subtext).

67. Eddie-baby's utopian dream is in this sense consistent with the values of early Soviet culture, in which daring experimentations and theories in the spheres of gender, sexuality, and social politics coexisted with a widespread idealization of masculinity and comradeship. See Borenstein, *Men without Women*.

68. Limonov, "Molodoi negodiai," 331. All quotations from "Molodoi negodiai" and "U nas byla velikaia epokha" are taken from the Russian edition of the *Kharkov Trilogy* published under the title *Russkoe*.

69. Limonov, "Molodoi negodiai," 329. The names are all plays on words, which in English would sound something like "Blankettov," "Drunkov," "Lemonov."

70. Limonov, "Ne putaite menia s Limonovym."

71. Borden, *The Art of Writing Badly*, 242.

72. Limonov, "Ne putaite menia s Limonovym."

73. See Matich, "Eduard Limonov."

74. Limonov, "Molodoi negodiai," 350–53, 362–68.

75. Limonov, *Drugaia Rossiia*, 91.

76. Limonov, "Molodoi negodiai," 368.

77. Limonov, "Molodoi negodiai," 323–24.

78. Limonov, "Molodoi negodiai," 354. Here the narrator is referring to Kharkov's famous State Industry Building (known by the acronyms Gosprom, in Russian, or Derzhprom, in Ukrainian).

79. Limonov, *Memoir of a Russian Punk*, 4.

80. Limonov, "U nas byla velikaia epokha," 39.

81. Limonov, "Molodoi negodiai," 501.

82. Limonov, *Drugaia Rossiia*, 141–52.

83. I am borrowing the term "chronotope" from Mikhail Bakhtin's classification of literary genres on the basis of their relationship with time and space, but I am also using it loosely to refer to different cultural trends and aesthetic visions in the contemporary cultural landscape. See Bakhtin, "Forms of Time and of the Chronotope in the Novel"; Epstein, *The Transformative Humanities*, 43–44; and the introduction, 20–21.

84. See "Eduard Limonov (interv'iu)."

85. See "Eduard Limonov: Vstrecha v kontsertnoi studii Ostankino."

86. "Eduard Limonov (interv'iu)."

87. Limonov, "U nas byla velikaia epokha," 11: "Мой взгляд—не глазами жертвы эпохи, ни в коем случае не взгляд представителя интеллигентского класса, но из толпы народной. В известном смысле, мой вариант эпохи—фольклорный вариант."

88. Kukulin argues that Vladimir Putin shares with Limonov's populism (which also characterized other forms of Russian popular culture in the late 1980s) the cult of masculinity and nostalgia for the Soviet past. I would add that Putin also inherits from

Limonov a certain "countercultural credit," although I believe that Putin's "law and order" and the idea of the "strong leader" that is associated with his figure are quite different from Limonov's desire "to shock the bourgeoisie" at all costs. See Kukulin, "Longing for Fear and Darkness."

89. Narodnyi Kommissariat Vnutrennykh Del (Popular Commissariat of Internal Affairs, NKVD) was the name of the Ministry of Interior and, by extension, of the Soviet police, between 1917 and 1946.

90. Limonov, "U nas byla velikaia epokha," 11–12.

91. Limonov, "U nas byla velikaia epokha," 84–85.

92. See Limonov, *Moia politicheskaia biografiia*, 84–85.

93. See these works by Limonov: *Moia politicheskaia biografiia*, 25–26; *Inostranets v smutnoe vremia*; *Ischeznovenie varvarov*; *Ubiistvo chasovogo*; *Anatomiia geroia*. See also the following articles by Limonov published in *L'idiot international*: "Projets sculpturaux pour Paris," no. 14, August 16, 1989, "Conversation imaginaire," no. 15, August 23, 1989; "Pour comprendre l'Europe de l'est," no. 16, August 30, 1989; "Discours sur les droits et les libertés," no. 17, September 6, 1989; "La désinformation occidentale," no. 23, October 18, 1989; "Terre d'asile," no. 24, October 25, 1989; "Carnet de bord: est ouest," no. 25, November 11, 1989; "Orgasmes collectifs à la télé," no. 26, November 8, 1989; "Le mur est mort, vive le mur," no. 27, November 15, 1989; "Appel à l'insurrection," no. 28, November 22, 1989, available at limonow.de, accessed April 19, 2016.

94. See Limonov, *Moia politicheskaia biografiia*, 25–26.

95. See Pawlikowski, *Serbian Epics*. The war in the former Yugoslavia and Limonov's impressions from his trips to war zones during those years are also the subject of the later collection of short stories *SMRT (rasskazy)*.

96. See, for instance, the explicit criticism of Limonov's political shift in Keith Gessen, "Monumental Foolishness." On Limonov's exclusion from recent scholarship on contemporary Russian literature, see Matich, "Eduard Limonov."

97. "Ischeznovenie varvarov" and "Distsiplinarnyi sanatorii" were written and published in French translation, respectively, in 1984 and 1988. They appeared in Russia for the first time in 1992 in Limonov, *Ischeznovenie varvarov.*

98. Limonov, *Drugaia Rossiia*, 86.

99. See Karskens, *Chronological Bibliography of the Works of Michel Foucault.*

100. Incidentally, the character of Stierlitz—who wore an SS uniform for most of the show—is often associated with the peculiar aesthetic fascination with Nazi Germany in late Soviet popular culture.

101. See Limonov, *Anatomiia geroia* and *Ubiistvo chasovogo*; Dodolev, *Limoniana.* All of Limonov's articles from this period were republished in these collections. For an account of his return to Russia, see also Limonov, *Inostranets v smutnoe vremia.*

102. Limonov, "Ne putaite menia s Limonovym." That of the "death of literature" became a recurring theme of Limonov's public statements. See, for instance, Viktor Erofeev, "Literatura i politika"; Limonov, "Pisatel'—ne professiia."

103. See Kron, "Pro babochku"; Matich and Heim, *The Third Wave*; Carden, "Limonov's Coming out"; Matich, "The Moral Immoralist"; Ryan-Hayes, *Contemporary Russian Satire*; Simmons, *Their Fathers' Voice.* Patricia Carden significantly defined *Eto ia—Edichka* as "the quintessential novel of the Russian third wave emigration" (see "Limonov's Coming Out," 221).

104. See Mogutin, "Eduard Limonov, sovetsko frantsuzskii natsional'nyi geroi";

"Vospominaniia russkogo panka"; *30 Interv'iu*; M. Gessen, *Dead Again*, 165–85; Essig, *Queer in Russia*, 3–25, 123–61.

105. Essig, *Queer in Russia*, 95.

106. See Limonov, *Anatomiia geroia*, 125–57; Limonov, *Moia politicheskaia biografiia*, 5–72. Lisa Ryoko Wakamiya argues that after returning to Russia and becoming involved with radical nationalist politics, Limonov distanced himself from his previous "exilic identities," embracing "particularly defined canons . . . [and] narrowly defined national traditions." In post-Soviet Russia, according to Wakamiya, Limonov "asserts his 'inherited' and 'authentic' qualities, among them an exaggeratedly heteronormative sexuality, which he defines in narrative forms that exploit hierarchical and patriarchal structures" (see Wakamiya, *Locating Exiled Writers*, 109–12.) In fact, Limonov's close association with Mogutin, and the fact that his novels were first published by Shatalov's publishing house, demonstrates that "heteronormative" might not be the best definition to describe the making of his post-Soviet public persona (see Essig, *Queer in Russia*, 146–49, 95, 123–61). Certain elements of Limonov's writing before and after his return to Russia can indeed be interpreted as masculinist and misogynist, and the aesthetics of the NBP was indeed based on a peculiar cult of war and masculinity. However, after his return to Russia, Limonov harshly criticized "traditional family values," and the position of the NBP in the sphere of gender and social politics has been far from straightforward. In addition, both Limonov and the NBP have been very critical of Russian cultural institutions and literary tradition, and they have promoted a fairly eclectic and cosmopolitan cultural and literary canon (see Limonov, *Drugaia Rossiia*, 7–43, 91–104, 167–73). For a more detailed discussion of these issues, see also chapters 2 and 3.

107. For a general introduction to the history of the NBP and its key figures, see Shenfield, *Russian Fascism*; Savel'ev, *Goriachaia molodezh' Rossii*; Rogachevskii, "The National-Bolshevik Party (1993–2001)"; Verkhovskii and Kozhevnikova, *Radikal'nyi russkii natsionalizm*, 287–99.

108. See "Reshenie Mosgorsuda" (verdict of the Moscow City court from April 19, 2007, that established the legal ban on the NBP in the Russian Federation); Verkhovskii, "Pochemu sleduet otmenit' reshenie o zaprete NBP."

109. See Kozhevnikova, Verkhovskii, and Veklerov, *Ultra-nationalism and Hate Crimes in Contemporary Russia*, 124–28; "Napadenie na natsbolov v Moskve"; "Pravozashchita/Programmy: Podderzhka politzakliuchennykh/Dela natsbolov." On the NBP's "political style" and specific approach to violence, see Mikhail Sokolov, "Natsional-bol'shevistskaia partiia"; Gromov, *Ulichnye aktsii*. The *Kratkii kurs istorii natsbolov* (The short course on the history of the *natsboly*), a brochure published by Limonov's organization in 2016, lists approximately 160 "political prisoners" in the NBP's history, with prison terms ranging from two weeks to eight years and some activists being incarcerated several times with different charges. The document also lists fifteen activists who died throughout the history of the organization, of which ten died in mysterious circumstances likely related to police brutality (beaten to death, thrown out the window of a prison administration office or under a train, committing suicide in prison, etc.); two died while fighting as volunteer soldiers in Eastern Ukraine; one was stabbed by local skinheads; one died during a brawl; and one (Andrey Sukhorada, who had joined the NBP for some time at the age of sixteen and a few years later became one of the members of the Primorskie partizany, an illegal group that waged a guerrilla war against the local police) committed suicide to avoid arrest during a police raid in 2010. See *Kratkii kurs istorii natsbolov*, 11–30, 56–69.

110. See Yakemenko, *Limonov o Limonove*; "Sud nad prizrakom."
111. See Verkhovskii and Kozhevnikova, *Radikal'nyi russkii natsionalizm*, 196–206.
112. See Horvath, "'Sakharov Would Be with Us.'"
113. Later collected in Limonov, *Propovedy*.
114. See "Moskva: 'Strategiia 31,' Triumfal'naia Ploshchad' 31.05.14."

Chapter 2. Making Post-Soviet Counterpublics

An earlier version of this chapter was published as Fabrizio Fenghi, "Making Post-Soviet Counterpublics: The Aesthetics of *Limonka* and the National-Bolshevik Party," *Nationalities Papers* 45, no. 2 (2017): 182–205, and is reproduced with permission from Cambridge University Press. First epigraph: "В Очемчире умереть—красиво / Солнечная долька на губах / В роще ароматных апельсинов / Гладя как любимую автомат / Забыв весь страх / Что улицы Москвы беззаконны / Идёшь как будто раздетым / Зло и Добро невесомы . . . // Поедем на Войну!"

1. Fraser, "Rethinking the Public Sphere," 68–69.
2. Bourdieu, *Distinction*, 7.
3. Fraser, "Rethinking the Public Sphere," 67.
4. Fraser, "Rethinking the Public Sphere," 67.
5. On publics and counterpublics, see also Cody, "Publics and Politics"; Spivak, "Can the Subaltern Speak?"; Felski, *Beyond Feminist Aesthetics*; Calhoun, *Habermas and the Public Sphere*; Taylor, *Philosophical Arguments*; Benhabib, *Democracy and Difference*; Asen, "Seeking the 'Counter'"; Warner, *Publics and Counterpublics*.
6. For a general introduction to early post-Soviet history, politics, and everyday life, see Kagarlitsky, *Restoration in Russia*; Mau and Starodubrovskaia, *The Challenge of Revolution*; Roy Medvedev, *Post-Soviet Russia*; McFaul, *Russia's Unfinished Revolution*; Sogrin, *Politicheskaia istoriia sovremennoi Rossii*; Shevtsova, *Russia Lost in Transition*, Humphrey, *The Unmaking of Soviet Life*; Volkov, *Violent Entrepreneurs*.
7. *Limonka* is a slang name for a hand grenade, and a play on words on Limonov's own pseudonym, also derived from the word *limon*/"lemon."
8. See Warner, *Publics and Counterpublics*.
9. Here I am borrowing the expression that the writer Zakhar Prilepin, an old-time member of the NBP, used to describe the aesthetics of the movement when I interviewed him. Zakhar Prilepin, personal interview, August 8, 2013.
10. See Yurchak, *Everything Was Forever, Until It Was No More*; Yurchak, "A Parasite from Outer Space"; Boyer and Yurchak, "AMERICAN STIOB."
11. See Austin, *How to Do Things with Words*.
12. See Yurchak, *Everything Was Forever, Until It Was No More*, 126–57.
13. A series of different views on these issues, building on Yurchak's theories, can be found in Fürst and McLellan, *Dropping out of Socialism*.
14. Quoted in Yurchak, "A Parasite from Outer Space," 328. On Kurekhin and his interactions with the NBP, see chapter 5.
15. Mischa Gabowitsch describes "fascist *stiob*" as a way of compensating for the impossibility "to express political dissent or social critique in straightforward, politically constructive ways, through party competition and public debate." See Gabowitsch, "Fascism as *Stiob*," 8. *Stiob* has also been seen as a central component of Russian political culture in general, and of Russian nationalism in particular. See Hemment, *Youth Politics in Putin's Russia*; Noordenbos, *Post-Soviet Literature and the Search for a Russian Identity*.

16. See Oushakine, "In the State of Post-Soviet Aphasia."

17. See "Eduard Limonov. Vstrecha v kontsertnoi studii Ostankino"; Limonov, "My—natsional'nyi geroi," 61: "Одежда любой фирмы, которую одевает Лимонов, становится одеждой национального героя. Майки—лимоновки, носки-рубашки—лимонки, пиджаки—лимон, прически—айлимонов."

18. Limonov *Dnevnik neudachnika*, 52: "Я плачу о тебе в Нью-Йорке. В городе атлантических сырых ветров. Где бескрайне цветет зараза. Где люди-рабы прислуживают людям-господам, которые в то же время являются рабами. А по ночам. Мне в моем грязном отеле. Одинокому, русскому, глупому. Все снишься ты, снишься ты, снишься. Безвинно погибшая в юном возрасте—красивая, улыбающаяся, еще живая. С алыми губами—белошее нежное существо. Исцарапанные руки на ремне винтовки—говорящая на русском языке—Революция—любовь моя!"

19. I am here referring exclusively to the coup d'état attempt of August 19–22, 1991, which was relatively peaceful considering the premises (three civilians were killed). Of course this assessment does not take into account the numerous ethnic conflicts following the end of the Soviet Union.

20. See "Sobytiia 21 sentiabria–5 oktiabria 1993 goda"; "Spisok liudei, pogibshikh v Moskve 21 sentiabria–5 oktiabria 1993 goda."

21. These questions remain controversial to this day. See Shevchenko, *Zhertvy chernogo oktiabria*; "Oktiabr'skoe vosstanie 1993 goda." For an account of the standoff of October 1993 and its political premises, see Roy Medvedev, *Post-Soviet Russia*, 135–205; McFaul, *Russia's Unfinished Revolution*, 121–308.

22. See McFaul, *Russia's Unfinished Revolution*, 207–27; Wood, *Russia without Putin*, 1–28.

23. See Oushakine, *The Patriotism of Despair*, 1–78; Hemment, *Youth Politics in Putin's Russia*, 1–69.

24. See note 17.

25. Konstantin Chuvashev, personal interview, May 16, 2015. Chuvashev was responsible for the design of *Limonka* up to issue 33, February 1996. On the founding of *Limonka*, see also Limonov, *Moia politicheskaia biografiia*, 23–47.

26. Literally, "the aesthetics of the political poster." Limonov himself used this expression to describe the aesthetics of *Limonka*. Eduard Limonov, personal interview, August 15, 2013.

27. See Limonov, "Limonka protiv stukachei-intelligentov."

28. Limonov's pseudonym was also used, interchangeably, by one of Dugin's close collaborators, Andrey Karagodin, as well as by other members of the NBP. Therefore, it is not really possible to establish the authorship of each article. See, among others, the following pieces by Polkovnik Ivan Chernyi: "Pokhishchenie i kazn' Al'do Moro" (on the Italian terrorist group Red Brigades); "Pivnoi putsch. Munich, 1923"; "Rozhdenie partii" (on the beginnings of the National Socialist Party in Germany); "Bog voiny-Makhagala" (on Baron Ungern-Shternberg); "Skachka na tigre" (on Italian right-wing terrorism in the 1970s and 1980s); "Noch' dlinnykh nozhei"; "Val'kiriia revoliutsii" (on Bol'shevik leader Larisa Reisner); "Stalin. Molodye gody"; "Nash Lenin"; "Pervye fashisty" (on the beginnings of the Italian Fascist Party).

29. See Sil'nyi, "Bol'shoi belyi chelovek" (on Arnold Schwarzenegger); Melent'eva, "Chernyi messiia Menson: 'Ia boikotiruiu vash mir'"; Klimova, "Nash Lui-Ferdinand Selin"; Dugin, "Gi Debor Mertv. Spektakl' prodolzhaetsia"; Kondratovich (translator),

"Zhan Zhene. Otryvki iz poslednego interv'iu"; Pavel Vlasov (pseudonym of Aleksey Tsvetkov), "Doktor Gerbert Markuze"; Limonov, "Poslednii den' komandante Che"; Burroughs, "Dikie mal'chiki" (translated fragments from the novel *Wild Boys*); "Ekspress na planetu Nova" (fragments from the novel *Nova Express*).

30. See note 28.

31. Dugin, "Novye protiv starykh."

32. Dugin, "Kontrelita," Dugin here is also referring to Italian sociologist Vilfredo Pareto's theory on the circulation of elites (on this, see also chapters 4–5).

33. See chapter 4.

34. Laura Ilina, personal interview, March 26, 2015. On the Polushkin Brothers and the beginnings of Russian alternative fashion, see also Baster, *Al'ternativnaia moda*; Kostrova, "Kontrkul'tura SSSR."

35. As I was able to verify, Limonov personally wrote (mostly by hand) extensive sections of the newspaper at least until the beginning of 1996.

36. Limonov, *Moia politicheskaia biografiia*, 238–40; on the role of fashion within the NBP, see also Ferelov, "Moda NBP"; Limonov, "'Punk and National-Bolshevism.'"

37. Sell, *The Avant-Garde*, 41.

38. "Aktsiia."

39. See "Maloletka iznasilovala pensionera"; "Vstretil El'tsyna i ispugalsia"; "Inostranets s"eden mafiei"; "O chem povedala luna"; "Kto ne rabotaet, togo ediat." This section was a parody of the popular column from the newspaper *Moskovskii komsomolets*, "Srochno v nomer" (Straight to the press).

40. "Kto ne rabotaet, togo ediat." The title of this piece is a parody of the famous early Soviet slogan "Kto ne rabotaet, tot ne est" (Those who do not work shall not eat), which, ironically, was originally an aphorism from the New Testament.

41. See Dubshin, "Vsiakaia morda blagorazumnogo fasona vyzivaet vo mne nepriatnye oshchushcheniia"; on the affinities between Limonov and Kharms and the Oberiuty, see Limonov, "Gruppa 'Konkret'"; Brodskii, "Posleslovie."

42. See Kamennyi, "ALLE GEGEN ALLE"; on the use of totalitarian aesthetics in the performances of Laibach, see Žižek, "Why Are Laibach and NSK Not Fascists?"; Monroe, *Interrogation Machine.*

43. See Yurchak, *Everything Was Forever, Until It Was No More*, 249–53.

44. See Richardson, "Neue Slowenische Kunst"; Laibach, "Art and Totalitarianism"; Laibach, "XY—UNSOLVED." Laibach is still active and keeps causing scandal with its work. In 2015 it became the first Western rock band to perform in Pyongyang, North Korea, on the occasion of the seventieth anniversary of the country's independence. Laibach members played several of their classic covers and original songs, as well as a cover of "The Sound of Music," which they considered an ideal piece to play in front of the North Korean audiences. On their return, the band members did not praise the regime unconditionally, but they did not overtly criticize it either, claiming, for instance, that they could not find any cynicism, sarcasm, irony, vulgarity, or other "Western characteristics" in the eyes and behavior of North Korean people. See Grow, "What Laibach Learned in North Korea."

45. See Žižek, "Why Are Laibach and NSK Not Fascists?"

46. On Sergey Kurekhin's TV hoax, see Yurchak, "A Parasite from Outer Space."

47. On Dugin's campaign, see Kushnir, *Sergey Kurekhin*, 198–218; Kan, *Kurekhin: Shkiper o kapitane*, 257–79; "Tainoe stanet iavnym"; "Politologi Ibis i Anubis."

48. Quoted in Kushnir, *Sergei Kurekhin*, 85.

49. See Kushnir, *Sergei Kurekhin*, 116–17.

50. Kan, *Kurekhin: Shkiper o kapitane*, 262.

51. See Kushnir, *Sergei Kurekhin*, 84–143.

52. Kushnir, *Sergei Kurekhin*, 72–78.

53. Kushnir, *Sergei Kurekhin*, 144–73.

54. Kushnir, *Sergei Kurekhin*, 144.

55. Kushnir, *Sergei Kurekhin*, 144–52. As an example of Kurekhin's taste for mystification and conspiracy theories, see also the experimental film *Dva kapitana 2* (Two Captains 2, 1992).

56. See Veig, "Pop-Mekhanika 418."

57. See "Politologi Ibis i Anubis."

58. Quoted in Kushnir, *Sergei Kurekhin*, 200.

59. See Dugin, "Iz kolybeli revoliutsii"; Kushnir, *Sergei Kurekhin*, 198–218; Kan, *Kurekhin: Shkiper o kapitane*, 257–79.

60. Kurekhin, "Esli vy romantik—vy fashist!"

61. Quoted in Kushnir, *Sergei Kurekhin*, 208.

62. Kushnir, *Sergei Kurekhin*, 209.

63. See Kan, *Kurekhin: Shkiper o kapitane.*

64. On this, and on the connection between Dugin's Eurasia Movement and Timur Novikov's New Academy, see chapters 4–5.

65. Dugin, "Vsia vlast' severu."

66. Dugin, "Gi Debor mertv. Spektakl' prodolzhaetsia."

67. See Rogatchevski and Steinholt, "Pussy Riot's Musical Precursors?"; Sandalov, *Formeishen.*

68. See Letov, "Eto znaet moia svoboda"; Letov, "Imenno tak vse i bylo." Letov's original term for shock is "epatazh," which more clearly evokes the original bohemian (and futurist) motto "épater les bourgeois."

69. See Dugin, "K zhenshchinam"; Timur Bonch (General Brusilov), "K chlenam NBP"; "SEX-trenazher elitnogo partiitsa"; "SEX-trenazher zhenshchiny partii."

70. Mogutin, "Bez intelligentov. Utopiia."

71. Mogutin, "Bez intelligentov. Utopiia.": ". . . в ближайшем будущем интеллигенция должна быть ассимилирована и уничтожена как класс."

72. I am here borrowing Viktor Shklovsky's term *ostranenie* (estrangement or defamiliarization), commonly used to describe the specific type of experience produced by the reading of literary texts. See Shklovsky, "Art as Device."

73. Medvedeva, "Oda russkomu muzhiku." The word *muzhik*, "peasant," is a colloquial term for a "common man," or just "a man," with a more or less derogative connotation depending on the context.

74. "Razdavit' dvukh zmei."

75. Sontag, "Fascinating Fascism."

76. "Fashizm ili ne fashizm: Konkurs."

77. Aleksei Tsvetkov, personal interview, March 15, 2015. On Tsvetkov's political career, see also Tsvetkov, *Dnevnik gorodskogo partizana.*

78. See Tsvetkov, "Chudotvornyi uzhas"; "THE Alekseia Tsvetkova." The pseudonym Pavel Vlasov is an allusion to the revolutionary hero from Maksim Gorky's novel *Mother* (*Mat'*, 1907); Ian Geil refers to Wayne Gale—the opportunistic journalist who

turns serial killers Mickey and Mallory Knox into celebrities in Oliver Stone's 1994 film *Natural Born Killers* (as Tsvetkov explained to me, in the Russian VHS version of the film the name Wayne sounded like "Ian"); Fridmen is a reference to the Montana Freemen, the American anti-government militia that got into a prolonged armed standoff with the FBI in 1996; Doktor Zig Khailer is a made-up name based on the Nazi salute *Sieg Heil* (transliterated into Cyrillic: *Zig khail'*).

79. Gruppa kommunisticheskii realizm (pseudonym of Aleksei Tsvetkov), "K novoi rechi—rechi bessmertnykh liudei."

80. See Groys, *The Total Art of Stalinism.*

81. See Benjamin, "The Work of Art."

82. On the history of Moscow Actionism, see Kovalev, *Rossiiskii aktsionizm*; Obukhova, *Performans v Rossii*; Baskova, *Devianostye ot pervogo litsa*; Kulik and Surkov, *Oleg Kulik.*

83. Tsvetkov gave me an account of these interactions in online correspondence via email and Facebook Messenger. Anatoly Osmolovsky confirmed this account when I interviewed him on June 26, 2015. See also the following texts about and by Moscow Actionists published in *Limonka*: Limonov, "Est' takaia partiia"; "Nazvat' presidenta pi. .rasom stoit 417 novykh rublei" (unsigned); Osmolovsky, "O stabil'nosti"; Osmolovsky, "Tvoi vybor sdelan." See also the following texts by Brener: "Nenavizhu"; "Obossanyi pistolet"; "Otkrytoe pis'mo o kholuistve"; "Palestintsam"; "Sovety informatsionnykh Luddistov."

84. Tsvetkov (pseudonym Ian Geil), "Zrelishche—lovushka nomer odin."

85. Tsvetkov (pseudonym Pavel Vlasov), "Ekstremizm—obraz zhizni."

86. See Tsvetkov (pseudonym Pavel Vlasov): "Proshchai anarkhiia," "Sindikalizm," "Terrorizm"; Tsvetkov (pseudonym Ian Geil): "Antigeroi," "Molodoi kommunist," "Revoliutsiia," "Ekologiia"; Tsvetkov (pseudonym Doktor Zig Khailer): "Fashizm—eto gor'kii shokolad," "Moia militsiia"; Tsvetkov (signed with his real name): "Anarkhizm," "Fusion Conspiracy."

87. See Tsvetkov (pseudonym Pavel Vlasov), "Vooruzhennyi rai."

88. See Tsvetkov (pseudonym Pavel Vlasov), "Bakunin kak superagent."

89. See Tsvetkov (pseudonym Ian Geil), "Marie-Madeleine De Brinvillier."

90. See Tsvetkov (pseudonym Pavel Vlasov), "Skinkhedy." On Dugin's ideology, see chapters 4 and 5.

91. On Stierlitz and the TV series *Seventeen Moments of Spring*, see chapter 1, 53 and note 100.

92. See Tarasov et al., *Levye v Rossii*, 56–59.

93. See Kokh, "Ubiistvo Pazolini"; "Skol'ko zhe evreev pogiblo?"; "Dnevnik Anny Frank—fal'shivka."

94. "SEX-trenazher elitnogo partiitsa." See also "SEX-trenazher zhenshchiny partii."

95. See Timur Bonch (General Brusilov), "K chlenam NBP"

96. See Dugin, "K zhenshchinam"; Limonov, *Drugaia Rossiia*, 13–24, 179–86.

97. See *Programma Natsional bol'shevistskoi Partii*, 1–10; 30; Limonov, "Manifest rossiiskogo natsionalizma"; Limonov, "Izvrashcheniia natsionalizma"; Limonov, "Razmyshleniia o natsionalizme."

98. See Gastello, "P.S."; Gastello, "SS-Pati"; Gastello, "Chto takoe partiia"; Ivanenko, "Negry i niggery."

99. *Dérive* was the improvised and subversive movement through urban space that was supposed to disrupt the routine and habits of capitalist society.

100. "Art-khronika."

101. Osmolovsky, "Antifashizm i anti-antifashizm," 9.

102. Osmolovsky, "Antifashizm i anti-antifashizm," 4.

103. Both Jones and Osmolovsky used the term *fashizm* as a synonym of German Nazism (as it is common in Russian).

104. Osmolovsky, "Antifashizm i anti-antifashizm."

105. Osmolovsky, "Antifashizm i anti-antifashizm," 6. Here Osmolovsky was referring to Russian communist or Stalinist organizations, such as the Communist Party of the Russian Federation, which during the 1990s shifted to conservative (and, often, strongly antisemitic) positions.

106. Osmolovsky, "Antifashizm i anti-antifashizm," 7.

107. Osmolovsky, "Antifashizm i anti-antifashizm," 8.

108. Osmolovsky, "Antifashizm i anti-antifashizm," 8.

Chapter 3. Bohemianism, Political Militancy, and Resistance to Modernity

Fourth epigraph: "Пластмассовый мир победил / Макет оказался сильней / Последний кораблик остыл / Последний фонарик устал, / а в горле сопят комья воспоминаний // Оо- моя оборона / Солнечный зайчик стеклянного глаза / Оо- моя оборона / Траурный мячик нелепого мира / Траурный мячик дешёвого мира // Пластмассовый мир победил."

1. Boltanski and Chiapello, *The New Spirit of Capitalism*, 37–38.

2. Boltanski and Chiapello, *The New Spirit of Capitalism*, 37.

3. Boltanski and Chiapello, *The New Spirit of Capitalism*, 38.

4. Boltanski and Chiapello, *The New Spirit of Capitalism*, 419.

5. See Masha Gessen, "NBP liubit vas"; Kozhevnikova et al., *Ultra-nationalism and Hate Crimes in Contemporary Russia*, 124–28; Verkhovskii and Kozhevnikova, *Radikal'nyi russkii natsionalizm*, 287–99; Bennetts, *Kicking the Kremlin*, 30–43. The NBP has also collaborated with several leftist and anarchist organizations and has counted several leftists among its members since its foundation (see Tarasov et al., *Levye v Rossii*, 56–59).

6. Julius Evola (1898–1974) was an Italian mystical philosopher, strongly anti-egalitarian and strongly antidemocratic, who was at different points close to Italian Fascism and German Nazism. In the postwar period, Evola became a source of inspiration for the European New Right. For a general introduction to Evola's thought, see Furlong, *Social and Political Thought of Julius Evola*; Griffin, *Modernism and Fascism*, 15–42; Griffin, *The Nature of Fascism*, 161–79; Gregor, *The Search for Neofascism*, 83–110. Evola was also an important source for Dugin's version of neo-Eurasianism. See chapter 4.

7. In the context of Soviet history, the Maiakovskie chteniia are commonly seen as a symbol of the power of civic poetry in Russia, of the temporary and spontaneous popular reappropriation of public places, and of the brief emergence of new possibilities of public expression after Khrushchev's de-Stalinization.

8. See "Programma Natsional-bol'shevistskoi Partii"; Limonov, "Razmyshleniia o natsionalizme"; Zhvaniia, *Put' khunveibina*, 262–415.

9. See chapter 2, note 73.

10. See Turner, *The Ritual Process*.

11. Lev Losev, personal interview, May 28, 2015.

12. See Zhvaniia, *Put' khunveibina.*

13. Aleksandr Lebedev-Frontov, personal interview, May 26, 2015; Zhvaniia, "Aleksandr Lebedev-Frontov."

14. Lebedev-Frontov described his own style as "national-conceptualism." Zhvaniia once defined it as "futurist surrealism." See Zhvaniia, *Put' khunveibina.*

15. Rodionov, personal interview, March 17, 2015; Rodionov, *Igrushki dlia okrain*; Rodionov, *Liudi beznadezhno ustarelykh professii*; Vsevolod Emelin, personal interview, April 14, 2015; Emelin, *Götterdämmerung*; Emelin, *Istoriia s geografiei*; Emelin, *Politshanson.* On Emelin's career and popularity see also Tsvetkov, "A Political Guide to Contemporary Russian Poetry"; Leibov, "Occasional Political Poetry and the Culture of the Russian Internet."

16. See Masha Gessen, *Dead Again*, 187–90; 197–202; Vitukhnovskaia and Tkachenko, *Delo Aliny Vitukhnovskoi*; Alina Vitukhnovskaia, personal interview, April 15, 2015.

17. Vitukhnovskaia, *Mir kak volia i prestuplenie*, 114.

18. Vitukhnovskaia, "Liubit' Avroru i Reikhstag." The source of some of the motifs of Vitukhnovskaya's poems is to be found in the "metaphysical realism" of writer Yuri Mamleev (see chapter 5).

19. Mikhail Roshniak, personal interview, May 22, 2015; Oleg Kulik, personal interview, June 9, 2015; Nikitina, "Pervyi moskovskii festival, performansa"; Rukavishnikov, "Pasynki beschest'ia" (minutes 54–56 document the NBP protest in front of the exhibition space at Kashirka).

20. Nikitina, "Pervyi moskovskii festival performansa"; "Limonovi performans."

21. "Limonovi performans."

22. Dugin, "Opyt svastiki."

23. Kuskov, "Vystavka-proekt ekstremizm i erotika."

24. Nechaev, the author of *Catechism of a Revolutionary*, was a source of inspiration for radicals around the world throughout the twentieth century. He also famously inspired one of the characters in Dostoevsky's novel *Demons.*

25. See Hemment, *Youth Politics in Putin's Russia*, 177–213, here 188–89; Sperling, *Sex, Politics, and Putin.*

26. See chapter 2.

27. Polkovnik Ivan Chernyi, "Val'kiriia revoliutsii."

28. I cross-checked these numbers with several current and former activists and leaders of the NBP/Drugaia Rossiia. The print runs of *Limonka* were published on the last page of each issue. Between 1998 and 2006, NBP activists applied for registration as a political party to the Ministry of Justice five times, and each time they were denied. According to the Russian legislation, the *natsboly* had to collect a minimum of five thousand signatures in 1998, and a minimum of fifty thousand in 2006 (the new legislation was approved in December 2004). The *natsboly* collected between six and seven thousand signatures in 1998, and more than fifty-five thousand in 2006. On the basis of the number of signatures collected by the NBP at the time, Viacheslav Likhachev estimates a party membership of approximately seven thousand in the early 2000s (see Likhachev, *Natsizm v Rossii*). Stephen Shenfield replicated this estimate in his book (see Shenfield, *Russian Fascism*). However, as several NBP party leaders confirmed, those numbers indicate the people who agreed to support the party registration, not the actual active members. Despite some disagreements among my informants about these numbers,

following a conservative estimate it is probably safe to assume that at its peak during the first decade of the 2000s the NBP counted anywhere between one and three thousand active members throughout Russia. Since these were all highly commited activists, who devoted a significant amount of time and energy to their work in the party, these numbers actually made the NBP a serious political force in Russia, especially in terms of street politics. See also "Natsbolam piatyi raz za poslednye vosem' let otkazali v registratsii partii"; "Gosduma priniala zakon ob uvelichenii minimal'noi chislennosti partii do 50.000."

29. On the schism in the NBP, see also Limonov, *Moia politicheskaia biografiia*, 140–56; Limonov, "NBP—partiia priamogo deistviia, a ne sekta intellektualov"; Dugin, "O Limonove, NBP, i neofashizme"; "Dugin: Pravda o Limonove."

30. Misha Verbitsky quoted in Sandalov, *Formeishen*, 280.

31. On the NBP and Moscow punk subculture, see Sandalov, *Formeishen*; Rogatchevski and Steinholt, "Pussy Riot's Musical Precursors?"

32. On the *natsboly*'s lifestyle, see also Semenov, *Fuck off, Mr. Bond!*; Polunina, *Da, smert'!*; Polunina, *The Last Revolutionaries*.

33. For a list of the main direct actions organized by the NBP, see *Kratkii kurs istorii natsbolov*, 31–55; Rogachevskii, "The National Bolshevik Party (1993–2001)"; "Politzakliuchennye natsboly (polnyi spisok)"; Likhachev, *Natsizm v Rossii*."

34. See M. Sokolov, "Natsional-bol'shevistskaia partiia."

35. See "Zakrytyi biulleten' NBP-INFO, no. 3." Some of the NBP-INFO bulletins became available after the end of Limonov's term on the party website, nbp-info.com, which was later shut down by the authorities. However, parts of the website can still be accessed at archive.org.

36. On the "Altai project" and on Limonov's trial, see Limonov, *Moia politicheskaia biografiia*, 255–92; Gofman, *Patrick Gofman présente l'affaire Limonov: Le dossier*; "Politzakliuchennye natsboly (polnyi spisok)"; "Sud prigovoril Eduarda Limonova k 4 godam."

37. See "Zakrytyi biulleten' NBP-INFO, no. 4" and note 5.

38. For further details on this transition, see chapter 1, 53–55.

39. See Tanya's comment quoted in the epigraph to the chapter.

40. On November 25, 1970, the writer Yukio Mishima, an important role model for Limonov and the National Bolsheviks, occupied the headquarters of the Japanese army with a small militia. Mishima intended to lead the army in a coup d'état aimed at establishing a political system based on his specific conception of imperialism and traditionalism. He gave a speech to the soldiers gathered in front of the building, which was supposed to inspire them to revolt. However, the soldiers did not take him seriously, and explicitly ridiculed him. In response to that, Mishima went back inside the building and, with the help of one of his followers, commited seppuku, the traditional ritual suicide. For a comparison between Limonov's and Mishima's works and careers, see Chantsev, *Bunt krasoty*.

41. See chapter 1, note 109.

42. See "Lichno v ruki. Spisok ubitykh i presleduemykh oppozitsionerov, peredannyi Garri Kasparovym Baraku Obame"; Verkhovskii and Kozhevnikova, *Radikal'nyi russkii natsionalizm: Struktury, idei, litsa*, 124–28; "Napadenie na natsbolov v Moskve"; "Pravozashchita/Programmy: Podderzhka politzakliuchennykh/Dela natsbolov."

43. Anatoly Tishin, personal interview, May 1, 2015.

44. Khodorkovsky was an important oligarch who at the time owned Yukos, then the main Russian oil company, and was incarcerated that same year, allegedly because

he intended to enter Russian politics and run against Putin. Economic reasons also most likely played an important role in his persecution.

45. See Politkovskaya's coverage of the trial for *Novaia Gazeta*: "Natsbolov v sude skovali tsepiami"; "8 let kolonii za 12 tysiach"; "Sud boleet. U nego 39"; "'Politicheskie' i 'ugolovnye'"; "Dekabristy vse eshche sidiat"; "I seif za 12 kopeek"; "Obviniaemye khorom sheptali svideteliu: 'vrushka, vrushka'"; "Okhrannik otgibal pal'tsy"; "Aziatskii sud po pravam cheloveka"; "V strane poiavilis' politzakliuchnnye? Bez uslovno"; "Kto el shashlik s 'nashimi'?" (on the violent assaults against members of the NBP). In 2006, Anna Politkovskaya was murdered in the entry hall of her building in Moscow. Although those who ordered the murder were never found, there were strong allegations of the direct involvement of Russian politicians and intelligence in the crime and even rumors about death threats to Politkovskaya from the president himself. See Sergei Sokolov, "Osvedomiteli—agenty spetssluzhb—sredi organizatorov ubiistva Anny Politkovskoi"; "PACE Rapporteur on Media Freedom Expresses His Deep Frustration at the Lack of Progress in Investigating the Murder of Anna Politkovskaia in Russia."

46. See Magun, *Negative Revolution*, 1–72.

47. See Epshtein, *Total'naia "voina."*

48. On the art collective Voina, see Epshtein, *Total'naia "voina."* On the complex relationship between art and politics in contemporary Russia, see also Dziewańska et al., *Post-post-Soviet?*; Ryklin, *Svastika, krest, zvezda*; Ryklin, *Svoboda i zapret*; Epshtein, *Iskusstvo na barrikadakh*; Epshtein et al., *Dukhovnaia bran'*; Bernstein, "An Inadvertent Sacrifice"; Valerie Sperling, *Sex, Politics, and Putin*, 222–93; Gabowitsch, *Protest in Putin's Russia*, 160–94.

49. The lectures have never been documented, but both Osmolovsky and Tishin, who was at the time one of the leaders of the party, confirmed that they took place. Anatoly Osmolovsky, personal interview, June 25, 2015; Anatoly Tishin, personal interview, May 1, 2015.

50. On the art groups Voina and Pussy Riot, and on the new wave of Moscow "art-aktivism," see Epshtein, *Total'naia "voina"*; Epshtein, *Iskusstvo na barrikadakh*; Dziewańska et al., *Post-post-Soviet?*; Masha Gessen, *Words Will Break Cement*.

51. See "Nadia Tolokno—Format voiny dolzhen stat' zhanrom."

52. "Nadia Tolokno—Format voiny dolzhen stat' zhanrom."

53. See Epshtein, *Total'naia "voina,"* 23–33.

54. Quoted in Masha Gessen, "NBP liubit vas": "Я, воин НБП, приветствую новый день. / И в этот час единения партии я со своими братьями! / Чувствую мощную силу всех братьев партии, / Где бы они сейчас ни находились. / Пусть моя кровь вольется в кровь партии, / Пусть мы станем единым телом. / Да, смерть!"

55. Kas'ian, "Moskovskii khudozhnik Anton Nikolaev demonstrativno vstupil v zapreshchennuiu NBP"; Anton Nikolaev, personal interview, June 14, 2015.

56. On the motivations and circumstances of this long standing political passivity, see Magun, *Negative Revolution*.

Chapter 4. Aleksandr Dugin's Conservative Postmodernism

1. Dugin, *Geopolitika postmoderna*, 71–72.

2. See Shekhovtsov, "Aleksandr Dugin's Neo-Eurasianism"; Shekhovtsov, *Russia and the Western Far Right*.

3. On Dugin's academic appointment and on the work of his Center for Conservative Investigations, see Rossman, "Moscow State University's Department of Sociology." On the events of May 2, 2014, see "Ukraine's Murky Inferno"; "How Did Odessa's Fire Happen?" On Dugin's removal from his academic position, see the following: "Rektor MGU uvolil Aleksandra Dugina"; "V MGU oprovergli uvol'nenie 'evraziitsa'"; Alekseev, "Ubivat', ubiva', ubivat'"; "Aleksandr Dugin: 'Ubivat', ubivat', i ubivat'!"

4. To this day, Dugin has published approximately fifty-five books (for a list, see the website of Dugin's online bookstore/publishing house: evrazia-books.ru). These include collections of articles and essays on philosophy, political theory, and geopolitics. Many of these were published by Dugin's own publishing house, Arktogeia; a few of them were published by the mainstream publishers Amfora and Akademicheskii proekt. Dugin's writing does not follow any specific academic standard: it freely switches from journalistic prose to philosophical lucubrations, literary reviews, and biographical notes. Some of his articles are republished in several collections, and all of his works are available online for free. This publication pattern seems to follow the principle of maximum possible circulation.

5. See some of the main websites connected to Dugin's organization: "Arktogeia—filosofskii portal"; "ARCTOGAIA"; "EVRAZIIA—Informatsionno-analiticheskii portal"; "Portal setevoi voiny"; "EVRAZIIA.TV"; "RUSSIA.RU—Televidenie"; "Katehon Think Tank. Geopolitics & Tradition"; "KNIGI EVRAZII."

6. See Laruelle, "Dangerous Liaisons"; "'Antioranzhevyi' miting"; "Aleksandr Dugin o situatsii"; Newman, "Russian Nationalist Thinker Dugin"; Volkov, "Dobrovol'tsy iz Rossii"; Bychenkova, "Dobrovol'tsy iz Rostova." Dugin was the first to use the word "genocide" in relation to Georgia's invasion of South Ossetia, before this became the Kremlin's official position on the subject (see Shekhovtsov, "Aleksandr Dugin's Neo-Eurasianism"). He was also the first to use the term "Novorossiia" in connection with the political crisis in Eastern Ukraine, claiming that a creation of an independent region in Southeastern Ukraine was an unavoidable step given the current political situation in Kiev. This was a month before the beginning of the conflict in Donbass and a month and a half before Putin used the term in an official statement for the first time (Clover, *Black Wind, White Snow*, 330; "Aleksandr Dugin: Bitva za Ukrainu"; "V strane idet voina terminov"; "Piat' gromkikh zaiavlenii Putina"). Several members of the Eurasian Youth Union confirmed that the Russian authorities gave them the task of gathering volunteers to be sent to Eastern Ukraine. These would be mostly street fighters and extremists, with or without previous military experience, who were recruited to destabilize the political situation in these territories in the early phases of the conflict.

7. See Barbashin and Thoburn, "Putin's Brain"; Neyfakh, "Putin's Long Game?"; Zubrin, "Dugin's Evil Theology." Historian Timothy Snyder has gone so far as to identify the ideology at the basis of the Eurasian Economic Union with Dugin's Eurasianism, and he has contrasted the illiberal nature of "Eurasianism" with the democratic foundation of the European Union (see Snyder, "Fascism, Russia, and Ukraine"). Such commentaries are wildly exaggerated, and they do not take into account the tendency, common among fringe far-right organizations, to publicly overstate their influence and political connections (see Laruelle, "Dangerous Liaisons" and "Is Russia Really 'Fascist'?"). Commentaries such as Snyder's also, paradoxically, reproduce Dugin's claims about his role as an éminence grise of Putin's empire and are based on a polarizing and essentialist worldview not so dissimilar from Dugin's own conspiracy theories. On this, see also Pinkham, "Timothy Snyder's Bleak Vision."

8. See Laruelle, *Russian Eurasianism*, 107–41; Sedgwick, *Against the Modern World*, 221–40. On the history of Russian Eurasianism, see Glebov, *From Empire to Eurasia*. On one of the most influential forms of "neo-Eurasianism," Lev Gumilev's, see Bassin, *The Gumilev Mystique*.

9. See Shenfield, *Russian Fascism*, 190–221; Ingram, "Alexander Dugin: Geopolitics and Neo-fascism"; Sedgwick, *Against the Modern World*, 221–40. See also the following by Umland: *Toward an Uncivil Society?*; "'Konservativnaia revoliutsiia'"; "Pathological Tendencies in Russian 'Neo-Eurasianism'"; "Aleksandr Dugin's Transformation"; and "Post-Soviet 'Uncivil Society.'" See also Shlapentokh, "Dugin's Eurasianism"; Shekhovtsov, "Aleksandr Dugin's Neo-Eurasianism" and "The Palingenetic Thrust of Russian Neo-Eurasianism"; Shekhovtsov and Umland, "Is Aleksandr Dugin a Traditionalist?" See also a more detailed discussion of this approach in the introduction, 14–17.

10. Limonov, *Moia politicheskaia biografiia*, 64.

11. Laruelle, "Is Nationalism a Force of Change in Russia?," 90.

12. On political technology, see the introduction, note 2.

13. In Dugin's writings, the terms "postmodern," "postmodernism," "postmodernity" or the "postmodern condition," "postmodern theory," and "postmodern art and culture" largely overlap. For him, postmodern culture and theory appear to be a symptom of postmodernity or of the emergence of a postindustrial society. In my exposition I maintain this terminological ambiguity, which is part of Dugin's own conception of postmodernism and postmodernity and of his political strategy.

14. See these works by Jencks: *The Language of Post-Modern Architecture*; *Post-Modernism*; *What Is Post-Modernism?* See also Venturi et al., *Learning from Las Vegas*.

15. Jameson, *Postmodernism*, X.

16. See Jameson, *Postmodernism*; Lyotard, *The Postmodern Condition*; Baudrillard, *Simulacra*; Baudrillard, *Selected Writings*, 185–219. See the following works by Bell: *The End of Ideology*; *The Coming of Post-Industrial Society*; *The Cultural Contradictions of Capitalism*.

17. See Barthes, *Mythologies*, 107–64.

18. Bell, *The Cultural Contradictions of Capitalism*.

19. Deleuze and Guattari, *Anti-Oedipus*, quoted in Harvey, *The Condition of Postmodernity*, 238.

20. Harvey, *The Condition of Postmodernity*, 238.

21. See Lyotard, *The Postmodern Condition*, 9–18.

22. See Boltanski and Chiapello, *The New Spirit of Capitalism*; and chapter 3, 99–100.

23. See Hardt and Negri, *Empire*

24. Hardt and Negri, *Empire*, 206.

25. Hardt and Negri, *Empire*, 214–18, 362–69.

26. See Foster, "Postmodernism"; Habermas, "Modernity—An Incomplete Project."

27. See Bokhari and Yiannopoulos, "An Establishment Conservative's Guide to the Alt-Right."

28. Bokhari and Yiannopoulos, "An Establishment Conservative's Guide to the Alt-Right."

29. See Solov, "Breitbart News Network."

30. See Radosh, "Steve Bannon, Trump's Top Guy"; Gray, "Behind the Internet's Anti-Democracy Movement."

31. See Bokhari, "Suck It Up Buttercups."

32. See Fuller and Mele, "Berkeley Cancels Milo."

33. See Horowitz, "Steve Bannon Cited Italian Thinker Who Inspired Fascists"; Michel, "Beyond Trump and Putin"; Michel, "Meet the Moscow Mouthpiece Married to a Racist Alt-Right Boss"; Gray, "A 'One-Stop Shop' for the Alt-Right." Significantly, the American right-wingers' main criticism of Dugin concerns his ambiguous position on race, which, at least formally, Dugin sees as a "social construct." See Tudor, "The Real Dugin."

34. See Epstein, *After the Future*; Lipovetsky, *Russian Postmodernist Fiction.*

35. See Groys, *The Total Art of Stalinism*; Groys, *Utopiia.*

36. See, in particular, Debord, *Society of the Spectacle*; Baudrillard, *Simulacra and Simulation.*

37. See Horkheimer and Adorno, *Dialectic of Enlightenment.*

38. Epstein, *After the Future*, 206–7.

39. Epstein, *After the Future*, 204.

40. Epstein, *After the Future*, 204.

41. See, in particular, Pelevin's *Generation P* and Sorokin's *Goluboe salo.* On the significance of these novels for post-Soviet culture and literature, see Genis, "Strashnyi son'"; Lipovetsky, "Goluboe salo pokoleniia"; Lipovetsky, *Paralogii.*

42. On the "canonization" of postmodern literature, its assimilation into mainstream culture, and the political consequences of such assimilation, see Medvedev, "Moi fashizm" (published in English as "My Fascism," in *It's No Good*, 117–48). An episode that symbolically marked this transition was Sorokin's "pornography trial," which was preceded by a series of public demonstrations organized against him and other "immoral" postmodern writers by the pro-government movement Idushchie vmeste (Walking Together). On this occasion, pro-Putin activists seemed to appropriate some of the strategies of postmodern performance: for one of the demonstrations, they built a gigantic papier-mâché toilet, threw copies of Sorokin's novels into it, and doused them with disinfectant. See Bershtein and Hadden, "The Sorokin Affair Five Years Later."

43. See Wilson, *Virtual Politics*; Ostrovsky, *The Invention of Russia*; Pomerantsev, *Nothing Is True and Everything Is Possible.*

44. See Prokhanov, *Gospodin Geksogen.* On Prokhanov, postmodern conspiracy theories, and the post-Soviet "legitimization of far-right discourses," see Kukulin, "Revoliutsiia oblezlykh drakonov"; Kukulin, "Reaktsiia dissotsiatsii"; Kukulin, "VRIO vmesto Klio"; Livers, "The Tower or the Labyrinth."

45. See, in particular, Krusanov's novels *Ukus angela*; *Amerikanskaia dyrka*; Noordenbos, *Post-Soviet Literature*, 111–44. Noordenbos describes the work of Krusanov as a form of "imperial *stiob.*"

46. See Elizarov, *Bibliotekar'* (published in English as *The Librarian*).

47. Dubovitskii (pseudonym of Vladislav Surkov), *Okolonolia* (published in English as *Almost Zero*). The independent experimental director Kirill Serebrennikov produced and directed a stage adaptation of Surkov's novel, providing another example of the strange overlap between "postmodernism of reaction" and "postmodernism of dissent" in contemporary Russian culture.

48. See Lipovetsky, *Paralogii*, 490–91, 499, 502–3, 526–27; Kukulin, "Reaktsiia dissotsiatsii"; Kukulin, "Revoliutsiia oblezlykh drakonov." This question and, in general, that of "conservative postmodernism," was also the focus of a special section of an issue

of the Moscow literary journal *Novoe literaturnoe obozrenie* published in the summer of 2018: Lipovetsky et al., "Postmodernizm v epokhu."

49. Laruelle, "Is Nationalism a Force for Change in Russia?," 89.

50. On Nashi's corporate patriotism, see Hemment, *Youth Politics in Putin's Russia*. On right-wing postmodernism and *stiob*, see also Gabowitsch, "Fascism as Stiob"; Noordenbos, *Post-Soviet Literature*, 111–45.

51. See Condee, *The Imperial Trace*, 28.

52. Medvedev, *It's No Good*, 126.

53. See Limonov, *Moia politicheskaia biografiia*, 63–71.

54. Clover, *Black Wind, White Snow*, 158.

55. On Pop-mekhanika 418, and on Dugin's electoral campaign in Saint Petersburg, see chapter 2, 75–78.

56. Mikhail Roshniak, personal interview, May 22, 2015; Aleksey Tsvetkov, personal interview, March 15, 2015.

57. See Dugin, *Osnovy geopolitiki*; Dunlop, "Aleksandr Dugin's 'Neo-Eurasian' Textbook"; Dunlop, "Aleksandr Dugin's Foundations of Geopolitics."

58. In particular, Dugin was invited by Guelman to work for Russia's state-run First Channel (Pervyi kanal), one of the Kremlin's main propaganda instruments. Among other things, Dugin and Guelman collaborated on the creation of the patriotic party Rodina (Motherland), which was allegedly planned as a means of taking votes from the Communist Party and reducing the political potential of the opposition. See Clover, *Black Wind, White Snow*, 267–305. On Guelman, Pavlovsky, and the Foundation for Effective Politics, see also introduction, 7 and note 2.

59. For a general introduction to de Benoist's ideas, see de Benoist, *Vue de droite*.

60. Quoted in Clover, *Black Wind, White Snow*, 259. On the beginnings of the Eurasia Movement, see also Laruelle, *Russian Eurasianism*, 107–40; Umland, "Post-Soviet 'Uncivil Society.'"

61. Dugin, *Pop-kul'tura*, 482–83.

62. Dugin, *Pop-kul'tura*, 378. On the role of conspiracy theories in Kurekhin's art project, see also chapter 2.

63. Groys, *The Total Art of Stalinism*, 12.

64. Groys, *The Total Art of Stalinism*, 9; chapter 2, 75–84.

65. Dugin, *Konspirologiia*, 33–34.

66. See note 51.

67. See Dugin, *Filosofiia traditsionalizma*, 15–96.

68. Dugin, *Tampliery proletariata*, 7.

69. Dugin, *Tampliery proletariata*, 5–89.

70. See Agursky, *The Third Rome*; Etkind, *Khlyst*; Etkind, *Sodom i Psikheia*. An abridged version of Agursky's book was published in Russian in Paris in 1980, under the title *Ideologiia natsional-bol'shevizma*. Etkind's *Sodom i Psikheia* and *Khlyst* were first published in Russia, in 1996 and 1998, respectively. These were in fact almost required readings for Dugin's "disciples" in the NBP and the Eurasia Movement. In his autobiography, Limonov ironically describes how Dugin would criticize young NBP activists for not having read Etkind's book. See Limonov, *Moia politicheskaia biografiia*, 151.

71. Smenovekhovstvo (changing signposts) was a political movement started by a group of conservative White émigrés who promoted the idea of a collaboration with

the Soviets in the hope that their ideology would eventually include nationalist and conservative elements. Scythianism was a current of thought promoted, among others, by symbolist writers Aleksandr Blok and Andrey Bely. The "Scythians" reclaimed Russia's "Asian identity," which they saw as creative, irrational, chaotic, and destructive. In their interpretation, the Russian Revolution was an expression of this rediscovered identity. The poet Kliuev's concept of "Red Rus'" combined the symbols and ideas of the revolution with Russian spiritual traditions preceding Peter the Great's Westernizing reforms.

72. See Dugin, *Tampliery proletariata*.

73. See Chytry, *The Aesthetic State*.

74. Dugin's historical vision was also not far, in many respects, from theories about the crucial role of "dual models" and "internal colonization," formulated by such scholars as Iurii Lotman, and, again, Aleksandr Etkind. See Lotman and Uspenskii, "Otzvuki kontseptsii 'Moskva-tretii Rim'"; Lotman and Uspenskii, "Rol' dual'nykh modelei"; Groys, Utopiia; Etkind, *Internal Colonization*; Etkind, *Khlyst*.

75. Dugin, *Tampliery proletariata*, 26.

76. On Dugin's "anti-globalism," see Dugin, *Osnovy geopolitiki*, 214–92; Laruelle, *Russian Eurasianism*, 115–20.

77. See "Novyi universitet." On the Iuzhinskii circle, see Laruelle, "The Iuzhinskii Circle"; Clover, *Black Wind, White Snow*, 151–75.

78. On Dugin's "leftist turn," see Tarasov et al., *Levye v Rossii*.

79. See de Benoist, *Vue de droite*; de Benoist, *Critiques*; de Benoist, *Le mai 68*; Steuckers, "La genèse de la postmodernité"; de Herte (pseudonym of de Benoist), "Faut-il être 'postmoderne'?"; O'Meara, *New Culture, New Right*; Spektorowski, "The New Right."

80. The title of Dugin's journal is a translation of the title of de Benoist's journal Éléments. De Benoist and Steuckers visited Dugin in Moscow in 1992, when the journal was founded. On the contacts between Dugin and members of the French New Right, see Shekhovtsov, "Aleksandr Dugin's Neo-Eurasianism"; Shekhovtsov, *Russia and the Western Far Right*.

81. See Dugin, "Kogda nikogo net"; Dugin, "Paradigma kontsa"; Dugin, "Postmodern?" Later republished in Dugin, *Pop-kul'tura*, 409–36; Steuckers, "La genèse de la postmodernité."

82. See Dugin, *Pop-kul'tura*, 414 and 415; Dugin, *Chetvertaia politicheskaia teoriia*, 15.

83. See Dugin, *Pop-kul'tura*, 414; Baudrillard, *Selected Writings*, 188–90; Steuckers, "La genèse de la postmodernité."

84. Dugin, *Pop-kul'tura*, 421–22.

85. Dugin, *Pop-kul'tura*, 425–26.

86. Dugin, *Pop-kul'tura*, 422–28.

87. See Barney (pseudonym of de Benoist), "Les nouveaux clivages du paysage intellectuel français"; Barni, "Intellektual'nyi peizazh."

88. Viktor Miziano, "Mir chrevat neoliberal'nymi simptomami."

89. See Deleuze, "Postscript on the Societies of Control"; Baudrillard, "Aesthetic Illusion"; Delez, "Obshchestvo kontrolia"; Bodriiar, "Estetika illiuzii, estetika utraty illiuzii."

90. Tarasov, "Godar kak Vol'ter."

91. Tsvetkov, "Shtirner-Prudon: dva poliusa anarkhii."

92. Verbitsky, personal interview, June 21, 2015; Verbitskii, "Khaos i kul'tura podpol'ia"; Parfrey, *Apocalypse Culture.*

93. Osipov, "Sadoeroticheskii natsional-satanizm."

94. In this section, I will focus on the following books by Aleksandr Dugin: *Pop-kul'tura*; *Geopolitika postmoderna*; *Chetvertaia politicheskaia teoriia.* I also reference Dugin's lectures and seminars published in Dugin, *Chetvertyi put'.* When possible, I will include references to the available English translations of some of these texts from Dugin, *The Fourth Political Theory*; Dugin, *The Rise of the Fourth Political Theory.*

95. See Dugin, *Pop-kul'tura*, 435–36.

96. His celebration of a "boundless and red fascism" was formulated in Dugin, "Fashizm, bezgranichnyi i krasnyi."

97. Dugin, *Chetvertaia politicheskaia teoriia*, 5–25; Dugin, *The Fourth Political Theory*, 11–31.

98. See Dugin, *Chetvertyi put'*, 270–316; Dugin, *Chetvertaia politicheskaia teoriia*, 100–112; Dugin, *The Fourth Political Theory*, 67–82.

99. See Dugin, *Chetvertyi put'*, 308–17; Dugin, *The Fourth Political Theory*, 67–70; Latour, *We Have Never Been Modern.*

100. See Dugin, *Chetvertyi put'*, 235–48; Dugin, *The Fourth Political Theory*, 177–83.

101. See Dugin, *Geopolitika postmoderna*, 39–76; Dugin, *Chetvertaia politicheskaia teoriia*, 187–97; Dugin, *The Fourth Political Theory*, 101–20.

102. See Dugin, *Chetvertaia politicheskaia teoriia*, 25–27, 219–42; Dugin, *Chetvertyi put'*, 235–48; Dugin, *Geopolitika postmoderna*, 48–76; Dugin, *The Fourth Political Theory*, 177–84. As I was able to verify, *Empire* became for the neo-Eurasianists what Etkind's cultural analyses had been for the old guard of "Duginites" in the 1990s: a canonical book authored by an ideological opponent that could be subversively interpreted and appropriated. However, whereas from Dugin's perspective Etkind (and Popper) belong to the adversary liberal camp, the Western New Left is for him a potential ally in the anti-globalist revolution, with the implication that ideological revolutions might need to be "resolved" after the revolution takes place. See Dugin, *Geopolitika postmoderna*, 48–76; Dugin, *Chetvertyi put'*, 633–37; Dugin, *The Fourth Political Theory*, 193–97.

103. See Dugin, *Geopolitika postmoderna*, 61–76; Dugin, *Chetvertyi put'*, 235–48; Dugin, *The Fourth Political Theory*, 156–83.

104. See Dugin, *Chetvertaia politicheskaia teoriia*, 5–27; Dugin, *The Fourth Political Theory*, 11–54.

105. Dugin, *The Fourth Political Theory*, 28–29; Dugin, *Chetvertaia politicheskaia teoriia*, 23–24.

106. Dugin, *The Fourth Political Theory*, 29; Dugin, *Chetvertaia politicheskaia teoriia*, 24.

107. Dugin, *The Fourth Political Theory*, 21–22; Dugin, *Chetvertaia politicheskaia teoriia*, 18–19.

108. Dugin, *The Fourth Political Theory*, 21; Dugin, *Chetvertyi put'*, 28–33.

109. Dugin, *The Fourth Political Theory*, 22–23; Dugin, *Chetvertaia politicheskaia teoriia*, 17–18.

110. Dugin, *Geopolitika postmoderna*, 69–71.

111. Dugin, *Chetvertyi put'*, 243–44.

112. Dugin, *Chetvertyi put'*, 235–44; *The Fourth Political Theory*, 182–83.

113. See Dugin, *Pop-kul'tura*, 121–63; Kurekhin, "Esli vy romantik—vy fashist!" Dugin's conception was clearly inspired by Kurekhin's interview published in *Elementy.*

114. Dugin, *The Fourth Political Theory*, 96–97 (modified translation). Original: Dugin, *Chetvertaia politicheskaia teoriia*, 96–97.

115. Dugin, *The Fourth Political Theory*, 172–73; Dugin, *Chetvertyi put'*, 170–72.

116. Dugin, *Chetvertyi put'*, 172–74; Dugin, *The Fourth Political Theory*, 173–74.

117. See Dugin, *Geopolitika postmoderna*, 66–71; Dugin, *Chetvertyi put'*, 249–70; Dugin, *The Fourth Political Theory*, 184–92.

118. Dugin, *The Fourth Political Theory*, 186.

119. Dugin, *The Fourth Political Theory*, 192.

120. Dugin, *The Fourth Political Theory*, 192.

121. Dugin, *The Fourth Political Theory*, 189.

122. Dugin, *The Fourth Political Theory*, 191.

123. Dugin, *Geopolitika postmoderna*, 152.

124. See Barthes, *Mythologies*, 107–64.

125. See Dugin, *Geopolitika postmoderna*, 198–273. Ethnopluralism has been seen by many as a form of "cultural racism" and, potentially, racial segregation. See Balibar and Wallerstein, *Race, Nation, Class*, 1–28; Taguieff, *Sur la nouvelle droite*; Spektorowski, "The New Right"; Shekhovtsov, "Aleksandr Dugin's Neo-Eurasianism."

126. Dugin, *The Fourth Political Theory*, 93.

127. Dugin, *The Fourth Political Theory*, 24, 36, 96; Dugin, *Chetvertaia politicheskaia teoriia*, 85, 94, 22.

128. See Dugin, *Geopolitika postmoderna*, 71–76.

129. See Pelevin, *Generation P* (translated into English as *Homo Zapiens*).

130. "Dugin's Guideline—In Trump We Trust."

Chapter 5. A Conservative Bohemia

Third epigraph: Evgeny Golovin, quoted at golovinfond.ru: "Тот, кто идет против дня, не должен бояться ночи."

1. On Kochetkov and his links with Dugin and the Russian government, see Shekhovtsov, "Far-Right Election Observation Monitors in the Service of the Kremlin's Foreign Policy."

2. The title of Gintovt's series is a reference to Lev Gumilev's definition of "passionaries," heroic leaders who are able to determine epochal changes in the history of their peoples or "ethnoses." These names and definitions were also popularized by an article by Dugin, published in a 1993 issue of his journal *Elementy*: Dugin, "Liudi dlinnoi voli." On Lev Gumilev, see Gumilev, *Etnogenez i biosfera zemli*; Bassin, *The Gumilev Mystique*.

3. Aleksey Beliaev-Gintovt, personal interview, March 31, 2015.

4. On the connection between Gintovt's art and the cult of war, violence, and "military dandyism" of such conservative interwar intellectuals as Julius Evola and Ernst Jünger, see also Engström, "Military Dandyism."

5. Verbitsky at the time considered nationalism the only revolutionary force within Russian society. When I interviewed him, he was very disillusioned with Eurasianism, vehemently anti-nationalist and anti-Putin (he ironically claimed to be a "Russophobe"). Verbitsky said that he had never believed that Eurasianists could "actually" go beyond their intellectual provocations and become allies of the current regime. Smirnov, "Mikhail Verbitskii: 'Ozhivit' vselennuiu!'"; Verbitsky, personal interview, June 21, 2015. Verbitsky was also one of the authors of the special issue of Dugin's journal *Elementy* about postmodernism, discussed in chapter 4.

6. Valery Korovin, personal interview, May 14, 2015.

7. Vladimir's was most likely an apocryphal reference to the hymn of the Fascist Party of Italy, "Giovinezza." The original lyrics are "Giovinezza, giovinezza, / primavera di bellezza, / nel fascismo è la salvezza della nostra libertà (Youth, youth, / Spring of beauty, / In fascism's the salvation / Of our freedom), although Vladimir's version, "the youth of our freedom" is actually much more evocative and multifaceted than the original.

8. Graña, "The Ideological Significance of Bohemian Life," 4.

9. Baudelaire, "The Dandy (1863)."

10. Benjamin, "On Some Motifs in Baudelaire," 197, n. 6. On the ideology, culture, and aesthetics of different types of Bohemia, see Graña and Graña, *On Bohemia.*

11. See Laruelle, "The Iuzhinskii Circle"; Clover, *Black Wind, White Snow*, 151–75. At the beginning of the 2000s, Dzhemal, Golovin, and Mamleev taught classes at Dugin's independent "New University." See "Arktogeia—Novyi universitet."

12. See Mamleev, *Vospominaniia*; "Yuri Mamleev: Pro tsenzuru i Iuzhinskii."

13. "Geidar Dzhemal' o sebe."

14. On traditionalism and its role in postwar right-wing culture, see Sedgwick, *Against the Modern World*; Gregor, *Mussolini's Intellectuals*; Goodrick-Clarke, *Black Sun.*

15. See Laruelle, "The Iuzhinskii Circle"; Laruelle, *Russian Eurasianism.*

16. See "Geidar Dzhemal' o sebe"; Vasily Shumov, personal interview, May 21, 2015.

17. On the real and alleged mystical origins of Nazism, see Goodrick-Clarke, *The Occult Roots of Nazism*; Goodrick-Clarke, *Black Sun.*

18. Laruelle, "The Iuzhinskii Circle," 573. Members of the Eurasia Movement periodically celebrate Von Ungern-Sternberg's memory to this day.

19. Conversation with an anonymous member of the Iuzhinskii Circle.

20. "В прекрасном утреннем настроеньи / В небесно-голубом кадиллаке / Мы едем по дорогам Европы, / Где так прекрасен утренний свет. // Небесно-голубые фашисты / Приветствуют нас правой рукою, / Ты даришь им лукавые взгляды / И радостно смеешься в ответ. // Небесно-голубые фашисты / В небесно-голубом кадиллаке, / На их повязках страшные знаки, / А в руках огромные коты." Recordings and lyrics of Dugin's song are available at "Arktogeia—Pesni Gansa Ziversa."

21. "Geidar Dzhemal' o sebe."

22. See Mamleev, "Shatuny"; Mamleyev, *The Sublimes* (English translation of *Shatuny*); Radashkevich, "Planeta nezasnuvshikh medvedei"; Vail and Genis, "S tochki zreniia gribov."

23. Dugin, *Tampliery proletariata*, 250.

24. Dugin, *Tampliery proletariata*, 251.

25. See Lotman and Uspenskii, "Novye aspekty izucheniia kul'tury drevnei Rusi."

26. Vernant, "Ambiguity and Reversal."

27. Andreeva and Podgorskaia, *Novye khudozhniki.* See these works by Yurchak: *Everything Was Forever, Until It Was No More*; "A Parasite from Outer Space"; "Post-post Communist Sincerity"; "Gagarin and the Rave Kids"; and Kushnir, *Sergei Kurekhin*; Mihailovic, *The Mitki*; Safariants, "Thank God We're Not Alive"; Shein, *Nol' ob"ekt.*

28. On the art of Timur Novikov and the New Academy, see Andreeva and Podgorskaia, *Novye khudozhniki*; Ippolitov and Kharitonov, *Novaia Akademiia*; Andreeva, "10 zhiznei Timura Novikova/Timur Novikov's 10 Lives"; Novikov, "Novyi russkii klassitsizm"; *Lektsii*; Andreeva, *Timur: Vrat' tol'ko pravdu!*; Engström, "Apollo against Black

Square"; Khlobystin, *Shizorevoliutsiia* (on the "New Serious" movement, see in particular 210–46).

29. On this, see Essig, *Queer in Russia*, and also the discussion of the post-Soviet reception of Limonov's work in chapter 2.

30. On the post-Soviet transformation of Moscow Conceptualism and its assimilation in the international art market, see Esanu, *Transition in Post-Soviet Art.*

31. On the concept of "new sincerity" in contemporary Russian culture, see Prigov and Shapoval, *Portretnaia galereia* (in particular, 9–26); Prigov, "What More Is There to Say?"; Epstein, *After the Future*, 328–39; Rutten, *Sincerity after Communism.*

32. Tupitsyna and Tupitsyn, "Beseda s Timurom i Afrikoi." On gay culture, queer aesthetics, and the New Academy, see also Campbell, "Homosexuality as Device"; Engström, "Apollo against Black Square"; "GAY.RU—Timur Novikov."

33. See Novikov, "Novyi russkii klassitsizm"; Novikov, *Lektsii*; Novikov and Brodsky, *Gorizonty.*

34. Novikov and Gurianov, "Sila krasoty"; Novikov, "Neskol'ko slov"; Novikov, "Georgii Gurianov"; Many of these ideas were also connected with broader international art trends. See Engström, "Metamodernizm."

35. See these works by Novikov: "Ideia totalitarnogo iskusstva"; "Novyi russkii klassitsizm"; "Soprotivlenie i vozrozhdenie."

36. Novikov, "Ideia totalitarnogo iskusstva"; Novikov, "Neskol'ko slov."

37. See Novikov, "Peterburgskoe iskusstvo 1990-kh godov."

38. Novikov and Brodsky, *Gorizonty.*

39. See Andreeva, "10 zhiznei"; Khlobystin, *Shizorevoliutsiia*, 31–41; Andreeva, "Novye idut."

40. See Novikov, "Georgii Gurianov."

41. These films followed quite faithfully the "prototypical plot" of socialist realist novels, dominated by a (metaphorical) father-son relationship, and a series of folkloric motifs. See Clark, *The Soviet Novel.*

42. See Medvedev and Novikov, *Belyi lebed'*; "Timur Novikov. White Swan."

43. See Khlobystin, *Shizorevoliutsiia*, 125–236; Shein, *Nol' ob"ekt.*

44. See Khlobystin, *Shizorevoliutsiia*, 210–46; Shein, *Nol' ob"ekt.* Gintovt sees Novikov's traditionalism as a strong revolutionary gesture, close to the spirit of the avant-gardes. See "Aleksei Gintovt o sovremennom iskusstve i evraziistve." Incidentally, Novikov also seemed to have a personal motivation for his turn toward a form of anti-Westernism conservatism. During one of their visits to New York, he and Gurianov contracted AIDS. Novikov gradually became blind and died prematurely in 2003; allegedly, in the last years of his life he interpreted his disease as a "curse" against his own sinfulness and that of Western civilization.

45. See Chechot, "Prozrachnyi sumrak"; Kushnir, *Sergei Kurekhin*; Zhvaniia, *Put' khunveibina*; chapter 2 of this volume.

46. See Novikov, "Neskol'ko slov"; Novikov, "Ideia totalitarnogo iskusstva"; Novikov, "Sever-Iug"; Medvedev, *Pokhishchenie Evropy*; Medvedev, *Pokhishchenie razuma.*

47. On the use of fascist and totalitarian aesthetics in the art of Laibach and NSK, see Žižek, "Why Are Laibach and NSK Not Fascists?"; Novikov et al., "Dogovor: Evropeiskoe obshchestvo klassicheskoi estetiki"; Monroe, *Interrogation Machine.* See also chapter 2 of this volume.

48. In a late interview, to explain how the "new seriousness" of the New Academy had predicted a broader change in Russian society, Novikov said that Putin did "not

joke" when he made such quasi-comical statements as "we'll whack them in the outhouse" (referring to the people responsible for the 1999 wave of terrorist attacks in Russia): Novikov, "Novye khudozhniki."

49. Khlobystin, *Shizorevoliutsiia*, 235.

50. Khlobystin, *Shizorevoliutsiia*, 231.

51. See "Aleksandr Dugin: Zakoldovannaia sreda."

52. In relation to the concept of "new seriousness," Maria Engström applies to Novikov, Gintovt, and the New Academy the term "Metamodernism." See Engström, "Metamodernizm."

53. I am here going against the Eurasianists' (or neo-academists') own statements and declarations. Dugin de facto claims to be using postmodernism as a "trick," aimed at fomenting a violent conservative revolution that "will put an end to the game" (see chapter 4). Novikov claims that Putin "is not joking" (see note 48). However, I am here looking at these different forms of "conservative postmodernism" as cultural practices rather than programmatic statements and manifestos. I believe that Dugin's, Gintovt's, and Novikov's art-political projects, in different ways, would cease to function or be effective if they were endowed with a straightforward "purely denotative" meaning. There are elements of "avant-garde posturing" in Dugin's and Gintovt's cult of violence, death, and heroism, and in Novikov's "everythingism" and "life-creation." Yet these projects also appear to be "intellectual games," in which players ended up being trapped, hence the perpetual oscillating between irony and seriousness. This, at least, was the opinion of a few of my informants, old-time Eurasianists who thought that Dugin's project had "gone too far" but that he had invested too much in it, and so "it was too late to go back." What makes these projects particularly radical and puzzling is, indeed, the application of these artistic strategies to grassroots politics and mainstream media.

54. For an introduction to Joseph Beuys's work and some of the main concepts related to his work and career, see Tisdall, *Joseph Beuys*. On the concept of *Gesamtkunstwerk*, with particular reference to the history of the NBP and Dugin's neo-Eurasianism, see chapter 2 and chapter 4 of this volume.

55. On Gintovt's art project in general, and on its links with Novikov's New Academy and Dugin's imperialism, see also Engström, "Military Dandyism"; Engström, "Apollo Against Black Square"; Engström, "Metamodernizm."

56. Doze, "Novonovosibirsk."

57. Krasok, "Aleksei Beliaev-Gintovt."

58. See Beliaev-Gintovt, *Aleksei Beliaev-Gintovt*; Beliaev-Gintovt, *Parad pobedy 2937*; Beliaev-Gintovt, *55°45′20.83″N, 37°37′03.48″E*; "DOKTRINA" (Gintovt's personal website). (The catalogs of *Parad pobedy 2937* and *55°45′20.83″N, 37°37′03.48″E* are also available online, doctrine.ru/delo/victory/victory.pdf; doctrine.ru/delo/block/block.pdf.)

59. See Paperny, *Architecture in the Age of Stalin*; Schlögel, *Moscow, 1937*; Ryklin, "'The Best in the World.'"

60. Tikhonov, "Aleksei Beliaev-Gintovt" (quoted in Engström, "Military Dandyism," 112). On the religious subtext of Stalinist architecture, see Paperny, *Architecture in the Age of Stalin*.

61. See Sontag, "Notes on 'Camp'"; Benjamin, "The Work of Art."

62. An image of this painting is accessible at doctrine.ru/delo/rodina-doch/?i=5.

63. See "Aleksei Gintovt o sovremennom iskusstve i evraziistve."

64. See Kukulin, "VRIO vmesto Klio."

65. Degot', "Mog li ul'trapravyi natsionalist ne poluchit' premiiu Kandinskogo?"

66. Osmolovskii, "Zaiavlenie Osmolovskogo."

67. "Chto vy dumaete o marshe protiv degenerativnogo iskusstva?"

68. See chapter 2.

69. Conversations with several students of Osmolovsky's art school BASA; Anatoly Osmolovsky, personal interview, June 26, 2015.

70. See chapter 4, note 58.

71. Plutser-Sarno, "Aleksei Beliaev-Gintovt."

72. Kurina, "Anatolii Osmolovskii: '90 protsentov sovremennogo iskusstva—voobshche ne iskusstvo.'"

73. Engström, "Military Dandyism," 106.

74. In this regard, Engström argues that the goal of Gintovt's "'flickering aesthetics" is to force the spectator or reader to formulate an opinion and "define" her own position. See "Military Dandyism."

75. Kuznetsova, "Utopiia goszakaza."

76. On Tsvetkov, see chapters 2–3.

77. On Nashi, see Hemment, *Youth Politics in Putin's Russia*; Lassila, *The Quest for an Ideal Youth.*

78. I am grateful to Aleksandr Verkhovsky, director of the SOVA Center for Information and Analysis in Moscow, for his guidance on the relationship between nationalist movements and the presidential administration in Russia today. See also "Misuse of Anti-extremism/SOVA."

79. See chapters 2 and 3.

80. On the basis of Dugin's (and de Benoist's) theories about cultural hegemony. See chapter 4.

81. Dugin, "Zaria v sapogakh."

82. See Dugin, "Evraziiskaia oprichnina."

83. "Programma Evraziiskogo soiuza molodezhi"; "Katekhizis chlena Evraziiskogo soiuza molodezhi."

84. See, for instance, Dugin, *Tampliery proletariata*; Dugin, *Russkaia veshch'.*

85. See Dugin, *Tampliery proletariata*, 125–28.

86. Dugin, "Iosif Stalin," 465. Incidentally, the cult of death and heroism is for many what makes Dugin close to the "original fascists." See Laruelle, *Russian Eurasianism*, 134–35; Shekhovtsov, "The Palingenetic Thrust."

87. See "Ob eskhatologicheskom lagere *FINIS MUNDI*"; "Finis Mundi. Konets illiuzii"; Speranskaia, *ENDKAMPF.*

88. See chapter 4.

89. *Berezki* literally means "little birches" and *matushka Rossiia* "little mother Russia," although (as evidenced by the latter expression) in Russian diminutives are not associated with size but are used as terms of endearment. Hence, a loose translation of *berezki* could be "dear little birches" and *matushka Rossiia* could be freely translated as "mama Russia" or "mom Russia." These expressions are part of the vocabulary of children's literature and fairy tales. In the context of the painting's gloomy and menacing appearance, they are particularly out of place.

90. For a survey of NOD's activities in recent years, see Ofitserova and Litavrin, "Napadeniia na oppozitsiiu."

91. See Knorre-Dmitrieva, "Aktivisty NOD napali na uchastnikov shkol'nogo konkursa."

92. See "Napadenie na Naval'nogo."

93. See Popkov, "*NODu krupno povezlo.*"

94. See Televidenie narodno-osvoboditel'nogo dvizheniia, "5.2.2015 E. Fedorov i I. Strelkov."

95. See Epshtein et al., *Dukhovnaia bran'.*

96. Allegedly, Gennady Zyuganov, the current secretary of the Russian Communist Party, has borrowed many elements of Dugin's ideology. See Laruelle, *Russian Eurasianism,* 11.

97. See Dugin, *Osnovy geopolitiki,* 74–79; Dugin, *Chetvertaia politicheskaia teoriia,* 198–212.

98. See Dugin, *Osnovy geopolitiki,* 629–47. Dugin uses the image of a "flourishing complexity" to define Eurasianist imperialism as an alternative to the leveling global hegemony of the capitalist West. Leont'ev's "flourishing complexity" can also be considered his version of de Benoist's "ethnopluralism," which determines, for instance, what Laruelle has defined as an "antisemitic Zionism." In short, although he admires deeply Jewish traditional culture and takes Israel as the only example of a government based on its own religious tradition and identity, Dugin believes that converted, cosmopolitan Jews are at the center of a global capitalist conspiracy. See Laruelle, *Russian Eurasianism,* 135–41. As mentioned, ethnopluralism is a very problematic concept in that it disregards the interdependence between the colonizer and the colonized.

Conclusion

1. Cacciari, "Perché Antigone?"

2. Latour, *We Have Never Been Modern,* 7; Chakrabarty, *Provincializing Europe,* 45.

3. Latour has more recently made such an attempt, in *An Inquiry into Modes of Existence.* On "metanarratives" and the legitimization of science and modernity, see Lyotard, *The Postmodern Condition.*

4. See Latour, *We Have Never Been Modern,* 27–32.

5. See Barthes, *Mythologies,* 109–73.

6. Latour, *We Have Never Been Modern,* 9.

7. The extended quote is from Kirill Medvedev, *It's No Good,* 139–40. Original Russian available in Medvedev, "Sait poeta Kirilla Medvedeva."

8. See Michel, "Beyond Trump and Putin."

9. See Gray, "A 'One-Stop Shop' for the Alt-Right"; Bruk, "Richard Spencer's Russian Wife Talks Trump, Utopia"; Michel, "Meet the Moscow Mouthpiece Married to a Racist Alt-Right Boss."

10. See Allen, "Meeting the European Fighters at War in Ukraine"; Clapp, "Why American Right-Wingers Are Going to War in Ukraine"; "A Donetsk sono arrivati volontari italiani per combattere le truppe di Kiev"; Antonova, "Ukraine Crisis: Meet the Foreign Nationals Fighting for the Donetsk People's Republic"; Dragosei, "Venticinque italiani indagati per aver combattuto in Ucraina."

11. See Pucciarelli, "Dugin (Il filosofo di Putin)"; "Sovranisti ma di sinistra"; Salvia, "Come la destra italiana sta rubando le icone della sinistra a suon di bufale"; Salvia, "Populismo, sovranità e meme su Putin"; Mattioli, "Quando i rossobruni diventano mainstream."

12. Prilepin, *San'kia* (published in English as *Sankya*).

13. Zakhar Prilepin, personal interview, August 8, 2013. In his "provincial attitude," Prilepin claimed to have used the writer Maksim Gor'ky as a source of inspiration.

14. See Prilepin, "Noveishaia istoriia. Novyi realizm."

15. See Krusanov, *Amerikanskaia dyrka.*

16. See "Russian Winter Olympics Campaign Branded 'Fascist'"; Arkhakova, "Svetloe ariiskoe budushchee." The exhibits featuring works of patriotic artists close to the New Academy and/or Gintovt's "conservative bohemia" included the following exhibits: "Pobeda kak novyi epos," Akademiia khudozhestv, Moscow, Spring 2015; "Obogashchenie real'nosti," Galereia A3, Moscow, Spring 2015; Mikhail Rozanov, "Iasnost' tseli," Muzei Moskvy, Spring 2015; Aleksei Beliaev-Gintovt and Mikhail Rozanov, "Poriadok," Ruarts Gallery, Moscow, Fall 2017; "Aktual'naia Rossiia: Sreda obitaniia," Muzei sovremennoi istorii Rossii, Moscow, December 2017.

Works Cited

Articles from *Limonka*, the National Bolshevik Party's Newspaper

"Aktsiia." *Limonka* 20 (August 1995).

"Art-khronika." *Limonka* 47 (September 1996).

Bonch, Timur (General Brusilov). "K chlenam NBP." *Limonka* 52 (November 1996).

Brener, Aleksandr. "Nenavizhu." *Limonka* 45 (August 1996).

———. "Obossanyi pistolet." *Limonka* 93 (June 1998).

———. "Otkrytoe pis'mo o kholuistve." *Limonka* 44 (July 1996).

———. "Palestintsam." *Limonka* 41 (June 1996).

———. "Sovety informatsionnykh luddistov." *Limonka* 104 (November 1998).

Burroughs, William. "Dikie mal'chiki." *Limonka* 39 (May 1996).

———. "Ekspress na planetu Nova." *Limonka* 41 (June 1996).

"Dnevnik Anny Frank—fal'shivka." *Limonka* 39 (May 1996).

Dubshin, Daniil. "Vsiakaia morda blagorazumnogo fasona vyzivaet vo mne nepriatnye oshchushcheniia." *Limonka* 29 (December 1995).

Dugin, Aleksandr. "Gi Debor mertv. Spektakl' prodolzhaetsia." *Limonka* 14 (May 1995).

———. "Iz kolybeli revoliutsii." *Limonka* 22 (September 1995)

———. "Kontrelita." *Limonka* 2 (December 1994).

———. "K zhenshchinam." *Limonka* 25 (November 1995).

———. "Novye protiv starykh." *Limonka* 1 (November 1994).

———. "Vsia vlast' severu." *Limonka* 11 (April 1995).

"Fashizm ili ne fashizm: Konkurs." *Limonka* 11 (April 1995).

Gastello, Oleg. "Chto takoe partiia?" *Limonka* 58 (February 1997).

———. "P.S." *Limonka* 52 (November 1996).

———. "SS-Pati" *Limonka* 55 (December 1996).

"Inostranets s"eden mafiei." *Limonka* 7 (February 1995).

Ivanenko, Aleksei. "Negry i niggery." *Limonka* 93 (June 1998).

Kamennyi, Aleksandr [Andrei Karagodin]. "ALLE GEGEN ALLE: Interv'iu nashego korrespondenta s gruppoi Laibach." *Limonka* 3 (January 1995).
Klimova, M., comp. and trans. "Nash Lui-Ferdinand Selin" *Limonka* 9 (March 1995).
Kokh, El'za. "Brener i Kulik." *Limonka* 33 (February 1996).
———. "Ubiistvo Pazolini." *Limonka* 38 (May 1996).
Kondratovich, T., trans. "Zhan Zhene. Otryvki iz poslednego interv'iu." *Limonka* 15 (June 1995).
"Kto ne rabotaet, togo ediat." *Limonka* 6 (February 1995).
Letov, Egor. "Eto znaet moia svoboda." *Limonka* 1 (November 1994).
———. "Imenno tak vse i bylo." *Limonka* 2 (December 1994) and *Limonka* 3 (January 1995).
Limonov, Eduard. "Est' takaia partiia." *Limonka* 44 (July 1996).
———. "Limonka protiv stukachei-intelligentov." *Limonka* 2 (December 1994).
———. "NBP—partiia priamogo deistviia, a ne sekta intellektualov." *Limonka* 90 (April 1998).
———. "Poslednii den' komandante Che." *Limonka* 36 (April 1996).
———. "Razmyshleniia o natsionalizme." *Limonka* 33 (February 1996).
Limonov, Eduard [pseudonym: Polkovnik Ivan Chernyi, which was also at times used by Andrei Karagodin and possibly other party members]. "Bog voiny-Makhagala." *Limonka* 15 (June 1995).
———. "Nash Lenin." *Limonka* 30 (January 1996).
———. "Noch dlinnykh nozhei." *Limonka* 22 (October 1995).
———. "Pervye fashisty." *Limonka* 37 (April 1996).
———. "Pivnoi putsch. Munich, 1923." *Limonka* 13 (May 1995).
———. "Pokhishchenie i kazn' Al'do Moro." *Limonka* 12 (April 1995).
———. "Rozhdenie partii." *Limonka* 14: (May 1995).
———. "Skachka na tigre." *Limonka* 17 (July 1995).
———. "Stalin. Molodye gody." *Limonka* 28 (December 1995).
———. "Val'kiriia revoliutsii." *Limonka* 25 (November 1995).
"Maloletka iznasilovala pensionera." *Limonka* 7 (February 1995).
Medvedeva, Nataliia. "Oda russkomu muzhiku." *Limonka* 2 (December 1994).
Melent'eva, Nataliia. "Chernyi messiia Menson: 'Ia boikotiruiu vash mir.'" *Limonka* 7 (January 1995).
Mogutin, Iaroslav. "Bez intelligentov. Utopiia." *Limonka* 1 (November 1994).
"Nazvat' presidenta pi. .rasom stoit 417 novykh rublei." *Limonka* 93 (June 1998).
"O chem povedala luna." *Limonka* 12 (April 1995).
Osmolovsky, Anatolii. "O stabil'nosti." *Limonka* 42 (June 1996).
———. "Tvoi vybor sdelan." *Limonka* 44 (July 1996).
"Razdavit' dvukh zmei." *Limonka* 29 (December 1995).
"SEX-trenazher elitnogo partiitsa." *Limonka* 55 (December 1996).
"SEX-trenazher zhenshchiny partii." *Limonka* 56 (January 1997).
Sil'nyi, Daniil [Daniil Dubshin]. "Bol'shoi belyi chelovek." *Limonka* 3 (December 1994).
"Skol'ko zhe evreev pogiblo?" *Limonka* 39 (May 1996).
"THE Alekseia Tsvetkova." *Limonka* 69 (July 1997).
Tsvetkov, Aleksei. "Anarkhizm." *Limonka* 85 (February 1998).
———. "Chudotvornyi uzhas." *Limonka* 44 (July 1996).
———. "Fusion Conspiracy." *Limonka* 86 (March 1998).

Tsvetkov, Aleksei [pseudonym: Doktor Zig Khailer]. "Fashizm—eto gor'kii shokolad." *Limonka* 63 (April 1997).
———. "Moia militsia." *Limonka* 64 (May 1997).
Tsvetkov, Aleksei [pseudonym: Gruppa kommunisticheskii realizm]. "K novoi rechi—rechi bessmertnykh liudei." *Limonka* 41 (June 1996).
Tsvetkov, Aleksei [pseudonym: Ian Geil]. "Antigeroi." *Limonka* 55 (December 1996).
———. "Ekologiia." *Limonka* 59 (February 1997).
———. "Marie-Madeleine de Brinvillier." *Limonka* 55 (December 1996).
———. "Molodoi kommunist." *Limonka* 56 (January 1997).
———. "Revoliutsiia." *Limonka* 57 (January 1997).
———. "Zrelishche—lovushka nomer odin." *Limonka* 60 (March 1997).
Tsvetkov, Aleksei [pseudonym: Pavel Vlasov]. "Bakunin kak superagent." *Limonka* 52 (November 1996).
———. "Doktor Gerbert Markuze." *Limonka* 25 (November 1995).
———. "Ekstremizm—obraz zhizni." *Limonka* 12 (May 1995).
———. "Proshchai anarkhiia." *Limonka* 18 (July 1995).
———. "Sindikalizm." *Limonka* 54 (December 1996).
———. "Skinkhedy." *Limonka* 61 (March 1997).
———. "Terrorizm." *Limonka* 68 (June 1997).
———. "Tupak Amaru—khronika priamogo deistviia i vooruzhennoi propagandy." *Limonka* 60 (March 1997).
———. "Vooruzhennyi rai." *Limonka* 35 (March 1996).
"Vstretil El'tsyna i ispugalsia." *Limonka* 10 (March 1995).

All Other Sources

"A Donetsk sono arrivati volontari italiani per combattere le truppe di Kiev." *Rai News*, June 10, 2014.
Agurskii, Mikhail. *Ideologiia natsional-bol'shevizma*. Paris: YMCA-Press, 1980.
Agursky [Agurskii], Mikahil. *The Third Rome: National Bolshevism in the USSR*. Boulder, CO: Westview, 1987.
Aksenov, Vasilii. "Zvezdnyi bilet." *Iunost'* 6 (1961). Translated into English by Andrew R. MacAndrew as *A Ticket to the Stars* (New York: New American Library, 1963).
"Aleksandr Dugin: Bitva za Ukrainu—Eto bitva za nash narod, nashu istoriiu, nashu dushu!" *Ekspress Gazeta*, February 20, 2014. eg.ru/politics/41948/.
"Aleksandr Dugin o situatsii na Ukraine." *Dobroe utro*, April 14, 2014. Pervyi kanal. 1tv.ru /shows/dobroe-utro/pro-ukrainu/aleksandr-dugin-o-situatsii-na-ukraine.
"Aleksandr Dugin: 'Ubivat', ubivat' i ubivat'!" YouTube, June 15, 2014. youtube.com /watch?v=sX4r1eXpUSI.
"Aleksandr Dugin: Zakoldovannaia sreda 'Novykh Imperii.'" *Khudozhestvennyi zhurnal*, no. 54 (2004).
Alekseev, Andrei. "'Ubivat', ubivat', ubivat', kak professor ia tak shchitaiu' (A. Dugin)." *Cogita.ru* (blog), June 16, 2014.
"Aleksei Gintovt o sovremennom iskusstve i evraziistve." YouTube, December 5, 2012. youtube.com/watch?time_continue=763&v=ogZxU8nxWmg.
Allen, Christopher. "Meeting the European Fighters at War in Ukraine." *Vice*, August 25, 2015.

Anderson, Benedict. *Imagined Communities: Reflections on the Origin and Spread of Nationalism.* London: Verso, 1991.

Andreeva, Ekaterina. "10 zhiznei Timura Novikova/Timur Novikov's 10 Lives." In *Timur: Nauchnoe izdanie*, edited by Ekaterina Andreeva, Ivan Chechot, and Kseniia Novikova, 8–57. Moscow: Moskovskii Muzei Sovremennogo Iskusstva, 2013.

———. "Novye idut/The New Artists Are Coming." In *Novye khudozhniki*, edited by Ekaterina Andreeva and Nelli Podgorskaia, 7–26. Moscow: Moskovskii muzei sovremennogo iskusstva, 2012.

———. *Timur: "Vrat' tol'ko pravdu!"* St. Petersburg: Amfora, 2007.

Andreeva, Ekaterina, Ivan Chechot, and Kseniia Novikova, eds. *Timur: Nauchnoe izdanie.* Moscow: Moskovskii muzei sovremennogo iskusstva, 2013.

Andreeva, Ekaterina, and Nelli Podgorskaia, eds. *Novye khudozhniki.* Moscow: Moskovskii muzei sovremennogo iskusstva, 2012.

"'Antioranzhevyi' miting na Poklonnoi gore sobral okolo 138 tysiach chelovek." *Novosti*, February 4, 2012. Pervyi kanal. 1tv.ru/news/2012-02-04/103828-antioranzhevyy_miting_na_poklonnoy_gore_sobral_okolo_138_tysyach_chelovek.

Antonova, Maria. "Ukraine Crisis: Meet the Foreign Nationals Fighting for the Donetsk People's Republic." *The Independent*, October 19, 2015.

"ARCTOGAIA." arctogaia.com/.

Arkhakova, Anna. "Svetloe ariiskoe budushchee." *Chastnyi korrespondent*, May 18, 2011.

"Arktogeia—Filosofskii portal." arcto.ru/.

"Arktogeia—Novyi universitet—Arkhiv lektsii." arcto.ru/article/1029.

"Arktogeia—Pesni Gansa Ziversa." arcto.ru/article/1116.

Asen, Robert. "Seeking the 'Counter,' in Counterpublics." *Communication Theory* 10, no. 4 (2000): 424–46.

Austin, J. L. *How to Do Things with Words.* Cambridge, MA: Harvard University Press, 1962.

Averintsev, Sergei Sergeevich. "Bakhtin, smekh, khristianskaia kul'tura." In *M.M. Bakhtin kak filosof*, edited by L. A. Gogotishvili and P. S. Gurevich, 7–19. Moscow: Nauka, 1992.

Bakhtin, Mikhail. "Forms of Time and of the Chronotope in the Novel." In *The Dialogic Imagination*, 84–258. Austin: University of Texas Press, 1981.

Balibar, Étienne, and Immanuel Wallerstein. *Race, Nation, Class: Ambiguous Identities.* London: Verso, 2011.

Barbashin, Anton, and Hannah Thoburn. "Putin's Brain." *Foreign Affairs*, March 31, 2014.

Barney, David [Alain de Benoist]. "Les nouveaux clivages du paysage intellectuel français." *Éléments: Pour la civilisation européenne*, May 1992, 3–11.

Barni, David [David Barney/Alain de Benoist]. "Intellektual'nyi peizazh." *Elementy* 9 (2000).

Barthes, Roland. *Mythologies.* New York: Farrar, Straus and Giroux, 1972.

———. *The Rustle of Language.* Translated by Richard Howard. Oxford: Blackwell, 1989.

Baskova, Svetlana, ed. *Devianostye ot pervogo litsa.* Moscow: A & D Studiia/Baza, 2015.

Bassin, Mark. *The Gumilev Mystique: Biopolitics, Eurasianism, and the Construction of Community in Modern Russia.* Ithaca, NY: Cornell University Press, 2016.

Baster, Misha. *Al'ternativnaia moda do prikhoda gliantsa: 1985–1995.* Moscow: "Garazh," 2011.

Baudelaire, Charles. "The Dandy (1863)." In *On Bohemia: The Code of the Self-Exiled*, edited by César Graña and Mari Graña, 576–79. New Brunswick, NJ: Transaction, 1990.
Baudrillard, Jean. "Aesthetic Illusion and Disillusion." In *The Conspiracy of Art*, 111–32. New York: Semiotext(e), 2005.
———. *Selected Writings*. Stanford: Stanford University Press, 1988.
———. *Simulacra and Simulation*. Ann Arbor: University of Michigan Press, 1994.
Beliaev-Gintovt, Aleksei [Aleksey]. *Aleksei Beliaev-Gintovt*. Exhibition catalog. Moscow: Galereia Triumf, 2008.
———. "DOKTRINA." *doctrine.ru*, August 31, 2018.
———. *55°45′20.83″N, 37°37′03.48″E*. Exhibition catalog. Moscow: Galereia Triumf, 2012. doctrine.ru/delo/block/block.pdf.
———. *Parad pobedy 2937*. Exhibition catalog. Moscow: Galereia Triumf, 2010. doctrine.ru/delo/victory/victory.pdf.
Bell, Daniel. *The Coming of Post-Industrial Society: A Venture in Social Forecasting*. New York: Basic Books, 1973.
———. *The Cultural Contradictions of Capitalism*. New York: Basic Books, 1976.
———. *The End of Ideology: On the Exhaustion of Political Ideas in the Fifties*. Cambridge, MA: Harvard University Press, 1962.
Benhabib, Seyla. *Democracy and Difference: Contesting the Boundaries of the Political*. Princeton, NJ: Princeton University Press, 1996.
Benjamin, Walter. "On Some Motifs in Baudelaire." In *Illuminations: Essays and Reflections*, edited by Hannah Arendt, translated by Harry Zohn, 155–200. New York: Schocken Books, 1969.
———. "The Work of Art in the Age of Its Mechanical Reproduction." In *Illuminations: Essays and Reflections*, edited by Hannah Arendt, translated by Harry Zohn, 217–51. New York: Schocken Books, 1969.
Bennetts, Marc. *Kicking the Kremlin: Russia's New Dissidents and the Battle to Topple Putin*. London: Oneworld, 2014.
Bernstein, Anya. "An Inadvertent Sacrifice: Body Politics and Sovereign Power in the Pussy Riot Affair." *Critical Inquiry* 40, no. 1 (2013): 220–41.
Bershtein, Evgenii, and Jesse Hadden. "The Sorokin Affair Five Years Later: On Cultural Policy in Today's Russia." *ARTMargins*, June 26, 2007.
Bodriiar, Zhan. [Baudrillard, Jean] "Estetika illiuzii, estetika utraty illiuzii." *Elementy* 9 (2000).
Bokhari, Allum. "Suck It Up Buttercups: Dangerous Faggot Tour Returns to Colleges in September." *Breitbart*, July 6, 2016. breitbart.com/milo/2016/07/06/milo-yiannopoulos-dangerous-faggot-tour-returns-campuses-fall/.
Bokhari, Allum, and Milo Yiannopoulos. "An Establishment Conservative's Guide to the Alt-Right." *Breitbart*, March 29, 2016. breitbart.com/tech/2016/03/29/an-establishment-conservatives-guide-to-the-alt-right/.
Boltanski, Luc, and Ève Chiapello. *The New Spirit of Capitalism*. London: Verso, 2007.
Borden, Richard C. *The Art of Writing Badly: Valentin Kataev's Mauvism and the Rebirth of Russian Modernism*. Evanston, IL: Northwestern University Press, 1999.
Bourdieu, Pierre. *Distinction: A Social Critique of the Judgement of Taste*. Cambridge, MA: Harvard University Press, 1984.
Boyer, Dominic, and Alexei Yurchak. "AMERICAN STIOB: Or, What Late-Socialist

Aesthetics of Parody Reveal about Contemporary Political Culture in the West." *Cultural Anthropology* 25, no. 2 (2010): 179–221.
Brodskii [Brodsky], Iosif. "Posleslovie." In *Moi otritsatel'nyi geroi: Stikhi 1976–1982 godov, N'iu-Iork-Parizh*, by Eduard Limonov, n.p. Moscow: Glagol, 1995.
Bruk, Diana. "Richard Spencer's Russian Wife Talks Trump, Utopia: Full Interview." *Observer*, September 19, 2017.
Burawoy, Michael, and Katherine Verdery, eds. *Uncertain Transition: Ethnographies of Change in the Postsocialist World.* Lanham, MD: Rowman & Littlefield, 1999.
Bürger, Peter. *Theory of the Avant-Garde.* Minneapolis: University of Minnesota Press, 1984.
Butler, Judith. *Excitable Speech: A Politics of the Performative.* New York: Routledge, 1997.
———. *Gender Trouble: Feminism and the Subversion of Identity.* New York: Routledge, 1990.
Bychenkova, Anastasiia. "Dobrovol'tsy iz Rostova gotovy podderzhat' Ukrainu za den'gi." Interview with Vladimir Propenko. *Donnews.ru*, March 5, 2014.
Cacciari, Massimo. "Perché Antigone?" *Antigone. Bimestrale di critica dell'emergenza*, March 1985.
Calhoun, Craig J., ed. *Habermas and the Public Sphere.* Cambridge, MA: MIT Press, 1992.
Campbell, Thomas. "Homosexuality as Device: Necrorealism and Neoacademism." *Ante Projects* 5 (2007): 68–79.
Carden, Patricia. "Limonov's Coming out." In *The Third Wave: Russian Literature in Emigration*, edited by Olga Matich and Michael Heim, 221–35. Ann Arbor, MI: Ardis, 1984.
Carrère, Emmanuel. *Limonov.* Paris: P.O.L., 2011.
———. *Limonov: The Outrageous Adventures of the Radical Soviet Poet Who Became a Bum in New York, a Sensation in France, and a Political Antihero in Russia.* Translated by John Lambert. New York: Farrar, Straus and Giroux, 2014.
Chabal, Patrick, and Jean-Pascal Daloz. *Culture Troubles: Politics and the Interpretation of Meaning.* Chicago: University of Chicago Press, 2006.
Chakrabarty, Dipesh. *Provincializing Europe: Postcolonial Thought and Historical Difference.* Princeton, NJ: Princeton University Press, 2012.
Chantsev, Aleksandr. *Bunt krasoty: Estetika Iukio Misimy i Eduarda Limonova.* Moscow: Agraf, 2009.
Chechot, Ivan. "'Prozrachnyi sumrak, blesk bezlunnyi . . .' Zametki o Timure Novikove / 'Transparent Twilight, Moonless Glow . . .' Some Remarks on Timur Novikov." In *Timur: Nauchnoe izdanie*, edited by Ekaterina Andreeva, Ivan Chechot, and Kseniia Novikova, 61–85. Moscow: Moskovskii muzei sovremennogo iskusstva, 2013.
"Chto vy dumaete o marshe protiv degenerativnogo iskusstva?" *Osmopolis.ru*, May 29, 2008.
Chytry, Josef. *The Aesthetic State: A Quest in Modern German Thought.* Berkeley: University of California Press, 1989.
Clapp, Alexander. "Why American Right-Wingers Are Going to War in Ukraine." *Vice*, June 20, 2016.
Clark, Katerina. *The Soviet Novel: History as Ritual.* Bloomington: Indiana University Press, 1981.
Clifford, James, and George E. Marcus, eds. *Writing Culture: The Poetics and Politics of Ethnography.* Berkeley: University of California Press, 2010.
Clover, Charles. *Black Wind, White Snow: The Rise of Russia's New Nationalism.* New Haven, CT: Yale University Press, 2016.

Cody, Francis. "Publics and Politics." *Annual Review of Anthropology* 40, no. 1 (2011): 37–52.

Condee, Nancy. *The Imperial Trace: Recent Russian Cinema*. Oxford: Oxford University Press, 2009.

de Benoist, Alain, ed. *Critiques: Théoriques*. Lausanne: L'Age d'Homme, 2003.

———. *Le mai 68 de la nouvelle droite*. Paris: Labyrinthe, 1998.

———. *Vue de droite: Anthologie critique des idées contemporaines*. Paris: Copernic, 1977.

Debord, Guy. *Society of the Spectacle*. Detroit, MI: Black & Red, 2000.

Degot', Ekaterina. "Mog li ul'trapravyi natsionalist ne poluchit' premiiu Kandinskogo?" *Openspace.ru*, December 11, 2008.

de Herte, Robert [Alain de Benoist]. "Faut-il être 'postmoderne'?" *Éléments: Pour la civilisation européenne* 60 (Fall 1986).

Deleuze, Gilles. "Postscript on the Societies of Control." *October* 59 (1992): 3–7.

Deleuze, Gilles, and Félix Guattari. *Anti-Oedipus: Capitalism and Schizophrenia*. New York: Viking Adult, 1977.

Delez, Zhil' [Deleuze, Gilles]. "Obshchestvo kontrolia." *Elementy* 9 (2000).

Dobrenko, E. A. *The Making of the State Reader: Social and Aesthetic Contexts of the Reception of Soviet Literature*. Stanford: Stanford University Press, 1997.

Dodolev, E. *Limoniana, ili neizvestnyi Limonov*. Moscow: Zebra E, 2012.

Doze, Pierre. "Novonovosibirsk." *Citizen K International* (Fall 2000): 199–200.

Dragosei, Fabrizio. "Venticinque italiani indagati per aver combattuto in Ucraina." *Corriere della Sera*, April 19, 2018.

Dubovitskii, Natan [Vladislav Surkov]. *Okolonolia*. Moscow: Russkii pioner, 2009.

Dugin, A. *Konspirologiia*. Moscow: Arktogeia, 1993.

Dugin, Aleksandr. *Chetvertaia politicheskaia teoriia: Rossiia i politicheskie idei XXI veka*. St. Petersburg: Amfora, 2009.

———. *Chetvertyi Put': Vvedenie v chetvertuiu politicheskuiu teoriiu*. Moscow: Akademicheskii proekt, 2014.

———. *Elementy*. Moscow, 1992–2000 (10 issues). Now available online: elements.lenin.ru/.

———. "Evraziiskaia oprichnina vosstanovit v Rossii sakral'nuiu vlast'." *Evraziia: Informatsionno-analiticheskii portal*, February 29, 2005.

———. "Fashizm, bezgranichnyi i krasnyi." 1997. arctogaia.com/public/templars/arbeiter.htm#fash.

———. *Filosofiia traditsionalizma: Lektsii novogo universiteta*. Moscow: Arktogeia-tsentr, 2002.

———. *The Fourth Political Theory*. London: Arktos, 2012.

———. *Geopolitika postmoderna*. St. Petersburg: Amfora, 2007.

———. "Iosif Stalin: velikoe 'da' bytiia." In *Russkaia veshch': Ocherki natsional'noi filosofii*, 1:468–78. 2 vols. Moscow: Arktogeia, 2001.

———. "Kogda nikogo net." *Elementy* 9 (2000).

———. "Liudi dlinnoi voli." *Elementy* 4 (1993).

———. *Misterii Evrazii*. Moscow: Arktogeia: 1996.

———. "O Limonove, NBP, i neofashizme." *Arktogeia—Filosofskii Portal*, April 14, 1999. arcto.ru/article/861.

———. "Opyt svastiki." Festival, Performansa pri uchastii zhurnala *Elementy*, *Al'-Manakh*; Moscow, November 7–11, 1994.

———. *Osnovy Geopolitiki: Geopoliticheskoe budushchee Rossii*. Moscow: Arktogeia, 2000.

———. "Paradigma kontsa." *Elementy* 9 (2000).

———. *Pop-kul'tura i znaki vremeni.* St. Petersburg: Amfora, 2005.
———. "Postmodern?" *Elementy* 9 (2000).
———. *The Rise of the Fourth Political Theory: The Fourth Political Theory.* Vol. 2. London: Arktos, 2017.
———. *Russkaia veshch': Ocherki natsional'noi filosofii.* Moscow: Arktogeia, 2001.
———. *Tampliery proletariata: Natsional-bol'shevizm i initsiatsiia.* Moscow: Arktogeia, 1997.
———. *Tseli i zadachi nashei revoliutsii.* Moscow: Fravarti, 1995.
———. "Zaria v sapogakh (Ideal'naia spetssluzhba)." *Zavtra* 13 (March 27, 2000).
"Dugin: Pravda o Limonove." *Vzgliad*, May 18, 2007.
"Dugin's Guideline—In Trump We Trust." YouTube, March 4, 2016. youtube.com /watch?v=aOWIoMtIvDQ.
Dunlop, John. "Aleksandr Dugin's Foundations of Geopolitics." *Demokratizatsiya* 12, no. 4 (Winter 2004): 41–57.
———. "Aleksandr Dugin's 'Neo-Eurasian' Textbook and Dmitrii Trenin's Ambivalent Response." *Harvard Ukrainian Studies* 25, no. 1/2 (2001): 91–127.
Dzhalogoniia, V. and B. Chekhonin. "Eto gor'koe slovo 'razocharovanie.'" *Nedelia* 8 (1976): 23–29.
Dziewańska, Marta, Ekaterina Degot', Ilia Budraitskis, and Anna Aslanyan, eds. *Post-post-Soviet? Art, Politics and Society in Russia at the Turn of the Decade.* Chicago: University of Chicago Press, 2012.
"Eduard Limonov (interv'iu)" (with Viktor Erofeev). *Ogonek* 7, no. 3264 (February 10–17, 1990).
"Eduard Limonov: Vstrecha v kontsertnoi studii Ostankino." Pervyi kanal Ostankino. Moscow, Russian Federation, February 1992.
Elizarov, Mikhail. *Bibliotekar'.* Moscow: Ad Marginem, 2008.
———. *The Librarian.* London: Pushkin Press, 2015.
Emelin, Vsevolod. *Götterdämmerung: Stikhi i ballady 1991–2009.* Moscow: Ad Marginem, 2010.
———. *Istoriia s geografiei.* Moscow: AST: 2011.
———. *Politshanson.* Moscow: Falanster: 2014.
Engström, Maria. "Apollo against Black Square: Conservative Futurism in Contemporary Russia." In *International Yearbook of Futurism Studies*, vol. 6, edited by Günter Berghaus, 328–53. Berlin: De Gruyter, 2016.
———. "Metamodernizm i postsovetskii konservativnyi avangard: Novaia akademiia Timura Novikova." *Novoe literaturnoe obozrenie* 3, no. 151 (2018). magazines.russ.ru /nlo/2018/3/tajnoe-stanet-yavnym-no-tolko-bez-kritiki.html.
———. "Military Dandyism, Cosmism and Eurasian Imper-Art." In *Russia's New Fin De Siècle: Contemporary Culture Between Past and Present*, edited by Birgit Beumers, 99–119. Bristol, UK: Intellect, 2013.
Epshtein, Alek. *Iskusstvo na barrikadakh: "Pussy Riot," "Avtobusnaia Vystavka" i protestnyi art-aktivizm.* Moscow: "Kolonna Publications," 2012.
———. *Total'naia "voina": Art-aktivizm epokhi tandemokratii.* Jerusalem: Georgy Eremin—Umlaut Network, 2012.
Epshtein, Alek, Viktor Bondarenko, Evgeniia Mal'tseva, and Sergey Popov. *Dukhovnaia bran'.* Moscow: Galereia Guelman, 2012.
Epstein, Mikhail. *After the Future: The Paradoxes of Postmodernism and Contemporary Russian Culture.* Amherst: University of Massachusetts Press, 1995.

———. *The Transformative Humanities: A Manifesto*. New York: Bloomsbury, 2012.

Erofeev, Viktor. "Literatura i politika." Radio Svoboda, *Entsiklopediia russkoi dushi*, October 1, 2005.

Esanu, Octavian. *Transition in Post-Soviet Art: The Collective Actions Group Before and After 1989*. Budapest: Central European University Press, 2013.

Essig, Laurie. *Queer in Russia: A Story of Sex, Self, and the Other*. Durham, NC: Duke University Press, 1999.

Etkind, Aleksandr. *Internal Colonization: Russia's Imperial Experience*. Cambridge, UK: Polity, 2011.

———. *Khlyst: Sekty, literatura i revoliutsiia*. Moscow: Novoe literaturnoe obozrenie, 1998.

———. *Sodom i Psikheia: Ocherki intellektual'noi istorii serebrianogo veka*. Moscow: "ITS-Garant," 1996.

"EVRAZIIA—Informatsionno-analiticheskii portal." evrazia.org/.

"EVRAZIIA.TV." evrazia.tv/.

Felski, Rita. *Beyond Feminist Aesthetics: Feminist Literature and Social Change*. Cambridge, MA: Harvard University Press, 1989.

Ferelov, Andrei. "Moda NBP." *Zavtra* 39, no. 827 (September 23, 2009).

"Finis Mundi. Konets illiuzii." *Vimeo*. Accessed July 28, 2017. https://vimeo.com/24243791.

Foster, Hal. "Postmodernism: A Preface." In *The Anti-Aesthetic: Essays on Postmodern Culture*, edited by Hal Foster, ix–xvi. Port Townsend, WA: Bay Press, 1983.

Fraser, Nancy. "Rethinking the Public Sphere: A Contribution to the Critique of Actually Existing Democracy." *Social Text* 25/26 (1990): 56–80.

Fuller, Thomas, and Christopher Mele. "Berkeley Cancels Milo Yiannopoulos Speech, and Donald Trump Tweets Outrage." *New York Times*, February 1, 2017.

Furlong, Paul. *Social and Political Thought of Julius Evola*. New York: Routledge, 2011.

Fürst, Juliane, and Josie McLellan, eds. *Dropping out of Socialism: The Creation of Alternative Spheres in the Soviet Bloc*. Lanham, MD: Rowman & Littlefield, 2016.

Gabowitsch, Mischa. "Fascism as Stiob." *Kultura*, no. 4 (December 2009).

———. *Protest in Putin's Russia*. Cambridge, UK: Polity, 2017.

"GAY.RU—Timur Novikov: '. . . Nevynosima legkost' bytiia.'" Accessed August 30, 2018. gay.ru/people/star/russian/xx-xxi/timur-novikov-nevynosima.html.

Geertz, Clifford. *The Interpretation of Cultures: Selected Essays*. New York: Basic, 1973.

"Geidar Dzhemal' o sebe, 'Iuzhinskom kruzhke' i Evgenii Golovine." Accessed August 29, 2018. youtube.com/.

Genis, Aleksandr. "Strashnyi son. O romane Vladimira Sorokina 'Goluboe salo'" (October 1999). Srkn.ru.

Gessen, Keith. "Monumental Foolishness. The Decline and Fall of a Man Who Once Seemed Poised to Become the Next Great Émigré Writer." *Slate*, February 20, 2003.

Gessen, Masha. *Dead Again: The Russian Intelligentsia after Communism*. London: Verso, 1997.

———. *The Future Is History: How Totalitarianism Reclaimed Russia*. New York: Riverhead, 2018.

———. "NBP liubit vas." *Bol'shoi gorod*, January 31, 2005.

———. *Words Will Break Cement: The Passion of Pussy Riot*. New York: Riverhead, 2014.

Glebov, Sergey. *From Empire to Eurasia: Politics, Scholarship, and Ideology in Russian Eurasianism, 1920s–1930s*. DeKalb: Northern Illinois University Press, 2017.

Gofman, Patrick. *Patrick Gofman présente l'affaire Limonov: Le dossier*. Paris: Dualpha, 2003.

Gol'dshtein, Aleksandr. "Eduard velikolepnyi." In *Rasstavanie s nartsissom: Opyty nominal'noi retoriki*, 328–49. Moscow: Novoe literaturnoe obozrenie, 1997.

Golynko-Vol'fson, Dmitrii. "Chert s mladentsem, ili vzroslenie nartsissa." *Novoe literaturnoe obozrenie* 56 (2002): 310–16.

Goodrick-Clarke, Nicholas. *Black Sun: Aryan Cults, Esoteric Nazism, and the Politics of Identity*. New York: New York University Press, 2003.

———. *The Occult Roots of Nazism: Secret Aryan Cults and Their Influence on Nazi Ideology*. Reprint edition. New York: New York University Press, 1993.

Gork'ii, Maksim. *Mat'*. 1907. Reprinted in *Vospominaniia*. Moscow: Khudozhestvennaia literatura, 1982. Translated into English by Margaret Wettlin as *Mother: A Novel in Two Parts*, by Maxim Gorky (Moscow: Foreign Languages Publishing House, 1954).

"Gosduma priniala zakon ob uvelichenii minimal'noi chislennosti partii do 50.000." *News.ru*, 3 December 2004.

Graña, César, and Mari Graña, eds. "The Ideological Significance of Bohemian Life." In *On Bohemia: The Code of the Self-Exiled*, edited by César Graña and Mari Graña, 3–12. New Brunswick, NJ: Transaction, 1990.

———. *On Bohemia: The Code of the Self-Exiled*. New Brunswick, NJ: Transaction, 1990.

Gray, Rosie. "Behind the Internet's Anti-Democracy Movement." *The Atlantic*, February 10, 2017.

———. "A 'One-Stop Shop' for the Alt-Right." *The Atlantic*, January 12, 2017.

Gregor, A. James. *Mussolini's Intellectuals: Fascist Social and Political Thought*. Princeton, NJ: Princeton University Press, 2009.

———. *The Search for Neofascism: The Use and Abuse of Social Science*. Cambridge: Cambridge University Press, 2006.

Gregor, A. James and Andreas Umland. "Dugin Not a Fascist? A Debate with A. James Gregor (6 texts)." *Erwägen Wissen Ethik* 15, no. 3 (2004): 424–29; *Erwägen Wissen Ethik* 15, no. 4 (2004): 591–95; *Erwägen Wissen Ethik* 16, no. 4 (2005): 566–72.

Griffin, Roger. "From Slime Mould to Rhizome: An Introduction to the Groupuscular Right." *Patterns of Prejudice* 37, no. 1 (2003): 27–50.

———. *The Nature of Fascism*. New York: Palgrave Macmillan, 1991.

———. *Modernism and Fascism: The Sense of a Beginning under Mussolini and Hitler*. Basingstoke: Palgrave Macmillan, 2007.

Gromov, Dmitry. *Ulichnye aktsii: Molodezhnyi politicheskii aktivizm v Rossii*. Moscow: Institut etnologii i antropologii RAN, 2012.

Grow, Kory. "What Laibach Learned in North Korea." *Rolling Stone*, August 15, 2015.

Groys, Boris. *The Total Art of Stalinism: Avant-garde, Aesthetic Dictatorship, and Beyond*. Princeton, NJ: Princeton University Press, 1992.

———. *Utopiia i obmen*. Moscow: Izd-vo Znak, 1993.

Gumilev, Lev. *Etnogenez i biosfera zemli*. Leningrad: Izd-vo Leningradskogo universiteta, 1989.

Habermas, Jürgen. "Modernity—An Incomplete Project." In *The Anti-Aesthetic: Essays on Postmodern Culture*, edited by Hal Foster, 3–15. Port Townsend, WA: Bay Press, 1983.

———. *The Structural Transformation of the Public Sphere: An Inquiry into a Category of Bourgeois Society*. Cambridge, MA: MIT Press, 1989.

Hardt, Michael, and Antonio Negri. *Empire*. Cambridge, MA: Harvard University Press, 2001.

Harvey, David. *The Condition of Postmodernity: An Enquiry into the Origins of Cultural Change*. Oxford: Wiley-Blackwell, 1991.

Hemment, Julie. *Youth Politics in Putin's Russia: Producing Patriots and Entrepreneurs*. Bloomington: Indiana University Press, 2015.

Horkheimer, Max, and Theodor W. Adorno. *Dialectic of Enlightenment*. Stanford, CA: Stanford University Press, 2007.

Horowitz, Jason. "Steve Bannon Cited Italian Thinker Who Inspired Fascists." *New York Times*, February 10, 2017.

Horvath, Robert. "'Sakharov Would Be with Us': Limonov, Strategy-31, and the Dissident Legacy." *Russian Review* 74, no. 4 (2015): 581–98.

"How Did Odessa's Fire Happen?" *BBC News*, May 6, 2014.

Humphrey, Caroline. *The Unmaking of Soviet Life: Everyday Economies after Socialism*. Ithaca, NY: Cornell University Press, 2002.

Huntington, Samuel P. *The Clash of Civilizations and the Remaking of World Order*. New York: Simon & Schuster, 1996.

Iakemenko, B. G. *Limonov o Limonove: I ne tol'ko*. Moscow: Krug, 2006.

Ingram, Alan. "Alexander Dugin: Geopolitics and Neo-fascism in Post-Soviet Russia." *Political Geography* 20, no. 8 (2001): 1029–51.

Ioffe, Dennis. "Modernism in the Context of Russian 'Life-Creation': 'Lebenskunst' and the Theory of 'Life ⇔ Text' Sign Systems." *New Zealand Slavonic Journal*, no. 40 (2006): 22–55.

Ippolitov, Arkadii, and Aleksandr Kharitonov, eds. *Novaia Akademiia. Sankt-Peterburg: Katalog vystavki*. Moscow: Fond kul'tury "Ekaterina," 2011.

Jameson, Fredric. *Postmodernism, or, the Cultural Logic of Late Capitalism*. Durham, NC: Duke University Press, 1992.

Jencks, Charles. *The Language of Post-Modern Architecture*. London: Rizzoli, 1977.

———. *Post-Modernism: The New Classicism in Art and Architecture*. New York: Rizzoli, 1987.

———. *What Is Post-Modernism?* London: Academy Press, 1996.

Johnson, Lena. *Art and Protest in Putin's Russia*. New York: Routledge, 2015.

Johnson, Reuben. "The Putin Jugend." *The Weekly Standard*, July 30, 2007.

Kagarlitsky, Boris. *Restoration in Russia: Why Capitalism Failed*. London: Verso, 1995.

Kamardin, Artem. "Ubei menia, opolchenets!" *Stikhi.ru*, 2015.

Kan, Aleksandr. *Kurekhin: Shkiper o kapitane*. St. Petersburg: Amfora, 2012.

Karskens, Machiel. *Chronological Bibliography of the Works of Michel Foucault*. foucault.info, June 2014.

Kas'ian, Aleksei. "Moskovskii khudozhnik Anton Nikolaev demonstrativno vstupil v zapreshchennuiu NBP." *Pravda.ru*, July 10, 2008.

"Katehon Think Tank. Geopolitics & Tradition." July 26, 2017. katehon.com/.

"Katekhizis chlena Evraziiskogo soiuza molodezhi." *Rossiia 3—Evraziiskii soiuz molodezhi*, n.d.

Khlobystin, Andrei. *Shizorevoliutsiia: Ocherki peterburgskoi kul'tury vtoroi poloviny XX veka*. St. Petersburg: Borei Art, 2017.

"KNIGI EVRAZII." July 26, 2017. evrazia-books.ru/.

Knorre-Dmitrieva, Kseniia. "Aktivisty NOD napali na uchastnikov shkol'nogo konkursa 'Memoriala' v Moskve i oblili zelenkoi Ulitskuiu." *Novaia Gazeta*, April 28, 2016.

Kostrova, Natal'ia. "Kontrkul'tura SSSR: Petliura i kompaniia o podpol'noi mode v SSSR." *Afisha*, April 29, 2011.

Kovalev, Andrei. *Rossiiskii aktsionizm: 1990–2000*. Moscow: World Art Museum, 2007.

Kozhevnikova, Galina, Aleksandr Verkhovskii, and Eugene Veklerov. *Ultra-nationalism and Hate Crimes in Contemporary Russia: The 2004–2006 Annual Reports of Moscow's SOVA Center*. Stuttgart: Ibidem-Verlag, 2008.

Krasok, Iuliia. "Aleksei Beliaev-Gintovt: Vse mechty vosstaiut." *Advertology.ru*, October 4, 2012.

Kratkii kurs istorii natsbolov. Moscow: Drugaia Rossiia, 2016.

Kron, Andrei. "Pro babochku poetinogo sertdsa." *Kovcheg* 3 (1979): 89–96.

Krusanov, Pavel. *Amerikanskaia dyrka*. St. Petersburg: Amfora, 2005.

———. *Ukus angela*. St. Petersburg: Amfora, 2003.

Kukulin, Il'ia. "Longing for Fear and Darkness: 'Oppositional Grassroots Stalinism' of the 1970s–1980s and Its Influence on Legitimizing Political Elites in Today's Russia." Translated by Philip Redko. In *Post-Soviet Nostalgia: Confronting the Empire's Legacies*, edited by Otto Boele, Boris Noordenbos, and Ksenia Robbe, 89–114. New York: Routledge, 2019.

———. "Prigov i Limonov: k poniatiiu postmodernistskogo zhiznetvorchestva." Forthcoming.

———. "Reaktsiia dissotsiatsii: Legitimizatsiia ul'trapravogo diskursa v sovremennoi rossiiskoi literature." In *Russkii natsionalizm: Sotsial'nyi i kul'turnyi kontekst*, edited by Marlène Laruelle, 257–338. Moscow: Novoe literaturnoe obozrenie, 2008.

———. "Revoliutsiia oblezlykh drakonov: Ul'trapravaia ideia kak imitatsiia nonkonformizma." *Polit.ru*, April 8, 2007.

———. "VRIO vmesto Klio: Obrazy istorii v dvukh literaturno-istoricheskikh polemikakh 2008 goda." *Pro et Contra* 13, no. 1 (February 2009): 20–35.

Kulik, Oleg, and Yuri Surkov. *Oleg Kulik: The Mad Dog, or Last Taboo Guarded by Alone Cerberus*. Bielefeld: Kerber, 2013.

Kurekhin, Sergei. "Esli vy romantik—vy fashist! Interv'iu c Sergeem Kurekhinym." *Elementy* 8 (1996).

Kurina, Aksin'ia. "Anatolii Osmolovskii: '90 protsentov sovremennogo iskusstva—vobshche ne iskusstvo.'" *Ukrainskaia pravda*, February 9, 2009.

Kushnir, Aleksandr. *Sergei Kurekhin: Bezumnaia mekhanika russkogo roka*. Moscow: Berstel'man Media Moscau, 2013.

Kuskov, Sergei. "Vystavka-proekt *ekstremizm i erotika*. 24.11—24.12.1995. Galereia Limonova." Moscow, November 20, 1995 (Mikhail Roshniak personal archive).

Kuznetsova, Ol'ga. "Utopiia goszakaza." *ArtKhronika* 5–11 (March 2002): 58–61.

Laibach. "Art and Totalitarianism Are Not Mutually Exclusive." *Official Laibach*. Accessed September 8, 2018. laibach.org/statements/.

———. "XY—UNSOLVED." *TV Weekly*, Ljubljana, June 24, 1983. laibach.org/xy-unsolved/.

Laruelle, Marlène, "Dangerous Liaisons: Eurasianism, the European Far Right, and Putin's Russia." In *Eurasianism and the European Far Right: Reshaping the Europe-Russia Relationship*, edited by Marlène Laruelle, 1–32. Lanham, MD: Lexington, 2015.

———. *Eurasianism and the European Far Right: Reshaping the Europe-Russia Relationship*. Lanham, MD: Lexington, 2015.

———. "Is Nationalism a Force for Change in Russia?" *Daedalus* 146, no. 2 (March 27, 2017): 89–100. https://doi.org/10.1162/DAED_a_00437.

———. "Is Russia Really 'Fascist'? A Comment on Timothy Snyder." *PonarsEurasia*, September 5, 2018. ponarseurasia.org/memo/russia-really-fascist-reply-timothy-snyder.

———. "The Iuzhinskii Circle: Far-Right Metaphysics in the Soviet Underground and Its Legacy Today." *Russian Review* 74, no. 4 (2015): 563–80.

———. *Russian Eurasianism: An Ideology of Empire*. Washington, DC: Woodrow Wilson Center, 2008.

Lassila, Jussi. *The Quest for an Ideal Youth in Putin's Russia II: The Search for Distinctive Conformism in the Political Communication of Nashi, 2005–2009*. Stuttgart: Ibidem-Verlag, 2014.

Latour, Bruno. *An Inquiry into Modes of Existence: An Anthropology of the Moderns*. Cambridge, MA: Harvard University Press, 2013.

———. *We Have Never Been Modern*. Cambridge, MA: Harvard University Press, 1993.

Leibov, Roman. "Occasional Political Poetry and the Culture of the Russian Internet." In *Digital Russia: The Language, Culture and Politics of New Media Communication*, edited by Michael Gorham, Ingunn Lunde, and Martin Paulsen, 194–214. New York: Routledge, 2014.

Letov, Egor. "Moia oborona." 1989. *Grazhdanskaia oborona, Ofitsial'nyi sait gruppy*. gr-oborona.ru/texts/1056898718.html.

"Lichno v ruki. Spisok ubitykh i presleduemykh oppozitsionerov, peredannyi Garri Kasparovym Baraku Obame." *Kasparov.ru*, July 8, 2009.

Likhachev, Viacheslav. *Natsizm v Rossii*. Moscow: Panorama, 2002.

Limonov, Eduard. "The ABSOLUTE BEGINNER ili Pravdivaia istoriia sochineniia 'Eto ia—Edichka.'" In *Eto ia—Edichka*, 323–34. Moscow: Glagol, 1990.

———. *Anatomiia geroia*. Moscow: Rusich, 1997.

———. "Distsiplinarnyi sanatorii." In *Ubiistvo chasovogo*, 181–360. Moscow: "Molodaia gvardiia," 1993.

———. *Dnevnik neudachnika—Diary of a Loser* [Russian and English versions]. Moscow: Literaturnyi institut im. A. M. Gor'kogo, 2002. First edition: *Dnevnik neudachnika*. New York: Index Publishers, 1982.

———. *Drugaia Rossiia*. Moscow: Ul'tra. Kul'tura, 2003.

———. *Eto ia—Edichka*. New York: Index Publishers, 1979; Moscow: Glagol, 1990.

———. "Gruppa 'Konkret.'" In *Apollon-77*, edited by Mikhail Shemiakin, 43–46. Paris: M. Chemiakine, 1977.

———. *Inostranets v smutnoe vremia*. 1993. Reprint, St. Petersburg: Amfora, 2007.

———. *Ischeznovenie varvarov: Stat'i, esse*. Moscow: Glagol, 1993.

———. *It's Me, Eddie. A Fictional Memoir*. New York: Random House, 1983.

———. "Izvrashcheniia natsionalizma." *Novyi vzgliad* 34 (August 7, 1993).

———. *Limonov v fotografiiakh s kommentariiami, napisannymi im samym! Ego blizkie, ego roditeli, ego voiny, ego zheny*, edited by Boris Gusev. Moscow: Stompo, 1996.

———. *Mal'chik, begi! Stikhotvoreniia*. St. Petersburg: Limbus-Press, 2009.

———. "Manifest rossiiskogo natsionalizma." *Sovetskaia Rossiia* (June 12, 1992).

———. *Memoir of a Russian Punk* [Podrostok Savenko]. Translated by Judson Rosengrant. New York: Grove Weidenfeld, 1990.

———. *Moia politicheskaia biografiia*. St. Petersburg: Amfora, 2002.

———. *Moi otritsatel'nyi geroi: Stikhi 1976–1982 godov*. Moscow: Glagol, 1995.

———. "Molodoi negodiai." In *Russkoe*, 323–543. Moscow: Ad Marginem, 2005. First edition: *Molodoi negodiai*. Paris: Sintaksis, 1986.

———. "My—Natsional'nyi geroi." In *Apollon-77*, edited by Mikhail Shemiakin, 57–62. Paris: M. Chemiakine, 1977.

———. "Ne putaite menia s Limonovym." Interview by Andrey Vandenko. *Novyi Vzgliad* 12 (April 4, 1992).

———. "Neterpimost'." *Novoe russkoe slovo*, January 13, 1976.

———. "Pisatel'—ne professiia." *Nezavisimaia gazeta*, November 13, 2014.

———. "Podrostok Savenko." In *Russkoe*, 129–322. Moscow: Ad Marginem, 2005. First edition: *Podrostok Savenko*. Paris: "Sintaksis," 1983.

———. Pro'povedi. *Protiv vlasti i prodazhnoi oppozitsii*. Moscow: Eksmo, 2013.

———. "Punk and National-Bolshevism." *The eXile*, January 26, 2007.

———. "Razocharovanie." *Novoe russkoe slovo*, November 21, 1975.

———. "Russkaia oppozitsiia i zapad." *Novoe russkoe slovo*, November 2, 1975.

———. *Russkoe*. Moscow: Ad Marginem, 2005.

———. *SMRT (Rasskazy)*. St. Petersburg: Amfora, 2008.

———. *Ubiistvo chasovogo: Stat'i*. Moscow: Molodaia gvardiia, 1993.

———. "U nas byla velikaia epokha." In *Russkoe*, 7–129. Moscow: Ad Marginem, 2005. First Russian edition: "U nas byla velikaia epokha," *Znamia* 11 (November 1989): 4–77. First Russian book edition: *U nas byla velikaia epokha*. Edited by Yaroslav Mogutin. Moscow: Konets Veka, 1994. First published in French: *La grande époque*. Paris: Flammarion, 1989.

———. "Zhit' ne po lzhi." *Novoe russkoe slovo*, July 6, 1975.

"Limonovy Performans. Bunker NBP (1995)." YouTube, 2011. youtube.com/watch?v=TRZt1YbSKTY.

Lipovetsky, Mark. "Goluboe salo pokoleniia, ili dva mifa ob odnom krizise." *Znamia* 11 (November 1999): 207–15.

———. *Paralogii: Transformatsii (post)modernistskogo diskursa v russkoi kul'ture 1920–2000-kh godov*. Moscow: Novoe literaturnoe obozrenie, 2008.

———. *Russian Postmodernist Fiction: Dialogue with Chaos*. New York: M. E. Sharpe, 1999.

Lipovetsky, Mark, Jonathan Brooks Platt, Ellen Rutten, Maria Engström, and Kevin Platt. "Postmodernizm v epokhu 'pravykh povorotov' i populizma." Special Section in *Novoe literaturnoe obozrenie* 151, no. 3 (2018).

Livers, Keith. "The Tower or the Labyrinth: Conspiracy, Occult, and Empire-Nostalgia in the Work of Viktor Pelevin and Aleksandr Prokhanov." *Russian Review* 69, no. 3 (July 2010): 477–503.

Lotman, Iurii [Yuri]. "Dekabrist v povsednevnoi zhizni (bytovoe povedenie kak istoriko-psikhologicheskaia kategoriia)." In *Izbrannye stat'i v trekh tomakh*, vol. 1, 296–337. Tallinn: Aleksandra, 1992.

———. *Istoriia i tipologiia russkoi kul'tury*. St. Petersburg: Iskusstvo-SPb, 2002.

———. "Literatura v kontekste russkoi kul'tury XVIII veka." In *O russkoi literature: Stat'i i issledovaniia 1958–1993*, 118–60. St. Petersburg: Iskusstvo, 1997.

———. "Poetika bytovogo povedeniia v russkoi kul'ture XVIII veka." In *Istoriia i tipologiia russkoi kul'tury*, 248–69. St. Petersburg: Iskusstvo-SPb, 2002.

———. "Rol' dual'nykh modelei v dinamike russkoi kul'tury (do kontsa XVIII veka)." In *Istoriia i tipologiia russkoi kul'tury*, 88–116. Saint Petersburg: Iskusstvo-SPb, 2002.

Lotman, Iurii, and Boris Uspenskii. "Novye aspekty izucheniia kul'tury drevnei Rusi." *Voprosy literatury*, no. 3 (1977): 1959–61.

———. "Otzvuki kontseptsii 'Moskva-tretii Rim' v ideologii Petra Pervogo (k probleme srednevekovoi traditsii v kul'ture barokko)." In *Istoriia i tipologiia russkoi kul'tury*, by Iu. M. Lotman, 349–62. Saint Petersburg: Iskusstvo-SPb, 2002.

Lyotard, Jean-François. *The Postmodern Condition: A Report on Knowledge*. Minneapolis: University of Minnesota Press, 1984.

Magun, Artemy. *Negative Revolution: Modern Political Subject and its Fate after the Cold War*. New York: Bloomsbury Academic, 2013.

Mamleev, Iurii. "Shatuny." In *Sobranie sochinenii*, 1:7–235. Moscow: Eksmo, 2016.

———. *Vospominaniia*. Moscow: Traditsiia, 2017.

Mamleyev, Yuri [Iurii Mamleev]. *The Sublimes* [Shatuny]. Translated by Marian Schwartz. Independently published, 2016.

"Manifest molodezhnogo dvizheniia 'NASHI.'" *Nashi.su*, October 25, 2005.

Marcuse, Herbert. *Eros and Civilization: A Philosophical Inquiry into Freud*. Vintage Books, 1961.

Mathyl, Markus. "The National-Bolshevik Party and Arctogaia: Two Neo-fascist Groupuscules in the Post-Soviet Political Space." *Patterns of Prejudice* 36, no. 3 (2002): 62–76.

———. "Nationalisme et contre-culture jeune dans la Russie de l'après-perestroïka." In *Le rouge et le noir: Extrême droite et nationalisme en Russie*, edited by Marlène Laruelle, 115–33. Paris: CNRS Éditions, 2007.

———. "Natsionalizm i kontrkul'tura v postperestroechnoi Rossii." In *Russkii natsionalizm v politicheskom prostranstve*, edited by Marlène Laruelle, 76–100. Moscow: Franko-Rossiiskii tsentr gumanitarnykh i obshchestvennykh nauk, 2007.

Matich, Olga. "Eduard Limonov: Istoriia avtora i ego personazha." *Oktiabr'* 11 (2013).

———. "The Moral Immoralist: Edward Limonov's *Èto Ja—Èdička*." *Slavic and East European Journal* 30, no. 4 (1986): 526–40.

Matich, Olga, and Michael Heim, eds. *The Third Wave: Russian Literature in Emigration*. Ann Arbor, MI: Ardis, 1984.

Mattioli, Valerio. "Quando i rossobruni diventano mainstream." *Not. Nero Editions*, October 9, 2017. https://not.neroeditions.com/crobuzon-1-rossobruni/.

McFaul, Michael. *Russia's Unfinished Revolution: Political Change from Gorbachev to Putin*. Ithaca, NY: Cornell University Press, 2001.

Medvedev, Aleksandr. *Pokhishchenie Evropy: Iskusstvo, torgovlia, voina*. St. Petersburg: Khudozhestvennaia volia, 1999.

———. *Pokhishchenie razuma: Zhertvy iskusstva. Nasledniki khrama*. St. Petersburg: Khudozhestvennaia volia, 2001.

Medvedev, Aleksandr, and Timur Novikov. *Belyi lebed': Korol' Ludvig II Bavarskii*. St. Petersburg: Novaia akademiia iziashchnykh iskusstv, 2002.

Medvedev, Kirill. *It's No Good: Poems / Essays / Actions*. New York: Ugly Duckling Presse, 2012.

———. "Moi fashizm." In *Bunt gumanizma*. Moscow, 2004. kirillmedvedev.narod.ru/my-fascism--.html.

———. "Sait poeta Kirilla Medvedeva." kirillmedvedev.narod.ru/.

Medvedev, Roy. *Post-Soviet Russia: A Journey through the Yeltsin Era*. New York: Columbia University Press, 2000.

Medvedeva, Nataliia. "Poedem na voinu!" 1995. YouTube, July 29, 2011. youtube.com/watch?v=PkZsZX4DTxA.

Michel, Casey. "Beyond Trump and Putin: The American Alt-Right's Love of the Kremlin's Policies." *The Diplomat*, October 13, 2016.

———. "Meet the Moscow Mouthpiece Married to a Racist Alt-Right Boss." *Daily Beast*, December 20, 2016.

Mihailovic, Alexandar. *The Mitki and the Art of Postmodern Protest in Russia*. Madison: University of Wisconsin Press, 2018.

"Misuse of Anti-extremism/SOVA." Report by SOVA Center for Information and Analysis, July 26, 2016.

Miziano, Viktor. "Mir chrevat neoliberal'nymi simptomami." *Elementy* 9 (2000).

Mogutin, Iaroslav. "Eduard Limonov, sovetsko-frantsuzskii natsional'nyi geroi." *Novyi Vzgliad* 101 (1992): 1.

———. *30 interv'iu*. St. Petersburg: Limbus, 2001.

———. "Vospominaniia russkogo panka, ili, avtoportret bandita v molodosti." In *U nas byla velikaia epokha*, edited by Eduard Limonov, 158–87. Moscow: Konets Veka, 1994.

Monroe, Alexei. *Interrogation Machine: Laibach and NSK*. Cambridge, MA: MIT Press, 2005.

"Moskva: 'Strategiia 31,' Triumfal'naia ploshchad' 31.05.14." *Drugros.ru*, June 2, 2014. drugros.ru/galeries/4086.0.html.

"Nadia Tolokno—Format voiny dolzhen stat' zhanrom, k kotoromu budut pribegat' ispytivaiushchie potrebnost' v proteste." *Novoe Vremia—The New Times* (Moscow), April 11, 2011.

"Napadenie na natsbolov v Moskve." Report by SOVA Center for Information and Analysis, July 30, 2005.

"Napadenie na Naval'nogo v Moskve." News. *Mediazona*. zona.media/chronicle/zelenka.

"Natsbolam piatyi raz za poslednie vosem' let otkazali v registratsii partii." *Newsru.com*, January 30, 2006.

Newman, Dina. "Russian Nationalist Thinker Dugin Sees War with Ukraine." *BBC News*, July 10, 2014.

Neyfakh, Leon. "Putin's Long Game? Meet the Eurasian Union." *Boston Globe*, March 9, 2014.

Nikitina, Tania. "Pervyi moskovskii festival performansa." Moscow, 1994 (Mikhail Roshniak personal archive).

Noordenbos, Boris. *Post-Soviet Literature and the Search for a Russian Identity*. New York: Palgrave Macmillan, 2016.

Novikov, Timur. "Georgii Gurianov." In *Novyi russkii klassitsizm*. St. Petersburg: Novaia akademiia iziashnykh iskusstv, 1998. timurnovikov.ru/library/knigi-i-stati-timura-petrovicha-novikova/.

———. "Ideia totalitarnogo iskusstva i antichnost'." In *Novyi russkii klassitsizm*, 53–70. St. Petersburg: Novaia akademiia iziashchnykh iskusstv, 1998. timurnovikov.ru/library/knigi-i-stati-timura-petrovicha-novikova/.

———. *Lektsii*. St. Petersburg: Novaia akademiia iziashchnykh iskusstv, 2003. timurnovikov.ru/library/knigi-i-stati-timura-petrovicha-novikova/.

———. "Neskol'ko slov po povodu takogo strannogo iavleniia kak neoakademizm." In *Novyi russkii klassitsizm*. St. Petersburg: Novaia akademiia iziashchnykh iskusstv, 1998. timurnovikov.ru/library/knigi-i-stati-timura-petrovicha-novikova/.

———. "Novye khudozhniki." In *Lektsii*. St. Petersburg: Novaia akademiia iziashchnykh iskusstv, 2003. timurnovikov.ru/library/lektsii.

———. "Novyi russkii klassitsizm." In *Novyi russkii klassitsizm.* St. Petersburg: Novaia akademiia iziashchnykh iskusstv, 1998. timurnovikov.ru/library/knigi-i-stati-timura-petrovicha-novikova/.

———. "Peterburgskoe iskusstvo 1990-kh godov." In *Lektsii.* St. Petersburg: Novaia akademiia iziashchnykh iskusstv, 2003. timurnovikov.ru/library/lektsii.

———. "Sever-Iug." 1997. timurnovikov.ru/library/knigi-i-stati-timura-petrovicha-novikova/.

———. "Soprotivlenie i vozrozhdenie: Klassicheskie traditsii iskusstva i istoriia fotografii." Kommentarii k vystavke v gosudarstvennom russkom muzee, 1994. newacademy.spb.ru/Timur/soprivoz.html.

Novikov, Timur, and Iosif Brodskii. *Gorizonty.* St. Peterburg: Institut istorii sovremennogo iskusstva, 2000.

Novikov, Timur, Aleksandr Dugin, and Miran Mohar. "Dogovor: Evropeiskoe obshchestvo klassicheskoi estetiki." In *Velikaia khudozhestvennaia volia: Ezhegodnik muzeia novoi akademii iziashchnykh iskusstv.* St. Petersburg: Kare, 1999.

Novikov, Timur, and Georgii Gurianov. "Sila krasoty." *Novyi russkii klassitsizm.* St. Petersburg: Novaia akademiia iziashchnykh iskusstv, 1998.

"Novyi universitet." nu.evrazia.org/index.html.

"Ob eskhatologicheskom lagere *FINIS MUNDI*: Dugin na Russia.ru." *Evrazia.tv,* November 21, 2011.

Obukhova, Aleksandra. *Performans v Rossii, 1910–2010: Kartografiia istorii. Katalog.* Moscow: Tsentr sovremennoi kul'tury "Garazh," 2014.

Ofitserova, Evgeniia, and Maksim Litavrin. "Napadeniia na oppozitsiiu, pomoshch' separatizma i konspirologiia. Chto nuzhno znat' o NOD." *Openrussia.ru,* April 13, 2016.

"Oktiabr'skoe vosstanie 1993 goda." 1993. sovnarkom.ru.

O'Meara, Michael. *New Culture, New Right: Anti-Liberalism in Postmodern Europe.* Bloomington, IN: 1stBooks, 2004.

Ong, Walter J. "The Writer's Audience Is Always a Fiction." *PMLA* 90, no. 1 (1975): 9–21.

Osipov, Georgii. "Sadoeroticheskii natsional-satanizm." *Elementy* 9 (2000).

Osmolovskii, Anatolii [Anatoly Osmolovsky] (exhibition curator). *Antifashizm i anti-antifashizm.* Moscow: Molodezh' protiv rasizma v Evrope, gazeta Rabochaia demokratiia, Tsentr sovremenngo iskusstva, zhurnal Radek, 1996.

———. "Zaiavlenie Osmolovskogo o vruchenii premii Kandinskogo Alekseiu Beliaevu-Gintovtu." *Osmopolis.ru,* 2008.

Ostrovsky, Arkady. *The Invention of Russia: The Rise of Putin and the Age of Fake News.* New York: Penguin, 2017.

Oushakine, Serguei. "In the State of Post-Soviet Aphasia: Symbolic Development in Contemporary Russia." *Europe-Asia Studies* 52, no. 6 (2000): 991–1016.

———. *The Patriotism of Despair: Nation, War, and Loss in Russia.* Ithaca, NY: Cornell University Press, 2009.

"PACE Rapporteur on Media Freedom Expresses His Deep Frustration at the Lack of Progress in Investigating the Murder of Anna Politkovskaia in Russia." *PACE: All the News.* Parliamentary Assembly. Counsel of Europe, February 20, 2009.

Paperno, Irina, and Grossman, Joan Delaney, eds. *Creating Life: The Aesthetic Utopia of Russian Modernism.* Stanford, CA: Stanford University Press, 1994.

Paperny, Vladimir. *Architecture in the Age of Stalin: Culture Two*. Cambridge: Cambridge University Press, 2002.

Parfrey, Adam, ed. *Apocalypse Culture*. Portland, OR: Feral House, 1990.

Pawlikowski, Pawel, dir. *Serbian Epics*. London: BBC, 1992.

Pelevin, Victor. *Generation P.* Moscow: Vagrius, 1999.

———. *Homo Zapiens*. New York: Penguin Books, 2002.

"Pervyi moskovskii festival' performansa—Programma vystavki." Moscow, November 25–27, 1994.

"Piat' gromkikh zaiavlenii Putina ob istorii Ukrainy." *BBC News*, October 10, 2014.

Pilkington, Hilary. *Russia's Youth and Its Culture: A Nation's Constructors and Constructed*. New York: Routledge, 1994.

Pinkham, Sophie. "Timothy Snyder's Bleak Vision." *The Nation*, May 28, 2018.

Plutser-Sarno, Aleksei. "Aleksei Beliaev-Gintovt sozdal khudozhestvennoe ob"edinenie FSB—'Front Spokoinogo Blagodenstvii.'" *Plucer Live Journal* (blog), December 15, 2008. https://plucer.livejournal.com/124476.html.

Poggioli, Renato. *The Theory of the Avant-Garde*. Cambridge, MA: Harvard University Press, 1968.

Politkovskaia [Politkovskaya], Anna. "Aziatskii sud po pravam cheloveka." *Novaia Gazeta*, October 6, 2005.

———. "Dekabristy vse eshche sidiat." *Novaia Gazeta*, August 18, 2005.

———. "I seif za 12 kopeek." *Novaia Gazeta*, September 19, 2005.

———. "Kto el shashlik s 'nashimi'?" *Novaia Gazeta*, September 1, 2005.

———. "Natsbolov v sude skovali tsepiami." *Novaia Gazeta*, July 4, 2005.

———. "Obviniaemye khorom sheptali svideteliu: 'vrushka, vrushka.'" *Novaia Gazeta*, August 22, 2005.

———. "Okhrannik otgibal pal'tsy." *Novaia Gazeta*, September 5, 2005.

———. "'Politicheskie' i 'ugolovnye.'" *Novaia Gazeta*, August 1, 2005.

———. "Sud boleet. U nego 39." *Novaia Gazeta*, July 18, 2005.

———. "8 let kolonii za 12 tysiach." *Novaia Gazeta*, July 11, 2005.

———. "V strane poiavilis' politzakliuchnnye? Bez uslovno." *Novaia Gazeta*, December 12, 2005.

"Politologi Ibis i Anubis (Dugin i Kurekhin). Vybory 1995." YouTube. youtube.com/watch?v=cdiLQLEeLUs.

"Politzakliuchennye natsboly (polnyi spisok)." *Drugros.ru*. Politicheskaia partiia Drugaia Rossiia, March 23, 2011.

Polunina, Alena, dir. *Da, smert'!* Russia, 2004. youtube.com/watch?v=DcSvTo2J2rU.

———. *The Last Revolutionaries*. Estonia/Finland, 2008.

Pomerantsev, Peter. *Nothing Is True and Everything Is Possible: The Surreal Heart of the New Russia*. New York: PublicAffairs, 2014.

Popkov, Roman. "NODu krupno povezlo." Blog post. *Openrussia.ru*, April 28, 2016.

Portal setevoi voiny. rossia3.ru/.

"Pravozashchita/Programmy: Podderzhka politzakliuchennykh/Dela natsbolov." *Mezhdunarodnoe obshchestvo Memorial*, June 24, 2011.

Prigov, Dmitrii [Dmitry], and Sergei [Sergey] Shapoval. *Portretnaia galereia D.A.P.* Moscow: Novoe literaturnoe obozrenie, 2003.

Prigov, Dmitry. "What More Is There to Say?" In *Third Wave: The New Russian Poetry*, edited by Kent Johnson and Stephen Ashby, 101–3. Ann Arbor: University of Michigan Press, 1992.

Prilepin, Zakhar. "Noveishaia istoriia. Novyi realizm." *Sobaka.ru*, May 3, 2012. sobaka.ru/oldmagazine/glavnoe/11550.

———. "Portret evropeitsa na fone russkikh kentavrov." *Svobodnaia Pressa*, December 8, 2012.

———. *San'kia*. Moscow: Ad Marginem, 2006.

———. *Sankya*. Ann Arbor, MI: Disquiet, 2014.

"Programma Evraziiskogo soiuza molodezhi." *Rossiia 3*. rossia3.ru/programma.html.

Programma Natsional-bol'shevistskoi partii. Moscow: MP Paleia, 1994.

Prokhanov, Aleksandr. *Gospodin Geksogen*. Moscow: Ad Marginem, 2002.

Pucciarelli, Marco. "Dugin (Il filosofo di Putin): 'Con la Russia e contro le élite la rivoluzione populista italiana.'" *la Repubblica*, June 24, 2018.

Radashkevich, Aleksandr. "Planeta nezasnuvshikh medvedei: Beseda s Iuriem Mamleevym v sviazi s frantsuzskim izdaniem romana *Shatuny*." Editorial. *Russkaia mysl'*, September 5, 1986.

Radosh, Ronald. "Steve Bannon, Trump's Top Guy, Told Me He Was 'a Leninist.'" *Daily Beast*, August 22, 2016.

"Rektor MGU uvolil Aleksandra Dugina." *Lenta.ru*, June 27, 2014.

"Reshenie Mosgorsuda o zapreshchenii NBP ot 19.04.2007." Report by SOVA Center for Information and Analysis, July 30, 2007.

Richardson, Joanne. "Neue Slowenische Kunst: Miran Mohar, Borut Vogelnik and Eda Zufer." ARTMargins, June 16, 2000.

Ries, Nancy. *Russian Talk: Culture and Conversation during Perestroika*. Ithaca, NY: Cornell University Press, 1997.

Rodionov, Andrei. *Igrushki dlia okrain*. Moscow: Novoe literaturnoe obozrenie, 2007.

———. *Liudi beznadezhno ustarelykh professii*. Moscow: Novoe literaturnoe obozrenie, 2008.

Rogachevskii, Andrei. *A Biographical and Critical Study of Russian Writer Eduard Limonov*. Lewiston, NY: Edwin Mellen Press, 2003.

———. "The National-Bolshevik Party (1993–2001): A Brief Timeline." *New Zealand Slavonic Journals* 41 (2007): 90–112.

Rogatchevski [Rogachevskii], Andrei, and Yngvar Steinholt. "Pussy Riot's Musical Precursors? The National Bolshevik Party Bands, 1994–2007." *Popular Music and Society* (2015): 1–17.

Rogers, Douglas, "Postsocialisms Unbound: Connections, Critiques, Comparisons." *Slavic Review* 69, no. 1 (Spring 2010): 1–15

Rossman, Vadim. "Moscow State University's Department of Sociology and the Climate of Opinion in Post-Soviet Russia." In *Eurasianism and the European Far Right: Reshaping the Europe-Russia Relationship*, edited by Marlène Laruelle, 55–76. Lanham, MD: Lexington, 2015.

"Roundtable with Edward Limonov." *The eXile* (Moscow), April 16, 2004.

Rukavishnikov, Filipp. "Pasynki Beschest'ia." YouTube, 2015. youtube.com/watch?v=LkziMXOknbw.

"RUSSIA.RU—Televidenie." Accessed July 26, 2017. tv.russiaru.net/.

"Russian Winter Olympics Campaign Branded 'Fascist.'" *The Telegraph*, May 17, 2011.

Rutten, Ellen. *Sincerity after Communism: A Cultural History*. New Haven, CT: Yale University Press, 2017.

Ryan-Hayes, Karen L. *Contemporary Russian Satire: A Genre Study*. Cambridge: Cambridge University Press, 1995.

———. "Limonov's *Eto ia—Edichka* and the Failure of an American Dream." *Canadian Slavonic Papers* 30, no. 4 (1988): 438–59.

Ryklin, Mikhail. "'The Best in the World': The Discourse of the Moscow Metro in the 1930s." In *The Landscape of Stalinism: The Art and Ideology of Soviet Space*, edited by Evgeny Dobrenko and Eric Naiman, 261–76. Seattle: University of Washington Press, 2003.

———. *Svastika, krest, zvezda: Proizvedeniia iskusstva v epokhu upravliaemoi demokratii.* Moscow: Logos, 2006.

———. *Svoboda i zapret: Kul'tura v epokhu terrora.* Moscow: Logos, 2008.

Safariants, Rita. "Thank God We're Not Alive: Rock Stardom in Soviet and Post-Soviet Cinema." In *Ruptures and Continuities in Soviet/Russian Cinema: Styles, Characters and Genres before and after the Collapse of the USSR*, edited by Birgit Beumers and Eugenie Zvonkine, 90–107. Routledge, 2017.

Salvia, Mattia. "Come la destra italiana sta rubando le icone della sinistra a suon di bufale." *Vice*, July 19, 2018.

———. "Populismo, sovranità e meme su Putin: Nella testa dei rossobruni italiani." *Vice*, June 15, 2017.

Sandalov, Feliks. *Formeishen: Istoriia odnoi stseny.* Moscow: Common Place, 2016.

Savel'ev, Viktor Alekseevich. *Goriachaia molodezh' Rossii: Lidery, organizatsii i dvizheniia, taktika ulichnykh bitv, kontakty.* Moscow: Kvanta, 2006.

Schlögel, Karl. *Moscow, 1937.* Reprint, Cambridge, UK: Polity, 2014.

Sedgwick, Mark J. *Against the Modern World: Traditionalism and the Secret Intellectual History of the Twentieth Century.* Oxford: Oxford University Press, 2004.

Sell, Mike. *The Avant-Garde: Race, Religion, War.* London: Seagull, 2011.

Semenov, dir., *Fuck Off, Mr. Bond!* 2003. youtube.com/watch?v=MOLAuBVccCQ.

Shein, Aleksandr, dir. *Nol' ob"ekt.* 2014.

Shekhovtsov, Anton. "Aleksandr Dugin's Neo-Eurasianism: The New Right à La Russe." *Religion Compass* 3, no. 4 (2009): 697–716.

———. "Far-Right Election Observation Monitors in the Service of the Kremlin's Foreign Policy." In *Eurasianism and the European Far Right: Reshaping the Europe-Russia Relationship*, edited by Marlène Laruelle, 223–45. Lanham, MD: Lexington, 2015.

———. "The Palingenetic Thrust of Russian Neo-Eurasianism: Ideas of Rebirth in Aleksandr Dugin's Worldview." *Totalitarian Movements and Political Religions* 9, no. 4 (2008): 491–506.

———. *Russia and the Western Far Right: Tango Noir.* New York: Routledge, 2017.

Shekhovtsov, Anton and Andreas Umland. "Is Aleksandr Dugin a Traditionalist? 'Neo-Eurasianism' and Perennial Philosophy." *Russian Review* 68, no. 4 (2009): 662–78.

Shemiakin, Mikhail, ed. *Apollon-77.* Paris: M. Chemiakine, 1977.

Shenfield, Stephen. *Russian Fascism: Traditions, Tendencies, Movements.* Armonk, NY: M. E. Sharpe, 2001.

Shevchenko, Valerii. *Zhertvy chernogo oktiabria 1993.* Moscow: Algoritm, 2013.

Shevtsova, Lilia. *Russia Lost in Transition: The Yeltsin and Putin Legacies.* Washington, DC: Carnegie Endowment for International Peace, 2007.

Shklovsky, V. "Art as Device." In *Theory of Prose*, 1–14. Elmwood Park, IL: Dalkey Archive, 1990.

Shlapentokh, Dmitry. "Dugin Eurasianism: A Window on the Minds of the Russian Elite or an Intellectual Ploy?" *Studies in East European Thought* 59, no. 3 (2007): 215–36.

Simmons, Cynthia. *Their Fathers' Voice: Vassily Aksyonov, Venedikt Erofeev, Eduard Limonov, and Sasha Sokolov.* New York: P. Lang, 1993.
Skidan, Aleksandr. "Limonov. Protivitel'nyi soiuz." *Kriticheskaia massa,* no. 1 (2005). magazines.russ.ru/km/2005/1/li7.html.
Smirnov, Andrei. "Mikhail Verbitskii: 'Ozhivit' vselennuiu!'" *Zavtra* (blog), October 26, 2005. zavtra.ru/blogs/2005-10-2671.
Snyder, Timothy. "Fascism, Russia, And Ukraine." *New York Review of Books,* March 20, 2014.
"Sobytiia 21 sentiabria–5 oktiabr'ia 1993 goda: Organizatory, ispolnitely i zhertvy politicheskogo protivostoianiia." Doklad Kommissii Gosudarstvennoi Dumy Federal'nogo Sobraniia Rossiiskoi Federatsii po dopolnitel'nomu izucheniiu i analizu sobytii, proiskhodivshikh v gorode Moskve 21 sentiabria–5 oktiabr'ia 1993 goda. Moscow, 1999 [Report of the Russian State Duma Commission on the events of September 21–October 5, 1993].
Sogrin, V. V. *Politicheskaia istoriia sovremennoi Rossii.* Moscow: Ves' Mir, 2001.
Sokolov, Mikhail. "Natsional-bol'shevistskaia partiia: Ideologicheskaia evoliutsiia i politicheskii stil'." In *Russkii natsionalizm: Ideologiia i nastroenie,* edited by Aleksandr Verkhovskii, 139–64. Moscow: Sova, 2006.
Sokolov, Sergei. "Osvedomitcli—agenty spetssluzhb—sredi organizatorov ubiistva Anny Politkovskoi." *Novaia Gazeta,* April 7, 2008.
Solov, Larry. "Breitbart News Network: Born in the USA, Conceived in Israel." Breitbart, November 17, 2015. breitbart.com/big-journalism/2015/11/17/breitbart-news-network-born-in-the-usa-conceived-in-israel/.
Sontag, Susan. "Fascinating Fascism." *New York Review of Books,* February 6, 1975.
———. "Notes on 'Camp.'" In *Against Interpretation and Other Essays,* 275–92. New York: Farrar, Straus & Giroux, 1966.
Sophocles. "Antigone." In *The Three Theban Plays,* 55–128. Translated by Robert Fagles. New York: Penguin Books, 1984.
Sorokin, Vladimir. *Goluboe salo.* Moscow: Ad Marginem, 1999.
"Sovranisti ma di sinistra: Chi sono i 'rossobruni.'" *La Repubblica,* June 24, 2018.
Spektorowski, Alberto. "The New Right: Ethno-Regionalism, Ethno-Pluralism and the Emergence of a Neo-Fascist 'Third Way.'" *Journal of Political Ideologies* 8, no. 1 (February 1, 2003): 111–30. doi:10.1080/13569310306084.
Speranskaia, Natella. *ENDKAMPF: Misterionsophia Nihiladeptus.* Moscow, 2010.
Sperling, Valerie. *Sex, Politics, and Putin: Political Legitimacy in Russia.* New York: Oxford University Press, 2014.
"Spisok liudei, pogibshikh v Moskve 21 sentiabria–5 oktiabria 1993 goda." Pravozashchitnyi tsentr "Memorial" / Memorial Human Rights Center. memohrc.org/ru/reports/spisok-lyudey-pogibshih-v-moskve-21-sentyabrya-5-oktyabrya-1993-goda. [Official list of people who died in connection with the events of September 21–October 5, 1993. Redacted by the non-governmental human rights organization Memorial.]
Spivak, Gayatri Chakravorty. "Can the Subaltern Speak?" In *Marxism and the Interpretation of Culture,* edited by Cary Nelson and Lawrence Grossberg, 271–313. Chicago: University of Illinois, 1988.
Steuckers, Robert. "La genèse de la postmodernité." *Vouloir,* no. 54/55 (July 1989).
Sud nad prizrakom. Telekompaniia "Ostankino." Moscow, Russian Federation, 2002.

YouTube, May 29, 2016. [Documentary on the NBP broadcast on Russian television in 2002.]

"Sud prigovoril Eduarda Limonova k 4 godam, priznav, chto terroristom ego schitali po oshibke." *NEWSru.com*, April 15, 2003.

Surkov, Vladislav. *Almost Zero*. New York: Inpatient Press, 2017.

Taguieff, Pierre-André. *Sur la nouvelle droite: Jalons d'une analyse critique*. Paris: Descartes & Cie, 1994.

"Tainoe stanet iavnym." YouTube. youtube.com/watch?v=tqGjyMGhdqU.

Tarasov, Aleksandr. "Godar kak Vol'ter." *Elementy* 9 (2000).

Tarasov, Aleksandr., G. Iu. Cherkasov, and T. V. Shavshukova. *Levye v Rossii: Ot umerennykh do ekstremistov*. Moscow: Institut eksperimental'noi sotsiologii, 1997.

Taylor, Charles. *Philosophical Arguments*. Cambridge, MA: Harvard University Press, 1995.

Televidenie narodno-osvoboditel'nogo dvizheniia. "5.2.2015 E. Fedorov i I. Strelkov: 5-ia kolonna vo vlasti—ugroza gosperevorota v Rossii!" YouTube, February 9, 2015.

Tikhonov, Andrei. "Aleksei Beliaev-Gintovt: 'Mne viditsia kommunizm s nechelovecheskim litsom.'" *Rossiia 3*, June 4, 2010. rossia3.ru/smi/nechelovechesko.

"Timur Novikov. White Swan: KING LUDWIG II OF BAVARIA." timurnovikov.ru/index.php?option=com_content&view=article&id=98:timur-novikov-white-swan-king-ludwig-ii-of-bavaria-8&catid=6:2010-06-17-11-24-54&lang=ru&Itemid=0.

Tisdall, Caroline. *Joseph Beuys*. Solomon R. Guggenheim Museum, 1979.

"A Tribute to Alexander Sumerkin." *Cardinal Points* 12, no. 2 (2010): 126–51. stosvet.net/12/sumerkin/.

Tsvetkov, Aleksei. *Dnevnik gorodskogo partizana*. St. Petersburg: Amfora, 2008.

———. "A Political Guide to Contemporary Russian Poetry." In *Post-post-Soviet? Art, Politics and Society in Russia at the Turn of the Decade*, edited by Marta Dziewańska, Ekaterina Degot, and Ilya Budraitskis, 221–34. Warsaw: Museum of Modern Art in Warsaw, 2013.

———. "Shtirner-Prudon: dva poliusa anarkhii." *Elementy* 9 (2000).

Tudor, Lucian. "The Real Dugin." *Radix Journal*, August 30, 2014. radixjournal.com/journal/2014/8/30/the-real-dugin.

Tupitsyna, Margarita, and Viktor Tupitsyn. "Beseda s Timurom i Afrikoi." *RISK: Almanakh* 1 (1995): 79–82.

Turner, Victor W. *The Ritual Process: Structure and Anti-structure*. New Brunswick, NJ: Aldine Transaction, 2008.

Tynianov, Iurii. "O literaturnoi evoliutsii." In *Poetika, istoriia literatury, kino*, 270–81. Moscow: Nauka, 1977.

"Ukraine's Murky Inferno." *The Economist*, May 8, 2014.

Umland, Andreas. "Aleksandr Dugin's Transformation from a Lunatic Fringe Figure into a Mainstream Political Publicist, 1980–1998: A Case Study in the Rise of Late and Post-Soviet Russian Fascism." *Journal of Eurasian Studies* 1, no. 2 (2010): 144–52.

———. "'Konservativnaia revoliutsiia': Imia sobstvennoe ili rodovoe poniatiie?" *Fond noveishei vostochnoevropeiskoi istorii i kul'tury* 1 (2006).

———. "Pathological Tendencies in Russian 'Neo-Eurasianism': The Significance of the Rise of Aleksandr Dugin for the Interpretation of Public Life in Contemporary Russia." *Russian Politics and Law* 47, no. 1 (2009): 76–89.

———. "Post-Soviet 'Uncivil Society' and the Rise of Aleksandr Dugin: A Case Study of the Extraparliamentary Radical Right in Contemporary Russia." PhD diss., University of Cambridge, 2007.

———. *Toward an Uncivil Society? Contextualizing the Recent Decline of Extremely Right-Wing Parties in Russia.* Cambridge, MA: Weatherhead Center for International Affairs, Harvard University, 2002.

Vail, Petr, and Alexander Genis. "S tochki zrenii gribov." In *Sobranie sochinenii,* by Iurii Mamleev, 689–700. Moscow: Eksmo, 2016.

"Vasilii Iakemenko: 'NASHI—dvizhenie oppozitsionnoe deistvuiushchei elite.'" *Nashi. su,* October 25, 2005.

Veig, Sol. "Pop-Mekhanika 418. V pamiati Aleister Crowley (fragmenty). Kurekhin, Dugin, Limonov. Osen' 1995." YouTube, June 18, 2013. youtube.com/watch?v=X26mgR3wQxo.

Venturi, Robert, Steven Izenour, and Denise Scott Brown. *Learning from Las Vegas: The Forgotten Symbolism of Architectural Form.* Cambridge, MA: MIT Press, 1977.

Verbitskii, Mikhail. "Khaos i kul'tura podpol'ia." *Elementy* 9 (2000).

Verdery, Katherine. *What Was Socialism, and What Comes Next?* Princeton, NJ: Princeton University Press, 1996.

Verkhovskii, Aleksandr. "Pochemu sleduet otmenit' reshenie o zaprete NBP." Report by SOVA Center for Information and Analysis, August 4, 2007.

Verkhovskii, Aleksandr, and Galina Kozhevnikova, eds. *Radikal'nyi russkii natsionalizm: struktury, idei, litsa.* Moscow: Sova, 2009.

Vernant, Jean-Pierre. "Ambiguity and Reversal: On the Enigmatic Structure of Oedipus Rex." *New Literary History* 9, no. 3 (1978): 475–501.

Vitukhnovskaia, Alina. "Liubit' Avroru i Reikhstag." *Den' literatury* 64, no. 13 (2001). you-books.com/book/G-Denliteratury/Gazeta-Den-Literatury-N-64-2001-13.

———. *Mir kak volia i prestuplenie: Poeziia, proza, publitsistika.* Moscow: Opustoshitel', 2014.

Vitukhnovskaia, Alina, and Aleksandr Tkachenko. *Delo Aliny Vitukhnovskoi: Sbornik materialov.* Moscow: Izdatel'stvo russkogo PEN-tsentra, 1996.

"V MGU oprovergli uvol'nenie 'evraziitsa' Aleksandra Dugina." *RBK.ru,* June 28, 2014.

Volkov, Konstantin. "Dobrovol'tsy iz Rossii gotovy vyekhat' na pomoshch' vostochnoi Ukraine." Editorial. *Izvestiia.ru,* February 25, 2014.

Volkov, Vadim. *Violent Entrepreneurs: The Use of Force in the Making of Russian Capitalism.* Ithaca, NY: Cornell University Press, 2002.

"V strane idet voina terminov." *Ekspress Gazeta* (Moscow), March 3, 2014.

Wachtel, Michael. "Zhiznetvorchestvo: The Conflation of Art and Life." In *Russian Symbolism and Literary Tradition: Goethe, Novalis, and the Poetics of Viacheslav Ivanov,* 143–56. Madison: University of Wisconsin Press, 1994.

Wakamiya, Lisa Ryoko. *Locating Exiled Writers in Contemporary Russian Literature: Exiles at Home.* New York: Palgrave Macmillan, 2009.

Warner, Michael. "Publics and Counterpublics." *Public Culture* 14, no. 1 (2002): 49–90.

———. *Publics and Counterpublics.* New York: Zone Books, 2014.

Wilson, Andrew. *Virtual Politics: Faking Democracy in the Post-Soviet World.* New Haven, CT: Yale University Press, 2005.

Wood, Tony. *Russia without Putin: Money, Power and the Myths of the New Cold War.* New York: Verso, 2018.

Yurchak, Aleksei. *Everything Was Forever, Until It Was No More: The Last Soviet Generation.* Princeton, NJ: Princeton University Press, 2005.

———. "Gagarin and the Rave Kids: Transforming Power, Identity, and Aesthetics in Post-Soviet Nightlife." In *Consuming Russia: Popular Culture, Sex, and Society Since Gorbachev,* edited by Adele Marie Barker, 76–109. Durham, NC: Duke University Press, 1999.

———. "A Parasite from Outer Space: How Sergei Kurekhin Proved That Lenin Was a Mushroom." *Slavic Review* 70, no. 2 (2011): 307–33.

———. "Post-post Communist Sincerity: Pioneers, Cosmonauts, and Other Soviet Heroes Born Today." In *What Is Soviet Now? Identities, Legacies, Memories,* edited by Thomas Lahusen and Peter Solomon, 257–76. Berlin: Lit, 2008.

"Iurii Mamleev: Pro tsenzuru i Iuzhinskii." YouTube. youtube.com/yts/jsbin/player-vflZ8°BLt/en_US/base.js.

"Zakrytyi biulleten' NBP-INFO, no. 3." *Nbp-info.ru,* September 24, 2008.

"Zakrytyi biulleten' NBP-INFO, no. 4." *Nbp-info.ru,* September 24, 2008.

Zholkovskii, Aleksandr. "Grafomanstvo kak priem (Lebiadkin, Khlebnikov, Limonov i drugie)." In *Bluzhdaiushchie sny i drugie raboty.* Moscow: Nauka–Vostochnaia literatura, 1994.

Zhvaniia, Dmitrii. "Aleksandr Lebedev-Frontov: 'Shum pogruzhaet cheloveka v sostoianie vremennoi smerti.'" *Sensus Novus,* March 30, 2013. sensusnovus.ru/interview/2013/05/30/16466.html.

———. *Put' khunveibina: Khroniki poslednei russkoi revolutsii.* St. Petersburg: Amfora, 2006.

Žižek, Slavoj. "Why Are Laibach and NSK Not Fascists?" *M'ars* 5, nos. 3–4 (1993): 3–4.

Zubrin, Robert. "Dugin's Evil Theology." *National Review Online,* June 18, 2014.

Index

CPSIA information can be obtained
at www.ICGtesting.com
Printed in the USA
LVHW081651251022
731537LV00004B/604